hold dear, I as always

Edited by Adolf E. Schroeder
and Carla Schulz-Geisberg

Translated from German by Adolf E. Schroeder

Jette, a German Immigrant Life in Letters

University of Missouri Press
Columbia, 1988

Copyright ©1988 by
The Curators of the University of Missouri
University of Missouri Press, Columbia, Missouri 65211
Printed and bound in the United States of America
All rights reserved
First paperback printing, 2011
5 4 3 2 1   15 14 13 12 11

Library of Congress Cataloging-in-Publication Data
Schroeder, Adolf E.
   Hold dear, as always: Jette, a German immigrant life in
letters / edited by Adolf E. Schroeder and Carla Schulz-Geisberg.
   P   cm.
Includes index.
ISBN 978-0-8262-1928-2 (pbk.: alk. paper)
I. Bruns, Henrietta, b. 1813—Correspondence. 2. German-Americans—Missouri—
Correspondence. 3. Immigrants—MissouriCorrespondence. 4. Missouri—Emigration
and immigration—History—19th century. 5. Westphalia (Germany)—Emigration and
immigration—History—19th century. I. Schulz-Geisberg, Carla. IL Tide.
F475•G3 1988
977.8.00431—dc19   87-22382 CIP

∞™ This paper meets the minimum requirements of
the American National Standard for Permanence of Paper
for Printed Library Materials, Z39.48, 1984.

This book is dedicated to
the memory of
Henriette Anna Elisabeth Geisberg Bruns
born in Stromberg in the Province of Westphalia
28 October 1813
married in Stromberg
24 May 1832
settled in Westphalia, Missouri
All Souls' Day
2 November 1836
died in Jefferson City, Missouri
7 November 1899

and to Becky
who contributed immeasurably
to this telling of Jette's story.

Acknowledgments

The remarkable body of letters and other documents from which this life story of a nineteenth-century German immigrant woman was drawn has been preserved by three generations of the Geisberg family of Münster in Westphalia, West Germany. The collection consists of over 270 letters, covering seventy-two years, from June 1827 to November 1899; an autobiography written by Henriette Geisberg Bruns some time after the Civil War for her children and relatives in Germany; and photographs and papers relating to the Geisberg family in Germany and America. The Geisberg collection is owned by Carla Schulz-Geisberg of Nienberge, Kreis Münster, West Germany, coeditor of the present volume and granddaughter of the recipient of most of the letters.

I first learned of Henriette (Jette) Geisberg Bruns from one of her great-great-granddaughters, Lynn Albin Osvold, on the occasion of the day-long observance held in Westphalia, Missouri, on 2 June 1974 to commemorate the centennial of the death of Father Ferdinand Helias, the Jesuit missionary to central Missouri who founded the Westphalia and other churches in the "Osage Country." At that time Lynn showed me copies of several letters Jette wrote home to Münster from the Westphalia Settlement, which had been sent to members of the family in St. Louis who had tried to locate and help relatives in Germany after World War II. Later, in continuing her research on her family history, Lynn learned of the private Geisberg family archives in Münster-Nienberge, in which Carla Schulz-Geisberg has collected, organized, and preserved her extensive collection of family papers and photographs. The original letters from America have been placed in protective covers, and each has been transcribed from the Gothic script and typed by Carla or her daughter, Eva-Maria Westermann. Detailed notes on family relations and activities, photographs of family members gathered from various private and public collections in Germany, and other family memorabilia supplement the correspondence in the Schulz-Geisberg archive. The materials brought together constitute a unique record of three generations of one family wrenched apart by the emigration fever sweeping Germany in the 1830s.

During a sabbatical semester granted by the University of Missouri–Columbia in the fall of 1975, and with the assistance of a grant from the Deutsche Akademische Austauschdienst of the Federal Republic of Germany, I was able to visit Nienberge and see the Geisberg archives. Carla gave me permission to copy some of the early letters to translate and make available to American family members and the Westphalia, Missouri, Historical Society. It soon became apparent that the letters not only provided valuable new information for researchers compiling church and community histories and family historians tracing early settlement of immigrant forebears, but they also offered a rare insight into an experience shared by nameless thousands of immigrants who settled on the western frontier in the nineteenth century and sought to make new lives for themselves and preserve their cultural values and traditions in a strange and often hostile environment.

With the assistance of a Summer Research Grant from the University of Missouri–Columbia, I visited with Mrs. Schulz again in May and June of 1978, and we decided to prepare the correspondence and autobiography for possible publication. In the years since that time, we have frequently consulted by mail and several times in person, and she has provided extensive information on people, places, and events in Germany. She has also provided seventy photographs of members of the family who are mentioned in this correspondence. We were able to reproduce a small selection of those in this book.

I have continued to receive much assistance from Lynn Osvold, who has researched family history in America. Patricia Hilkemeyer of Westphalia, Missouri, has been of inestimable assistance, locating many county and church records to confirm or supplement information in the letters. Additional letters relating to the Geisberg and Bruns families in America and Germany have been made available by the Decker families of St. Louis and Jefferson City and Mrs. Joseph Dubbert and Mrs. Ted Borgmeyer of Martinsburg in Montgomery County. Although many of the letters in the Schulz-Geisberg, Decker, Dubbert, and Borgmeyer collections could not be included in the present volume because of space considerations, all have contributed to our knowledge of the Bruns-Geisberg families in Missouri.

I would like to express my appreciation to Mrs. Schulz-Geisberg and her family; to Lynn Osvold and Patricia Hilkemeyer; to Ernest William Decker IV and Vera Decker; to the Dubbert and Borgmeyer families; and to Mr. Norbert Redel of Westphalia, who patiently allowed me to see the Bruns house on many occasions. Father William B. Faherty, S.J., and Mrs. Nancy Merz of the Jesuit Missouri Province Archives in St. Louis, Sister Laura Northcraft of the School Sisters of Notre Dame, and the Chancery of the Diocese of Jefferson City were unfailingly helpful. The Office of the Adjutant General, Missouri National Guard, the Archives Service, Office of the Secretary of State, the State Historical Society of Missouri, and the Western Historical Manuscript Collection–Columbia provided much assistance. Maxine Roberts, former secretary of Germanic and Slavic Studies, University of Missouri–Columbia, transcribed taped translations. Colleagues who read early versions of the manuscript made many thoughtful suggestions that have contributed substantially to the value and readability of the book. My thanks to them and all who have helped.

A. E. S.
Columbia, Missouri
December 1987

As a member of a family which for generations has been imbued with a strong sense of tradition, I have always hoped to make the letters of my grandfather's sister, Henriette Bruns, née Geisberg, accessible to the American relatives whose ancestor she is.

These letters bear witness to the strong personality and great will power of this woman. Her fate is touching, her characteristics are impressive, and her ability to endure inspiring.

May a feeling of belonging together arise in her numerous descendants as they get to know her. It has been a joy and an obligation for me to have contributed to the bridge still lasting between the United States and Germany.

Carla Schulz Geisberg
Am Kalthof 11
4400 Münster-Nienberge
West Germany
December 1987

Contents

Introduction

by Adolf E. Schroeder

I

Most immigrant women came to America as wives and mothers. Our view of them has almost always been through the eyes of their husbands, sons, or other male observers, who tended to see them as one-dimensional stereotypes, heroic in many cases, but silent and stoic figures in the background of the drama of immigration.

Our first detailed view of German immigrants in Upper Louisiana was provided by Timothy Flint, a New England cleric and missionary to the western states and territories. In 1819–1820 Flint lived for more than a year near a settlement on the Whitewater River in southeast Missouri that had been founded in 1800 by Mennonite and Lutheran immigrants from North Carolina, who were later joined by settlers from Germany and Pennsylvania. He found the Whitewater community "German in all its habits" and reported that the settlers' wives had no taste for parties and teas. "Silent, unwearied labor and the rearing of their children are their only pursuits."[1] Some of Flint's perceptive vignettes of domestic, religious, and social life in the settlement illuminate qualities of the women that contrast with this view of their characteristics, however. His landlady and advocate, "Madame Ballinger,"[2] far from silent, engaged the German minister, who had been banished from the community for drunkenness, in a lively argument when he came to her home to criticize the English clergyman, who had found favor with the German minister's former congregation. Flint might not know one word of "Dutch," she conceded, but he "does not trink one trop of whiskey!" During a stay in the Whitewater River settlement, Flint counted forty-five female dresses hanging around his sleeping room, "all of cotton, raised and manufactured and coloured in the family." He adds ambiguously, "The ladies of the cities are not more inwardly gratified with the possession of the newest and most costly furniture, than these good, laborious, submissive and silent housewives are, in hanging around their best apartment fifty male and female dresses, all manufactured by their own hand."

Whether the women caught up in the massive nineteenth-century immigration from Germany to Missouri were "silent and submissive," or whether they came from duty or inclination, is rarely known. There is ample evidence that their husbands and fathers were often so mesmerized by Gottfried Duden's vision of a new *Germania* in Missouri that common sense had left them.[3] Gert Goebel, who arrived in 1834 with the Giessen Emigration Society, reported that he had known men so convinced they were coming to a tropical climate that they wanted to leave their featherbeds at home. In some cases, at least, the

---

1. *Recollections of the Last Ten Years, Passed in Occasional Residences and Journeyings, in the Valley of the Mississippi, from Pittsburg and the Missouri to the Gulf of Mexico, and from Florida to the Spanish Frontier, in a Series of Letters* (Boston: Cummings, Hilliard and Company, 1826), pp. 236–37.

2. Flint's variant spelling of *Bollinger*, a family name still prominent in southeast Missouri.

3. *Bericht über eine Reise nach den westlichen Staaten Nordamerika's und einen mehrjährigen Aufenthalt am Missouri (in den Jahren 1824, 25, 26 und 1827), in Bezug auf Auswanderung und Ueberbevölkerung* (Elberfeld: Sam Lucas, 1829). My quotations are taken from an English translation of Duden's work: *Report on a Journey to the Western States of North America and a Stay of Several Years Along the Missouri (During the Years 1824, '25, '26, and 1827)*, ed. James W. Goodrich et al. (Columbia: University of Missouri Press, 1980).

women prevailed, the featherbeds were brought, and, faced with a long Missouri winter, the men had to be grateful for their wives' foresight.[4]

Duden, a lawyer and civil servant from Remscheid in the Ruhr Valley, arrived in St. Louis in October 1824 on a self-appointed mission to find a favorable location in the Far West for the large-scale emigration that he believed was the only solution to the economic, political, and social ills in his homeland. Convinced that the problems he had dealt with as an officer of the Prussian Court were caused by overpopulation, poverty, and oppression, he wanted to write a practical guide for prospective emigrants to help them make new lives for themselves and their families in America. He and his travel companion, Ludwig Eversmann, bought adjoining farms of government and improved private land on Lake Creek, in what is now Warren County, and Duden spent almost three years gathering the practical and detailed information he hoped would prepare emigrants for conditions in the Far West.

Unfortunately for the Duden followers who flocked to Missouri in the 1830s, his experience was somewhat exceptional. During his stay in Warren County he reported three mild winters and two pleasant and temperate summers. He was able to hire his American neighbors to build his cabin and put up his fences, clear his land and cultivate his fields, and even to hunt wild turkeys for his table, while he spent his time reading, writing, and walking in the forests. Thoroughly imbued with the notions of German romanticism of his time, Duden was so inspired by the majesty of the land and the potential it offered for a better life for his countrymen that his romantic descriptions of the natural wonders of Missouri tended to overshadow the practical advice he conscientiously included for prospective emigrants. To the poor of Germany, who were either crowded onto ever-diminishing patches of worn-out land or had no land at all, to middle classes taxed and persecuted by intransigent and corrupt ruling princes, and especially to intellectuals and revolutionaries, who saw the freedoms they had been accorded after the Napoleonic wars eroding with each new student uprising, Duden's Missouri must have been nearly irresistible. As he declared in his Thirteenth Letter, one could roam through the beautiful countryside for hundreds of miles "to select land with a cover of wood and meadow in accord with one's own desires." There was room for millions of fine farms along the Missouri River, where the industry of a few hands could provide abundance for whole families. He believed that in only a few years a new and better Germany could be established on the western frontier of America.

Duden's *Report* was published in Elberfeld in 1829 at the author's own expense. It appeared in a pirated edition in 1832 in St. Gallen, Switzerland, and in 1834 was published in a revised edition in Bonn. By 1834 Duden was trying to answer the many critics of his book who had come to Missouri to see his paradise themselves and accused him of luring his readers to a life of certain misery on the frontier. In spite of his efforts to be objective, he had evoked a land of limitless opportunity, in which the new settler could become quickly established in a benevolent environment, crops would thrive in a soil so rich it would not require fertilizer for a hundred years, little cash would be necessary, and family harmony would naturally prevail as man was ennobled by nature.

The first known group of Duden followers to settle in Missouri, the members of the Berlin Society, seem for a time to have achieved a way of life that, although somewhat incongruous

4. *Länger als ein Menschenleben in Missouri* (St. Louis: C. Witter, 1877), p. 7.

in the environment, approximated Duden's vision and their own of life in a new *Germania*. Observers reported enthusiastically on the hospitality of the wife and five daughters of Baron von Bock, a prominent member of the society, who settled near Duden's farm in the early 1830s and established the town of Dutzow, named for his estate in Mecklenburg. We know from Frederick Gustorf's 1836 account[5] that the von Bock home was decorated with German engravings, a piano, and a small collection of books. Gustorf reported that the daughters entertained visitors graciously, serving good coffee in beautiful cups with "real German cream puffs," and chatted with their visitors about English literature, last week's ball, and the ways of their American neighbors, to which they could not become accustomed. A young neighbor played the piano exquisitely, and after a bountiful dinner they all sang German songs as darkness fell over the Missouri forest. Gustorf remarked that he could not believe that "women of such culture have come here to milk cows," but we know very little of the day-to-day life of the von Bock family on the frontier. The baron had built a log club-house with billiard tables before he built a dwelling for his family, as neighbor Friedrich Münch reported disapprovingly, and his considerable fortune slipped through his fingers in lavish entertaining and impractical ventures. However, his daughters were said to have married well and took care of their parents in their old age.[6]

The idealistic members of the Giessen Society, who had dreamed of establishing a model political and social German state in America to demonstrate the virtues of democracy and inspire revolution at home, saw in their wives and mothers a saintly forbearance and dedication to duty, as they took on the milking of cows and other work as a matter of course.

> They were the most unpretentious and modest women and never demanded of their husbands comforts and unessential conveniences to which they had certainly become accustomed, but which the financial situation of their husbands precluded. These women, who never lost sight of their genuine feminine dignity, considered it no disgrace to do their own washing and scrubbing, to milk the cows, in other words to do work the like of which they had previously never been obliged to do.[7]

Most women had been helplessly swept along by their husbands' dream that, as Friedrich Steines wrote, "in the still seclusion of the Missouri forests, where nature still reigns supreme, there it must be better. There many hearts shaken by storms will find peace."[8] Steines's brother Hermann had been sent to America in 1833 to investigate conditions there and advise his family as to whether it would be desirable to emigrate. He had learned in Baltimore that Missouri was in very bad repute among immigrants, and after arriving in St. Louis he found that conditions in many ways justified this reputation. He was concerned about women members of the family.

> Now a few words to you, my mother and my sisters. .... If you feel strong enough in body to endure the hardships of the journey, and buoyant enough in spirit to participate in ... the fond

5. *The Uncorrupted Heart: Journal and Letters of Frederick Julius Gustorf, 1800–1845,* ed. Fred Gustorf and Gisela Gustorf (Columbia: University of Missouri Press, 1969), p. 137.
6. Goebel, *Länger als ein Menschenleben in Missouri,* p. 8.
7. Ibid., p. 68.
8. As quoted by William G. Bek, "The Followers of Duden," *Missouri Historical Review* (hereafter cited as *MHR*) 15 (April 1921): 521.

dream of your men folks, then we shall all be happy and greatly benefitted. The older members of our family will not be materially benefitted by coming here, but your interest in your children must be the deciding factor if you take this step. You women must have a clear understanding with your men.[9]

Strong in body and buoyant in spirit as they may have been in starting their journey, many of the women, like the men, fell victim to dangers they could not have imagined in Germany. They had worried about the exotic: Indian raids, wild beasts of the forests, and rattlesnakes. They suffered, and often died, of common illnesses. Friedrich Steines was not to be dissuaded from emigration by his brother's cautionary advice. He arrived in St. Louis with his family and other members of the Solingen Emigration Society in early July 1834. At first his family seemed to have withstood the trip well, but before the month was out his four children, his wife, and a sister-in-law had died of cholera.

The early settlers of Hermann, who had dreamed that their town would soon outdistance St. Louis, suffered enormous disappointment and hardship in establishing their colony. Jacob Naumann, an early visitor, reported that "things were pitiful in Hermann."

> One can imagine, a family newly arrived, living with another family in a house that was built only for the needs of the owner and his family, and only one heated room. Then there is sickness in both families, there is discouragement when in the cold, unfriendly days of winter, with the fire in the stove or the fireplace burning brightly, the water standing at the opposite wall freezes in the bucket.[10]

Such hardships of frontier life took a heavy physical and psychological toll. When Gustav Koerner visited the prosperous Berlin settlement at Dutzow on his 1833 walking tour of Missouri, he reported that although their homes were comfortable, some even of brick, and their farms well cultivated, there was sickness in almost every family, "it being the malaria season."[11] Frederick Gustorf observed that the lives of the educated upper-middle class and minor nobility even in Belleville, Illinois, one of the earliest and most successful of the German settlements in the Mississippi Valley, were by no means idyllic by European standards. In one household "a brave, hospitable woman . . . talked very praiseworthily about German social life in Illinois, in contrast to German social life in Missouri." However, Gustorf thought that even in Illinois social life was limited to prosperous and related families visiting each other on Sundays, drinking coffee within the family circle, and reminiscing about the past. The Illinois family he visited owned a beautiful, well-furnished, and roomy house surrounded by a "romantically located" farm, but the man of the house was ill with fever. On another farm near Belleville, he found Baron von Haxthausen struggling to maintain his farm, run a "small and ill-equipped distillery," and build a mill, but nothing was going well. The educated immigrants often could not manage without experienced farm tenants, and Gustorf heard many sad stories about the suffering and hardship of middle-class German families in Illinois and Missouri.

9. Quoted in Bek, *MHR* 14 (October 1919): 70.
10. [Jacob Naumann], *My Journey to America, 1836–1843,* ed. Anna Hesse (Hermann, Mo.: Privately printed, 1969), pp. 36–38.
11. *Memoirs of Gustave Koerner, 1809–1896,* ed. Thomas J. McCormack (Cedar Rapids, Iowa: The Torch Press, 1909), p. 320.

Their experiences are beyond imagination. With their wives, sons, daughters they live wretched lives. Imagine people from the finest German classes living in miserable huts! Previously they had lived in comfortable houses, and now they have to eat the plainest of food and do the hardest work in the fields, surrounded by black forests and cut off from society and all the conveniences of life. They live in memory of the sweet past, in contrast with the miserable present, and in contemplation of a sad future. . . . Their despair can be read in the deep, dark lines of their faces.[12]

Even decades after the hard early days had passed and a modest prosperity had been wrested from the frontier, so that settlers could surround themselves with the accouterments of the life they remembered, homesickness sometimes could not be held at bay. Jessie Benton Frémont reports an incident that occurred in the fall of 1853, when she grew impatient with the progress of her steamboat and got off at Washington to continue overland to St. Louis. She was told that only Germans lived in Washington, but she declared that she felt at home anywhere in Missouri and was deposited on the bank among the crowd who had come to watch the arrival of the boat. Asking for a hotel, she was led into the "clean, ugly, comfortable town" and taken to a large house, where she was welcomed by the mistress and her daughters, who "came forward and made me as quietly welcome as though they knew me. . . . Their faces, the furniture, the violins and guitar, and high pile of music books; the pretty light hair of the women, too-tightly-plaited, all were Germany itself. I pleased myself by accepting this unquestioned hospitality as it was given, and still did not give my name." She was shown to her room and had taken off her hat and gloves when the mother of the family suddenly became convinced that her guest was from Germany and was overwhelmed with grief and homesickness for her old homeland.

"Ah, dear God! You are a lady from my country;—you are from Hesse-Cassel. The ladies in my country wear these gloves when they go hunting with the king. They have stopped in their carriages at my door, and I carried them drink. It is twenty-four years since I have come away from my country; but I love it best . . ." and then she let the tears downfall, for the lost home.

Jessie identified herself, and her hostess soon regained her composure and "seemed as pleased as if I had been a lady hunting with the king" to welcome the daughter of former senator Thomas Hart Benton, who even in defeat was revered by most Germans. The visitor shared in the celebration of the wedding anniversary of her hosts and enjoyed what seemed to be their habitual evening recreation:

After the early supper, they all gathered in the large room, which was positively elegant from its glistening cleanliness. . . . Each took his instrument and place by the table,—sons and sons-in-law,—the father and several of the younger women taking their music, and then followed piece after piece of such music as only Germans can play rightly,—occasionally all joining in a lovely song.[13]

The illuminating glimpse Jessie Benton Frémont gives of an exemplary German housewife pouring out her grief to her visitor provides a dimension of frontier life generally missing in the early writings of settlers, visitors, and observers. In Friedrich Münch's assess-

12. *The Uncorrupted Heart*, pp. 108, 77.
13. Jessie Benton Frémont, *The Story of the Guard: A Chronicle of the War* (Boston: Ticknor and Fields, 1863), pp. 55–59.

ments of the contributions of the wives of the intellectuals who came to Missouri in the 1830s, the women appear stoic in the face of hardships and disappointments, carrying out their duties as homemakers without complaint.

> Our wives here have an important and difficult task, but they are aware of their importance and are never plagued by boredom and are satisfied with what they accomplish for the welfare of their families. They keep their houses clean and in good order, they take care of all the cooking, baking, washing, knitting, mending, sewing, . . . take care of the children, milk the cows, make butter and cheese, dry vegetables, make soap, tend to the flower and vegetable garden, take care of the chickens, and in spite of everything they do not cease to live as educated human beings.[14]

As their father had, the sons of Louise Münch saw their mother as symbol rather than person. Julius Muench wrote:

> [She was the] faithful companion who, born and raised amidst refined surroundings, left home and friends and family and all that was dear to her in a land where she had been happy and contented, and, without complaint, followed him to an uncertain future in a New World, true to her promise, "for better or for worse." She devoted herself to lessening his burdens, and did it gladly, and she believed, with him, in the motto, that "the noblest thing of all is to have devoted an entire lifetime to the benefitting of mankind."[15]

Hugo Muench understood the trauma the "immigrant woman" must have endured, but he saw her as an idealized composite:

> We may all understand how the men of those days, with their political hopes crushed, their religious convictions trampled upon, and the material progress in the land of their fathers apparently forever halted, could turn their backs to the civilization of centuries, sever all ties of blood and friendship, and be prepared to bear all the hardships of a new life in the wilderness of the West; but what about the women of that period? In most instances they were compelled to exchange rather comfortable surroundings for the discomforts and trials of a frontier life; they left all that was dear to them by way of kinship and culture to follow the fortunes of a husband who in fact knew but little of the dangers into which he was leading his dear ones. . . . Is it not marvelous that under such stress of discouraging conditions, without the aid of an active intercourse with the dear ones beyond the seas, these women should have maintained a stout heart, should have borne uncomplainingly the whole burden of an almost uncivilized life, and yet never have failed to lift high the ideals of their youth, and buoy up the flagging courage of their oft times despairing husbands?[16]

Henriette Bruns, who speaks for herself in the autobiography and letters in this collection, may well not have recognized herself in Hugo Muench's idealized portrait of the immigrant woman. She wished for the kind of perfection he saw in his mother and other wives of early immigrants (and no doubt saw in her). But although she longed for the strength to offer her husband and brothers the steadfast support she believed it was her duty to provide, she often found herself wanting. She frequently resolved to be more patient, but patience was not

14. *Der Staat Missouri, geschildert mit besonderer Rücksicht auf teutsche Einwanderung* (New York and St. Louis: Farmers' and Vine Growers' Society, 1859), p. 100.
15. "A Sketch on the Life and Work of Friedrich Münch," Muench Papers, Missouri Historical Society, St. Louis.
16. "The Early German Immigration to St. Louis and Vicinity," Muench Papers, Missouri Historical Society.

given to her. She was often lonely and weary, sometimes angry and distraught, often plagued by boredom. She scolded her brothers and sisters at home in Germany because they would not write her of the social activities she missed so much—then was helplessly envious when they did write of their trips, attendance at balls, and family gatherings. Complaining of the hardships of the frontier, shaken by the tragedies in her life and the lives of others, grieving for her lost country, she brings an immediacy to the immigrant experience lacking in other writings. If no less heroic than her idealized compatriots because she was not always (or even very often) satisfied with what her husband, her brothers, or she herself accomplished in America, she did not suffer her adversities in silence and never became reconciled to the losses emigration brought. On 15 May 1857, after more than two decades in America, she wrote to her brother Heinrich Geisberg: "I have reproached myself bitterly that I did not object more strongly to a move to a country to which I had never had any particular attraction and which robbed me for life of many pleasures." She served as a traditional pioneer housewife because no other role was possible, but she wished for the kind of freedom her husband and brothers had, longing to go seek gold in California or simply move away from Westphalia, once exclaiming impatiently to Heinrich that she wished she "could be Bruns for a while." Her letters to her brother reflect her day-to-day worries and disappointments, but also illuminate her strong influence on the lives of her husband, brothers, children, and grandchildren. She represents the role of the frontier woman in shaping the character and values of her time.

II

Born in 1813 into a large, closely knit, devoutly Catholic family that belonged to what she referred to in her autobiography as the "so-called distinguished people" of the Westphalian city of Oelde, daughter of the mayor and tax collector of that city, Henriette Bruns (called "Jette" by her family and friends) was brought up in a family devoted to reading and music. After her mother died in childbirth in 1827 when Jette was thirteen, she was sent to Münster to be educated in languages, homemaking, and the social graces. There she lived for two years in the home of her father's brothers, an extensive establishment on the River Aa with elaborate gardens, which she was able to recall in the most exact detail in her old age in Missouri. Upon her return to Oelde in 1831 to take care of her ill father and six younger brothers and sisters, she met the "young doctor from Lohne," Dr. Bernhard Bruns, actually fifteen years her senior, who was establishing his practice in Oelde, Stromberg, and the surrounding area. In spite of objections from the Münster relatives because of her youth (they reminded her that her mother's marriage at sixteen and subsequent child-bearing had led to her death at thirty-two), plans for the marriage had been completed when her father died in November 1831, shortly after her eighteenth birthday. The wedding took place the following year.

On 5 January 1835 the twenty-two-year-old Jette wrote to her brother Heinrich about her plans to emigrate to America with her husband and young son. The expectations, doubts, hopes, and fears of a sheltered young woman facing the prospect of a long and perhaps permanent separation from her family are reflected in this and other long, agonized letters she wrote her brother before her departure from Germany. Her expectations were not great.

The Bruns family was not going to America "to seek a glittering fortune." But "over there" land could be bought cheaply, the soil was fertile enough to provide for all household needs, and there were almost no taxes. Every reader of Gottfried Duden's *Report* knew of the advantages of life in the New World, where there would be no worries about one's station in life and, most important of all, better opportunities for the children abounded. Although she was persuaded of all the reasons for emigrating, the thought of leaving family, friends, and familiar surroundings to venture into a new and strange world was not easy to contemplate.

There seems to have been no political necessity for the young Bruns couple to emigrate. They had settled down in Jette's parents' home to look after some of her younger brothers and sisters, and she hoped to bring the rest of the scattered family together as soon as possible. As she was to regret for all her life, this was not to be. Dr. Bruns's decision to emigrate to America was based partly on the widespread poverty he encountered in the course of his practice; as his wife confided to her brother, he was tired of "having to extort his fees," knowing that when he finally got paid, the patient had deprived himself of the little he had for his own family in order to pay the doctor's bill. In addition to having to collect fees from patients who could not afford to pay them, which his wife believed was the beginning of the dissatisfaction that led him to think of emigrating, Dr. Bruns had suffered embarrassment because of widespread gossip relating to the pregnancy of a young woman in a nearby town, the daughter of a magistrate, whom he had tried to help. Although the rumors were generally conceded to be unfounded, even by the woman's parents,[17] the situation had occasioned considerable letter-writing among members of the Geisberg family and their friends before his marriage to Jette, and he seems never to have been able to win the complete confidence of the uncles in Münster, who took a familial interest in the prospects of their niece after the death of her father. There was a barely suppressed doubt that the doctor from Lohne could adequately support their brother's eldest daughter, and a lingering disapproval of the marriage that Jette felt deeply for years afterward.

Evidently, another factor contributed significantly to Dr. Bruns's restlessness and determination to seek a new life for his family: the pervasive emigration fever then gripping the country. "It was in the air," Jette wrote in her autobiography, "and we talked a lot about it." In June 1835 Bruns set out for America to find a home for his wife and son, accompanied by his brother Hermann and another traveling companion. After a brief stay in Baltimore, the brothers proceeded to St. Louis, where by chance they met Nicolaus Hesse, himself a recent immigrant, who had settled with his wife and six daughters on the Maries River in what is now Osage County, an isolated location he had discovered on his explorations into the interior of Missouri from St. Louis. Hesse, who had served as a local official in the area of Warburg in Westphalia, had a comfortable livelihood in Germany, but like Dr. Bruns, whom he persuaded to visit the Westphalia Settlement, he was sensitive to the poverty and suffering he saw around him. Like Bruns, he had fallen victim to the emigration fever sweeping Germany, fostered by Duden's *Report* and other accounts of life in America. His group included a teacher, a secretary, workmen, and a maid, and he had plans to establish a distillery and other businesses in Westphalia at a time when fields had not yet been cleared, as Jette later observed.

17. Letter dated 10 January 1832, from Clemens-August Wesemann in Oelde to Caspar Geisberg, Carla Schulz-Geisberg Archive, Nienberge.

Dr. Bruns was very favorably impressed with Hesse's plans and the area in which he had settled. Writing to Jette from St. Louis on 3 October 1835, describing the site on the Maries River he had chosen for their future home, he demonstrated his thorough familiarity with Duden's *Report*, telling of the fertility of the soil and the beauty of the landscape with an intermingling of practical observation and romantic description worthy of Duden himself.

Dr. Bruns returned to Germany for his wife and son, and just over a year after his discovery of the site on the Maries River, on All Souls' Day, 2 November 1836, the Bruns family arrived in the Westphalia Settlement. Their party included two of Jette's younger brothers, Franz and Bernhard Geisberg, Bruns's brother David, and a maid and her daughter. The sea voyage had taken sixty-six days, and the trip overland and by boat to the Maries another six weeks. In her autobiography Jette recalled her first home in America: "Our shelter was in the middle of a field, a simple log cabin with two bedsteads, one table, four chairs, and one bench." To Heinrich she wrote on 14 November 1836 that the cabin had one window and was "the size of our living room at home." As winter came on, the disadvantages of life on the frontier became apparent. "When it rains it is just too sad in these log cabins," she wrote. "I frequently think back to our comfortable living room." More depressing than the discomfort, however, was the loneliness of being separated from family and friends with little opportunity to make new acquaintances.

The area Dr. Bruns had chosen for his new home was for a number of reasons to remain isolated for many years. Gert Goebel wrote of early Westphalia some years later:

> At a very early time, even before the founding of Hermann, we heard from time to time of a German settlement on Maries Creek, and of a certain Dr. Bernhard Bruns. The region in which this settlement was established was little known at that time, and communication with it was difficult, because approaching it from the east, the Gasconade had to be crossed and from the west the Osage.[18]

Undaunted at first by the isolation and primitive conditions on the Maries, and with their vision of a new life firmly in place, the Bruns set out to build a house in the Westphalia Settlement as nearly like those at home as possible. Still standing today on a hill above a bend in the Maries, Jette's American home bears a ghostly resemblance to the early-nineteenth-century residences of Oelde and Stromberg, but she was to wish many times before it was finally completed that they had chosen to build a simple log house. She was destined to enjoy little opportunity to develop a social circle in the fifteen years she spent in Westphalia; instead, her home was often crowded with workmen and relatives and plagued with sickness.

A serious setback in the expectations of the newcomers occurred when the Hesses decided to return to Germany in April 1837, less than two years after settling in Missouri and little more than five months after the Bruns family arrived. Hesse had found it impossible to carry out his ambitious plans, partially because of his wife's disabling homesickness.

Although the Hesses' departure only steeled Jette's resolve to stay in America, the years in Westphalia were to become more and more difficult, not only because of crop failures, floods, and the epidemic illnesses that marked the late 1830s and early 1840s in Missouri, but

18. *Länger als ein Menschenleben in Missouri*, p. 50.

also because of the longing for her family, an emptiness that letters from home could not fill. Historian Oscar Handlin, himself the son of immigrants, who has written movingly of the "interruptions of a familiar life, separation from known surroundings, the becoming of a foreigner and ceasing to belong . . ." that was central to the immigrant experience, has observed that the "history of immigration is a history of alienation and its consequences."[19]

Soon after returning to Germany, Nicolaus Hesse wrote of his life on the frontier in terms that could only alarm Jette's family in Münster and annoy Jette herself, but his assessment of the illness that had caused the collapse of his own dreams evoked with some accuracy the problems suffered by her brother Bernhard and a condition she herself had to fight frequently, and not always successfully:

> The memory of relatives, friends, and old acquaintances causes a longing which in many, especially tender-hearted women, creates a homesickness that often degenerates into real melancholy that cannot be cured by any medicine. The cause is not in a faulty judgment of the conditions of the old and new home, but rather the love of the original home, which is common to all people of the earth.[20]

Handlin has characterized the immigrant condition as a severe and continuing trauma: "The immigrants lived in crisis because they were uprooted. In transplantation, while the old roots were sundered, before the new were established, they existed in an extreme situation. The shock, and the effects of the shock, persisted for many years, and their influence reached down to generations which themselves never paid the cost of crossing."[21] The psychological suffering inherent in the immigrant experience was intensified on the frontier by unaccustomed deprivations and hardships, inexorable forces of nature, and debilitating diseases. Jacob Naumann reported from Hermann in August 1839 that "the fever was worse than ever" and described the often-tragic results: "With many this illness settled on the eyes and ears, and in serious cases, strength of mind. They become listless and weak and often irrational. They dream while awake and sneak around like ghosts in the night. If the fever stays with them for a long time they are apt to keep the after effects for the rest of their lives."[22]

Hesse had learned that there was a vast difference between the European dream of plenty and the American reality. Noting the prevalence of noxious insects and wild animals, the time and hard labor required to clear land, and the difficulties in raising and caring for livestock, he concluded that "whoever is well situated in Europe, or even somewhat satisfactorily situated, should not move,"[23] warning his readers that America was not the *Schlaraffenland* of German myth, where the trees are laden with fruit, the brooks flow with milk and honey, and roasted doves can be plucked from the air.

The warning came too late for the Bruns family and the Geisberg brothers, struggling to establish a foothold for themselves on the Maries River. Brought up to respect work, Jette sometimes found great satisfaction in her accomplishments in those early days, as she wrote

---

19. *The Uprooted* (New York: Grosset & Dunlap, 1951), p. 4.
20. *Das westliche Nordamerika, in besonderer Beziehung auf die deutschen Einwanderer in ihren landwirtschaftlichen, Handels-und Gewerbverhältnissen* (Paderborn: Joseph Wesener, 1838), p. 208.
21. *The Uprooted*, p. 6.
22. [Naumann], *My Journey to America*, p. 38.
23. Hesse, *Das westliche Nordamerika*, p. 187.

Heinrich on 3 December 1836: "You cannot believe how satisfying it is to work. I probably have had very few days in which I was ever as busy as I am here, that is, having to work, but I am quite happy in doing this and like all the others I have a tremendous appetite and sleep soundly." But in her dreams she returned to the old familiar surroundings. "It is strange, but almost every night now I have dreamed of our father, and then I am still a child with him and spend beautiful hours in my dream."

The struggle to accommodate to the new environment and give new form and meaning to their disrupted lives, often under harsh and hostile circumstances, was harder than they had anticipated. Jette was not yet twenty-four, and sometimes her burdens and responsibilities overwhelmed her, as she reported sadly to her brother in August 1837. "We have had very little luck with anything we have tackled this year. . . . Now we have many people and little to eat. A great worry for the housewife. . . . Well, what else should I complain about? That I am very often vexed? That I feel doubly annoyed with all these misfortunes? That it is no fun to represent cook, nursemaid, and housewife in one person?"

Split-rail fences were washed away when the Maries flooded, the potato crop was ruined by drought, and little pigs froze in the winter or floated away in floods. The construction of the house proceeded so slowly that "the whole world [was] amazed," and at night when the workmen sat around the fire, she had to go to bed with the children to get out of the way. Like Duden, Dr. Bruns had envisioned a natural social harmony developing in the Missouri woods, and writing to Heinrich on 18 January 1836, before her departure for America, Jette had reported that her husband had spoken of the harmonious atmosphere in the Westphalia Settlement, where deprivations borne together were a "lot of fun" and many happy hours were spent working together. Actuality turned out to be otherwise. Her brother Bernhard grew worse, often sick with fever, imagining "thousands of voices in the air," and many times unable to work. The maid, Jenne, disappointed with America, lived in a state of outrage, attacking the children, the chickens, the animals, and inanimate objects, and giving Jette another cross to bear in the New World.

Tragedy often visited the little community, and life sometimes took on a surrealistic quality, for Jette as well as for her brother Bernhard. "A little time ago I went to Lisletown," Bernhard wrote, "but, oh, the city was empty. . . . Do you also have cities with one inhabitant in Germany?"[24] In 1838 Jette wrote about the "two Swedes" who kept a store on the Osage River. One night the men inexplicably locked their doors, got into a boat, and disappeared without a word. One body was later found in the Missouri River near St. Charles. The other had apparently been swept away. The fever struck again and again, six times in the summer of 1838.

By 1839 Westphalia seems to have become a thriving village with a carpenter, a cabinetmaker, a blacksmith, a gunsmith, a butcher, and a shoemaker and was expecting a tailor; but in June 1840 Jette wrote: "How lonely I am. No female being who thinks as I do, with whom now and then I can share my feelings when I need that kind of relief, when I want to forget my daily troubles and sorrow, when these could be set aside for a little while."

Simple satisfactions were transitory, her losses lasting. She loved her garden and "dyeing things blue," and she took immense pleasure in her children: Hermann, the German-born

24. Letter to his brother Heinrich, 4 May 1839, Carla Schulz-Geisberg Archive, Nienberge.

son who had emigrated with his parents; Max, born in Westphalia on 27 February 1837, less than four months after their arrival; Johanna, named for Jette's sister in Germany, born 3 March 1839; and Rudolph, born 26 January 1841. But in 1841, just before her twenty-eighth birthday, three of the children, those born in America, died within three weeks of each other of dysentery, Johanna on 13 September, Max on 19 September, and the baby Rudolph, who seemed at first to be recovering, suddenly on 2 October. The deaths of her children, for whose future she had left her home, devastated her. Her brother's romantic elegy on the deaths of the three children in Westphalia reflects a grief calmed by faith and family love, but the "heart's pure and serene peace" for which she longed did not come to her. In the years following the loss of her children, Jette was often, as she put it, at odds with the whole world. She was left alone for long periods while Dr. Bruns kept up his widely scattered practice, bills for which he often found as difficult to collect as in Germany. Her husband's differences with church officials and various business partners intensified her feelings of alienation. Her continuing concern for the young sisters and brothers she had left behind in Germany led to misunderstandings with her uncle and aunt in Münster, which hurt her deeply. Stories circulating in the Westphalia Settlement and among family members at home that the Bruns were planning to return to Germany angered, frustrated, and saddened her. Hard times persisted, and in 1842 she wrote Heinrich that the piano they had bought from the Hesses in 1837 was sold for one hundred fifty dollars because there was no money at all and she did not play it anyway.

In 1843, after a long struggle with his personal demons that had alternately grieved his sister and aggravated her beyond measure, Bernhard Geisberg went back to Germany. As Jette had feared, he was no better able to function at home than in America, and she soon learned that he had been sent to an institution, where he was to spend the rest of his life. It was to torture her for many years that she had not been able to wrest him, body and mind, back from the "Hell that rattled in him," as Heinrich's romantic poem "Fantasy Based on Bernhard's Tale" put it. Another loss in 1843 was the death of a fellow Westphalian from their hometown of Oelde. Riding from Lisletown at night, Fritz Schwarze had been thrown from his horse and suffered fatal injuries, leaving his wife and six children destitute. "He was the only friend we had from Oelde," Franz Geisberg wrote his brother. "[He] had cleared almost thirty acres of new land . . . and now that he could enjoy the fruits of his work, he is taken out of this world."[25]

Although her brother Franz and her husband frequently wrote of their farms, or "plantations" as Dr. Bruns liked to call their holdings, in glowing terms and always expected the next venture—whether a store, a mill, or a distillery—to be the successful one, life remained unrewarding for Jette. They eventually became well situated in Westphalia, "yes, indeed better situated than in Oelde; we have furniture, we are even not without some luxuries, as for instance, a carpet, a fine lamp, vases, etc. . . . But all this does not please me." She worried about her brother Franz, working hard but unable to achieve the same kind of comforts she had, and about her cousin, Arnold Boner. She had known Boner in her youth as a dashing young officer arranging balls and serving as her faithful messenger when she had been exiled to Münster; in America she coped with an ill, distraught man who had emigrated to Westphalia in 1845 after the death of his wife and hatched one impractical plan

25. Letter of 14 May 1843, Carla Schulz-Geisberg Archive, Nienberge.

after another from which Dr. Bruns had to try to dissuade him. In 1847 her brother's wife died of tuberculosis after a long and harrowing illness; her cousin Boner died just as he finally got settled on a large farm; and in August she lost another child, a son, born prematurely, who lived only eight days. In 1849, more than a dozen years after settling in Westphalia, Jette still felt herself a stranger in a strange land: "You cannot imagine how hard it is to become accustomed to things here," she wrote Heinrich in February of that year. "The customs, the morals, the language, people without feeling, everything is foreign and cold." She had written the previous year in confidence to her uncle in Münster, asking him to urge Bruns to give up his widespread practice in Westphalia before it ruined his health. "I often say that we will have to try something different so that Bruns could have his . . . practice . . . somewhere else. But Bruns enjoys our beautiful farm, and he fears the uncertainty."[26] She longed to go to California to seek gold, but instead became responsible for her brother's three children while Franz went to seek a fortune.

In 1851, finally determining to make a new start, Dr. Bruns moved his family to a large farm across the Osage at Shipley's Ferry, where they lost another child, a five year old, to sunstroke. The grief over her lost children and the recurrent illnesses had taken their toll on Jette. In January 1853, a few months after her thirty-ninth birthday, she described herself to Heinrich as a "still, sad, indifferent figure, without interest, with aged features, a mouth without teeth." Franz came back from California without having found "the glittering fortune" he had seen others find, and after long discussions the family decided to move to Jefferson City. Hermann, the oldest son, and Franz favored the move. Jette had been undecided what to do, she wrote Heinrich in September 1854, but she thought life in the city would be better for the children. It seemed at first that they had made a serious mistake. Dr. Bruns, who had a genuine love for "plantation" life, if little business sense, fell into such a severe depression that Jette later recalled this period as the worst in her life. In temporary quarters and as isolated as she had ever been in Westphalia, struggling to take care of her own five children and her brother's three and at the same time bring her husband back from what seems to have been a self-imposed withdrawal, she "chatted" and suggested and urged. Her husband put on a frosty face, she wrote Heinrich, and her brother remained monosyllabic, having no idea what he wanted to do. Dr. Bruns developed pneumonia, and various doctors came and prescribed medicines, which he refused to take. Jette was very frightened, but eventually he effected a cure for his illness himself.

After his recovery, Dr. Bruns built a store with an apartment upstairs for the family, and business seemed to thrive. In 1856 he was able to take Jette back to Germany. At last she realized her dream of seeing again the brothers and sisters she had left behind twenty years before. Ironically, yet perhaps not unexpectedly, the trip home brought sorrow as well as joy. After twenty years in America, she at first felt disoriented in her homeland. "Everything seems so strange to me and yet so familiar," she wrote in May 1856 on her arrival in Germany. "It makes me sad. I would almost like to turn around and go back to Missouri to my children." When they visited the hospital where Bernhard had been confined for many years, only Dr. Bruns was allowed to see him. It was an experience that intensified her grief for her lost brother.

Upon their return to Jefferson City, Dr. Bruns built an imposing residence on High Street

---

26. Letter to Caspar Geisberg of April 1848, Carla Schulz-Geisberg Archive, Nienberge.

across from the State Capitol, on the site where the U.S. Post Office now stands. Three stories high, each floor with nine rooms, it provided an excellent view of the Capitol grounds and government activities. Franz Geisberg built a store nearby on High Street near Broadway and settled there with his three children. At last the family seemed to be in reach of a secure and comfortable life. Dr. Bruns, who had been politically active even in Westphalia, became prominent in local and state political and business circles. An ardent supporter of Thomas Hart Benton, he was one of the organizers of the Jefferson City Land Company, which planned to establish a new community west of Jefferson City based on "Bentonian" principles.[27] In 1858, however, Jette suffered the loss of her last link in Missouri with the Geisberg family. Her brother Franz, the "boy" who had given her many worrisome hours and whose health had been weakened by his years of farming in Westphalia and searching for gold in California, died after a brief illness. He was forty-two and had never been, as she wrote Heinrich in November, "as long as he has been here so satisfied and full of hope." The orphaned Geisberg children, Caspar, Henriette, and Heinrich, ranging in age from thirteen to seventeen, became her care again.

The approach of the Civil War brought uneasy times to the capital city. As pro-Union sympathizers tried to wrest the state government from the hands of elected officials sympathetic to the South, Jette's two boys, her own son Heinrich and her brother's son Caspar, went off to St. Louis to join the Union army. With Confederate flags flying from the State Capitol and Confederate troops camped on the Capitol grounds, rumors circulated regarding possible retaliation against Germans, who were known to oppose slavery. Local officials moved the seat of government to Boonville in June 1861 as Gen. Nathaniel Lyon approached Jefferson City; Jette considered moving with the children to a "free state," but the family stayed together. Their primary concern was for the soldiers, Caspar with the First Regiment of American Zouaves and Heinrich with Col. Franz Sigel's Third Regiment. The news about Caspar came first. He was seriously wounded near Fort Donelson in March 1862 and hospitalized at Mound City, Illinois, where his arm was amputated. He wrote that he wanted to come home, and Dr. Bruns went to get him, but Caspar died a few days after arriving in Jefferson City. He was twenty-one. Heinrich reenlisted in a cavalry unit and died in battle near Iuka, Mississippi, the next year, on 7 July 1863, two months before his twenty-first birthday.

Dr. Bruns, serving as a Union major, was active in political and military affairs in the state capital during the war, but he had little time to devote to business. When he died in 1864, while serving as mayor of Jefferson City, his affairs were left in disarray. Jette found herself alone with four of her own children (Wilhelm, the youngest, had been born at Shipleys Ferry in November 1853), two of Franz's children, many debts, and almost no resources. To support herself and the children, she let rooms and ran a boarding house, which was patronized by many prominent German legislators. Judge Arnold Krekel called her dining room the "radical corner" because of the political persuasion of her boarders, and others referred to it as "the German Diet." Judge Hugo Muench, who accompanied his father to Jefferson City as a teenager, later recalled that although he was allowed to sit at the table with his elders if he kept quiet, the political discussions often got so intense that the diners forgot to pass food to

27. Letter to the editor, *Jefferson City Inquirer,* 7 November 1857.

him, and he left the table with extensive information on political problems but still hungry. During the many years she boarded legislators and other officials, Jette sometimes took "Americans," but not Democrats or former secessionists.

Although intensely interested in politics throughout her life, in the years after the war she had little time to visit with her distinguished guests as she tried to unravel the complex financial problems Dr. Bruns had left her. Still defending her husband to Heinrich, she suffered the unkind remarks of his creditors as best she could. It was only with the assistance of her brother-in-law Hermann Bruns, who still lived in Westphalia, of Judge Krekel, who got a small pension for her from the Land Company, and of a stipend from a family foundation in Germany that she was able to keep her home, where she worked and raised her children, educating them to the best of her ability.

The settlement of the estates, Dr. Bruns's and her brother's, dragged on for years with suits by creditors and many embarrassments and disappointments. She was shocked to find that money borrowed from her uncle and brother Heinrich in the 1830s had never been completely repaid and interest payments had lapsed years before. In the early 1890s, twenty-seven years after Dr. Bruns's death, when she finally received a pension for his service as a medical officer in the Union army, she immediately committed this income to Heinrich to repay loans from him that had weighed on her mind for many years.

In the last decades of her long life, Jette lived with her children, visiting them in Ohio, St. Louis, Seattle, and back in Jefferson City, suffering their griefs and disappointments, worrying about her grandchildren, and always sharing her worries with Heinrich. Her daughter Effie was widowed in 1871, with three children to support. In 1872, when Jette was fifty-nine, Hermann, her oldest son, the one born in Germany and perhaps the most troubled of her children, died at age thirty-eight. Her daughter Ottilie's husband, Carl Hess, spent long months in Colorado in a mining venture, and mother and daughter kept up large gardens and orchards and took care of chickens and livestock while he was away.

In the 1880s, when Jette was in her mid-seventies, she and Wilhelm, who had never found his "place in life," started a farm near Jefferson City. She planted one hundred fifty mulberry trees and planned to raise silkworms, but Wilhelm soon grew discouraged with the farm and went to join his brother in Seattle. Jette moved back with Ottilie, where she grew flowers, read Thomas à Kempis, and continued to write to her family in Germany until her failing eyesight made it impossible to write, read, or distinguish flowers from weeds. She died on 7 November 1899, sixty-three years and one week after her arrival in the Westphalia Settlement. Her daughter Ottilie Hess, writing in 1891 of her hope that her mother would bring her autobiography up to date, observed that it would not be pleasant reading, for "these were difficult, worrisome years in which she, a woman standing by herself, had to create an existence for herself and her children. But it will be . . . an example of what will power can achieve."

With their determination to survive only strengthened by the adversities they faced, Jette and her contemporaries made a lasting mark on the frontier, holding faithfully to their values and strong sense of family. Orphaned children of their brothers, sisters, and cousins were taken into their households as a matter of course, along with parents and other aging or ill relatives. They valued education and saw that their children, girls as well as boys, had the best schooling possible. They took an active interest in American politics and local affairs, but perpetuated the German traditions that seemed a last tie to their homeland. Refusing to accommodate to the melting-pot concept of American history even during times of virulent nativism when it would have been easier to do so, they insisted that their children learn the German language, carry on German traditions, and keep in touch with the relatives at home. As a consequence, the small centers for German culture that Duden, Münch, and Follenius[28] envisioned did in fact arise in Missouri and elsewhere and had a profound effect on the state and the nation.

The letters Jette wrote to her brother often discuss local, state, and national political developments and give her views of the events she experienced and observed during six decades in the United States. However, they are primarily a very personal and intimate document of her own emotional and spiritual life from her impetuous youth to her reluctant accommodation to the infirmities of old age. They reflect the tensions in family relationships and the predicament of cultural minorities facing societal pressures to assimilate. The stress of the acculturation process that eventually occurs in the second and third generations of an immigrant family stranded her between cultures. In November 1879, over forty years after arriving in Missouri, Jette complained from Ottilie's home in Jefferson City that writing was getting more difficult for her because she was living "in foreign circles." Throughout her long life she held to her family in Germany, sometimes scolding them for not writing but always concerned about them.

Like most personal letters, these were intended only for the eyes of the recipient, usually not even to be shared with family members, and certainly not for readers of another time. Jette was much given to self-examination and reported her shortcomings to her brother in great detail, but sometimes could not resist criticism of others. She wrote down whatever was on her mind, and not having the time or energy to recopy her letters to omit comments she regretted, sent them off with their imperfections, sometimes admonishing her brother to forget her comments immediately! Nevertheless, in her autobiography and in the remarkable letters to her brother Heinrich, Jette speaks for her silent contemporaries, offering an intimate view of nineteenth-century German family life on the American frontier. Not only in her strength and will power, but also in her losses and disappointments she represents an important feminine experience during a critical time in our national development. Her story, personal and unique as it may be, is the story of many women.

---

28. Paul Follenius, cofounder with Friedrich Münch of the Giessen Emigration Society.

A Note on Language

Spelling variations are common throughout the Geisberg-Bruns letters. Nineteenth-century German was a language in flux, and the spelling of names differed from one day to the next or even from one paragraph in a letter to the next, as in *Adolph-Adolf, Caspar-Kasper, Catherine-Katharina, Carl-Karl.* When verification of a name was not possible, the spelling given by the writer was retained, and normalization was not attempted. Americanization of names affected spelling in later years. Jette generally spells names such as *Hermann* and *Ernst* the German way, even when the person with the name had changed it. Her son-in-law Ernest Decker had Americanized his name and named his son *Ernest,* but to Jette her son-in-law and grandson were always *Ernst.* The names *Gustave* and *Theodore* may appear with or without the final *e.* Infants were given multiple Christian names, and Jette's relatives sometimes used one and sometimes another name at different times in their lives.

Other proper names in the text often reflect the preference of the person, as with Friedrich *Münch* and his son, Hugo *Muench.* In the case of Gustav *Körner,* the spelling of the name in later years appears as *Koerner,* particularly in connection with his political life in Illinois. On the other hand, the German poet's name is naturally written as *Körner.* German towns are written as they appear on standard German maps of the time, for example, *Münster* and *Osnabrück,* but *Oelde.*

Jette's German was excellent, but obviously during the span covered by the 151 letters, from her thirteenth year to her eighty-seventh, changes in style occurred that are reflected in the translation. As she grew further in years from her homeland, her children spoke English, correspondence with her family decreased, and it became more difficult for her to write her native language. In her autobiography, selections from which appear here as introductories to the periods of her life covered by the letters, she reached far back into her past to bring up a German at once more formal and tinged with her local dialect. A few letters from members of Jette's family were included when they contributed to the telling of her story. Letters written by her father, Max Geisberg, to his sister and to Jette present a curious contrast: that to his sister a passionate expression of his agony at the death of his wife, those to Jette loving but pragmatic.

The translator has tried to achieve a more or less idiomatic English in word order, verb form, prepositional choice, and punctuation, trying, however, not to affect the spontaneity or the mood of the letter. Jette's letters are informal and personal writings in which a woman's life experience is recounted to a close family member. Whether writing immediately, as in the letters, or retrospectively, as in the autobiography, Jette said things her own way.

Home of Jette's parents in Oelde. Pen sketch by Max Geisberg,
son of Jette's brother Heinrich.

Henriette Geisberg Bruns. Photograph taken
in Jefferson City about 1863–1864.

Dr. Bernhard Bruns, Jette's husband.
Photograph shows him as major in U.S.
Army Surgeons Corps, about 1863.

Jette's 1850 sketch (redrawn by Frank Stack) of the half-timbered house she and Dr. Bruns built in Westphalia in 1836–1838. The two following photographs (used courtesy of the Missouri Department of Natural Resources) show the house as it appeared in the mid-1980s.

Heinrich Geisberg, Jette's brother and the recipient of most of the letters.

Pastor Hermann Bruns of Wadersloh, Jette's brother-in-law, who performed her marriage ceremony in 1832.

Dr. Bruns and Jette.

Franz Geisberg, Jette's oldest brother, who emigrated with her to Westphalia.

Caspar Geisberg, Franz's oldest child, who was wounded at Fort Donelson and died in Jefferson City in March 1862.

Heinrich Geisberg, Jette's brother, who became a lawyer and archivist in Münster, and his wife Auguste, whom he married in 1872, when he was fifty-four years old.

Johanna, Jette's sister, and her husband, Caspar Offenberg, who was lord mayor of Münster.

Therese, Jette's youngest sister, and her husband, Franz von Hatzfeld, who was a court counselor in Münster.

Hermann Bruns, Jette's only child born in Germany, and his wife, Nettie Holtschneider, who was also born in Oelde.

Heinrich (Henry) Bruns, Jette's son, who was killed in battle in 1863 at Iuka, Mississippi.

Euphemia (Effie), Jette's daughter, and her husband, Ernest William Decker II, St. Louis lawyer and state representative.

Louis David Bruns, Jette's son, and his wife, Emily Louise Sander.

Ottilie, Jette's youngest daughter, and her husband, Carl E. Hess, first superintendent of the power and light company in Jefferson City.

Wilhelm Bruns, Jette's youngest son.

Arnold Boner, Jette's cousin, who emigrated to Westphalia in 1845 and died there two years later.

24

Jette with her three youngest children, Wilhelm, Louis, and Ottilie (from left to right). This photograph was taken after the death of her husband.

Heinrich Geisberg with his wife, Auguste, and their two children, Max and Maria. Photograph taken in 1876.

Max Geisberg. This photograph shows him as an art history and archaeology student in Münster; he became professor of art history and director of the State Museum for the Province of Westphalia in Münster.

Jette with her brother Heinrich and sisters Therese (at far left) and Johanna (at far right) during her visit to Germany in 1882.

Jette in her old age. She died at age eighty-seven in 1899, in Jefferson City, having gradually lost her eyesight in her last five years.

Missouri's state capitol in Jefferson City, with Lohman's Landing in the foreground. From a lithograph published in the mid-1860s by Hermann J. Meyer, 164 William Street, New York City.

St. Joseph Catholic Church in Westphalia, Missouri. Courtesy of the State Historical Society of Missouri.

Father Ferdinand Helias, S.J., first pastor at Westphalia. Courtesy of *The Catholic Missourian*.

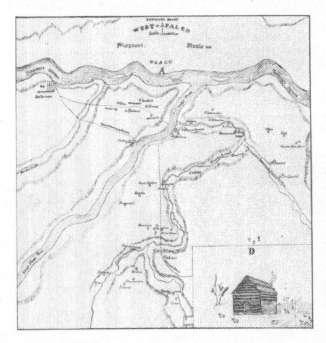

Map of the Westphalia Settlement as it appeared in 1837–1838; this map, provided by the Westphalia Historical Society, was drawn from one by Nicolaus Hesse that was published in his *Das westliche Nordamerika* (Paderborn, 1838).
The sketch at lower right shows Hesse's cabin.

Residence of Dr. Bruns at Washington and High streets, Jefferson City, from an Eduard Robyn lithograph. Courtesy of the Missouri Department of Natural Resources.

B. Bruns and Company store, High Street, Jefferson City. Courtesy of the Missouri Department of Natural Resources.

Bruns-Geisberg Family

I,1. Maximilian Friedrich Geisberg
11 Aug 1774–20 Nov 1831 Oelde
m. 14 Oct 1812 (7 children)
Maria Johanna Hüffer
23 Mar 1796–1 Jun 1827 Oelde

II,1. Anna Elisabeth Henriette Bernadine
Geisberg (Jette)
28 Oct 1813–7 Nov 1899 Jefferson City
m. 24 May 1832 (11)
Johann Bernard (Dr.Bernhard) Bruns
22 Dec 1798–1 Apr 1864 Jefferson City

2. Franz Friedrich Geisberg
5 Jan 1816–28 Oct 1858
m. 5 Nov 1840 (4)
Gertrude Stiefermann
d. June 1847 Westphalia

3. Heinrich Engelbert Geisberg
17 Sep 1817–14 May 1895 Münster
m. 4 Apr 1872 (3)
Auguste Josephine Boner
28 Mar 1840–27 May 1924 Münster

4. Bernhard Geisberg
17 Aug 1819–18 Aug 1880 Obermarsberg

5. Johanna Maria Geisberg
27 Feb 1822–10 Oct 1902
m. 3 Sep 1840 (11)
Caspar Offenberg
4 Feb 1809–3 Mar 1879

6. Wilhelm Geisberg
16 Jul 1824–19 Apr 1865 Hamburg

7. Therese Geisberg
31 May 1827–27 Mar 1909
m. 12 May 1853 (7)
Franz von Hatzfeld
15 Oct 1819–7 Apr 1886

III,1. Hermann Ludwig Bruns
20 Oct 1833 Oelde–22 Jun 1872 St.Louis
m. 1862 (1)
Maria Cath. Holtschneider (Nettie)
10 Feb 1843 Oelde–23 Oct 1918

2. Maximilian Bruns
27 Feb 1837–19 Sep 1841 Westphalia

3. Johanna Clotilde Euphemia Bruns
3 Mar 1839–13 Sep 1841 Westphalia

4. Rudolph Gerhard Johannes Bruns
26 Jan 1841–2 Oct 1841 Westphalia

5. Heinrich Gottfried Hermann Bruns
19 Sep 1842–7 Jul 1863 at Iuka, Miss.

6. Euphemia Anna Bruns (Effie)
3 May 1844–30 Sep 1937 Jefferson City
m. 24 May 1866 (3)
Ernest W. Decker II
26 Nov 1838–6 Dec 1871 St. Louis

7. Albert Christoph Bruns
11 Dec 1845–24 Aug 1851 Westphalia

8. Adolph Bruns
7 Aug 1847–15 Aug 1847 Westphalia

9. Ludwig David Bruns (Louis)
17 Jul 1848–   1909 Skagway, Alaska
m. 3 Sep 1879 (5) Emily Louise Sander
8 Oct 1861–19 Jan 1912 Mercer Island,
Wash.

10. Ottilie Therese Bruns
23 Apr 1851–19 Jul 1934 Jefferson City
m. 22 May 1880 Carl Edwin Hess
30 Apr 1839–22 Dec 1904 Jefferson City

11. Wilhelm Georg Bruns
24 Nov 1853–21 Dec 1916 Seattle, Wash.

III. Children of Franz Geisberg and Gertrude
Stiefermann born in Westphalia, MO

1. Johann Caspar Geisberg
30 Sep 1841–18 Mar 1862 Jefferson City
Wounded at Ft. Donelson, Tenn.

2. Maria Henriette Geisberg (Jette)
3 Feb 1843–1 Sep 1926 Jefferson City
m. 2 May 1867 (6) Henry C. Nitchy
23 May 1834–5 May 1894 Jefferson City

3. Heinrich Christoph Geisberg (Henry)
13 Jun 1845–9 Oct 1921 Jefferson City
m. 10 Feb 1876 (1) Amelie J. Guyot
1851–1912

4. John Peter Mathias
22 Jan 1847–25 Jan 1847

III. Children of Heinrich Engelbert Geisberg
and Auguste Boner

1. Maria Josephine Geisberg
11 Apr 1873 Münster–25 Mar 1933 Wesel
m. 29 May 1900 Clemens Kochs
1869–1952

2. Johanna Amalie Maria
21 Sep 1874; died the same day

3. Max Franz Heinrich Geisberg
9 Oct 1875–5 June 1943 Münster
m. 11 Apr 1907 (4)
Maria (Mia) Overhues 1881–1967

Bruns Family from Lohne near Lingen, Parish of Schepsdorf

I. Hermann Heinrich Bruns (heir to farm at Lohne)
30 Mar 1763–27 Oct 1825
m. 9 Nov 1790 (9)
Catharina Euphemia Gosling
16 Feb 1768–18 Mar 1836

II,1. Margaretha Aleid Bruns
11 June 1792–22 June 1838 Lohne

2. Hermann Heinrich Bruns (heir to farm)
18 Apr 1794–26 Dec 1857
m. 23 Nov 1824 (2)
Euphemia Gesina Hermeling
30 Jul 1801–24 Jul 1828

3. Johann Hermann Bruns (pastor in Wadersloh)
11 Sep 1796–14 Nov 1874

4. Johann Bernard (Dr. Bernhard) Bruns
22 Dec 1798–1 Apr 1864
m. 14 May 1832 (11) (see Geisberg Family above) Henriette Geisberg
28 Oct 1813–7 Nov 1899

5. Bernard Hermann Bruns (Hermeling)
16 Jan 1802–4 Jan 1878 Drievorden
m. 1824 (4)
Euphemia Christina Hermeling
4 Feb 1794–14 Oct 1874 Drievorden

6. Johann Gerard Bruns
15 Jul 1804–
m. 18 Feb 1832
Maria Elisabeth Hamm
11 Sep 1794–

7. Johann Heinrich Bruns (deaf and dumb)
6 Nov 1806–19 Aug 1877

8. Johann Bernard David Bruns
21 Apr 1809–3 Nov 1857
m. 21 Sep 1845
Christina Blumberg
remarried 17 Feb 1858
Gerhard Hilkemeier
–28 Feb 1888

9. Gerard Hermann Bruns
24 Dec 1811–14 Jul 1876
m. 23 Apr 1840 (9)
Anna Maria Lückenhoff
25 May 1819 Oelde–22 Aug 1859
Westphalia

III. Children of Johann Bernhard Bruns and Jette Geisberg (see Bruns-Geisberg Family above)

III. Children of Gerhard Hermann Bruns and Anna M. Lückenhoff of Westphalia, MO

1. Bernard Joseph Bruns
25 Feb 1841–20 Jun 1858

2. Elizabeth Bernadine Catherine Bruns
24 Apr 1842–8 Jan 1903
m. 6 Apr 1864 (13)
Hermann Adrian
3 Mar 1836–6 Jun 1888

3. Henriette Elizabeth Bruns
5 Jan 1845–

4. Catherine Maria Francesca Bruns
5 Jul 1846–27 Mar 1916
m. 8 Jun 1875 Joseph Dubbert (6)
14 Feb 1847–10 Feb 1922

5. Joseph Christian Bruns
16 Feb 1848–

6. Maria Katharina Henriette Bruns
21 Jul 1850–20 Mar 1889
m. 23 Apr 1872
John Hilkemeyer

7. Maria Christina Elizabeth Bruns
13 Dec 1852–21 Sep 1855

8. Maria Catherine Wilhelmina Bruns
2 May 1856–14 Mar 1941
m. 2 Sep 1879
Bernard Hageboeck

9. Maria Bertha Bruns (Sister Hedwig)
16 Jan 1858– Nov 1954

prologue

In Germany, 1813–1836

"I am so terribly frightened, and I cannot tell Bruns.
But I do not waver for a moment."

Jette Bruns, 5 January 1835,
to her brother Heinrich

From the Autobiography

In a Koerdinck[1] calendar which I discovered after my father's death, I found the beginning of an autobiography, written in Grandfather's hand. . . . This was a hundred years ago, and I now follow his example. At the request of my children, I have to go very far back, I have to try to refresh my memory and begin to see before me the time when I was a small child.

I am Henriette, the oldest daughter of Max Friedrich Geisberg, Licentiate of Law, and Johanna Hüffer.[2] Father's forebears had been tax collectors in Stromberg[3] for several generations. Thus my grandfather, Franz Friedrich Geisberg, whose wife was Elisabeth Wernekink from Metelen, was also a tax collector. After a childless marriage of twelve years, my grandparents had six children. My father was the oldest son, born in 1774. Soon thereafter Grandfather accepted the call of the Elector of Westphalia and settled permanently in Münster. The second son, Bernhard, studied in Göttingen; he caught nervous fever,[4] and remained very withdrawn. In the course of the years this lessened somewhat, so that he became a little more accessible to his relatives, and in his room and otherwise in the small family circle he was very kind and participated in everything. He had not completed his ordination, but he was a canon and drew a canon's salary. The third son,[5] Adolf, wanted to pursue a career as a merchant in Bremen, but at his father's request he returned during the unrest of the war and took over his position. (Westphalia was ruled by the French at that time.) His wife, Therese, née Lohkampf, was a lively, good woman. Since she had no children she had all kinds of diversions and always had students in the house, generally the adolescent sons in the family. I, too, spent several years with them. She was just the right person for the two uncles who stayed with them in the grandparents' house. The fourth son, Franz, a handsome, personable officer, was married to Marianne Westendorf from Oedingberge. Later, he became the tax collector for the Minister vom Stein at Castle Cappenberg.[6] The fifth of the children was the daughter, Ursula. She was

1. Koerdinck was a book printer and publisher in Münster. His *Almanach* appeared from 1750 to 1900 and continues as the Regensberg *Münstrischer Almanach*.
2. Max Friedrich Geisberg, who was born 11 August 1774 at Stromberg, was a mayor of Oelde and tax collector. He died 20 November 1831 at Oelde. Johanna Hüffer was born 23 March 1796 and married Max Geisberg at Liesborn on 14 October 1812, when she was sixteen. She died 1 June 1827 after the birth of her seventh child.
3. Stromberg is a small fortified town approximately three miles south of Oelde.
4. The German term, at that time, for typhoid fever. The name *typhoid fever* was coined in 1837 to distinguish the disease from typhus.
5. Family records indicate that Adolf Victor was actually the fourth son, born 14 April 1779, while Franz Heidenreich, born 1 December 1777, was the third.
6. Baron Heinrich Friedrich Karl vom und zum Stein (1757–1831) studied law at the University of Göttingen and entered Prussian governmental service in 1780. Following Prussia's crushing defeat by Napoleon at Jena in October 1806, Stein was appointed prime minister in October 1807. He at once issued the Edict of Emancipation, which abolished serfdom in Prussia, and worked to promote land reform and institute local self-government, but his career as prime minister ended when a letter expressing his hope for the liberation of Germany fell into the hands of the French. He fled to Austria, and in 1812 went to Russia where he served as advisor to Alexander I during the Napoleonic invasion. He continued to work for the liberation and unification of Germany but was defeated by Metternich and others at the Congress of Vienna in 1815. Following this, he went into virtual retirement and died at Cappenberg, Westphalia.

married to the court counselor, Max Boner, and they lived first in Oelde, then in Liesborn, and finally in Münster. Uncle Caspar, the youngest son, was delicate as a child. He was a scholar and for many years was archivist in Münster.

My mother's parents were the linen merchant Heinrich Andreas Hüffer of Stromberg and his wife Elisabeth Hellweg of Münster. (Half-brothers of Grandfather were Hermann, who had a large bookstore in Münster, and Brother Wilhelm, who was prior and, after the monastery was closed, became pastor in Liesborn. The third moved to Eupen at the Belgian border and became a rich factory owner. His half-sister married an Eylardi in Bremen.) My grandfather's only full sister was Johanna, who was married to the banker Ludwig Niedieck in Stromberg. (The Hellwegs in Münster were a big family. I became acquainted with Grandmother's brothers and sisters later on. They were the cloth merchant Andreas, our uncle, the canon, our aunts Oberschmidt, Funke, Schmedding, Brüning, and von Zurmühlen.) Grandfather was H. A. Hüffer, a lively, energetic man. He died early. My mother, born in 1796, and her brother, Heinrich, born in 1798, were the only children.

During the war our father came to *Haus Geist*[7] and Oelde and Stromberg. He became tax collector and mayor of Oelde. When he was thirty-eight years old, he married sixteen-year-old Johanna Hüffer. At first they lived in Grandmother's house. But soon after my birth (I was born on 28 October 1813) they moved to Oelde. And now I begin to remember how I was often at Grandmother's and how she gave me presents and loved me. A Christmas tree, which in those days was very rare, glittered with many candles at Christmas time. At her death in 1820 I felt my first great pain.

From then on I remember how the stork stopped in at our house. We were seven brothers and sisters. Franz, a weak child, Heinrich, Bernhard, Johanna, Wilhelm, and Therese.[8] We children had a happy youth. Father was serious. He had a considerable library and read a lot. Mother was lively, energetic, and the soul of the house. She was always busy in the household with the servants and with us children and in the garden; she was ambitious and inventive. I remember that I attempted to help her in the garden. As a rarity she had several kinds of Indian corn as well as some colorful beets. In the little garden behind the house we three oldest ones had our plots. A sand path surrounded the oval center of the space like a crescent and was edged on both sides by flowers. Then there were beds with plants, and at one side there was a sundial, and under it was the well for the pump for the house. We had a piano, a grand piano from Grandmother, who was probably a virtuoso. There was a box full of music beside it. At an early age I received lessons in piano and particularly in voice. Mother and I sang duet, I always alto, and since she was a member of a singing society, I helped her study her part. That made me proud. In school I learned well, I believe, and I was also instructed at home. In class I was always the youngest but not always the best-behaved, since I remember being punished several times. As a hobby I cut quills for writing, and for that purpose I always had a fine sharp knife which earned me the thanks of my classmates. And when Father once asked me for a sharpened quill, since he no longer could see so well, I felt very

7. *Haus Geist,* an old castle about two and a half miles northwest of Oelde, was formerly the Monastery of the Holy Ghost. The family of Chief Forester von Bachofen, friends of the Geisbergs, lived there.

8. Jette's brothers and sisters were: Franz Friedrich, born 5 January 1816; Heinrich Engelbert, born 17 September 1817; Bernhard, born 17 August 1819; Johanna Maria, born 27 February 1822; Wilhelm, born 16 July 1824; and Therese, born 31 May 1827.

important. In school the bigger boys and girls were instructed in grafting trees. On special days we were led to the separate nurseries, and there we were allowed to show our skill. We also learned to sing from notes, and I did well in that and was allowed to sit next to the music teacher in church to assist her; she had asthma. The boys sat with a teacher in the choir loft, and we sat below. We took our turns singing. I loved the songs from the Verspoell song book[9] very much. I always remembered them, and even now I often hum these melodies. In the home of the widow of the surgeon Schlieff I had lots of company, and she always had books to read. And her daughters and I profited by that. There were many things that were beyond our horizon, but we were very proud. She had the plays of Shakespeare; on the title page from Macbeth, the Queen was dashing out of the burning castle shouting, "Oh flame, consume me, but at the same time destroy my spirit." Later, when I returned from Münster, little Fränzchen, who was the dearest to me, was dead.

A treat to which we looked forward for a long time was the trip to Liesborn during vacations. On the first of every month my father made his rounds as tax collector. In September we three oldest were allowed to accompany him. In front was the tax messenger, Michaelis, with a basket on his back in which books and the necessary supplies were kept. Father always carried a loaded rifle. And we swarmed around him. The first stop was in Diestedde. After several hours, which he spent with his duties and we by looking and running around, we had a good meal at the inn. At four o'clock Father was finished, and then we set out toward Liesborn. Our uncle, Pastor Hüffer, received us kindly. Upstairs in the old monastery we had big, splendid rooms. (Father roomed at the inn.) It was so solemn there, so serious, still according to the old custom of the monastery. But Uncle and the other priests were so good and tried to please us in every way imaginable. I believe they liked to see us young people. In the evening we went to visit Dr. Vehring, a long-time, faithful friend of our father and an excellent doctor, who would not be deprived of having dinner with Father every month. These trips, the most beautiful of vacations, were repeated for several years. And even after the death of our uncle, his successor, Father Josephus Zumsande, insisted that we come as we had done earlier. My cousins Marie Geisberg and Max Boner[10] were included, and under the supervision of the latter we were allowed to go on longer excursions. How quickly the week went by when we traveled back from Watersloh.[11] Another extremely pleasant tour during the vacation took us to Münster. Our parents engaged the city drummer, Deppe, who had a little donkey and a little wagon with two side steps and two upholstered seats. We departed early one beautiful morning, Arnold Boner,[12] my two brothers, Carl Geisberg, and I. Naturally we were in a good mood, but our leader increased our pleasure by his tales of the French War. He taught us *oui, qui vive,*[13] and many other short sentences. After four hours we passed Warendorf, and then at the next inn we took a break.

9. C. B. Verspoell, *Gesänge beim Römisch-Katholischen Gottesdienste, nebst angehängtem Gebetbuche,* 6th ed. (Münster: Aschendorff, 1820).

10. Marie, born in 1814, was the daughter of Franz Heidenreich Geisberg and his wife Maria Anna Westendorf. Her brother Carl, born in 1817, later emigrated to America and settled in Milwaukee. Max Boner, born in 1809, was the son of M. Ursula Geisberg and Max Friedrich Boner, court counselor in Münster.

11. Usually spelled *Wadersloh,* the town is about eight miles south of Jette's home town of Stromberg.

12. Arnold Boner (1800–1847), Jette's cousin, was revenue collector for Count Nesselrode Reichenstein at Herten near Recklinghausen. He emigrated to Westphalia in 1845 and bought a farm there, where he died on 27 July 1847.

13. French challenge, "Who's there?"

The donkey found plenty of food. For us pancakes were baked and we drank milk. Perhaps Deppe found something too. Eventually we were ready again. We were not the least bit bored and often ran beside the wagon, and then rode again, and if we saw something special we stopped. From Telgte we had a highway, and finally at the end of a trip which had taken ten hours we were in Münster. I don't recall anything else about this except that soon a letter arrived from Mother, the only one I still have, in which she admonished me that we should be well-behaved and that I should watch the boys.

I was now thirteen years old and had graduated from school. A few weeks later our dear mother suddenly died after the birth of a little sister. She was thirty-one years old. A hard blow! If only it could have a happened a few years later! The relatives sent us a housekeeper and a wet nurse.

Jette to her aunt, Therese Geisberg of Münster, after the death of her mother

Oelde, June 1827

Dear Aunt:

I do hope that you got home safely. We certainly wish so. Now, right away, I have a request for you which we cannot take care of, which is to put a notice in the paper concerning the birth of Threschen[14] and the death of Mother. I shall now acquaint you with a few of the details.

Little Threschen was born on 31 May, at half-past nine in the evening. During the night, at half-past one, my mother was provided with the last rites. She had severe cramps and lost strength rapidly, and finally on the first of June at 9:30 in the morning she died, gently and calmly. On the 24th of March she had become thirty-one years old, and for fifteen years, since the 14th of October 1812, she was the happy wife of my good father. My heart is full and yet I have to compel myself to put something reasonable onto paper. Perhaps this will suffice to write up a death notice. You probably know that it would be very hard on Father if he would have to work this out himself, and therefore you probably will be good enough to grant me this request. Father has come home again, and he is still very well. However, he is often very sad. Time will ease everything. Things are working out quite well with the nanny. Threschen is getting cuter every day. Very often she has her eyes open, and then she looks as if she were I don't know how old. She has already smiled once. The poor little worm does not feel her loss. The household is working out fairly well. Jenne[15] is trying very hard, but Mother is still missed everywhere very much. It would be good if we could get a good person as a housekeeper. The sooner the better. The duties I now have toward Father and my brothers and sisters I shall try to fulfill well. However, I still feel much too weak. I shall trust firmly in God. He will not desert us. Now I must close. Many greetings to the aunts and uncles from Father and my brothers and sisters. From your loving,

Henriette Geisberg

P.S. Don't take it amiss that I have written so poorly, I was much too upset. The next time I shall try to do better. Write as soon as possible and tell Uncle Caspar that I shall write him as

14. Form of endearment, "little Therese."
15. The maid, probably the same Jenny Jurgens who accompanied the Bruns family to America in 1836.

soon as possible. Father would also have liked to write, but he has absolutely no time for it now.

From Max Geisberg to his sister Ursula, a month after the death of his wife

Liesborn
2 July 1827

Dear Ursel:

My soul rages within me and I am so sad, but how can it be any other way? For here I am at Liesborn, in the bedroom of our late uncle, far away from my seven children. There is the bed in which the pastor died and where Jänne slept when she was here after his passing. Everything around evokes memories of him and of her in me.

Here I sit, lonesome and tired from the trip, in the most oppressive summer heat, and I meditate and don't know what I want. . . . But it is true, is it not, that I am not alone? He, the loving Father, who alone can protect me, alone can console me, is indeed with me. And my name is written in His hand, and when I, encouraging myself, sacrifice to Him all this grief anew, already convinced that it will be for my good, and I thank Him, oh, then He will forgive me these few tears which escape me and which He Himself in pity gave us to relieve oppressed hearts.

It rages in me, it presses and presses until after shedding hot tears in my quiet little room I turn over everything and myself to Him. I feel worst when I have occasion to look for something among her things. I recently opened a little box and found little slips of paper with inscriptions, for instance, "hair of my dear Max, Johanna, and Wilhelm."

I cried like a child and could not compose myself. Oh, dear, dear Jänne!

However, when I am with others, then I pull myself together and am calmer, and gradually I am learning to overcome the violence of my grief. Truly, you would be surprised at me. At home the children come closer and closer to me, feeling that they have in me now their only support, so I now frequently go out with them. . . .

I thank you, dear Ursel, very sincerely for the loving letters you have sent me in my sad situation. They have really been true consolations during my grief-filled travels and have uplifted my bowed head to the Father of Love. Only to you will I say it, so that you will love me even more and will ask the All-loving for forgiveness for me because of my great grief. Oh, I am so bowed down, yet You, oh God, will not reject my crushed, bowed heart.

This letter comes at a bad time when my heart is completely dissolving. Take it thusly, read it, burn it, and believe surely that at different times it is quite different with me, absolutely.

I shall answer dear Marianne[16] in the near future. Tell her she should not hold my being late against me. I am, after all, firmly resolved to practice what I advised that dear one in an earlier similar situation.

Farewell and regards to all! Hold dear and write your mourning and yet calmed,

Max

16. This seems to refer to Maria Anna Westendorf, whose husband, Franz Heidenreich Geisberg, had died in 1825.

From the Autobiography

After half a year they took me to Münster to the home of my uncle, Adolf Geisberg, for further education. I had lessons in sewing, and in the afternoon I had to go to the Chaplain Neuvöhner, where we six young girls had private instruction in world history, geography, and composition. Lena Honthumb[17] and I would meet Marie Geisberg at the Cathedral Court and go to the Rectorate of St. Aegidi together. And then we still had French lessons with Miss Bucholz at the Martini School. I also had instruction in music and drawing. In the winter we had dancing lessons. During the second year we had cooking instruction in the morning, and studying for all this could really fill the time. However, I was often taken along in the afternoon by Uncle and Aunt to see the surrounding country. In the winter my aunt gave whist parties in the evenings, and if I felt too lonely I then went to visit the Boners or to the Geisbergs of Cappenberg, who had moved to Münster after Grandfather's death. My cousin Marie was a very close friend. We were always together. And Lena Honthumb was often with us.

Uncle Adolf had taken over our grandparents' house, and the two unmarried brothers, Bernhard and Caspar, lived there. They had their rooms upstairs, but at noon and in the evenings they came down for their meals. The Geisbergs were all well-meaning, noble people, but rather quiet and reserved.

At times Uncle Adolf had to attend a land sale in the country. Then Grandfather's big family coach was hitched up, and we all had to go along. Uncle Caspar and my aunt rode in the back, and Uncle Adolf and Vicar Lagemann (an uncle of my aunt's, a good and cheerful man) were on the back seat. I was shoved in between, and Uncle Bernhard sat on the driver's seat beside the coachman. Those were magnificent days!

The house on Neubrücken Street was roomy. A big gate led to the paved courtyard. To the left was the door of the house, where downstairs there were four rooms, the kitchen, and the room for the domestic. Above the gate there were two bedrooms for students; a wide stairway led up to the hall on the first floor, where besides some large offices for my uncle there were six other rooms, among them the living room and bedrooms for my unmarried uncles. In the back part of the house, near the River Aa, there was first a student room, then a laundry room, then near the road the horse stable, and over that there were rooms for the hired hand. In the front was the shed for two coaches, and beside that was the woodshed. To the left in front of the windows of the living room there was a little garden with dwarf fruit trees and strawberries. Straight ahead you came to the bridge over the Aa, and only then came the big garden, which covered the space along the water for the length of four of the houses on the street. There were magnificent high fruit trees bordering it. And to the left, in the rear, were shrubs down to Dr. Roer's garden, high bushes, hedges, winding and sand-covered paths, then currant bushes in long rows, and several arbors with stone tables.

There were beds of asparagus and vegetables surrounded by the flowers. To the right there was a little gate in the hedge leading out to the promenade and the city. This was used only by the two uncles, but almost every day, so that Uncle Bernhard should not always be alone.

17. Lena Honthumb, Jette's girlhood friend, was the daughter of Ludwig Honthumb, counselor at the Supreme Court in Münster.

This note from Max Geisberg to his fifteen-year-old daughter on Christmas Eve 1828 was addressed to "Demoiselle Henriette Geisberg," Münster auf Neubrücken, marked "Frei," and sealed with red wax. Postal services were not free but were owned by private families at the time.

Dear Jette:

For the wonderful New Year's presents from little Thereschen, I give to her my sincere thanks. This evening, bowls should be set out, and tomorrow you can see what the Christ Child has brought. For you a little something shall be put aside in your pouch, for even though you are not present, you are close to my heart.

Your loving father,
Max Geisberg

24
———28
12

Give the enclosed little letter to Aunt Therese and don't forget to give my greetings to Caspar on his Saint's Day.[18]

Marginal note

A Merry Christmas!
A Happy Entrance into the New Year!
And the Day of the Three Kings!

Max Geisberg to Jette

Oelde
29 March 1829

Dear Jette:

To be sure I have not yet answered a few of your last letters in writing, but rather by deed, by twice sending you clothes. (1) A blue silken and (2) a blue cotton dress, besides (3) shirts, and then (4) a black silken dress. In your letter you did not express yourself clearly enough, for naturally I know nothing about a cloak-party dress. Therefore if this is not right, send it back to us for Johanna, and the irritating cloak or party dress will follow. I ask you, however, to take good care of them and to imitate the person who wore them before you and knew how to take especially good care of them so that they would last a long time. Think of her as a guardian angel. I can easily imagine that you really liked the *Heister Peter,*[19] which was your first ball, but with the false locks you must really have looked foolish. I have no objection to that, but with clothing that is decent and fitting for us and not expensive, one does not have to appear weird and conspicuous by not being up with the latest fashion. The false lock business is and will remain ridiculous and comical. It is too bad that the curling of your own hair takes too much time, for time is, after all, precious.

18. 6 January. According to church tradition, Caspar was one of the three kings who came bearing gifts for the Christ Child. Emperor Frederick I (1123–1190), Barbarossa, is said to have brought Caspar's relics (after the capture of Milan, Italy, in 1164) to Cologne, where they were enshrined in the Cathedral.
19. A popular ball in Münster.

However, now the time of fasting is here, and so we want to collect ourselves and prepare for a happy resurrection at Easter. Here everybody is still quite lively and well. Thereschen's rash has decreased a lot, it is almost gone in her face, only around the upper lip she has an inch-long scar which looks red, but I hope that it will disappear completely since the redness is already decreasing.

We have already been busy in the gardens, sowing and digging, and I've also had about twenty young fruit trees planted in the new garden. —Since the time you wrote me something of Uncle Adolf's illness, I have been quite worried and even though you reported in the last letter that the doctor had declared that the fever had left him completely, this has not been enough to satisfy me. I have inquired of everybody who returned from Münster as to his health, and have always received good news, the last from Krebs. It is good that he has pretty well recovered, thank God! Go to him and tell him that your father sends his best greetings and expresses his sincerest brotherly sympathies for all his suffering and thinks of him very, very often.

Farewell, dear! Write to me soon about Adolf's health. Regards to all the aunts and uncles from your loving father,

Max Geisberg

From the Autobiography

After a two-year stay in Münster I was supposed to go home again. But before that Uncle Adolf took a vacation trip, and they decided it would be quite agreeable to them, and particularly for me, to go along. And so we set out, always by special coach. At first through the Wupper Valley toward Hagen, and then toward Cologne. Then up the Rhine, and we took in everything that was worth seeing. My stout uncle even climbed up with me to the Stolzenfels.[20] And then we went to Bingen, Rüdesheim, Mainz, and toward Frankfurt, where we stayed for a while. It was the time of the fair.[21] Paganini[22] gave his world-famous concerts, and then we went on to Kassel and gradually back.

Then I thought "you can cheer up Father and show what you can do keeping house." I was prevented for a time from doing the latter. I was looked upon as a grown up. Father therefore let himself be persuaded to introduce me to our relatives and acquaintances. These included the Wesemanns, the Osterlinks, the Wenners, the Gessners, the Volmers, the Zumnordens, the von Bruchhausen, von Bachofen, Speiths, and others. One Sunday morning as we were going out in spite of the rain we met the young doctor[23] on the street. He greeted us very cordially and went on. Mrs. Volmer was very friendly and always remained very much devoted to me since she had been an intimate friend of my mother. At the request of my

20. A castle on the left bank of the Rhine south of Koblenz, built about 1244, frequently used as the residence of the archbishop of Trier. Destroyed by French troops in 1689, it was rebuilt from 1836 to 1845 and became the property of King Friedrich Wilhelm IV of Prussia.

21. Frankfurt had an annual trade fair.

22. Niccolo Paganini (1782–1840), Italian violinist and composer, gave hundreds of concerts in Europe's leading cities from 1828 to 1834.

23. Geisberg family records show that Dr. Johann Bernhard Bruns, Jette's future husband, was born in Lohne near Lingen in the province of Hanover on 23 December 1800. However, recently discovered church records of the parish of Schepsdorf/Lingen indicate that Johann Bernard [sic] Bruns was born 22 December 1798.

uncle from Münster I attempted to get Father to take walks in the afternoon. He went along with that, and so we roamed around the surrounding country. It seemed to be good for him and sometimes he even proposed more extensive trips.

I tried to make myself useful with sewing and made dresses for my little sisters and all kinds of things. And then I had a lot of social activities with school acquaintances and my three cousins. I liked Jenny the best. Jenny Wenner was a sister of Aunt Hüffer. It was so comforting to me that my mother's friends treated me in such a friendly way. A small place does indeed offer more social relationships in life. It was easy to become acquainted with people, and a few parties out of town were very pleasant. A well-to-do farmer, Meier Erdland, gave a so-called sheep-shearing party to which the neighbors were invited first of all, of course, because they allowed his sheep in first after the grass had been mown. And then from the city the clergy, the doctor, court officials, and well-known citizens were invited. Altogether there were a few hundred people. We were there. First a dinner was served inside and out in the hall, where tables and benches had been set up in long rows. We girls preferred to sit there, where we were able to get up between long courses. The meal lasted for several hours. Finally the music started, the cook came with a spoon, and offerings were made.[24] Immediately thereafter the tables and benches were cleared and cleaned, and the dance began. We danced on the big stone-covered threshing floor just as easily as in a ballroom. The doctor was attentive to me, and the young lawyers were also good dancers. This was a lively, easy-going life.

We also had a music club. Our good friend Wenner was the director. The members met every two weeks for choral practice. At times the people with instruments also joined us. Each time two members had to deliver a solo of their own choice. Once I sang a selection from the *Stummen*,[25] and Marie accompanied me. Another time Jenny Wenner and I sang a duet from *Don Juan* [*Don Giovanni*], the song "Reich mir die Hand mein Leben."

Everybody who could sing and belonged to society joined us. We had a lot of fun. In our group of alto voices there was an old lady, the wife of Dr. Hüger, who had a very strong voice and so we listened very closely and then soon outsang her. We had beautiful pieces. From Mozart, the *Twelfth Mass;* "The Easter Morning," "The Bell" (this was later presented at a concert). During the solo singing once a Miss Gessner sang, and she was a good actress, but too affected and too languishing. She had chosen for her presentation the aria from *Oberon,* "Ocean, Thou Mighty Monster," and as she began was so goggle-eyed and sang so high, well, I could not contain myself and neither could the first soprano, and we looked at each other and then burst out laughing. We had to leave the room ingloriously. Several gentlemen followed us. But she did not seem to take it amiss.

At Christmas time there was a ball at the Oberniers, which both the townspeople and people from out of town attended. My good father escorted me on the condition that we would leave at midnight. Old Mr. von Bruchhausen brought his daughters Dina and Nettchen. The old gentlemen sat in the room next door with a glass of wine. The clergymen were there for a while. It was a lively party. They had good dancers, but for us it was soon over. Resigned, we followed our fathers.

24. It was customary at the time for guests at such an affair to take up a collection to tip the cooks and other servants.
25. *Stummen* (the mute) refers to *La Muette de Portici* by D. F. E. Auber (1782–1871), which premiered in 1828.

On the third holiday[26] there was a punch evening, given by the wife of Dr. Speith, the usual place for a party for the men. But ladies and gentlemen were paired off, and there was all kinds of fun. These were the so-called distinguished people of the city with their wives and daughters, approximately forty people. We had about a dozen young people. The doctor of law, Ludwig Wenner, was a good friend of ours and was also related to us. I spent the most pleasant hours in their house. Jenny was so kind, but so fragile. There later I often met Dr. Bruns. Our governess always tried to get me together with him, which annoyed me so much that I became stubborn and kept my distance. However, in the course of the winter when he paid more attention to me and I became better acquainted with him I got to like him. At Mardi Gras there was another ball. After I had danced happily for several hours, my father appeared at the door. Without further comment I got myself ready to leave. Downstairs at the steps the doctor was waiting, and he asked Father whether he could accompany us. The latter nodded, and so we went. Father walked ahead, and Dr. Bruns kept his arm tightly around me. He was constantly doing something under the covering over my head. He himself was without a hat or any protection in a severe blizzard, and I couldn't do anything so as not to attract Father's attention. Some time later Father said to me: "I believe the doctor is paying attention to you. I hope he does not think that I am very rich." This startled me. It seemed to me that we liked each other very much, but what else? On another occasion the doctor said something, and I did not object. Without further discussion we developed a harmless relationship, only a little deeper, without other people noticing it.

However, in Münster they must have heard of it, for suddenly a letter arrived from Uncle Caspar, reproaching us bitterly that I, a sixteen-year-old girl, would harm myself with such a relationship. He said it would have to cease. Father was probably also reproached. (They had always blamed Mother's death on her early marriage.) Father spoke very seriously to me, but it was too late.

And now cousin Marie was to come to divert my thoughts and to assist me. And assist me Marie indeed did. As soon as she knew Bruns a little, she was very firmly on his side. The two of us could take walks with him and make secret dates. She beat me to it if I was slow. If he had been out and did not return until night—usually we knew that—she was the first to jump out of bed when the horse turned into our street. We waved a good night to him. He had spoken to Father, who had wished that for the time being we attract no attention to ourselves.

Then summer came and there was a visit by Aunt Therese and another lady. All kinds of excursions were planned, and we were always asked to go along. But we never went to the Wenners, and did not see anybody of interest. I must confess that Marie and I were very pleased when our aunt took sick and we had to send for the doctor. To be sure he cured her after a few days, and she confessed that she was quite, quite pleased with him.

During this summer there were great maneuvers on the heath near Lippstadt, approximately four hours from Oelde. Troops from everywhere moved in and had to find quarters. Then it began to rain, and it was so persistent that the soldiers had to be quartered in the surrounding villages during this emergency. Father voluntarily agreed to take the commanding officer, Major von Döring, with his orderlies. The 13th Regiment, which was under him,

26. In Germany Christmas Eve, First Christmas Day, and Second Christmas Day were celebrated.

consisted almost exclusively of reserve officers from Münster. We knew many of them. Our cousin Arnold Boner was with them. He was a handsome, slender man over six feet tall. A ball was organized under his direction. We were permitted to go, but he had promised that he would deliver us home at midnight, and so he did. This was life in a little village! After a week the troops moved on, and the arrival of the royalty was near. Father was at the reception. We were to join him with the Wenners and the people from Stromberg to see the parade. It was a happy trip on a beautiful day! After the King[27] and his entourage had taken their places on the heath, the regiments with the bands playing marched past, one after the other, endless in number. We remained in our coach in order to be able to see better. Suddenly our major came galloping toward us with his adjutant, saluted with his drawn saber, exchanged a few kind words, and then cantered after his companies. Marie and I were really proud. We got back to Stromberg to the Hüffers late at night.

During this summer Lena Honthumb and Trude Steinbicker (she later became the wife of Franz Geisberg Oels) were boarders at *Haus Geist* with the chief forester, von Bachofen. Since both of them were close friends of ours and we were well acquainted with the Bachofens, we went to see them several times a week. We read, played music, and had a great deal of fun together. Often we went on little trips through the surrounding country. Marie, who usually was very delicate and weak, had gotten her strength back very well. Then the news of her little brother Caspar's death reached us, and she had to go home.

A little later I received an invitation from Aunt Therese to spend the winter with them. They wanted me to get to see something of the big world. I did not really want to go, but Father decided in favor of the plan. Thus I had to leave Oelde for half a year. Bruns and I took the separation hard. Opposition brought more determination to continue our relationship. Even on the last evening he spoke with me at the window of my room.

I was outfitted in Münster. I frequently got to go out; I went with Marie to the Musical Society, and with uncle and aunt to the Civic Club. Uncle Caspar frequently presented us with tickets for the opera. Everything was done to cheer me up. A secret consolation came weekly from Oelde to a different address and was secretly handed to me by friends. Marie had been forbidden by her mother to participate in any way on my behalf. That, of course, she could not do. And it was very hard on me. However, my cousin Arnold Boner had no scruples. He was a faithful messenger.

Bruns's various university friends considered me one of them from the very beginning. They were my most frequent dancing partners and were well liked by my relatives. They were also my protectors if others approached me. As if that would have been necessary!

In the course of the winter Bruns had to take his surgical examination in Münster. I was immediately completely restrained. However, when he called on me before leaving, he happened to find me alone at home. The maid probably was eavesdropping and must have told my aunt. And so from then on the road was clear, without comment. Winter was soon over. I went back home, but Father thought that I could better practice keeping house at the Hüffers' and so I had to leave for Stromberg, an hour from home.

At the Wenners things looked sad. After the birth of their third child, Jenny had to stay in bed. Aunt Hüffer and I visited her several times a week. Bruns had to dedicate many an hour

27. Friedrich Wilhelm III (1770–1840) of Prussia.

to her. She did not even like to see him accompany me to Stromberg afterward. Father was happy to see me back, and he said to our governess that I should have the doctor. That was quite a satisfaction to me.

Jenny was approaching death. Wenner suffered tremendously. And we all grieved so much! A few weeks later the last boy died and Wenner stood alone. He was sick and confined to the house and sometimes asked that my sister, Johanna, come to give him some comfort. Bruns saw him often.

Then in November a letter from home arrived saying that I should come back because Father was seriously ill. My uncle immediately took me home. Father was happy that I was there. I sat up with him by myself all night long. The next morning a stroke put an end to his life. Now we were completely orphaned.

Cousin A. Boner was sent by our uncles to make the necessary arrangements. Three of my brothers were already attending the *Gymnasium*.[28] He was supposed to take along the three little ones and leave me with the Hüffers. I rebelled, and did not want to be separated from the children. The relatives from Stromberg, Uncle Hüffer and Grandfather Niedieck, got together with the Wesemanns at our house. They decided that the two uncles, Hüffer and Uncle Caspar, should take over the guardianship.

From a letter by Clemens-August Wesemann[29] of 10 January 1832 to Caspar Geisberg about the death of Max Geisberg

. . . The news of his death, which was so quick and unexpected, must have been a severe blow to you and the other brothers and sisters there, and I feel deeply with you. I know with what brotherly love the departed was attached to you and how much you were a consolation, a counselor, and a refuge to him. However, I know at the same time how uplifting the memory of his inspiring life must be to you and to your dear brothers and sisters. For God and religion were his dearest subjects of conversation, and his veneration of these was proven by his acts. On All Saints Day he celebrated his last feast in the church, and lately he held his morning and evening devotions in the bedroom, kneeling in front of a picture beside the portrait of his wife, and he is said to have been frequently found crying at those times. Certainly he had obtained the moral perfection for which his Creator had destined him! The orphans who are left behind can unfortunately not even fathom yet, except for the older ones, what they have lost in their father, who stood before them as a model of Christian virtue, full of sadness concerning the early loss of their mother, on whose account he had hoped not to leave his worries behind for them. I am very pleased that you have dedicated yourself, with Hüffer, to the care of the orphans. God will give his blessing to this . . .

Letters of 10 December 1831 and 6 February 1832 from Jette to her Uncle Caspar Geisberg defend her plan to marry Dr. Bruns, assuring her uncle that the decision was not a rash one and that although "we have very little money, of that we have been told for some time," Bruns believes and she believes that he will be

28. A nine-year secondary school, equivalent to high school and junior college. Graduation from the *Gymnasium* is a prerequisite for admission to a university.

29. Wesemann (1794–1875), law commissioner in Oelde, married Kathinka Niedieck in 1823. Their son married Agathe Offenberg, Jette's niece.

able to support her. She is distressed at the suggestion that the house and gardens be rented out and the children scattered and urges him to agree to let the household continue. She firmly denies the "disgusting rumor" that her uncle had heard concerning Bruns and a young woman in a nearby village. The scandal of the magistrate's daughter and rumors about the doctor are discussed in letters to Caspar from Heinrich Hüffer, Jette's maternal uncle, and Clemens Wesemann, who was involved in settling the Max Geisberg estate. Writing on 15 December 1831, Hüffer reports, "I have not heard anything recently of the rumor, and people of good intention who know B. better do not believe it at all." In a letter of 10 January, Wesemann concludes, "I at least have to consider myself morally convinced of the unreasonableness of the rumor which has circulated about him and which has seriously hurt him . . . and I may say that all who know Bruns will agree." Wesemann considers Bruns an excellent doctor: "Here he is generally esteemed and considered a very capable and thorough physician, even by doctors who are living in the neighborhood, who already praise him, particularly in regard to his very incisive diagnoses. He is lucky, has a rare medical practice, is available to anybody and everybody any hour of the day and night, and has a practice that extends over the whole area, for which his healthy and strong constitution serves him well." Hüffer reports, "B. confessed to me recently that he did not have a fortune, but that his position earns him a satisfactory income, so for instance last year he made 1,300 thaler. This may have been a somewhat high estimate; however, one can say that he should certainly be able to reach half of this amount in the future."

From the Autobiography

I was recognized as the fiancée of Dr. Bruns. The household was to continue with the governess and my two brothers and sisters until the wedding could take place after the first period of mourning. But little sister Therese was immediately asked for by Aunt von Hatzfeld.[30] There were many things pertaining to the estate to be taken care of that I could understand. And I had to take care of them, particularly since our guardians did not get along and Uncle Hüffer resigned. Uncle Caspar was faithful and cared for us like a father. He was a pillar my brothers and sisters could lean on after we left. . . .

Our wedding took place on the 24th of May 1832. I was deeply moved when on coming down from the church I saw the governess standing there crying. They all tried to cheer me up. Wenner and Iwan were groomsmen; Elise Brüning and sister Johanna were at my side. All the relatives from Stromberg were there. The Wesemanns, the Osterlinks, the Brünings, and others. I wished so much that Marie could have been with me.

After a few hours we started on our trip. I wanted to be introduced to my husband's relatives, who lived at Lohne near Lingen. We arrived there the second evening, and from every corner welcoming shots were fired, and a tall, slightly stooped lady stood at the door. It was my husband's mother. She came toward us with great cordiality. Brother Hermann Heinrich, the owner of the farm, was a widower with two small girls. His mother and his sister took care of the household. And then there was still a deaf and dumb brother with them.[31] We were taken to the relatives living nearby, and I noticed how the men all talked so wisely and knowingly even about things not related to agriculture. On the third day the brothers took us across the endless heath to Drivörden, where another brother lived in House Hermeling.[32] He and his wife,

---

30. Elisabeth Niedieck, from Stromberg, was married to Bernhard von Hatzfeld, commissioner of justice in Ahlen. Their son later married Jette's sister, Therese.

31. Johann Heinrich Bruns (1806–1877).

32. Bernard Hermann Bruns, called Hermeling (1802–1878), lived at Drievorden, approximately fifteen miles south of Lohne. Jette consistently wrote *Drivörden*.

Christina, were magnificently capable people. We very much liked being with them. We traveled home again by way of Bentheim and got there after eight days.

Bruns was in demand as a doctor, and I endeavored to be a housewife. The housekeeper had left, but my sister Johanna and my brother Wilhelm stayed with us. Therese, a good girl who had been at our house from the time when my mother was alive, was capable. We were quite happy. A lot of my happiness was because my husband was so good to my brothers and sister. During the vacation the three students came back home as they always had. We lived in our parents' home. It was something new for the boys, and they really enjoyed it that their oldest sister was so flighty around her husband.

During the first year of our marriage, Dr. Wenner showed a liking for little Nette von Bruchhausen, and he talked to me a lot about that. It was very difficult for me that I had to give him an opportunity to see her at our place. After the year of mourning for Jenny was over, he led her home. The bridal couple walked to the church from our house. But when we got back afterward, my aunt and I found a moment of privacy, and remembered the dear departed one with hot tears. They went to Stovern. They lived happily but Wenner's health was ruined, and he went downhill. A violent hemorrhage brought death to him in the first year. Nettchen was quite beside herself and was no longer responsible. Katinka and I sincerely tried to help her regain her composure until finally her father interceded and persuaded her to go home with him. We, too, missed Wenner very much.

In the second year a son was born to us, Hermann.[33] Back in my husband's home region there were no poor people, but there were many near us. That his income had to come from poor people was the beginning of his dissatisfaction, although his practice was extensive, and he enjoyed being held in high regard by everybody. At that time there was an emigration fever in the air and it was furthered by reports of Duden, von Martels, Löwe, and others.[34] Bruns kept himself well-informed, and we discussed it often.

For me it was a hard struggle between inclination and duty—anyway I thought it was. When the latter won, a big fuss broke out, but I had given my husband my promise to follow him to the New World. Katinka, who usually carried a lot of weight with me, said bluntly that it was a great wrong for me to agree to go. She thought that Bruns would not go without me. And she was probably quite right. I later mentioned this to Wesemann because he was so bitter, but he then agreed with me. To be sure, it was terribly difficult to leave my young brothers and sisters behind. I believe Bruns realized that he would have to be everything to me. But he remained firm, and thus the relatives had to yield. He wanted to go alone first so that he could provide a secure place for me. This was advisable, because first I had to be declared of age and the guardians had to agree. This also applied to my oldest brother, Franz, as well as to the younger, Bernhard, who wanted to go along. Together with a merchant, Bertelsmann from Bielefeld, Bruns went to Bremen, and they sailed on the *Elise*, a big ship bound for New York.[35] I received frequent letters. And after seven months he had bought property in the state of Missouri and came back for me.

33. Hermann Ludwig Bruns was born in Oelde on 20 October 1833.

34. For Duden, see Introduction, note 3. Heinrich von Martels, *Briefe über die westlichen Theile der Vereinigten Staaten von Nordamerika* (Osnabrück, 1834). Löwe probably refers to Gustav Löwig, *Die Freistaaten von Nord-Amerika: Beobachtungen und praktische Bemerkungen für auswandernde Deutsche* (Heidelberg and Leipzig, 1833).

35. Charles Bertelsmann from Bielefeld is listed as traveling cabin class with Dr. Bruns on the *Elise*, departing Bremen on 12 June 1835 and arriving in Baltimore on 6 August.

Jette to Heinrich

Oelde, 5 January 1835

Dear Heinrich:

My last letter was incomplete, and I really did not want to write all the things that I did, but before I knew it they were written; when I then wanted to take up some other points, I was prevented from doing it, and thus I let the letter be launched. A second letter was to follow immediately, but it was never written and now surely four weeks must have passed. I am diligently helping Bruns write New Year's wishes, and thus it happens that I have little time to write or do anything else; you must be indulgent.

The views expressed in your letters have pleased Bruns and me very much, and they are indeed not very far from our views. There is probably no absolute necessity that would motivate us to change our residence so radically. Bruns has a good practice and is not easily discouraged, but he also does not intend to sit still over there; the possessions one would like to have cannot easily be gotten here without resorting to forceful methods, and this is for him at least as much a burden as perhaps half of the practice. And if he then finally gets his bills paid, he knows only too well how the poor debtor has to suffer to satisfy his bill and often has to deprive himself of the little that he has to protect himself. In brief, my husband is sick of having to extort his fees. There is probably no hope that this can be remedied, and indeed one would have to fear the opposite. Regardless of that, we can now live quite decently, without abundance, but shouldn't we also consider our future? Will Bruns remain strong forever? We also have Hermann. I wish and hope that the Good Lord will bless us with a few more children! What are the prospects to have them educated according to their station, or even if Hermann would be our only one, would we see him well taken care of? This alone would concern us, for how many years will have to pass before a young man can have his own home after he has finished the necessary studies, whatever his profession? You yourself know this perhaps better than I; and how many parents sigh as they stand beside the cradle and wonder how they can raise their little ones. All of this is nothing special, and probably every emigrant would have told you this. But I wanted to say that for this reason only, without being in need, one would still have sufficient reason to undertake such a trip, without wanting to seek a glittering fortune and without expecting it. I can say that my expectations are certainly not too high. If I only consider that in the first place one can live over there almost without having to pay taxes, that one can buy land cheaply and can live on it, that the fertile soil will sufficiently provide the needs of a household, that the other necessities can be arranged as one wishes without having to worry about one's station and one's situation, then I find very little else to worry about. The practice would keep us adequately supplied with the few things we need. I think that with our modest wishes we cannot fare poorly.

When I now think of our departure from here, however, I have to say that since the New Year all courage has left me. But the decision will have to be made soon. I almost tremble when I think of it. We will have to take care of the renting of the house, of the gardens, letting the maids go, everything will have to be arranged. Johanna and Wilhelm will have to be provided for in Münster. With whom? Of course, it might be possible to take them along! Then all the furniture and all the things we cannot take along will have to be sold. Most of what was so dear and valuable to me in the house must be sold. I will have to leave the beloved home of our parents to strangers, perhaps never to step into it again. Oh, if I only think of all of those things! —And then you all are in Münster, and I am the only one and the oldest and the adult who is sailing across the wide ocean for a new home, leaving you behind and (I probably visualize the worst) leaving you exposed to all kinds of inconveniences and whims*—especially the little ones—which, even if I could not change, I could at least lessen, and I would know how you are getting along, and your free time would be left for me. And you will have to avoid Oelde when we are no longer here! Yes, it is a strange destiny that it was just we who thought of going, since after all there are many people who are alone and who perhaps live not half as well and are not thinking of it!

But I tell you this, Heinrich, you and Franz, you are both grown now, and I ask you to give me the assurance that would ease my mind (in case we should leave) that you will seek the confidence of your little brothers and sisters. Be indulgent with their small faults and admonish them kindly. Try to see them regularly and try to inform yourself about everything that they are doing. Wilhelm is particularly kind and gentle. He must not be led with severity. Johanna needs more firmness; she is clever and one will have to employ all kinds of precautions not to be deceived. —Yes, this is my most urgent request. Do not leave our brothers and sisters without care. Try to be more to them than I have ever been! —Will I ever be able to live through all this? I think of this often recently. I am so terribly frightened, and I cannot tell Bruns. But I do not waver for a moment. I almost wish that it had been decided, then this uncertainty would stop.

*Naturally I exclude our good relatives. Even if they are sometimes angry or in bad humor, that can be borne.

The end of the letter is missing.

Oelde, 18 March 1835

Dear Heinrich:

As Carl stepped into the room on the Saturday evening before *Fastnacht*[36] and I greeted him, keeping the door open, I looked into the kitchen because I believed I heard you. I could barely suppress my hurt feelings when Carl explained that he was alone. On Sunday we went to meet Johanna coming from *Haus Geist,* met her and hurried back, still nursing the slight hope of seeing you come back with the wagon. It came without you and drove slowly and sleepily on. Well, Easter will soon be coming and after thirty-one dreary fast days, which were hard on you, we will greet each other quite joyfully. Then the professor can really not say no!

For quite some time Uncle Caspar did not answer my letter. But then several weeks ago when I visited the Hüffers, our aunt told me everything that was in the letter. I became a little disturbed. I would certainly not have expected that from Uncle Caspar. For the time being I wanted to talk only with him. If I had wanted to confide in Uncle Hüffer, I was closer than he was. It annoyed me quite a bit. However, I endeavored to suppress my annoyance, since it is our father's brother who has done this to me, he whom I like quite well otherwise. Perhaps

36. Shrove Tuesday or Mardi Gras, the day before the Lenten season.

he did not quite understand my letter. —Now, a good week ago I received a letter from him in which there is quite a bit of disapproval. Some of it hurt me deeply. However, I did not weaken. I shall hold back with my answer until we have decided on some things. Perhaps this will take until Easter. Here only the Niediecks, Wesemanns, and Osterlinks, besides the Hüffers, know of our intention, but perhaps the whole town knows it already. However, now I don't care at all. Most likely Uncle Caspar will have received the old papers. Right now I do not have time to look over the book list, but in the near future I may perhaps ask for some of the books.

Regards to all and hold dear, as she does you,

Your sister Jette

Oelde, 28 May 1835

Dear Heinrich:

Yesterday I wrote to Bernhard, who did not know what to do with his impatience since all the rumors have upset him very much. Today it is your turn, and now this morning I have received your letter, and with the same mail Bruns received his passport. So there you have more news than I thought I would have today.

First I want to answer your next-to-last letter, since Bruns has the other one in his pocket. Johanna was really very pleased with Father's letter[37] and with your courtesy. May she remain as pious and good as we wish her to be, and as we want to help her to be by giving her the three prayer books, which will guide her and serve for her frequent edification. The first book, which she received the day before Holy Communion from her sister, is called *Maria,* the second is well known to you, the third one is *Hauber's Prayer Book* from Aunt Boner[38] and was accompanied by a ring. I shall send you Father's letter in the near future. The box will probably not be called for until next week. The girls had not gotten me anything earlier.

That Bruns wants to get away from here is, I believe, not a secret from a soul in Oelde any more, and we also talk about it openly; I probably need not tell you that therefore you may also do this without hesitation. He will leave in about eight days or perhaps two weeks, since the newly arrived passport now removes the greatest obstacle and he need only take care of his things now. I must not hold him back any more since he may regret any delay. In addition, a travel companion, the merchant Bertelsmann, has already left for Bremen and will send Bruns news very soon.

Pentecost Monday may perhaps be the designated time for his departure from here. I hope that Boner will not hesitate to give you his permission to come. Bruns will include a few lines, which you may give him if you wish. In case he does not give you permission after all, then Bruns will let you and Franz know when you can find him in Greven.[39] In this case you will have to inconvenience yourself that far on his account!

Now you have to answer me right away. If you are going to be here for Pentecost, you can ride with Bruns to Warendorf if the tour would be too much for you. —I now have to ask

37. A letter from Max Friedrich Geisberg, given to his daughter.
38. Johann Michael Hauber, *Gebetbuch für katholische Christen* (München, 1832). Ursula Boner, née Geisberg (1781–1848), was the sister of Jette's father. In 1799 she married Max Friedrich Boner, court counselor in Münster.
39. Greven, a town about ten miles north of Münster, was a convenient meeting place for the family as Bruns traveled from Oelde to Bremen.

your forgiveness for something; I have had the opportunity several times already to get what you wanted in Stromberg, but now it escapes me how highly "you think" it should be valued, therefore do write me again. In the near future, I resolve, I shall take care of all requests promptly.

The portraits will stay here for the time being. Osterlink must have seen Father's signet; perhaps he can give me information. However, we do not intend to use the seal which belonged to Father forever. But rather we had thought for some time of having two seals made in which a ram's horn stands beside a field on which *BB* has been engraved. Do try to get one from an engraver right away, but it should be done very nicely and it must be engraved very finely and daintily, not awkwardly. Order one according to your own ideas and bring the seal with you when you come here at Pentecost, otherwise it will be too late; therefore in any case . . .

The end of the letter is missing.

Jette to Bernhard Bruns

Oelde, 5 July 1835

Dear Husband:

Tomorrow you will have been away from me for a whole month! I have received your four letters and they have pleased me very much, particularly the last one, which I really did not expect. I thought that I would remain in the dark concerning your departure. Now since I know you are at sea I am much calmer. You were still very well, and I believe that you will not become seasick. —The delay of your departure was quite painful to me since I had accompanied you to sea in my thoughts for quite a long while, believing you to be sailing with favorable winds. Even if you do not get over there quite as quickly, you will have a pleasant voyage. —Since you are away, everything here in the house has become quite different. It is so quiet, so monotonous. In the first few days after your departure I had no desire to do the least bit. Now, however, I am most satisfied when I am hurrying around. I spend many an hour in the garden, and then I think that I am with you under God's open sky. Our boy is really extraordinarily lively. He is now learning a lot and succeeds in reproducing the sound of the word that is given him. He did not know anything of you in the first few days, and it bothered me very much when he always repeated *Pappe* or *Kappe*[40] when I said, "Papa." Now, however, especially when I show him a pipe, he says, "Papa gone" [*Papa weg*]. Just now I showed him your picture, and he laughed and repeated, "Papa, Papa," and preferred it to my picture. He wanted to look at it again and again. A few times it happened that I was having very gloomy thoughts and then he called to me with his sweet voice, "Mama," so that I seized him and pressed him to my heart. Yes, dear husband, I have a great consolation in our son.

His cough is pretty well. Recently I had the mixture refilled and I found afterward that he had little white worms. At my request Dr. Dreier gave me some powder, and after that I did not see any more. This morning after he had not taken any for several days there was again a little worm. Now I shall wait a little bit and then have your mixture refilled. It purges better,

40. *Pappe* means cardboard; *Kappe* means cap.

and the powder tasted so bad that I had to pour it down his throat. On the Feast of Sts. Peter and Paul[41] we took a ride in Nollmarg's little wagon to Stromberg with Hermann. He laughed with his whole little face and was very contented all day long. He was wearing a new little straw cap, which made Mama and Liebethchen somewhat vain. The Hüffer children received a drum, and I could not restrain myself and presented him with one too. —Our budget is now probably a little bit more limited than it was earlier. However, we do not lack anything since we have plenty of milk and fresh vegetables are coming in. In addition we have bacon and ham. In the evening we have soup or bread and butter with cottage cheese or some salad with meat or pancakes. I had my first roast since you have been gone, and now we cannot even finish it, and we eat from it at noon so that it will not spoil. Now I am in the process of making *Handkäse*.[42] Two weeks ago our cow gave nine-and-a-half liters of milk, but now the oats are getting too hard and she no longer yields as much. Every time we have fresh peas or beans I wish that you were here. How you would like them! There are also strawberries coming in now. And all of this you have to do without (I'm collecting the seeds of the strawberries in the garden). And now I have to tell you that Hermann likes to eat beans. This morning he nabbed a few from the strainer after they had been poured through, and at noon he takes a double portion. Everything in our garden is doing well. We are getting lots of vegetables. Perhaps I will need to buy only very few or no potatoes at all. However, that depends on when you say I have to give up the household. —You have to write me about this, but I would like to keep everything as long as possible. When we live with other people it will cost much more.

On Thursday I went in the evening to *Haus Geist* with Johanna. On the way I talked about our impending trip, and she said that she also would like to go with us. What do you think about that? I would have to write to Uncle Caspar about it. After you were gone he wrote me right away and even said that he had no doubt that some of my brothers would follow me. If he would only react favorably to my request, then she should go to Münster this fall to have more instruction.

Mr. von Bruchhausen wrote me last week that he wants to take Bernhard in. I am immensely pleased since he will be well taken care of there and can learn a great deal. If he should follow us later he will be secure. Do not forget, dear husband, to look out for possible prospects for Heinrich, so that he can get as much information as possible. I would like it so much if he could be in our vicinity.

Recently Wesemann told me that somebody had said to the Speiths that as a former demagogue you had good reason to leave Prussia. Should I perhaps inquire around? Be careful if there is something to be feared. Write me concerning this immediately because it disturbs me!

Chaplain Schniederjans visits me every day. He is extremely polite and good-natured; but he seems to have a great deal of free time, that is, if not making his visit here. He lives with Oenkhaus since he had some trouble with the Speiths. Nal had just moved to the Nennewalds. She was in constant turmoil with Mrs. Oenkhaus. She has visited me four to five times already. The first time was just after you had left. She was crying and very excited. A few days afterward she felt at liberty to accuse me of having known what you knew and said

41. 29 June.
42. A homemade cheese that is shaped by hand.

that the doctor should have done better by her. If she had known, she would have followed Bttsm[43] to Bremen right away. I replied evasively, upset that I, as so often happens, never force myself into your secrets if you do not consider it best to inform me. Since that time she has been somewhat more proper. She still complains very much concerning Bttsm. His letter did not seem to please her, and she has made up her mind to follow him if he does not come back. I urge you not to write anything to me that she is not supposed to know concerning him. She intends to stay in Oelde and will not return home at any cost. The child is lively and happy; as one can imagine, however, it cries a lot because of her anger. I wish she would leave here. It is quite annoying to me, but do not tell him anything of this!

Today Budde's house next to the apothecary's shop was raised, and consequently there is dancing at the Wemhoffs'. Our girls wanted to go for a while so much that I gave them permission to dance until 11:30. Now I have to stay up until that time, and I'm thinking I will spend the time best if I chat with you a little bit. (It will take double postage anyway to Bremen.) This noon Mrs. von Bachofen and her mother had lunch with me. They had notified me before. Afterward they went to the club. Since we want to do our laundry and will presoak tomorrow, I used this excuse to stay at home. This time there is still some of your laundry here. Next time there will be none. I am so afraid that you will not be here for New Year's. It is a long time. I probably told you that if you thought that you could accomplish more there than here you should not worry on my account. I now take this back, and I ask you very sincerely if it is at all possible to come back to me as quickly as possible. I want to go with you if you want to go, even if it's in the midst of winter—only do not leave me alone any longer! However, I am satisfied with what you decide, just as it probably should be. Sometimes I think how happy, how blissful I shall be when you are back and when you and we are all well and healthy. Right away, however, it occurs to me that this joy is almost too great to enjoy serenely, and I imagine all kinds of fears that may become reality. However, I do not let these troublesome spirits keep the upper hand for long, and I commend myself and all of us to the good Lord and to His fatherly grace. On Sunday, the 5th, I went to Holy Communion and there I prayed very sincerely for you too. On Sundays especially it always occurs to me that you do not have an opportunity to hear Mass, and consequently I have to make up for it, and I listen for you too and endeavor to be very reverent.

Osterlink announced on the 4th that bills are to be paid to him, and he made this announcement all over the area. Now I hope that we will soon get some money. I had to go and get some from Ost. a little while ago. —All show me a great deal of sympathy, and they all urge me to visit them; however, I am not in the mood for that yet. And besides I don't feel very free. —Hermann is getting livelier every day. He laughs and squeaks mightily. Oh, how you will enjoy him when you see him again. He is also getting much smarter, and he looks like a little darling in his straw cap. He is a good boy, with his white skin and flaxen hair and the pretty nails, which must not be forgotten.

I am so happy that I have only this child. Later I would be glad to have many more. Everybody is ahead of me now. Busch has a daughter. Dear, dear husband now I have to conclude and take leave. However, I will soon write you again.

I firmly hope that you and we will be well, and I will endeavor to be quite patient and wait

43. Abbreviation for *Bertelsmann;* see note 35 above.

for your letter. Do not worry too much. Postpone everything until we can be together. But look for a nice little spot for us, and the rest will work out. Write to me in detail concerning everything. Hermann kisses you with me, and my brothers and sisters all send their greetings. Once more, do not worry too much so that you remain healthy and strong for your son and your wife, who loves you from the bottom of her heart.

Jette

Our letters will probably cross. If you write as faithfully as you did here, I need not remind you.

Letters of 7–8 August and 12 August 1835 from Dr. Bruns to Jette describe his voyage on the Elise *and conditions in Baltimore. The voyage took forty-three days at sea and five days from the first sighting of land at Cape Henry to port. Baltimore was "full of Germans" and there was plenty of everything in the city. "Vegetables, particularly cabbage and beans. . . . potatoes taste as they do in Germany, also apples and pears, but the melons are not as tasty, and in addition they are eaten here with pepper and salt and I don't like that." He described in detail the unrest and violence related to the closing of the Maryland Bank. "If the directors of the bank had been caught, they would have been covered with tar and rolled in feathers naked and driven out of the city on a donkey. . . . Now on the second day after the unrest no one talks about it any longer, and only anecdotes about the happenings are retold and laughed about. In Germany something like this is unheard of, and probably German newspapers will find opportunities to describe it as if everything here is lawlessness and licentiousness."*

Oelde, 19 August 1835

Dear Heinrich:

First I have to tell you that I was happy to hear all the good news from you. So you expected instead of a letter from Frans[44] a letter from me first! I had not gotten around to it, although I wanted to write every evening. Look up the name of your oldest brother in the calendar. For brevity's sake I chose the little word *umgehend* (by return mail) although I hesitated a little and really wanted to say, "With the returning messenger." Is this wrong?

I am sorry that our aunt[45] did not receive my letter earlier. Perhaps she had not returned home by the beginning of the vacation. We probably must wait for her permission. I wrote to her that if she did not want to bring Threschen to Warendorf to meet me, you could come with the little one by mail coach. Opportunities are rare. On the 28th of August the pastor (from Oelde) will travel back to Münster, but school is probably not over by then. Uncle Caspar has been informed about Johanna. I think one will have to keep her present sojourn in mind.

When I received your letter I happened to be in a very serious mood, and it did not

44. Old-fashioned spelling of *Franz*. Evidently Heinrich misspelled his brother's name, and Jette was chiding him for his error.
45. Therese Geisberg, née Lohkampf, was married in 1814 to *Domänenrat* Adolf Viktor Geisberg. In their house at Neubrückenstrasse 28, she took care of her husband's unmarried brothers Bernhard, canon in St. Martini (1776–1841), and Caspar. Her marriage was childless. After the death of Max Friedrich Geisberg, she and her husband wanted to care for Jette's orphaned brothers and sisters, but Jette wanted to keep the children with her.

contribute to making me more cheerful. I like the little students' verse, but I try to interpret it, and that may well be the cause for the present dreary worry. However, Heinrich, what are you saying? "Up there"!? (Do you consider the value of your existence not important enough to ask the Good Lord to let you carry out a few good things here on earth yet?)[46]

I leave my brothers and sisters, and only this can ease my mind, that besides the other good relatives I have grown brothers who can take care of what I could do for the little ones. Franz has probably the best chance to be able to follow us, and whose turn will it then be to become the protector of our brothers and sisters?

Will I vainly cherish a favorite wish for a long time, perhaps for always, to see you near us? Only the thought that you would stand as a pillar of protection for my brothers and sisters whom I leave behind might make it possible for me to relinquish this wish and console myself somewhat. Let us leave everything to the Father in Heaven. What if I could not trust Him now any more!

The future will probably prove to be much brighter than we think. However, I must not flatter myself with too many hopes. My career is prescribed for me; if the Good Lord would only give me beautiful peace of mind! I quite frequently think now of the hereafter, but I always pray to God that He will keep me for my husband and child for a few more years!

Dear Heinrich, you probably will think that I have taken your words too seriously since you are now receiving a long sermon in exchange. Do not take it amiss!

Tell Threschen that I would like to have her here; I do not doubt that she will then ask Aunt's permission. I believe that this will be the last letter before the vacation. You will let me know the day of your arrival, won't you? I have never longed for the vacation to begin as much as I do now; at least I was more patient. Like you I wish a letter would arrive, but there will probably be some news while you are here. What joy! Or, no, I must not think of that!!! But I shall never again let my boy get so far away. Prudence doesn't seem so important to me now.

Now I hope you will stay well and not overtax yourself. And then above all I wish you much luck. Your loving sister

Jette

Many regards to our uncles and to Threschen from the three of us.

On 3 October 1835 Dr. Bruns wrote Jette from St. Louis: ". . . I have found a place which I like completely and which you will certainly also like. It is situated in Gasconade County,[47] approximately thirty hours from St. Louis, fifteen English miles from Jefferson, two miles from the Osage. . . . Here there flows a river, the Maria River,[48] which is as large as the Ems near Warendorf. It joins the Osage two hours from here. I like the Maria River and its landscape so much that I have resolved to make our future residence there. . . .

46. This remark is crossed out in the text of the letter, but rewritten on the margin in Heinrich's hand.

47. Gasconade County, organized by an act approved 25 November 1820 to become effective 1 January 1821, lay in east-central Missouri, bounded on the north by the Missouri River, on the east by Franklin County, on the south by Crawford and Phelps counties, and on the west by the Osage River. In 1841 the area west of the Gasconade River was separated and became Osage County.

48. German immigrants often referred to the Maries River as *Mariafluss,* the "Maria River." Robert L. Ramsay, *Our Storehouse of Missouri Place Names* (Columbia: University of Missouri Press, 1973), p. 9, notes that the name was spelled *Marais,* a French word for marsh or swamp, on early French maps.

It will be very pleasant for you that there are several German families, among them Hesse from Roesebeck,[49] *Grammatica . . ., Schröder, and Nacke."*[50]

Readers of Gottfried Duden's Report or those who had heard about Duden's Missouri would have recognized echoes in Dr. Bruns's letter of Duden's descriptions of the land and opportunity in the Far West. "The river has a very fertile bottom, so that it will not be necessary to add fertilizer to increase the yield for the next hundred years. . . . There is salable land . . . suitable for the erection of mills and distilleries." Dr. Bruns anticipated that he could build a good practice among his German and American neighbors. There were many animals, "stags, deer, quail, and wild boar." In short, the pleasantness of the site on the Maries River, the fertile soil, the favorable lay of river and hillside, fire and building wood, and healthy spring water persuaded him that he had found his American paradise. He had not seen any snakes, although he had walked or ridden in the forest every day.[51]

Oelde
1 December 1835

Dear Heinrich!

I have to tell you that recently I have been more than ever very moody and restless; and therefore I have abandoned English, but will soon begin again. However, for now, only German words! I had looked forward with endless longing to a letter from Bruns. Of course, it could hardly have arrived any earlier. However, it does contain what I expected and more than I could expect. I could thank our Father in Heaven from the bottom of my heart that He has guided everything for the best!

However, Heinrich, my joy was not pure, and it becomes clear to me that as long as I am still here I will have no peace. If only these last days could be made somewhat shorter! Bruns will write to me in about three weeks again, and he already indicates in this letter all kinds of things that should not be sold. After receipt of the next letter he thinks the sale ought to be held. And in January Bruns will be here. I am indescribably happy at how close this is! United with him, everything can be borne much more easily. And then I shall never be alone again. Time passes more quickly than one thinks in the beginning. Next Sunday it will be a half year that he has been gone. Bruns sends his greetings to the brothers and sisters who are vacationing.

49. Nicolaus Hesse, a political and administrative officer at Rösebeck, near Warburg, emigrated in 1835 with his wife and six daughters, settling on the Maries River in August 1835 and recording land in sec. 26 on 29 August 1835. Finding life on the frontier too difficult and discouraging, the family sold their property to Christian Boessen and left the Westphalia Settlement on 12 April 1837 to return to Germany. Hesse published *Das westliche Nordamerika, in besonderer Beziehung auf die deutschen Einwanderer in ihren landwirtschaftlichen, Handels, und Gewerbverhältnissen* (Paderborn: Joseph Wesener, 1838), in which he detailed the hardships as well as the opportunities of life on the frontier. The book caused Jette's family considerable anxiety.

50. Franz and Ludwig Gramatica are listed on the "Census of 1839" for Westphalia, Missouri, compiled by Father Ferdinand Helias, as sons of the widow Anna Maria Gramatica. Their ages were given as 28 and 31. Franz appears as Francis Gramatica on the abstract map of Township 43R10W in the south center of sec. 26, 29 August 1835. A Cole County naturalization record shows Francis Grammaticus [*sic*] taking the oath of intent to citizenship in June 1842. Father Helias also lists Hermann Schroeder, 18, the son of the widow Margaretha Schroeder, who, according to family records, emigrated in 1835 and Joseph Nacke, 36, his wife Maria Anna, 33, and three children, ages 1 through 10.

51. In explaining the enormous potential of the fertile Missouri soil, Duden had noted in his Thirteenth Letter that "good soil or first rate soil does not require fertilization during the first century" (*Report*, p. 55). He discussed snakes at length, including the report in his Fifteenth Letter that "Stories are told of snakes crawling into houses and even into beds," and conceded that the proximity of poisonous snakes in Missouri forests had some effect on everyone, "especially on women" (p. 76).

Hermann has sore eyes. The left one is quite bad. He cries a lot. Dr. Dreier has given us a salve that we rub on his neck to draw the matter away from his eye. The boy cannot stand the eyedrops at all. He always hides his head when I want to moisten his eye with them. He also has very little appetite and eats almost no vegetables. He does not sleep well at night, and then he catches up during the daytime. But his mother gets the short end of it. For a few weeks now he has been wearing pants, and he looks very cute in them.

According to the letter from Franz, your dancing lessons seem to have come to an end, which I regret very much. Both of you could have used more lessons.

Bernhard is quite satisfied with staying at the Bruchhausens'. If he is not especially summoned I see him only on Sundays, and even then he prefers to be back at noon unless young Bruchhausen can also stay a while. Bruchhausen wanted to send me an English letter for you, but he hasn't done so yet. It will probably be sent in the near future. You should, however, send the sixty songs. Didn't you retain a thaler for the notes? I am enclosing the amount of the bill from Coppenrath and an extra ten groschen.[52] The *Ballroom for Guitar* costs one thaler and ten groschen for four booklets, so it would be all right if you would add the one thaler. Later I can settle with you about the songs that have been received. Now I would very much like for you to give the two thaler and twenty-five groschen to Marie, as well as the enclosed letters. And then I will have taken care of all my debts in Münster.

Soon more; I have no time now. Regards to Franz, Threschen, and all the others, from your sister Jette.

I was advised to sell the grand piano right away; unless the offer is too low I shall probably accept.

Oelde, 3 January 1836

Dear Heinrich:

I have wished you all a very happy New Year from the bottom of my heart, to be sure without having said it. And since I do not consider myself blessed, I wanted to pray in quiet solitude for my dear ones, that the dear God may let it be for them happy or at least quite pleasant. I have sought to strengthen myself for the beginning of the New Year by taking Holy Communion, which I have always considered a big wall separating the youthful years, happily experienced, and the decisive future. Now this objective has been reached, and soon the great moment will come when I shall leave everything here—I still have no news from my husband, nor do I know for sure if and when he will return (and where he may be at this time). I wonder where he might be now? Will he experience the hard winter doubly while traveling? Or is he not writing to me any more because he is close to me? For several days I have been living in anxious anticipation. From all sides the latter prospect is made so probable to me that, particularly in the evening, any rattling of wagons excites me anew. And, Heinrich, at this very moment I think that every firm footstep on the street could be his. Perhaps I must still endure this illusion often, very often! As the heavens have decided. —However, no, I am not resigned, am no longer patient! This morning in church I said to myself: What if our Good Lord had

---

52. In the early nineteenth century the Prussian thaler was equivalent to thirty silver groschen at twelve pfennige each. A North American dollar was worth one thaler, twelve groschen, and ten pfennige (see Chr. Ad. Rise, *Fehlerfreier Faulenzer oder Schnellrechner* [Reutlingen: Fleischhauer & Spohn, 1846], pp. 83–84).

decided on a different fate for him, what if he had met with an accident, and I would never see him again on this earth? And then I felt so terribly bad; I tried to visualize so vividly God's kind providence, hoping that the Father of us all would also care for me, for my husband, and for my poor child; and then I thought again that the Good Lord could nevertheless in all His omniscience consider it better to take away my dear husband from me, and if it were so (if it should happen) then it would have to be for the best. But I was not at all satisfied with this, and I told myself again and again: it cannot be, it must not come to this, and I could not yield myself quite trustingly and resignedly today to His guidance of our fate. I hope to Heaven that I don't have to fear anything bad. If only I would not have to wait so long without news!

But thinking about it reasonably, I surely believe that a letter has been somewhat delayed; I do not believe that Bruns can come first and soon, for then he would not have announced another letter earlier.

Frau von Hatzfeld departed yesterday morning, and I'm still happy that I have not let myself be swayed or let my mind be changed. I am just too restless! How could I have stood it in Münster! Since the birth of Hermann he has not spent a night without me, and so I do not want to leave him now, as long as his father is so far away. I now think that Bruns will accompany me for a day or two to Münster. Tell everybody that it was quite a struggle for me to let this opportunity pass. But mainly the failure of a letter to arrive decided it for me. It ruined my mood so that I immediately resolved to stay here.

Vonneguts have gotten my piano, and I have become quite indifferent toward it now. Time blots out everything and softens everything! At first I cried for my grand piano, for I loved it so much! —It is late—until, until tomorrow!

4 January

Yesterday I was invited to *Haus Geist* to visit with Johanna and the young people of Stovern. We went, as requested, early in the morning, and after dinner there was hunting; there was also ice skating and sledding, and I tried skating again and it was really fun. Probably this was the last time here in Europe. Bernhard practiced hunting in a circle. The other Bernhard [Hüffer] was busily pushing the sled, L. R. Volmer took his turn, but finally we could push ourselves after I had taken off my ice skates because it was no longer so smooth and we could run quite quickly.

I was very much surprised that you were so little tired by the great tour, and therefore now you will not fear the trip for *Fastnacht*. If Bruns would only be here, so that you would see him right away! I am hoping! Regards to Franz; I shall write to him in the near future. Hold in love and answer soon,

Your sister, Jette.

Regards to all from me, especially to Uncle Caspar whom you have to congratulate on his name-day. The probate court sent a thick letter yesterday to the wife of Dr. Bruns, in which it is stated that her husband himself would have to consent.

Oelde
18 January 1836

Dear Franz and Heinrich!

Almost five days have already passed since my Bruns returned to me, and I use the first quiet moments to send you some news. Uncle Caspar will have gotten the note from Bruns in which he reported his arrival. On Wednesday the 13th I was sitting here by myself late at night. Firm footsteps approached and the doorknob was turned. Trembling, I thought of the possibility and sought to control myself and receive someone else calmly. Liebeth opened the bar and bolt, an exclamation of amazement escaped her, then deep silence, then he stood in front of me. —Yes, I have my husband back again; Eternal Providence led him happily through many dangers and difficulties back into my arms. Thanks, sincere thanks to the Good Lord! And should something happen to him now, then, dear brothers, he will never be alone! Calmly and bravely we shall go together toward the future. Bruns is healthy and well and is extremely satisfied with our situation in America; he reports many beautiful and good things about it. I really do not know what I should write.

If only you were here now, Bruns could talk to you for days, for he is full of information. And it seems to me that even those who are not concerned with America would have to find his reports interesting. He is much too much in demand by everybody here, which is not at all pleasing to me nor to Bruns. There is such activity in the house, which is so new and unusual to me, that it seems as if my head is no longer in its right place. However, that will improve!

I would have imagined that the place where Bruns bought property would be more comfortable and more lively, but even though Americans are already living in surrounding areas, where we shall live there seem to be only German immigrants. From everything he tells me one can see that there must be great harmony and that all have enough to live on. The deprivations, of which there are many in the beginning, are borne by all of them together, and they usually have a lot of fun doing that and spend many a happy hour working together. A church will be the center, a German priest will hold divine service. There is even a teacher already and a shoemaker. When we arrive, our house will be somewhat established, although Bruns is proceeding slowly in order to save expenses and only one carpenter, by the name of Kolk from Lohne, Keiser from Boesfeld (the parish of Herzebrock), and Bruns's brother are working on it.[53] I am agreeable to everything. I believe that I can be quite content with everything.

Hermann at first did not recognize his Papa and opened his eyes wide. And then he received some cake and gradually softened up, and now it has come so far that he says, "Father pick me up," and today he even said, "Mother away!" Then the good father laughed so heartily that I could not begrudge his being favored.

You do have to speak to Bruns by all means. I think that it could perhaps be arranged when he visits his mother soon. By the way, he is careful to avoid attracting a crowd. I believe more and more every hour that he will have to leave. During these last days I have not seen him for any two hours without some stranger. It is annoying, particularly since he has no intention of joining up with anyone for the trip.

For now good-bye, greetings to all from us, tell the relatives about this news and hold in love my only husband and his wife.

Marginal Notes: In the near future Franz will receive an American calendar, Heinrich an English book, and Threschen dolls to be dressed.

53. Dr. Bruns's brother Gerhard Hermann (1811–1876) accompanied him to Missouri, traveling on the *Elise* from Bremen, arriving in Baltimore on 6 August 1835. According to the ship's passenger list he traveled in steerage while the doctor and his traveling companion Bertelsmann were in cabin class. He purchased land on 20 April 1837 (Osage County abstract map 43R10W) and became a successful farmer in Westphalia. Theodor Kolk and Bernhard Kayser [also spelled *Keiser*] were listed on the same ship. Kolk listed his hometown as Büren, which is approximately thirty-five miles southeast of Oelde. The abstract map of Township 43R10W for Osage County shows Kolk recorded the purchase of land on 16 November 1835.

On 28 April 1836 Jette wrote a letter of farewell to her uncle Caspar, expressing her relief that her brothers Franz and Bernhard were accompanying her to America and begging his forgiveness that she is leaving her other brothers and sisters in his care. "To be sure, I believe that I am fulfilling my primary duty as a wife, and I hope to God that bitter remorse will not torture me in the future, but I fear that the heart's pure and serene peace will forever be denied me!"

Oelde, 10 May 1836

Dear Heinrich:

You will have heard from Aunt Therese that Bruns has chosen the *Ulysses*, which belongs to the Kuhlenkamp Brothers in Bremen, for our trip. The ship is now on its return trip from America, but has already been announced; we hope that it has arrived in the meantime. When it has been unloaded and loaded again it will start the voyage with us.

It is headed for Baltimore; New York would have pleased me just as well, however. The cabin will be occupied by twenty-four persons. They are:

Bruns and wife, their three brothers [Franz and Bernhard Geisberg and Bruns's brother],[54] Hermann, Jenne and Drückchen,[55] and the bride of carpenter Kolk. (9 persons)

The old Schwarze with wife and four children, one maid.[56] (7 persons)

Fritz Schwarze am Teich
Stephan Lücke
Hessler, a theologian
Mr. Rienermann
Chaplain Schniederjans[57]
the daughter of Feldmann am Berge
the daughter of Hambrock, from the parish of Stromberg.[58] (7 persons)

the son of the tenant farmer Binkhoff, from the parish of Ostenfeld is as good as certain. Mallinckrodt from Dortmund?[59]

54. Johann Bernard David Bruns appears on the passenger list of the *Ulysses*, arriving at Baltimore on 19 September 1836, as age 24, a native of Lohne. He was born 21 April 1809. According to church records of St. Joseph at Westphalia, he married Christine Blumberg on 21 September 1845.

55. The maid, Jenny Jurgens, and her four-year-old daughter, Gertrud.

56. The passenger list of the *Ulysses* shows G. Schwarze from Oelde, his wife and two children, Bernhard and Gertrud, ages 6 and 4, while Friedrich Müller in "Westfälische Auswanderer im 19. Jahrhundert" for the district of Münster #219, correctly lists Gottfried Schwarze from Oelde, innkeeper, born 16 December 1805, his wife Gertrud, née Kramer, and their four children ages 6, 5, 2, and 1 ½. The maid was presumably Elisabeth Vennewald, age 24.

57. Four on Jette's list appear on the passenger list, but Müller has more details and more accurate spellings: Müller #227, Gottfried Schwarze from Oelde, age 31, with passport for one year. According to the Schwarze firm's anniversary publication, *100 Jahre Brennerei-Tradition in einer westfälischen Familie,* [1664–1964] Friedrich Schwarze, Kornbrennerei, Oelde, Westf. (Stuttgart: Daco Verlag, n.d.), p. 13, the young man, known as Fritz, held a one-year travel permit and returned to Germany. Müller #229 lists Lücke from Oelde, journeyman miller, age 28, also having a one-year permit. Müller #220 lists Bernhard Hessler from Vellern, born 12 April 1811, but he appeared on the passenger list as age 30. The passenger list has Heinrich Rienermann, age 38, from Oelde, but he is not included by Müller. Since Chaplain Schniederjans is not listed on either of the two documents, he may have been considered a member of the ship's crew for the duration of the voyage.

58. The two women, apparently traveling together, Gertrud Hambruck from Stromberg, age 35, and Elisabeth Feldmann from Stinninghausen, age 20, are on the passenger list, but Müller fails to record either of them or W. Binkhoff from Ostenfelde, age 25.

59. The passenger list recorded him as "Conr. Mallinkrodt," age 27. His application for U.S. citizenship, entered in St. Charles Circuit Court, 10 December 1839, shows the name is correctly spelled *Mallinckrodt*. The ancestral home of the Mallinckrodt family still stands near the church in Jette's home town of Stromberg.

Dr. med. Köchling with wife and three children? from Steinheim in the district of Paderborn.

The latter had expressed their desire to travel with us earlier and will let us know within the next few days,[60] since Bruns will have to determine who the passengers in the cabin will be. The cabin will have to be enlarged. We will have steerage board and therefore will buy all kinds of additional things in Bremen and do some additional cooking. The fare per person will be forty-five thaler—Bruns has reserved thirty seats for steerage, but more likely than not there will be fifty people from this area who will get together on our ship. We have already packed half a box. Next week there will be more to pack. Oh, I wish we were finished with this! Then I would be much more at peace!

Seamstresses cannot be found in Oelde anymore. And therefore I will have to pack all kinds of things that are unfinished, which I do not like to do. In case we are still here next Pentecost, which now seems probable, we hope to see you here with us even if it is only for a short time. In case other orders arrive you will be notified early enough. Do send me the picture of Münster. It shall shine in America.

You can get a new pair of pants, or better yet, I will send you the material right away. I can tell you what it will cost later.* Now I hope you will stay well; soon more. All join me in sending greetings. Your sister, Jette.

Busch has moistened Bruns's pants to prevent them from shrinking in the laundry. — Bruns wishes, however, that you would not tell everybody the great number of people who plan to go with us.

Marginal note: There are four and one quarter Berlin ells; I have figured for your size one-quarter of an ell more; the ell costs eleven and a quarter groschen.

One corner of the following letter was torn off. The bracketed words are provided by the editors to reconstruct the letter.

Oelde, 18 May 1836

Dear Heinrich!

The clothing has arrived. I did not find a little note, although you did write the address. I therefore think that you will surely spend the Pentecost days here. —Uncle Caspar wrote to Bruns; the contents are very embarrassing to all of us and we would like to object somewhat, which you can perhaps convey to Uncle Caspar, using the most extreme consideration. The authorizations, statements, receipts, etc., will be taken care of as soon as the local court has received the papers. I doubt, however, very much that you will be able to turn over the money to us at Pentecost. It is very embarrassing for us that the payment will be drawn out to such an extent since we expect news from Bremen any day now. However, I am convinced that as soon as the papers have been returned to Münster there will be no further delay.

Now our uncle writes: "I have to note that I have paid the following from my own account: Because of the declaration of the majority of Franz, 9 thaler; taxes for real estate, 11 thaler, 3 groschen; the bill from the merchant Melcher, 100 thaler; and I shall also pay an additional 80 thaler, the balance of the 200 thaler I had designated for the brothers, for which I expect the bill from you, which includes the money for board with von Bruchhausen."

60. Dr. Köchling and family were not on the passenger list of the *Ulysses*.

The money to von Bruchhausen will amount to 55 thaler, for the seven months. At the shoemaker Stammes alone I have spent 17 thaler for shoes and boots, which makes a total of 72 thaler. Now this leaves only 8 thaler. Naturally Franz would be happy to take care of this with his own money. But what does Bernhard have now? He does not have a penny in his pocket to take care of the trip; he would have to get funds from us for every little package of tobacco, for every glass of beer. This would always be a very depressing situation for him. And for us and for Franz this would be even worse. The trip to Missouri will cost at least 100 thaler, and the expense for him would always come first; and even from here we would have to pay his debts. —We are not at all in a position to advance such considerable sums; many things will be lacking in our domestic arrangements until better times come. Many deprivations will be facing us anyway. —If Franz pays his travel expense from his money, if he purchases a farm for himself for 300 thaler, and should they later on have an opportunity to stay together and buy a farm for 500 thaler, then there will only be 500 thaler for him. Still he could advance funds to Bernhard from this money, but where is his prospect of getting it paid back, even if it were only in a year or perhaps in two years that he would be thinking of establishing his own business? If he wants to begin a business with Bernhard then 500 thaler is very little money and will not go very far. —Uncle Caspar promised at one time to advance Bernhard 300 thaler, and considering this as his board money, take back 100 thaler every year from his estate. Bernhard will remain a minor and must therefore draw on the estate money, and 100 thaler a year, here at least, is not sufficient. Therefore this estimate was not very high. —Later the uncle wrote that he wanted to give both of them a present of 200 thaler, and that they should take care of the things they needed for the trip. We were silent, even though this change did not please us, although a present could only be very pleasant. Now, however, from these 200 thaler all the bills that could belong to the estate are to be paid. The sum is therefore not given as a present to the brothers, but only to you. And they have nothing! —At that time we trusted Uncle's promise and were happy to hear that Bernhard could go along. Under these circumstances it would never have occurred to us to take along a brother like Bernhard, who is still in need of all his education; it would therefore have been much wiser for him to stay here for the time being. For Bruns and I can really not manage it now, truly. It would be, however, far from our wishes to leave Bernhard in the lurch now. That cannot be done either. I only want to say that if we had known earlier how things would turn out, it probably would not have happened this way. At least not for the time being.

Uncle Caspar should not, by the way, blame us for being ungrateful. No, certainly not! Indeed he means so well! But ask him whether the bills from Melcher and from von Bruchhausen could not be paid from the inheritance of the minor children. Then the purchases for the trip and the trip itself would be free for Bernhard. We would have to be satisfied with whatever else turns up. —There probably should be no discussion of the 300 thaler anymore. But will Bernhard's part of the inheritance be held for him? Or will everything be used to cover the still-existing debts? Probably the latter. But that too is [not quite] right. One can [probably] still assume that Bernhard [will return] in the future. Only it is rather [difficult] to send [him] so far [alone]. —I have to trust you, Heinrich, that you will inform Uncle Caspar as far a[s you consider] it wise. [He] must [not] be insulted at any cost. [If you] could only succeed in seeing that the aforementioned sums would not all [be withheld. Implore] him most seriously! There [isn't] a single farmhand who would start out with [such empty] pockets as Bernhard.

At Pentecost we will talk more about this.

Sincere greetings from Franz, Hermann, and your sister Jette.

For Heaven's sake do not tell the uncle anymore than [you consider wise].

Marginal note: I forgot that our uncle has also set aside another 50 thaler for us. These must therefore be spent for Bernhard first.

From the Autobiography

So we resolved to leave our home country. All preparations were made. Afterward Uncle Caspar appealed to the probate court and straightened out everything, and the brothers received permission to go along. Everything that had to be taken along was packed in boxes, and the other household things were sold. In the meantime Trude accompanied me to Warendorf, where Bruns was already waiting for me. After we had survived this, we soon were back in Oelde. Cousin Tine had taken care of the little one and of the girl. A dark house lay in front of us. Bruns was getting his key from the post office across the street when he received a letter. After we had light, he opened the letter in the empty house. It contained the news of his mother's death. That's all that we needed to shake our forced composure. We had a very bad night.

After that the last things were done quickly. Our brothers arrived, and travel companions reported in and then traveled ahead. Our departure was set for Sunday morning. We probably thought about it quite differently. The brothers found the wagon the eve before. When it arrived they jumped in, and we followed and away it went. Amazed and perturbed, the neighbors looked after us when they realized that we were waving good-bye. Our little son, who had just gotten rid of the measles, got very sore eyes upon the sandy roads. To be sure we had taken the road to Bremen by way of Bruns's home in order to bid farewell to the relatives on our way. At the Eylardi Inn in Bremen, we waited for the arrival of our goods, which were loaded on heavy wagons and traveled at a slower rate. We traveled to Bremerhaven in a rather big boat and waited for our ship but finally boarded a different one. This was the two-masted *Ulysses,* under Captain H. Spilker.

Bremerhaven, 11 July 1836
Monday

Dear Heinrich:

Since nine yesterday morning we have been here at the house of the master shipbuilder, Cornelius. Besides us, the following are staying here: Dr. Ordemann and wife, daughter, and son; the Apothecary Bellmer; Mr. Brakenbusch, M.D.; Mr. Böhme, M.D.; Mr. Mallinckrodt; Mr. Wenker;[61] Hessler; Fritz Schwarze; Franz; Bernhard; David Bruns; and we with Hermann, Jenne, and Drückchen. Except for the Ordemanns all of the above will be traveling with our group. Yesterday afternoon I went with Bruns on board the ship and saw

61. The passenger list of the *Ulysses* has Chr. Bellmer from Hoffstadt [Hovestadt], apothecary, age 59; Dr. Brakenbusch from Braunschweig, physician, age 25; Dr. John Böhme from Niederlahnstein, physician, age 25; C[arl] Wenker from Dortmund, farmer, age 25. Wenker and Mallinckrodt eventually settled in St. Charles County at New Dortmund near Augusta.

where we will be. As elegant as the cabin is, very little trouble was taken otherwise. The bedsteads are very spacious, therefore it is a good resting place. We have a new big table, and our boxes will make suitable chairs for us. Only the new pine wood is still giving off some scent, and in general it is quite close below and also in the cabin. We will have to stay mostly on deck during good weather.

Our trip to Bremen was quite hard on me. I had been able to bear parting from all of you with composure, but afterward it was that much worse. I could not get over it. It was embarrassing for me that strangers disturbed us in that moment. Now, even though I am constantly disturbed, I can think back on it with relative equanimity. Only for moments is my oppressed heart relieved. I fear for the future.

Again and again I think, "I shall never forget this as long as I live!" It is really indescribably difficult. And how often in my life may I be faced with a similar parting? For I will see all of you again, I am absolutely sure that I will see you again! But I will never again be able to think of Aunt Therese without bitterness. It pains me deeply in my soul; Little Therese is after all also the child of my mother. Nature placed her at my side. I have a greater right to her than our aunt has, than all the others except us. No, our aunt's character, as I would never have thought of her, has been so harshly revealed. I will never get over it!

12 July

Sunday, in the evening we arrived at Rheine. The next morning we set out early for Drievorden, and in the afternoon we proceeded from there to Lohne. Everybody had departed from there already, and so we hurried after them the next morning. It was a bad road, always cobblestone highway. In the evening we had reached the first station after Osnabrück at ten o'clock. A quarter of an hour from Osnabrück, Mamsell Piepmeyer caught up with us. She had heard from the people traveling from Oelde about our departure and had driven to Osnabrück, and since we had already left there she had given orders to drive on quickly. —At eight o'clock on Wednesday evening we arrived in Bremen. The Schwarzes and Viele were there and quite cheerful. The others had found quarters at Ordemann's. I was extremely exhausted and ready to collapse. I am not yet feeling well. But we did have constant hardships.

At three o'clock on Saturday morning we went to Ordemanns in order to go by riverboat to Bremerhaven. Our freight wagons had not arrived until Thursday evening. All the boxes were then loaded in the boat. The unfavorable west wind allowed us to cover only a short distance; in the evening we were not far beyond Vegesack. Anybody with a good appetite would have fared poorly, and whoever managed to prepare a somewhat tolerable resting place for himself on top of the boxes could rejoice because it was so cold on deck. Toward evening a few, among them we too, climbed into a small boat to seek shelter in a lone house and rest there till midnight since low tide had come. At half past nine the drunken boatman came and awakened us, quarreled with Ordemann, and went back cursing with the small boat, since we did not yet want to go along. At midnight we got up again, and finally at half past one our host rowed us to the riverboat. That was some night! The wind had gotten up, a few sails were hoisted, and, favored by the tide, we arrived here at eight in the morning in pouring rain. Yesterday the weather improved, and today we have a fresh wind from the east. We shall set sail at eleven.

Everything is so strange to me, but I shall board that ship courageously. Since I have left all of you, the land of my home is far away. What is this strange world to me? Why should Bremen fascinate me? Only Westphalia drew tears from me that will never dry again. I have no Fatherland any more. The wide world stands open for me!

Bruns is urging, he sends to you, my brothers and sisters, his sincerest regards. Give this letter to Johanna, read parts of it to Thereschen, and write Wilhelm about it. I cannot write any more.

So, now almost a quarter of a year will pass before you can hear from us. Remember us in your prayers and trust in the Highest. Be of good spirits! Hermann still has sore eyes, but otherwise he is quite frisky.

So farewell! Do write at the beginning of your vacation even though you will not have received a letter, and then follow us soon by way of Havre de Grace. Give our regards to all, all who know us, but particularly to Marie whom I will write, perhaps while aboard ship. The letters to our uncles are not quite finished yet. My indisposition did not allow me to get to them.[62] Give my special regards to our uncle and aunt. Do remember us in your thoughts!

Eternally and unchangingly dedicated to all of you with sincere love

Your sister Jette

Marginal note: Franz, who no longer can find time to write, also sends a thousand greetings to all of you. You will hear from him from America right away.

62. Jette was pregnant when the family left Germany.

life
in
America

I

The Years in Westphalia, 1836–1853

You cannot believe how satisfying it is to work. I probably have had very few days in which I was ever as busy as I am here, that is, having to do hard work, but I am quite happy in doing it, and like all the others I have a tremendous appetite and sleep soundly. (It is strange, but almost every night I dream of our father, and then I am still a child with him and spend beautiful hours in my dream.)

Jette Bruns to Heinrich
3 December 1836

From the Autobiography

On the 6th of July 1836 we set sail. Bruns had negotiated with the agent for us and our travel companions in advance. We were thirty people and traveled second cabin but had all the privileges of the first, which didn't have any passengers. We were allowed to do our own cooking if we did not like the food for the steerage class. All in all it was a good group. We were cruising for three weeks in the North Sea, but then we succeeded in getting through the Channel.

After 66 days we landed in Baltimore.

Baltimore
20 September 1836

Dear Heinrich:

Friday evening, 16 September, anchor was dropped and we had safely arrived in the harbor! It was a long and arduous voyage! However we were and are all well and thank the Father in Heaven that he has protected us so far! I had written down the events of the voyage for you, but to my great annoyance I am now missing the whole notebook; perhaps I will find it later.[1] As you know, we set sail on 12 July. By the afternoon, when the pilot left us, one after the other began to hold his head overboard; Bernhard, Mrs. Schwarze, the children, and others. The next morning I felt ill and remained in bed for two days, but during the whole time I only had to vomit four or five times; this was pretty much the same with most passengers. Later I was always spared.

The wind was adverse from the very first evening and remained so for almost three weeks; we did not pass the English Channel until 2 August and had to cope with very heavy stormy weather in the North Sea. On the open sea things went fine in the beginning; later we sailed southward and experienced a calm and great heat. The longing to reach land as soon as possible became greater and greater. The water was very bad, and the food was not very appetizing; how good that we had ham and sufficient wine with us. But there were lots of other things lacking. How I pitied others when I dined with Hermann at noon in the captain's cabin, and also when the heat was great and we sat down beside Mrs. Kirchberg. There was scarcely any other shade on deck. Mrs. Ossenbeck from Everswinkel was happily delivered of a son; Bruns was in attendance. He was baptized by the chaplain and received the name Johann Heinrich Bruno Ulysses. The godparents? Captain J. H. Spilker and Mrs. Bruns. A festive noon meal followed, in which Schniederjans and I participated.

1. The notebook is not known to have survived.

We saw only a few fish. Once a dolphin was caught and provided us with beef steak for two days; at least it could hardly be differentiated from beef. Otherwise the trip·was very monotonous. Great was everybody's joy when the pilot ship approached us at Cape Charles.[2] It was late the evening of the 12th when we entered the bay. And then there was another calm and we often had to lie at anchor. —Saturday, the 17th, after the doctor had left the *Ulysses,* the three cabin passengers, Bruns, and I with Hermann, Rienermann, Wenker, Mallinckrodt, Schwarze, and Lücke were put ashore. We were very sincerely happy to have firm soil under us and hurried here.* We immediately went and bought fruit and everything tasted magnificent. We spent the night here. On Sunday morning we went with Hermann to the Cathedral (Jenne was still aboard). I was deeply moved when I found myself in the really beautiful church, and I was able to tell the Good Lord so very much from the bottom of my heart in a few minutes. The church was empty; we were told that Mass would be held in an hour. Therefore Bruns and Mallinckrodt went to the bank; the chaplain and a few steerage passengers had, as they later told me, gone to a German Catholic church. Hermann and I had to wait patiently during this hour. Finally it was time! It was a musical Mass. The sexton or assistant accompanied me to a bench—otherwise all belonged to private people—but Bruns had to stay in the back with Hermann, as I later realized. That made me uneasy and I looked around several times, and suddenly both of them were gone. The Gospel was read, and since we could not understand it, we went home and Hermann was spared. By then Franz, Bernhard, David, and Viele, who had all hurried to Mass after the quarantine had elapsed, were also here.

I do not like it here in Baltimore; I have never known such heat as we have had in these days. It was not possible to write earlier because I could not collect any of my thoughts. Hermann causes me a great deal of trouble, and Bruns and the brothers are always busy. Yesterday morning they all left except for Bruns and me, Hermann, Mallinckrodt, Wenker, and Rienermann. The canal from Philadelphia to Pittsburgh is not passable, and thus the goods had to be transported by wagons. Franz and Bernhard have bought linen jackets and straw hats and, with a rifle on their backs, roam the country with the other hunters if they are not in the mood to sit on the slow freight wagons, onto which seats have been attached. I would very much like to be with the others, but Bruns did not want to leave me alone, and thus tomorrow we will travel to Philadelphia and New York. I shall write again in a few days, but I would like to give wings to this letter because you will certainly be waiting for it.

A thousand greetings to all, especially to the brothers and sisters and relatives. How often I thought of you on the desolate sea voyage. I shall write more details in another letter. The brothers will hardly be able to write before we reach our property. Once more greetings to the brothers and sisters, and to all the others from us. Your sister Jette, who loves you sincerely.

Marginal note: The William Tell Hotel, Mr. Exe, Pratt Street.

From the Autobiography

In Baltimore we separated. Our baggage went by heavy wagons up toward Pennsylvania; the women and children could ride. The men, among them my brothers, roamed around with their guns and inspected the country and the people and returned to our train in the evening.

2. Cape Charles, Virginia, about twenty miles northeast of Norfolk, is on the southern tip of the peninsula that separates the southern end of the Chesapeake Bay on the west from the Atlantic Ocean on the east.

We had to go and get our cousin, Heinrich Niedieck, in New York. Then with him we joined our companions in Philadelphia, from where we continued on canal boats over the Alleghenies. There were the gentlemen, Professor Conrad Mallinckrodt, Carl Wenker, Heinrich Rienermann. It was a wonderful trip, back on firm ground, traveling through beautiful country in a free nation. In Wheeling we had to wait a week for our wagons. Bruns alone was capable of using English. Thus it was up to him to send our caravan on. Besides the above-mentioned gentlemen there were the Schwarze, Zellerhof, Vennewald, and Westermann families,[3] and six young people. By way of Pittsburgh we went down the Ohio, but near Cincinnati we ran on a stump. Since the river was very low, we were pleased to be able to continue our trip on the little steamer *Cavalier.* My husband became sick and was very ill-humored. I was with the child in the ladies' cabin and could not always be with him. And the food was bad since the steamer was overcrowded. For the first time I tried to express myself in English and with some success. I was able to persuade the black cook to take me to the meat storage room, where I looked for some meat for soup. The maid and others of our group were on the cabin deck, and I was able to prepare some food there.

The *Cavalier* brought us to St. Louis without trouble. We arrived there in rainy weather. The city was overcrowded with people traveling home to the south, so we had to stay aboard our ship. Bruns took me to the Carstens[4] family, where Mr. Gottfried Schütz and Edward Eggers were working. Then we went to Dr. Pultes, who was a university friend who had come to St. Louis a year before. St. Louis had approximately seven thousand inhabitants at that time. There we purchased the most necessary things for our immediate needs, and then we traveled on the Missouri up to Jefferson City. Our companions had traveled on different steamers to Osage City. We went up the Osage River to the mouth of the Maries on flatboats. Now there were only the Zellerhof family and the maid with us. We disembarked at Mr. Henry Dixon's inn. Our things had been unloaded near the penitentiary, and there our people found some shelter until the new friends from Westphalia came from Lisletown to get us.[5] I was shocked at their appearance, genuine backwoodsmen in rough clothing and prepared for rough work. They were the Messrs. Huber, Gramatica, Höcker,[6] and others. It was certainly a great omen that they welcomed us in this manner. And they probably had very little choice. A wagon covered with a tarpaulin had arrived. Mr. John Shipley took us

3. The passenger list of the *Ulysses* has Edelbert Zellerhof from Oelde, age 38, and his wife Maria, age 31; Georg Vennewald from Oelde, 37, his wife Johanna, 37, and two children, Hermann, 4, and John, 3; H. Westermann from Oelde, 40, Maria Westermann, 38, Gertrud Westermann, 37, and three children, Bernhard, 10, Elisabeth, 7, Marian, 4. Müller does not list the Zellerhofs; he lists #226, Georg Vennewald, 36, born in Vellern, as having emigrated in 1836 with his wife Maria Gertrud Rickmeyer, as well as three children; he also lists #256, Georg Westermann from Oelde, born 22 August 1797 at Ennigerloh, his wife Gertrud Rhebaum, and five children ages 10 ½, 8 ½, 5 ½, 3 ½, and 1.

4. H. A. Carstens operated a drugstore in St. Louis. The City Directory of 1842 lists Carstens and Schuetze, Druggists, at 163 N. First Street. Gottfried Schütze, apothecary, age 32, arrived on the ship *Baltimore* at Baltimore on 19 June 1834.

5. The penitentiary to which Jette refers was in Jefferson City. Lisletown, a small settlement at the confluence of the Maries and the Osage, where today U.S. 50 crosses the Osage River, was named after Benjamin Lysle, who acquired the land in 1834.

6. Information regarding Karl (Charles) Huber's origin has not yet been located. The abstract map of Township 43R10W shows that his land was recorded in the southwest quarter of sec. 26 on 29 August 1835. Father Helias listed him on the Westphalia census as Carolus Huber, age 30. Höcker is listed on the map as Frederick Hoecker, owning land in the south center of sec. 23 on both sides of the Maries, 22 January 1836.

through thick and thin, often without any road, to his parents' farm on the Osage River. The next morning we were ferried across the river, and after a few hours we were at our new home. It was the second of November 1836.

Before I continue telling my story I shall say that this area remained our home for over fifteen years. In joy and sorrow, frequently ill, we lived there. We endured our often difficult fate, and among ourselves we were happy to have many children.[7] We had brought Hermann, our oldest, along.

Our first shelter was in the middle of a field, a simple log cabin with two bedsteads, one table, four chairs, and one bench. We were longing for rest and were not even surprised at the sparse furnishings. Before evening we had already taken care of our meal and our lodging for the night. Gradually we were as comfortably settled as possible. The carpenter for the house that we were planning to build made an additional bedframe to shove under the bed for our girl, and with his assistance a lean-to for the boxes was made of split boards. My brothers lived for the time being with us. My brother-in-law, Hermann, had already bought a place on the Little Maries. The carpenter Kolk and his wife, brother-in-law David, and big Jan[8] and his helper, Keiser, lived in a small cabin about a mile from the location we chose for our house. In the beginning we were supplied with bread and milk from there. The winter was upon us, and my brothers brought in firewood. Pigs had already been fattened for us, and they were soon butchered. Then we got a cow and soon thereafter our first riding horse. Thus we could keep house. And if we saw our travel companions now and then, we had already accomplished a lot.

The Hesse family lived near our farm. Mr. Hesse was a former official from the area around Paderborn. Bruns had lived with them during his first stay in this area on the Maries. And Hesse was the reason that the settlement was founded there. Bruns had met him in St. Louis at Carstens's store, after Hesse was already settled on his farm. Before Bruns returned to Germany, Hesse advised him and his brother to buy a small farm as well as some suitable government land.

Besides the Hesse family there were the other families—Huber, Gramatica, Höcker, Nacke.[9] Closer to the Osage were Clarenbach, who came in 1834, as well as the Zur Megede family.[10] On the Maries there was Mr. Scheulen[11] from the lower Rhine with a big family. He

7. The Bruns couple had eleven children, five of whom died in childhood. Although family and church records differ on some birth and death dates, letters and other sources provide the following information: Hermann was born 20 October 1833 in Oelde and died 22 June 1872 in St. Louis; Maximilian, born 27 February 1837 in Westphalia, died 19 September 1841; Johanna, born 3 March 1839 in Westphalia, died 13 September 1841; Rudolph, born 26 January 1841 in Westphalia, died 2 October 1841 (Max, Johanna, and Rudolph died within three weeks of each other from dysentery, which Hermann had contracted in Jefferson City and brought home); Heinrich was born 19 September 1842 in Westphalia and died in the battle of Iuka, Mississippi, 7 July 1863; Euphemia, born 3 May 1844 in Westphalia, died 30 September 1937 in Maplewood; Albert, born 11 December 1845 in Westphalia, died 24 August 1851 at Shipley's Ferry; Adolf, born 7 August 1847 in Westphalia, died 15 August 1847; Ludwig, born 17 July 1848 in Westphalia, died in 1909 in Skagway, Alaska; Ottilia, born 23 April 1851 at Shipley's Ferry, died 19 April 1934 in Jefferson City; Wilhelm, born 24 November 1853 in Jefferson City, died 21 December 1916 in Seattle, Washington.

8. Jan is most likely John Brüggink, who was listed on the passenger list of the *Ulysses* as a joiner from "Dehnenkamp" (actually Denekamp, Holland), age 28. He had worked for the Bruns family in Germany.

9. Joseph Nacke, age 36, his wife Maria Anna, 33, and their three children appear on Father Helias's 1839 census. Nacke recorded land in the southeast quarter, sec. 27, adjacent to Huber's property, on 1 October 1835.

10. Peter F. Clarenbach, or Klarenbach, was a member of the Solingen Emigration Society, led by Friedrich Steines, which sailed on the *Jefferson* from Rotterdam, arriving at Baltimore 5 June 1834. The group reached St.

had come with Mr. Aretz, a very well-to-do farmer, and a close relative of the Porth family that was to come soon thereafter. Mr. Aretz bought the Scheulen farm and some more land on the Osage. He, however, had gone back to Europe when we arrived. In the Maries bottom close to the mouth of the river was the family Messerschmidt, who were Pennsylvanians and very practical and fine people. Lisletown, at the mouth of the Osage, was our first connection with the world, and there a certain Adolf Menger lived, a very fine gentleman from Mainz who had established a store. Bruns, who from the very beginning entered into a sizable practice (unfortunately much too far spread), also went to the settlement on the Missouri called French Village. I remember that he brought a baking pot from there for us.

Our first visit to Mr. Hesse's upset me very much. The lady took Bruns aside, cried, and complained that she couldn't stand it here. They were the only refined family in the settlement. No doubt Mr. Hesse himself was to be blamed that he wasn't doing so well. He had brought with him a teacher, a secretary, workmen, and a maid. He wanted to establish a distillery at a time when there weren't even fields there. As soon as the people began to claim American wages, it didn't work. He would have liked to have seen it through and worked and become a surveyor. This was a big setback in our expectations. But as it often happens, instead of disappointing us it strengthened us and steeled us even more. We were not going to do as they had done. That was our firm resolve. The Hesses went back to Europe.

In the spring of 1837 many people from the Rhineland arrived, and most of them found temporary shelter with Mr. Scheulen. Then they gradually bought land and established farms. They also brought a clergyman along who, to be sure, was not so well fitted for a new community.[12] There were Mr. Dohmen, Bössen, Arend, Stievermann, Götz, Mertens, Brockerhoff, Kern, and others.[13]

Louis in July 1834 during a cholera epidemic that cost many lives. Steines lost his wife, four children, and a sister-in-law before the month was out. The group broke up, and by October 1834 some members, among them Joseph Arez, Carl Eduard Klönne, Sandfort, Johann Adolf Scheulen, Wilhelm Schmitz, and Caspar Carl, all listed on the *Jefferson*, moved west, where they bought land and settled near the Osage River. Two members of the Solingen Society who had settled in the Osage Country visited Steines at his farm in Frederick's Valley on Tavern Creek in Franklin County in July 1835 and reported that "Klarenbach has much work as a watchmaker and lives happily" (William Bek, in *Missouri Historical Review* 15 [April 1921], p. 677). Clarenbach first recorded land in the northeast quarter, sec. 15, 18 February 1836. Henry Zurmegede first recorded land in the southwest quarter, sec. 14, 6 February 1836.

11. Johann Adolf Scheulen was one of the two members of the Solingen Society who visited Steines in July 1835. Although the visitors spoke "in the highest terms" of the Osage Country, they indicated that they would like to buy land in Franklin County so as to be nearer St. Louis and have more German neighbors (ibid., p. 676). Joseph Arez, age 31, recorded the first of his land purchases in the northeast quarter, sec. 14, 14 May 1836, as well as the southwest quarter, sec. 13. Hermann Scheulen, the oldest son of Johann Adolf Scheulen, recorded land in the northwest quarter, sec. 35, 24 May 1838.

12. Father Johann H. Meinkmann, identified by Jette Bruns in her letter of 14 April 1837 as a native of Schöppingen, which is approximately twenty-five miles northwest of Münster, arrived in the Westphalia Settlement in the company of seven families. They had sailed on the brig *Charles Ferdinand* from Bremen and arrived at New Orleans on 15 February 1837. (A copy of the passenger list of that brig is in the Westphalia Historical Museum.) As the first resident pastor, Father Meinkmann is credited with establishing a log church and holding school for the children of the settlers. Because Meinkmann had failed to obtain the necessary release from his former parish in Germany, Bishop Joseph Rosati was reluctant to recognize his ministry, but he was eventually installed as pastor of Westphalia on 24 November 1837. In April 1839 Bishop Rosati transferred him to the newly established parish of St. Francis Borgia in Washington, Missouri. He later became pastor at Ferdinand, Indiana, where he served until his death on 25 August 1847.

13. The passenger list of the *Charles Ferdinand* included the following families who traveled with Father Meinkmann to Westphalia: Christian Bössen, 51, his wife, 53, and six sons, ages 25 to 10; John Caspar Artz, 33, his

Mr. Huber married the young daughter of Mrs. Schröder.[14] He knew how to take hold of things immediately. He had a wagon, and he employed people and got along. He had the misfortune to lose his wife in the first year.

Our next neighbor above us, Mr. Gramatica, from Paderborn, was not without means. He had with him a very old mother and a feeble-minded brother. He was always happy and wanted to work hard, and occasionally he did. He often came to us and told happy stories, was entertaining and carefree. As far as he was concerned things were going along fine. But his mother! She took care of his household, she cooked if there was something there, she complained little until she came to ask for some coffee. Anxiously she paid in advance. I was pleased to help her out. However, it had to be secretly. Fortunately, she soon died.

That year two travelers passed through, Dr. von Könige and Mr. Sutter.[15] They stopped at the Hubers' and visited us. They were very interesting men who had seen a lot and knew how to talk about it. The doctor was kind of forward, but Mr. Sutter was much more pleasant and knew how to entertain in many ways. Later he became famous by finding gold in California.

My older brother, Franz, had bought land not far from us and took care of it himself.[16] The younger brother, Bernhard, went to an American, John Robinson, in order to learn agriculture, as did Carl Zumnorde, a friend of Bernhard's youth from Oelde.

That summer when several workmen were already busily working on our new house the Maries flooded and caused us a great deal of damage. We lost the shingles and the bricks that had not yet been fired. We learned from that how high up we had to plant our potatoes, but for that year we had none to eat, nor did we have any vegetables. Usually one was able to buy

---

wife Anna, 28, and three daughters, ages 5 to 1; J. Dohmen, 40, his wife, 38, and four sons, ages 11 to 4 (the four year old was listed as having died on the voyage); W. Götzen, 34, his wife Maria, 36, and one daughter, 5 (Götzen recorded land in the southeast quarter, sec. 11, 26 May 1837); J. Mertins, 44, his wife, and three sons, ages 14 to 7; J. Stiefermann, 41, his wife Maria, 40, and six daughters, ages 15 to 1. Neither Brockerhoff nor Kern was listed although they appeared in the February 1839 manuscript census compiled by Father Helias. A Friedrich R. Bruggerhoff, 38, and two children, 13 and 12, appear on the passenger list of the *Jefferson,* arriving in Baltimore on 5 June 1834 with the Solingen Emigration Society. Henricus Brockerhoff, 50, is listed in Father Helias's census, as is Johannes Kern.

14. Margretha Schröder, née Versen, the widow of Franz Anton Schröder, who died in 1831, emigrated with her children in 1835. She recorded forty acres of land in the northwest quarter, sec. 26, 2 July 1838, adjoining the property of Charles Huber on the north. On 1 April 1841 Margretha married John Adolph Klassen.

15. Johann August Sutter (1803–1880) was born of Swiss parentage in the German village of Kandern in the Margravate of Baden. He appeared in the St. Louis German community in the autumn of 1834 and is known to have spent the winter in St. Charles, supported by a Westphalia immigrant, Johann August Laufkötter, who had opened a store there. When Sutter visited the Duden settlement in 1835, he claimed that he had been an officer in the Swiss Guard of Charles X and had been forced to flee Paris in the July Revolution of 1830. In other stories he claimed to have attended a military academy in Bern (there was no military academy in Bern) and to have served as a captain in the Swiss army (there was no Swiss army; each of the twenty-two Swiss cantons maintained militia troops). There was considerable interest in Missouri in Sutter's trade ventures, mounted with borrowed money which he invested in pistols, trinkets, and German students' jackets bought from St. Louis pawnshops for the Indian trade, particularly after he returned to St. Charles from his 1835 trip to Santa Fe with large profits. But his trip the following year, for which he and his companions had borrowed heavily, was financially disastrous. Goods in demand the previous year were impossible to sell, and there were heavy losses. Sutter left St. Charles and was reported to have traveled up the Missouri on the boat that brought Father Helias to mid-Missouri on 11 May 1838. See *Sutter: The Man and His Empire* by James Peter Zollinger (London: Oxford University Press, 1939), which is based on research in Switzerland, Germany, and the United States.

16. Franz Geisberg is listed as having recorded 120 acres in sec. 26 on 29 August 1835. This is obviously an error since he did not arrive at the Westphalia Settlement until November 1836. He recorded forty acres in the southwest quarter, sec. 27, 18 June 1837.

things, however. Once we had no flour since the Maries was so high and the mill was located ten miles from us. Fortunately Mrs. Zellerhof [17] was able to help us.

My cousin Niedieck was staying with Americans, a very nice family, and besides farming the man made shoes. One day Heinrich N. presented me with a pair of shoes he had made himself and wrote to his father that he could be proud of his son. This amused us. On Sundays we usually had a lot of visitors. Mr. Rienermann appeared regularly, and frequently Mr. Mengers or some other family would come.

We became impatient with the progress on the construction of our house, which was not getting on. In late fall after the timbers had been erected and the roof had been put on, we moved in. There was still no gable, no chimney, no floor, neither windows nor doors. But after we had gotten there, things went ahead. (If only we had let the big house go and had been satisfied with a few comfortable log cabins as other people were.)

Our son Max was born February 1837, and the boys were a joy to us. But often in the evening, when the workmen were sitting around the only fireplace, I went to bed with the children in order to be out of the way. In the spring after the seven rooms of the house had become livable, Bruns opened a store with Niedieck and Mr. Ferdinand Meier, who was from Münster.[18] In the beginning this went well, but Niedieck again became unreliable and withdrew, and Zumnorde took his place.

My brother Bernhard had gone to Augusta to Mr. Wenker to learn the tanning business. In the summer he came down with a fever, and Mr. Julius Mallinckrodt took him in. On the advice of Mr. Wenker, my brother Franz rode over there to get him. However, he was still too weak, and after quite some time Mr. Wenker brought him home himself. He must have suffered very much from homesickness and had become very melancholy and strange. When soon afterward he got a severe nervous fever, Bruns hoped that his emotional condition would improve. It became somewhat better, so that with some help he was able to work his own farm until he again became sick. Then he decided to go back to Europe. We agreed with him, and he embarked via New Orleans. After that, brother Franz built a house and took a wife, Gertrude Stievermann.[19] Brother-in-law Hermann took Marie Lückenhoff as his wife.[20]

Particularly sad events were that Rienermann was found drowned in the Maries. And then the horrible death of Mr. Gottfried Schwarze! He and young Schröder were madly riding home from Lisletown one night. Suddenly Schröder was alone and his companion lay on the ground with a broken head. He was taken home, but he never regained consciousness, and died after a few hours.

In our house a little girl arrived on the third of March 1839. Her name was Johanna. After a long sickness there was a bright sunbeam. I got well again, and the children were prosper-

17. According to the map drawn by Nicolaus Hesse in 1838, the Zellerhoff property lay either in sec. 12, 13, or 24 on the Maries.

18. Joseph Ferdinand Meyer, a merchant from Münster, born 25 August 1812, is listed by Müller #388 as emigrating in 1837.

19. Gertrude's surname is spelled differently by various members of the family, sometimes *Stiefermann* and sometimes *Stievermann*. In either case the German pronunciation is the same. The wedding took place 5 November 1840.

20. Müller recorded #340, Joseph Lückenhoff, from Oelde, 53, his wife Elisabeth Hülsmann, 41, five sons, 19 to 6 months, and four daughters, 17 to 2, of whom Anna Marie was born in Oelde on 25 May 1819. She married Gerhard Hermann Bruns in Westphalia 23 April 1840 and died 22 August 1859.

ing. I tried again and again to overcome the melancholy feeling of homesickness, which was that much deeper since I tried to hide it from my husband and he was away so very often.

A log church was being built by the settlers. After the first year we had a permanent priest, often even two. They were Jesuits and very respectable men who were well-suited for a new settlement. There were only four Protestant families there—the Clarenbachs, the Zur Megedes, the Höckers, and the Kleinsorgens.[21] They were all highly respected and were good neighbors. Especially with the Clarenbachs we had a very nice relationship. The settlement grew with each year. Strangely enough, for many years there was no inn there. The strangers who passed by or wanted to spend more time there were simply sent to the doctor's house. And thus it happened that we entertained many famous politicians, high clergymen, and candidates for office at our house.

Tuesday, 14 November 1836

Dear Heinrich:

We arrived here at eleven in the morning on All Souls Day. The log cabin was locked up, but Bruns broke the lock. It consists of one room the size of our living room with one window; in it there were a table, four chairs, and two bedsteads. So this was to be our home for the winter! I have to confess that I nevertheless felt good to have reached a safe asylum, and very uplifted by the firm knowledge that I want to stand everything with fortitude. The sun shone warmly and kindly through the leafless trees; soon a bright fire was burning, and for the noon meal we had some wonderful vegetables.

Our belongings could only be transported very slowly, and thus in the first week we lacked all kinds of things; however, I still am happy that with every day things will become better. Now the carpenter Kolk has built a shed onto the house in which the boxes can be stored. Our possessions, with the exception of a few things, arrived in good shape. Unpacking and airing things is a lot of work. Our next-door neighbors are Huber, Hesse, Nacke, and Gramatica, whom I have visited with Bruns.

Last Thursday and Friday we had Divine Service. A dignified young Jesuit (who is a native of Cleve)[22] read the Mass, and all received Holy Communion. In counting the Catholic community we arrived at seventy members. Only Bruns and I could go to Mass on the second morning. The rain poured down from heaven in buckets; it was a hard walk. After confession Mr. Huber was married,[23] and then the Mass began. We had coffee at the Hesses and started on our way back, but we almost got stuck. The water had gathered so much that we had trouble getting through. If by next summer we have a horse I shall certainly be able to

21. Hermann Heinrich Christoph Jürgen Kleinsorge (1795–1871), an assistant to the city council of Lemgo/Lippe from 1833 until he emigrated, sailed aboard the *Flavio* on 28 June 1848 with his wife, Anna Maria Sophie Elise Falke of Brake, and four sons. On 29 November 1848 they acquired the 120-acre farm of Charles and Elizabeth Huber on the western edge of Westphalia. Although he was an Evangelical Lutheran, his descendants converted to Catholicism and became members of the St. Joseph Church (Edward Bode in *St. Joseph Sequicentennial 1835–1985*, p. 173).

22. Records in the archives of the archdiocese of St. Louis show that one of the traveling Jesuit missionaries saying Mass at the Westphalia Settlement in 1836 was Father Cornelius Walters, a native of Kleve on the lower Rhine, who had been sent to America by the diocese of Münster.

23. Karl Huber married Christina Schroeder on 9 November 1836. She died at Westphalia on 14 March 1838. Huber married seventeen-year-old Elisabeth Lückenhoff on 8 May 1840.

use it; however, Bruns will probably have to buy one sooner because he has to get out almost every day. The Americans seem to have a great deal of confidence in him. If Bruns is not at home and an American comes, then, my dear Heinrich, it is a joy to see how beautifully we endeavor to speak English. It is really my greatest annoyance that I cannot use it. However, it will soon improve. On the first Sunday we were at the Hubers for lunch, along with another gentleman. In the course of the conversation he explained that he could not at all understand the lady in our house. Lady Jenne!? We really had a good laugh at this. She, by the way, had a great deal of fun in getting this title.

Sunday, 3 December

Still no letter has been dispatched to you! It seems to me that this delay is not quite right, although Bruns said that one really could not write until the Germans who had come with us had established a permanent place. I, however, think you will give us the first priority, and your sympathy will demand news from us.

During this time we all have been very busy. We have done our laundry, a hog was butchered, corn had to be harvested, etc. For approximately ten days now, and to my great joy, Franz and Bernhard, who had stayed with the Hubers until then, have been with us. Heinrich Niedieck went from us to an American by the name of Burns. He visited us today again, and he is quite satisfied. He is most likely to be the quickest to learn English. Now today we have rainy weather again, the third time since we have arrived here; for two weeks we had a freeze. It froze pretty heavily during the night, but during the daytime it always turned very pleasant and the sun shone warmly as it probably never did in Westphalia so late in the year. When it rains, it is just too sad in these log cabins; the one in which we live lies on a slope, and thus a little ditch had to be made so that the water would not run into the shed and even into the house. In cold weather one is a little hesitant to get up in the morning, and I frequently think back to our comfortable living room. However, here we just have to live through it.

There is one situation that makes me very cross. It is that Jenne is not at all adaptable. The thought that I will have to get along for years with this disorderly, clumsy person can discourage me any moment. Too often I am vexed about this, and I believe that she is a hopeless case. Thus it happens that I myself have to do most of the cooking and have to try to find work for her outside the house if possible. I shall commend this cross to Heaven!

You cannot believe how satisfying it is to work. I probably have had few days in which I was ever as busy as I am here, that is, having to do hard work, but I'm quite happy in doing it, and like all the others I have a tremendous appetite and sleep soundly. (It is strange, but almost every night now I dream of our father, and then I am still a child with him and spend beautiful hours in my dream.)

During the first days of our stay here Hermann was unwell and had fever every day. Soon, however, it dissipated, and the little rascal is very frisky and has a much greater appetite than ever before. When the weather is good he roams around outside.

Franz will probably take over the farm on which we now live from Bruns's brother because it is more adaptable to another business. The connection from the Osage to the Missouri River and back is easier here, and Hermann Bruns will move about three miles away from us, where he has bought an improved farm from an American by the name of Russet. David Bruns will be situated a little closer to us. He will buy some government land. In the next few days, after the corn has been harvested here, Bernhard will go to Mr. Scheulen, who has a mill and distillery. He is really itching to go. I have not yet seen very much of this whole area; however, the location of our farm is very pleasant, and the place where the house is going to stand is the best of all the locations. Yesterday I went there with Bruns in order to discuss a few changes concerning the construction of the house with Kolk. We will take two rooms less and instead will have a hall. If only we could be moved in! Who knows what will happen in the meantime!

[continued with red ink]

I hope that we will soon be able to call for a letter from you from the post office, for you certainly will have remembered that you wanted to write at the beginning of September. I yearn very much to hear from you, although I am for the time being at peace concerning you. Quite frequently we talk about where you might be at this time, in Bonn or Heidelberg? Surely you will have passed the final exams long ago while we were still rocking on the high seas.[24] It is disagreeable to us that letters cannot be sent directly to you; however, the uncles will surely forward them to you immediately. —Franz is sitting here with us and talking a blue streak and says I should write about this since I'm complaining about it: Bernhard is talking while he is lying in bed. Old Schwarze's Fritz, who lived in Shipley's log cabin with Vennewald, has bought some land approximately six miles from us between the Maria and the Missouri, eighty acres of land, of which twelve have been cleared and are planted in corn, for which he paid two hundred dollars. They all say that he lives too far away; however, he himself is mightily satisfied and is already living there and has taken over horses, cows, pigs, geese, and chickens valued at four hundred dollars. Vennewald came back only yesterday, from St. Louis, where he filed for eighty acres of government land. Hessler has also gone there in order to buy land. He will live approximately eight miles up the Maria from us. Fritz Schwarze am Teich is also in St. Louis and will file with Hessler; they say that if he lives there and wants to operate a distillery, he will not have such a good market there as compared to here. Rienermann is still with the Hesses, but he will probably soon move on. Zellerhoff is working at the Clarenbachs every day for one half dollar plus board, just as Westermann is. Some who really have great plans say that we are living too close to our neighbors, which will be detrimental for raising stock, and this is also the reason why H. Bruns (as a capable farmer) will move farther away. But we are a good fifteen minutes away from our new house, and almost the same distance from the Hubers and Hesses. Gramatica will probably be situated closest to us, but it seems to me that fifteen minutes is far enough to let a herd of pigs run wild. Franz and several other think likewise. By the way, we are unlikely to do any farming to any great extent—the medical practice is better. Bruns's two brothers live in the other house, as do the carpenter Kolk and Jan, who formerly was a hired hand with Bruns in Lohne. My husband has hired him for a year, and since he has some experience he is helping Kolk with the construction of the house. Kolk's fiancée, who is staying with us until the wedding, cooks in this house.

24. The examination, generally called the *Abitur,* was the final examination at the *Gymnasium.* Passing it qualified a student for admission to any university in Germany. Heinrich Geisberg passed the *Abitur* at the *Paulinum* in Münster in 1836 and subsequently studied law at the universities of Bonn and Berlin.

Now I want to tell you good-bye, and I shall soon write more. You will have received the first letter from New York. Greetings to all, especially to the brothers and sisters, to the uncles and aunts a thousand times; also the brothers and sisters Geisberg, the Boners, Lena, Trude,[25] and all our acquaintances! So many times I think of you back home!

Later when we have more peace we shall report in with more letters. You certainly are corresponding with Johanna, with Wilhelm and Threschen, aren't you? Do write me about them all, everything you know. I am thinking of sending a few enclosures for them in the next letter. Do keep up the good relations with them! They have to feel very close to you! And now dear, dear Heinrich I hope you are well. I am beginning to realize how great the separation is! Do not study too hard and do take some time for recreation and be careful with the wild activities of students. You have to answer me right after receiving this letter! Franz, Bernhard, Bruns, and Hermann send their sincere greetings, together with your loving sister, Jette.

On 3 March 1837 Jette wrote to her Aunt Therese and Uncle Adolf Geisberg to announce the arrival five days before of her second child, Max, a healthy boy "with a stub-nose and little black hair." She had not yet heard from her relatives. The letter is completed by Dr. Bruns, who reports that Jette is feeling very strong. He is highly satisfied with her condition. The immigrants from Westphalia are doing well in the New World, with fine plantations and good prospects. He has a lucrative practice, but "the one thing we lack is good company. This is particularly unpleasant for the women . . . ." On 5 March, Franz Geisberg wrote to his Uncle Caspar, reporting that he had bought eighty acres of land bordering that of Bruns. On 14 April, Bruns wrote Caspar of his land holdings on the Maries, the livestock he had acquired, and his successful practice. "I wish you could see our property here. You would exclaim! Here is a good place to live! The location is like paradise. The soil cannot be worn out." The winter had been quite unfriendly, but spring was arriving and everything seemed well in the Westphalia Settlement. On 30 May, Bernhard Geisberg wrote to Heinrich of his trip from Baltimore and the arrival on the Osage, "the most beautiful river which I have yet seen in America. . . . some maintain it is the most beautiful river in the United States."

Westphalia Settlement
August 1837

Dear Heinrich:

Today I was alone all day long with my little ones. And I thought that I would write you a lot. I talked with you in my thoughts all morning. But here comes an American on horseback, and I have to try to speak English with him. He is waiting for Bruns, who will not return until this evening. I have progressed with my English speaking so far that I can understand occasionally a few common little sentences and can reproduce them. I must really learn more, for it annoys me tremendously when I stand there like a blockhead and cannot answer.

I am being admonished by you and by Uncle Caspar to write more. Bruns is to be blamed that I have not answered the letter I received on 2 July until now. I had sat down a few times and had already written more than a page when my husband happened to read the letter and announced his verdict that it was not worth a penny. At first, I was absolutely furious, but

25. Gertrud Steinbicker (1814–1886) married Franz Geisberg (1808–1876), who was the son of Franz Heidenreich Geisberg and Marianne Westendorf.

then I thought it over and found that he was not quite wrong. It bears the imprint of my mood at that time. I had to force myself to put something down on paper; and therefore there's almost not a healthy thought in it. Now, however, only now, I shall and can write anew, but I must humbly ask that you do not immediately judge me. —On 2 July, I received the first letter from you. It was the second you had written, dated April 8th (therefore the first one is somewhere else). The time before receiving it was dragging on, and I was restless, especially since I counted on your punctuality. Your letter was in many ways quite touching for me. I often think of Cousin Johanna.[26]

It was somewhat puzzling to me that our Johanna has already gone to Stromberg; that, I thought, would be better at a later time. If a fine education is missed in these years, then it is hard to make up for it later, and I find it hard to believe that Miss Költchen accomplished this in one year. If there should be some change in her situation, then take care that special consideration is given.

Fritz Schwarze, who left here in June, had not received a letter from Dina F., and even now none has arrived. It does not seem to me to be quite right if she wants to change her mind. We are quite anxious to know and would hate to lose him.[27]

Heinrich Niedieck received a lot of letters recently, specifically a bank draft; everything was addressed to Bruns. He was very happy at this. He has to be treated with circumspection; he is not yet well. It is a shame that the address on the newspapers sent to Osterlink had gotten lost; it could easily have turned out that it was not Bruns who was the writer. —Well, our Mr. Brother does a little teasing, which really made me laugh heartily, and even little Max laughed and thought it would be high time that the faraway uncle learns of his arrival if he had received his name. If the heavens will consent and will bless us further we shall let it be known in time so that you can assist us in praying for a little Johanna.

Brother Bernhard has been in New Dortmund on the Missouri since the beginning of June to work in the tannery belonging to Mr. Wenker, our former traveling companion. He has not yet written; however, I have copied your letter for him and also admonished him to write.

Franz is with us. I really think he will have to live for a while among the Americans to learn English. In his leather pants he really looks like a farmer. Aside from a little slowness, he seems to me to be doing well and seems to get along fine with his work. Our household consists of Franz, Bruns, me, with my two boys, Jenne and Drüke, Kolk and wife, big Jan Brüggink, little Jan Hillen, and David Bruns. —Hermann Bruns has gone to St. Louis to spend some time there. For two weeks now three Rhinelanders have been making bricks, so David and little Jan are always here.

We have had very little luck with anything that we have tackled this year, and it takes a great deal of perseverance and patience not to lose courage. You know that we believed we would be able to occupy our house soon after our arrival. But still only the skeleton is

26. Johanna Geisberg (1816–1886), Jette's cousin, married County Court Director Üdinck from Werne. The daughter of Franz Heidenreich Geisberg and Marianne Westendorf, Johanna was first engaged to a forester named Stein who met with a fatal accident the day before their wedding. The reference probably relates to this.

27. According to the Schwarze firm's anniversary publication, Gottfried Schwarze embarked from Philadelphia on the *Amphitrite* in 1837 to return to Germany. He did not return to America, but instead became manager of the family distillery in Oelde in 1841 (Friedrich Schwarze, *300 Jahre Brennerei-Tradition in einer westfälischen Familie* [1664–1964][Stuttgart: Daco Verlag], p. 13).

standing, and a few shingles have been attached to indicate how the roof will be. Our carpenter, to be sure, has done his work well, but has proceeded so very slowly that the entire world is amazed. The shingles are being cut by someone else. In the bottom, down below the new house, there is a small field and a pasture for the cattle. However, we did not get around to finishing that, and so the field has remained almost desolate. The few things that have been planted have been destroyed by the flood. Here on Franzen's farm we planted two-thirds in corn and one-third in wheat. The corn stand is good, so we hope the corn will ripen, although it has received very little care. In the spring our horses suddenly got sick and we could not plow, and the weeds got out of hand, and so the corn had to be hoed, which was very troublesome and was not completed. The wheat grew very poorly and had to be stacked in a big pile since we still have no shelter for it. We could plant only very few vegetables because the little fellow took too much of my time. The few things on the stiff upper land did not succeed very well. Now we have many people and little to eat. A great worry for the housewife! Fresh potatoes have to be dug now, so that there is something here. In order to make the misfortune complete, our carpenter and his young wife were hit by the fever; Jenne now has been going there every morning for a week to cook and take care of the household. Well, what else should I complain about? That I am very often vexed? That I feel doubly annoyed with all these misfortunes and the domestic annoyance with Jenne etc. etc.? That it is no fun to represent cook, nursemaid, and housewife in one person? Away, away, with further song concerning these things. To say it in brief, I wish and hope that things will improve!

My boys sweeten many a disagreeable thing for me; unfortunately the big one has already begun to be quite unruly, but when that is past I really love him very, very much. And the little one is a complete little angel. All day long he is friendly, but he does not want to sit or lie down, and I always have to hold him. With his bare little head with the golden brown hair shining, lightly dressed, often wearing only a little shirt, he mumbles loudly with a strong voice and approaches Hermann, then looks at him cheerfully, and the latter jumps in front of him and makes him laugh loudly. Bruns also pays a great deal more attention to Max than he did earlier to Hermann; he is probably now used to them. Also, the good man has far more consideration for me; he probably thinks that I am now in greater need of it. When I express a wish, he seeks to fulfill it. His practice is a little too far, even though it earns that much more; today he is away in Portland on the Missouri, which is thirty-five miles from here. —A week ago I went for the first time to the Schwarzes. Franz took us there because Bruns was out. He has good corn, his wife has a clean household, she is active, and her Lisbeth is no less active; it makes me sad when I see how the latter assisted the mistress constantly, and Jenne has such a tremendous deliberateness when I struggle in her presence. (Bruns said that as soon as possible he wants to buy me a black girl, whom I could then teach.) The way to the Schwarzes, through Lisletown, is really not too far. I really had to laugh aloud at his ability to build; a very pretty fireplace, a kitchen, and a strange outhouse have been finished. Really these people become extremely skilled here.

Now I have to close. In the next few days I shall write a letter to you and send it by way of Münster, and later I shall write regularly every six weeks myself, or Franz, or Bruns. You mention very little of Wilhelm and Thereschen, tell me a little bit more of them the next time, and they also all have to write me. Greetings above all to the brothers and sisters; I hope they write you frequently because you have to know exactly what is happening with them. They have to give you their complete confidence. Do write whether I can send a letter now and then to Bonn.

And now farewell! Write frequently, even if it is only small details of what you do on this or that day, and then embellish it a little bit because I like that so much; and repeat a few things from the first letter which was lost.

Hold dear, as always, your faithful sister Jette.

Westphalian Settlement
7 September '37

Dear Heinrich:

At the beginning of August I sent my last letter to you. I've also sent a few pages to Johanna, which I gave to Schwarze to take along. It's little enough; however, it is getting better and better, just watch!

A quarter of a year ago now a very beautiful piece of furniture, which outshines all other items, a piano, found its way into our log cabin. (But perhaps you know this already, since Bruns has written to Uncle Caspar about it.) What a strange coincidence! How could I have imagined that just such an instrument as I had denied myself would be made available to me in America! Until a few days before the departure of the Hesses we had not thought of it; then the Hesses offered it. German price, German work, without the cost of transportation! Thus we agreed. However, I have to confess that the beautiful piano neither has a suitable place nor is it being properly used. Both will be taken care of better in the new house. It has a beautiful full sound, and the outside has brown finish; there is nothing lacking. The Swede, Mr. Blumenthal, was recently kind enough to tune it. The guitar kept very well on the trip.

Mr. Hesse—you mentioned him—started his return trip to Europe in the spring. A few weeks later he wrote to Bruns: in St. Louis his brother, who had been ill here for a long time, died. Later, on the train between Lancaster and Philadelphia, he lost his only little son; his wife was twice at the edge of her grave; however, she has recovered in the meantime, so he wants to embark for England. Thus he leaves America. Mr. Hesse came with great expectations; he brought along many people, and only average means. The people did not do what they were supposed to do, and his wife was not in accord with them; from domestic dissension there developed disgust; the people drifted away, Mr. Hesse toiled honestly in his field, but he alone, with his quick temperament, could not accomplish enough. The children were not directed to do anything; the mother lived only for her children and wished nothing more than to return. And here sat Mr. Hesse, without means, without help, without a prospect. It is true that only after long resistance did he decide to give in finally to the will of his wife. Perhaps in the end he secretly longed to return himself; however, without the strong urging of the latter he probably would never have decided to do it. He seemed to fear the return to Germany. I still see his sad, quiet face in front of me; in the last weeks he was extremely depressed. He did have weaknesses and faults, but he always remained a man worthy of respect. Envy can never take this name away from him, nor jealous ingratitude; nor the verdict of the jury. He returns over the ocean with a spotless reputation. We were very sorry that he did not satisfy the probably irresponsible claims of his former domestic help, but departed quietly from St. Louis. (He was not able to say no to anyone who asked for anything.) The state of health of the family did not allow him to seek justice publicly, nor perhaps did his already limited means. You see, we are inclined to think the best of him, as most of the others around here do. His farm has been taken over by a Rhinelander, a straightforward, simple man who, for the time being at least, makes us miss the former owner very much. There are fewer educated people around here than former country people, who probably for the time being will have the best of it. A great deal of patience and perseverance are necessary in the beginning; otherwise I am afraid that Mrs. Hesse will find all kinds of women who will follow her back.

Among the educated people we would count the family Huber, which consists of husband, wife, mother-in-law, and brother; Niedieck is also in their house; further, the family Clarenbach; the husband is in Germany at the present time, and I hold the wife in high esteem; she has three children and two brothers and a sister (a grown brother, the sister is smaller than Johanna). Then in Lisletown there is Mr. Menges, a merchant, and on the Osage there are a few Swedes who have a store, and very fine people by the name of Gramatica, the Schwarzes, and Linnemann here on the Maries, and thus it goes on.

In the middle of June we had a considerable flood here. The entire bottom along the Maries was under water, as was that along the Osage; we have heard that the Ohio was extremely high. All the little pigs floated away, and many hogs died. We ourselves had our new and Franzen's small field under water, and then we had to collect our split rails that were scattered in the woods and lug them back, and we also lost a few shingles. That was not much damage. Our corn remained in good condition. Some, however, who lived near the Maries had to evacuate their houses and lost most of their corn and their garden fruit. Our drying house for the bricks was soon repaired, and now approximately thirty thousand bricks are dry but have not yet been fired. I am full of anxiety and worry that the weather will change; otherwise they will be finished a week from today. And then the bricks will be laid, and as soon as the walls are there we will be able to move. I wish you could share my longing; we have to get there at any cost. Up there on the hill it is so airy, it will dry quickly; it will be a lovely spot where I shall feel at home again. Oh, how many annoying hours have I spent because of procrastinations; how slowly everything progressed with this carpenter; I would like to have the patience of an angel. But is it not really terrible that we have been building here now for two years? I can scarcely think of anything else, but have so much to worry about, and nothing has helped. Bruns is also quite glum. We are now firmly resolved that in case the bricks should fail we will make a few mud walls and move in anyway. We just cannot go on as we are now!

There is one other thing I want to tell you. Do you know that I also ride a horse? On the 4th of July I rode on a brand new side saddle to the Scheulens. Max was sitting very happily in my lap. There were several Americans and Germans there, and the noon meal took place in accordance with the American way. At first all ladies sat down, and several gentlemen served us. Soon after the meal there was some dancing. But there was only one fiddle there. American dancing is really quite boring, without a beginning and without an end, almost like contre dances but with no different couples. Finally they figured out that one could also waltz to the tune; and I even danced around a few times. In the end it almost turned too dark for us.

A few weeks ago a camp meeting took place near the post office. It lasted for over three days and is said to have been very crowded. In the beginning we also intended to go there; however, after some consideration, we thought it better to remain at home. Franz rode over there. Some women became enraptured, others moaned mightily (this is a special sign of reverence), others wept. There is constant preaching. When hunger calls, then food is served under the tents that have been pitched, and all who are at all known are invited to partake. For three days, Mr. Bensink (from Bielefeld) ate busily, drank, moaned, and shouted amen, but delayed his further conversion somewhat. Americans who do not believe in anything nevertheless ride there, shake their heads, and smoke, talk, chew, etc., which does not particularly please the preachers, who often have to ask them to quiet down.

We have also had some very warm days here, warmer than I have ever experienced, but not so sultry. One can sit quietly on a chair and the perspiration runs quietly down one's cheeks in drops, and I often wonder that I am so warm and feel it so little. To be sure, in these log cabins one is in very close contact with the heat of the sun; we have the sun standing almost all day at our front door. If one has a little shady spot outside, it is much easier to get along than at times in Germany. However, this summer is said not to be equal to the ones in former years; the last few weeks we again had cooler nights. The change in the weather is so sudden here that it is really amazing. Now it is again very warm, but last week I wanted to have somebody go and fetch our featherbeds from the new house.

A few weeks ago Kolk showed us a little nest of hummingbirds; it sat there attached to the extreme end of an oak branch and was as big as a walnut half. The pretty little bird buzzed around his little building. We regretted very much that the slender tree with its far-reaching branch prevented closer observation. Twice already Indians have been nearby. At first there was a group in Lisletown, where a Mr. Williams speaks their language. They drank mightily until someone finally thought it wise to show them the door. A little while ago again forty Indians with wives and children appeared in the Swedes' store on the Osage; they love whiskey very, very much. The women simply are told to go into the woods, where they make a fire and prepare their food until the men feel like eating or lying down. The men swam through the Osage on top of or alongside their horses, shouting wildly; all who saw it were amazed at their skill in guiding their canoes very quickly. There is no thought of danger or attack. They obey as soon as they are told. Unfortunately I heard of their stay at the Osage too late; otherwise I would have ridden over there because I have not seen any yet.

We have a few hundred plants of tobacco; it grew very well even though we did not have much time to care for it, nor did we plant it early enough. The big, heavy leaves hang down and can be taken off. The tobacco resembles the plant that we used to have in the little yard.

25 September '37

Fortune is smiling at me; two Sundays in succession now we have received letters. (It has now been four weeks that I have wanted to send this letter to you, and it is still not finished.) You have written something about Bonn and your stay there. Since your first letter was lost I only knew you were studying there. Do write frequently; your sister is not a stranger to the Rhine. Have you visited Stolzenfels yet? When you walk up the small, narrow, winding path you can think of me. I spryly followed our stout uncle, who finally arrived with me at the top completely exhausted. I was dizzy and I did not dare approach the edge of the precipice; but how beautiful was the friendly valley in front of us, how gently did the Lahn wind its way into the mighty stream. I still remember this scene vividly.

Will you stay in Bonn in the future? Do repeat a few of the things from the lost letter. What will Mr. Hesse be doing in Germany? Uncle Caspar announced his arrival. We would be interested in hearing from him—has Fritz Schwarze arrived? Will he return? —The immigrants here still have to suffer a great deal from the Missouri rash. The main cause is that they eat too much meat,[28] and then also they live on land that has not been cleared. Many of them do not know about this. Max and Hermann have little blisters on their hands and feet and are amazingly annoyed at this, which mother has to bear with patience. The fever, which was quite tolerable during the summer, now appears more frequently. In our house Bruns, Franz, David, Jenne, and little Max were spared. We others did have a taste of it. But I feel quite well again. It was bad in the other house, where the wife of the carpenter had three or four attacks. And then Jenne had to cook there, or the carpenters had to do it themselves. It is the usual cold fever.

Now farewell and remain well, write diligently; you see how quickly letters can fly across the ocean. I will soon be happy that we can converse with each other in this manner. Only too often, however, I lack the time to be able to write calmly. In the new house, where I can sit down by myself, it will be better, but when there is so much restlessness around me, I lack the peace. I often fear that I communicate to you the least interesting things; you will have to pass over this.

Bruns, who rode twenty-six miles today, sends his greetings from his bed. Franz is active and sends sincere greetings even though he is not at home right now. He went to get apples from the other side of the Missouri. He went by boat with the others. The fruit is cheap there and very nice. There are also a lot of peaches.

Hold dear, as always, your sister Jette.

On 13 October 1837 Heinrich wrote Jette, describing the dismantling of the family business in Münster. He reported rumors that "Bruns is said to have moved away because of an investigation concerning the Burschenschaft" {the student fraternity} and further that "Bruns is supposed to have remarked that if things do not turn out better he will return. It is not as good over there as he had imagined." Heinrich was frustrated that he could neither confirm nor deny the rumors.

On Christmas Day 1837, Jette wrote to Uncle Caspar, reporting that the family had moved into the new house six weeks before. They had the use of three rooms and cooked in a building next door. She had a second maid "to share the burden of the household." Franz was doing well as a farmer, but she was worried about Bernhard, who had been ill and was acting strangely.

Westphalia Settlement
1 March 1838

Dear Heinrich:

Mr. Lamken was kind enough to bring a letter for us to Lisletown from Jefferson. Mr. Niedieck brought it along here. I happened by chance to be unwell and had a severe head-

---

28. A similar observation was made by Gottfried Duden in his *Report:* "The too frequent eating of meat produces unpleasant results especially among the members of the feminine sex, because their household tasks demand far less of the exercise necessary for digestion than the men have . . . . A number of prevalent ailments are due merely to the excessive eating of fatty meat dishes" (Twenty-eighth Letter, p. 134).

ache, but I wanted to see it, and I read and I read, and I skimmed over many things, and I thought that I would have to read it again and then I went to bed. Until Niedieck said, "So this was already written in 1836?" And then I was very happy that this first letter had finally reached its destination.[29] —And brother Heinrich was still in very good spirits and probably while writing looked happier than his older sister when she saw brother Bernhard read the letter and make a strange face, almost tearful, then terribly serious, then stop at some spot for a long time, and finally look at me frequently without expression and without saying a word. —Bernhard has gained a lot of strength in the last few days; he has become almost as strong as he was before, and it seems he is physically completely healed. However, he has lost all his former urge to be active, he is distracted, and can sit all day long full of thoughts. The shyness is almost the same; only now and then a smile comes over his expressionless face, and he merely answers with a short yes or no to any question that is directed to him. I don't know what will become of him! Often I think when he sits there so quietly without taking part in what is going on that he is still very low; later when he speaks with me very reasonably and as usual, when I select this or that text that is appealing to him, then I think that everything will soon be fine again. Bruns shrugs his shoulders and is hoping for the best!

14 March

I've been waiting for a long time for a letter from you. In August we received your last letter. Now in the middle of March it has been six and one-half months. Heaven knows, if it does not get better soon, then it will make me nervous. And it is strange how every more cheerful turn of the mind is immediately depressed. For some time now I have written so many things in my thoughts and described to you the situations and the people of the settlement here, and it only required a few calm hours in order to find these thoughts again.

Today young Mrs. Huber was buried. It has been almost two weeks since she rushed into the arms of her husband already dying and completely enveloped in flames. She suffered tremendously. Her face, arms, and shoulders had been burned. Still affected by giving birth and by the death of her second son, she must have been overcome by dizziness, for she could give no other reason for the outbreak of the fire. Often I have admired her heavenly patience when she was suffering those severe pains. The wounds began to heal, she could see with both eyes, but the fever became stronger, the fire went inside, and she died last Monday. — How easily man's life is wiped out! She was not yet twenty years old. Not much of my work got done in those days.

I can see in my notes the name of Blumenthal; so for my and your diversion let me tell you a little bit more. Blumenthal and Pitterson were educated Swedes who spoke pretty good German (also English and French). The former was very musical. They established a store on the Osage above Vennewald's farm. They were well liked by the Germans and visited Hubers, us, and others at times. Pitterson traveled with his goods up the Osage for about a hundred miles, but his business went poorly. He had come back in the morning, and Blumenthal came to get medicine for him in the evening. He was monosyllabic and immediately left again. Bruns was not here. The next morning Mr. Shipley asked Bruns to come over because the store was closed. When they opened the door they found everything in good order; all the goods were there, only a few pieces of their clothing were missing, and their

29. The lost letter of 1836 arrived in February 1838.

canoe on the Osage was not there. Soon thereafter Mr. Menges read in the paper in St. Louis a report from St. Charles that a body had been found in the Missouri. The description fit Pitterson, but another body had been taken away by the Missouri. This event has occupied us very much.

But now something else! Now and then, when it occurs to us, we partake of the bag of nuts. They grow here in tremendous amounts. In an hour, in a space as big as our living room, I picked a whole big bag. Then one throws it on one's horse and trots casually home. While picking them I thought, if I could only bring them back to your study! The walnuts are not as good here—the shells are so tough and thick that it is not worth the trouble to crack them.

21 April

For two weeks now I have been in possession of a letter from you dated 6 November that was dispatched one month later. I was going to say that we had expected it earlier and then I found a little note to Bernhard: "Münster, September." It came from Niedieck's letter. So this is "the last letter" of which you wrote. Hmmm!!! Well, in compensation this one is also . . . — (three hours later) Curse the eternal distractions on Sunday, always visitors! Your letter is quite long and pleasant. But you have to write more frequently; seven months is really too long. Everything that you write is good and nice, but do say at random whatever occurs to you; the more joy, the more good spirits, the more your sister's eye will laugh, and the more happy we will be, all of us. Don't let the pen be drawn so rarely for us; how could you leave it unused many a day from six to eight in the evening! "I imagine your life is certainly idyllic." —Certainly, certainly, dear Heinrich, but let me sketch a little. Spring is as beautiful, I almost believe, as it is with you; I welcome it much more than I did last year; it is much prettier. Our farm is getting more friendly every day. From the bedroom where I am writing the yard forms the foreground, the red blossoms of the Judas tree and the white of dogwoods, the sprouting green between the rocks—then straight in front of me, approximately fifty paces gently down hill, is the little gate to the bottom field. Here is the garden where Mrs. Bruns has been busily occupied during the past two weeks and enjoys the sprouting peas, beans, and other plants by the hour. The garden forms the center of the field. To the right is a stretch of plowed field with oats, to the left there are some trees that have been killed, some bushes and low-lying land that I hope will be replaced by a few fields of corn this summer. Behind all this there is a stretch of forest that has not been cleared this year yet; thick green covers the ground as in the most beautiful meadow. If one directs the eye a little higher, then it meets a steep hill, a steep rock bank up the hill, and above it a wooded place that is embroidered with green. The Maries flows deep at the foot of the hill and forms the boundary to our field. However, I took the center first, and now I shall turn to the left. From the corner of the bottom field the property line runs upward for quite a distance; the area that had been fenced in has been divided into sections; the one at the slope is wooded and goes a good distance. It is used as a pasture for the working cattle and calves. The second space is also on the rise, the upland field that is planted with corn and potatoes. —On the right, the hill slopes downward, beginning gently and then, turning, the top gets very steep down to the bottom; the road winds down the hill to the bottom. A ditch runs into the creek, and on the other side of it is the bottom, which is flooded and is filled with sycamores, chestnuts, elm trees, etc.; there is not much underbrush there, but the trees are so wild, so slender. This part is the first to grow green. We also bleach our laundry there. (When looking at this, I like all of it very much, but I wonder whether you will also like it when you read about it? I do not know!) On the other side of the house, at a distance of approximately twenty paces, a steep precipice runs straight down. I sometimes think it would be nicer to have a cleared field down below and be able to see the fruit, but Bernhard says it would be nice to be able to look into the tops of the trees and to hear the cattle coming up from afar. To the right, away from the living room about twelve paces from the house, close to the steep slope, there are two log cabins, the smokehouse and the chicken house, and farther up there is a bigger one which is used as a stable for the horses. Farther on, the hill becomes broader so that one can no longer see its sloping. One can see the farm belonging to Gramatica in the distance on the upland field; it lies very close.

8 May

There I got another letter, as if it had come out of the clouds; it was completely unexpected, so that I feared some special occasion had forced you to write. Now this one should be dispatched immediately, even though I wanted to ask a lot of things; the continuation will begin right away. The bothersome fever may be a poor excuse for writing on this letter for two and one-half months, but it afflicted me again. But now I have determined that it will not come again all summer long. And, secondly, there were recently three families who stayed with us for several weeks, among them the parents of little Jan. Now they have been taken care of, except for the young couple who live with us in the small house. The woman helps us when necessary, and the man has cleared a few acres down in the bottom field so he can plant some corn; it was too late for him to begin for himself, and we are happy to have so much land cleared for the coming year.

Our church affairs, of which I have not yet written because I wanted to write so much about them, will be in order soon. Any day now we expect the superior of the Jesuit College, accompanied by Fr. Helias.[30] The latter, as the superior wrote to Bruns, will make his home here next to the church, and thus a school will also be started. Fr. Meinkmann, who had been employed as a pastor for the Westphalia Settlement earlier, has been dismissed by the entire community and lives with his favorite people, the Rhinelanders, on the other side of the Maries. I shall write more of this in the next letter. It must really be considered a great calamity that such a priest came over from Germany; I have never known one who acted and worked like Fr. Meinkmann.

And now something else concerning Bernhard! Recently he had the fever three times; it came very regularly, and then went by itself. Now he is quite well except for a few pecu-

30. Father Ferdinand Benedict Maria Ghislain Helias d'Huddeghem, was born at Ghent in Flanders on 3 August 1796. He entered the Society of Jesus in October 1817 and was ordained at Sitten, Switzerland, in 1824. He arrived in New York, accompanied by Father James Busschots, on 29 May 1833 after a forty-two-day voyage. Father Helias spent two years at the Jesuit Mission of White Marsh, Maryland, and in Pennsylvania before transferring to St. Louis, where he arrived on 22 August 1835. He taught French, German, canon law, and theology at St. Louis College, but in May 1838 his superior, Peter Verhaegen, sent him to central Missouri. Landing at Cote Sans Dessein on 11 May, he proceeded to the Westphalia Settlement, where he celebrated Mass on Sunday, 13 May. He was duly installed as pastor of the German congregation in the St. Joseph log church above the Maries River that Father Meinkmann had built the year before. In July he was joined by Father Busschots, who served as his assistant until 23 September 1839.

liarities that he had before. He is also much happier, and I hope that his recovery will proceed because then he will soon be able to take up the role of a capable farmer. He can no longer think of working in a tannery, and I also would not like to let him go so far, although Mr. Wenker is a magnificent man, so that Bernhard speaks of him and of the Mallinckrodts with the greatest sympathy. Bernhard really thinks he should own some property. Recently he wanted to go into the woods (a few miles from here near the Osage) and work there, and we talked him out of it with a great deal of effort. However, it was agreed that the land (eighty acres of government land, one hundred dollars) shall be entered in his name. If money could be deposited for Bernhard, the transfer of the same would be welcome. Bruns cannot raise it as easily during these bad times,[31] which are now very noticeable here in the country. Think this over with Uncle Caspar!—

Schwarzes have a little girl: Johanna Henriette Georgia. Now farewell, dear Heinrich, a thousand greetings to all. Write as diligently as your sister Jette wishes.

Bruns, Franz, Bernhard (all of whom want to improve), Hermann, Max, Mr. Niedieck send their regards.

We wish we could have Fritz Schwarze back again, but he probably will not return? Did the latter give you the rattle of a snake from us, seventeen rattles?

In a letter of 13 August 1838, Dr. Bruns wrote Caspar Geisberg that the crops in Westphalia were thriving. Franz was doing well as a farmer—"of all the Latin Farmers,[32] he is the most excellent." A farm had been purchased for Bernhard, who seemingly had recovered from the recurrent fevers without ill effects.

23 September 1838

On the 10th of this month we again received a letter from you, dear Heinrich. The beginning was enough for me, and I folded it quietly and laid it aside (since even without this, everything was swimming in front of my eyes and I had just forced myself to get out of the bed after attacks of fever). —Now after two weeks I can think about it a little more calmly. That my letter to Uncle Adolf has missed its purpose is indicated by "the two years of reproaches which were held back," and I see how little I may speak to his heart. It was an attempt on my part to establish a little more friendly, open relationship than we have had; I had thought that the distance between us would have made this a bit more possible. No, Heinrich, the few lines of your letter were sufficient to move me deeply, and I often thought of it but still would not like to say anything . . . .

6 November

What a long time has passed! First I shall try to get back to the text above. Every day now I expect a letter from our uncle; and therefore may you, before this letter arrives, become better acquainted with my thoughts concerning this matter, and in case the letter from the uncle turns out to be such that I would rather keep quiet forever, then you can tell him the

31. The depression that followed the Panic of 1837 affected Missouri less than many other states in the late 1830s, but its effects were obviously felt in Westphalia.

32. The term *Latin farmer* was used to describe scholarly German immigrants in Illinois and Missouri who because of their classical education and lack of practical experience seemed poorly suited for life on the frontier. Franz did not have the educational background of the "Latin farmers" in eastern Missouri.

parts in these lines that you find fitting for his ear, or, if you believe that it is better (for you), then be quiet and I shall in this case be able to accept it.

The fact that Thereschen stayed behind has always been on my mind from that time until this. I feel deeply hurt. The uncles seem to have taken our whole plan very lightly if they believed that we were trying to influence a child who was in the best hands (after the parents), even at that time, in favor of a land that only Bruns knew and to which my relationship with him rather than my own inclination drew me. We have children! The brothers are young men! Could we have offered the girl, even in the best case, a position equivalent to that in which she was living then? The uncles, of such thoughtful character, should at least not have believed us capable of the opposite! Since it was the aunt's idea, I always thought that I would be able to find in Uncle Adolf some compassion for sisterly love; and this I could not forget. I was struggling, I did not want to write, did not want to speak; it was in vain. If our uncle could be indifferent to me, I could have or I would have forgotten the obligations which I have not only on your account, but which I have for myself toward him and our aunt, and which it never occurred to me I would want to deny since, yes, then I would not have written, that's quite sure. Just because I respect him, treasure him very highly, and because I wanted to think of him in this life, in spite of the distance, in a friendly manner, and since his good will (without any ulterior motives) is not indifferent to me, therefore I wrote. Frankness, I thought, would not be misconstrued so easily. From youth on we were not accustomed to holding back whatever was close to us, and I did not think that we would want to appear differently now. Even Uncle does not like pretense; his just, straightforward mind is not compatible with that. Should he not have thought of this?

I am now twenty-five years of age, and I have been married for six years; has my behavior been so childish that I could not be permitted to speak of the deepest feelings of my heart? Was I expected to be quiet and thus, so to speak, deny them? Was I to be blamed for neglect of my brothers and sisters since the death of my parents? Certainly I am aware of many a weakness; however, my renewed efforts to work for their welfare continued. Who would be closer to me, who has a husband and children, than you all? I have had to deny myself so many things since my departure from Germany, and what would be left me if it weren't your love, your compassion? What am I to hope of my uncle and aunt? I know quite well that I have always been more attached to our uncles, that they were dearer to me than I was to them or could be to them. Uncle Adolf and our aunt have not always treated us very kindly since I have been a married woman; it hurt but I tried to make Bruns forget it, and when I thought of the deep love of Uncle for our father, then he was again high in my estimation. I have often kept quiet and have let things pass. —But there is a limit! I can still not forget Greven,[33] and I still find no wrong in having written about it to our uncle. I could not let it go, even out of consideration for you. His honest mind will not take it out on you, that I know. And then our uncle may forget the ingrates (as he thinks); I shall be quiet since I cannot better anything, and I shall pray for him. And Thereschen? No one can ever bar her from my heart even if she does not want to recognize me as her sister!

The remainder of the letter is missing.

33. In Greven Jette took leave from her brothers and sisters who remained in the care of relatives in Germany, Heinrich, Wilhelm, and Therese with their uncle and aunt, Adolf and Therese Geisberg, in Münster, and Johanna with the Hüffers in Stromberg.

21 October 1838

Dear Heinrich:

It is really a dumb thing to begin letters and leave them lying incomplete, and since my hindrances were somewhat embarrassing the Good Lord may assist me now in completing this sheet. However, the present time shall be discussed first and we in it! —Brother Bernhard has been down with a nervous fever for the past two weeks. It was probably not very serious, but it was still dangerous enough. Now Bruns thinks the biggest danger has passed, and today he was up and awake during the day and participated in our conversation. During the first eight days he was constantly hallucinating without having any bright moments; last week he often came to his senses again and inquired about many a thing, and now he still speaks quite a lot in his sleep; to be sure he now feels his weakness even more. But we can now expect with good reason some improvement daily, and thus we hope that this illness will soon be overcome, by the grace of God.

Mrs. Bruns believes she has the right as a patient to speak of herself now. The fever has been quite at home with us this summer; six times it reappeared. The last time was the worst. Perhaps my sensitivity contributed to that because of the constant illnesses I have had and the work that was left undone; now my strength does not want to come right back; the last few days I went to bed occasionally. My feet do not want to carry me up the hill again after I have gone down into the garden, and I cannot eat some things and have little appetite; and then the mind is so active and thinks about this and that which cannot be accomplished in time. Nothing but annoyance! However, this will surely improve; at least we will hope that it will. Bruns is chipper and was so during the entire summer. The long-lasting heat and drought are blamed for the frequent appearance of cold fever. But most of this is past now. For quite some time Bruns had to make so much medicine and had to visit so many sick people that he did not have enough time to visit the patients who lived farther away. If he was not at home then Mrs. Bruns always had to have some "fever medicine" ready and could advise the Americans on the time they were to take the medicine, the avoidance of sour milk, melons, etc., in a most learned manner. Bruns has to go to Jefferson now and then, and now an Irishman from there has been staying at the Hubers' for a few weeks and lets himself be treated by Bruns. Well, enough of bragging. If it is bragging.

Brother Franz was and is happy. This afternoon he rode to muster as a cavalryman; to be sure the way to the county seat[34] is a little far, twenty-five miles, and if all who have to serve appear, most will have to bivouac outside. Many Germans stayed at home before because it had not been taken seriously. This time, however, it is said that everybody who stays away is assessed a little monetary fine of one dollar. The militia is supposed to be reorganized in the entire state. H. Niedieck is even a sergeant with the infantry; I hope that this post will earn him something and will occupy his time, because that would be good. He has not been working at all again recently, and Bruns, who right from the very beginning of Niedieck's cobbler work was shaking his head, sees that his opinion is justified; Niedieck has brought it so far that he can even make himself a pair of shoes, if need be, and can repair them in order to be able to run around in them. Whiskey is again his master, frivolity has the upper hand, and Bruns, who has had nothing but trouble from the beginning of Niedieck's stay here and

34. Mount Sterling, at that time the seat of Gasconade County, is located on the eastern bank of the Gasconade River approximately twenty-eight miles from Westphalia.

has had annoyances and frustrations with him, sees that everything is in vain; he is of no account. Since this summer he has again been here in our house and is of little joy to us. He is always proper, especially when he has had too much to drink, and then he is gone for days. The worst is that he drinks secretly and has hidden bottles everywhere. Bruns, who canceled credit for him with several people, often did not know where he got the money for drink (that he has done so he had to learn from other people), and now we learn that he borrows from one, has taken goods from another and sells them again—all dumb pranks, what a terrible frivolity! I had already told Bruns that N. should really try to get on somewhere else in order to stop the expense, and suddenly here he appears and tells Bruns that he wants to go back to Germany! What a cowardly thing! To come back as such a miserable human being! Now he has been offering several people the money that was promised to him in writing at the time of his departure from Germany (also to Bruns). Nobody wants to buy this certificate. And now he is attempting to borrow money for the trip. He will probably not get it, and Bruns will not post bond for him. In the end if he does not succeed he will have to wait for an answer from home, and he can therefore spend the winter doing nothing again. You know yourself that these lines are not for everybody, dear Heinrich, but I did not want to pass up this particular subject deliberately, because many a thing is distorted when looking at it from a distance, and it is necessary that our uncles and you understand Bruns's way of operating and know his efforts, for it is possible that at some later time people will discuss with you the unhappy young man, and he himself may well appear later. I wish it would go better with him! It often makes me very sad.

Hermann is growing up, and he has a mighty interest in everything that grows in the fields and in the garden, and he already speaks somewhat more reasonably, but he is still fussing too much with the little one and lets himself be manipulated by Zellerhoff and Johann. Max is quite well and now has red cheeks; he speaks and chatters away and is quite a little madcap, so he is quite different from Hermann, and occasionally it earns him Father's severity. Then again he is so kind and shares everything that he has. His face, as I look at it, has a high forehead, long black eyelashes, the eyes of his mother, a little gray; when I have him in my arms and look into the mirror, it is clear that he has a crooked nose, almost like that of brother Bernhard, and a very strong little lower lip; in short, he has far more of a Geisberg face; however, the older Hermann gets, the more he resembles Bruns. These things often amuse me. Little Max is still sleeping in Mother's arms; the trough in which we persuaded him to sleep this summer he no longer likes, and although the boy will soon be two years old, Mother insists seriously on having a cradle for him!

Brother-in-law David is still with us and will spend at least the winter with us since he has for the time being no wife and will not get one either. His field bears him corn and potatoes, and thus he sits down at noon quite comfortably and fries some potatoes and eats the meat and bread he has brought along and returns home in the evening. The wages for a hired hand amounted to one hundred twenty dollars this year; and since others realize as well as we do that this was much too high a price compared to the small yield from a farm here, we might have had to let our Johann go. Now, however, we have found a way out; Johann is still clearing approximately four to five acres. He tills his land and does everything as before and will receive half the corn, a cow, and a sow. The animals will be given to him in the spring, and then they can stay here until he moves over to his farm next fall.

Our Jenne (the old one, as Hermann says when he is set on to her by Johann) not only remains incorrigible, but has even gotten much worse recently. Whether she perhaps has more than a just claim here in America or whether her hopes of marriage have contributed in recent times, at any rate she can scarcely spend one minute without violent attacks against the children, against the dogs, against the cows, the cats, the chickens, or inanimate objects. Mrs. Bruns has long gotten used to this and has learned to overlook things in order to keep her maid in good humor, and now she has had to have the bitter experience that even in sickness she has not the right to order this or that according to her needs, for in her crudeness Jenne dared to give me some coarse and improper answers. But my sensitivity made me silent, and my head had to suffer again, and the fever did not improve with this. Now we employ as much consideration as possible in order to get through the winter at least, and then toward Easter she can marry if she can, or she can do whatever else she wants to do. In order for us to recover our great expenses, she has legally promised to leave her Drükchen for several years in our service. She is a neglectful, stupid child, promising little. I knew already in Oelde that I would have nothing good with Jenne, and I wondered whether I was right in wanting to break the promise I had given her. I don't like to think about the things that happened between Oelde and Bremen and so on until here and then for two years afterward. Earlier I was able to have such good relationships with my girls and lived in such harmony with them, and both of them, Threse and Libeth, would have gone with us. The plan to take only Jenne along as an older faithful person who did not want to marry became a hard choice. However, this will soon be over and then it will hurt less!

Now that all persons of our household have been introduced to you, we will have to count our animals. You know that this includes Franz's. First, let's look at Bruns's riding horse. It is a beautiful gold-brown "bay" mare, too lively for Mrs. Bruns. Once it danced in full trot with me over branches, down the slope, and down into the bushes. Since that time I ride it only when Bruns is along. Now come two geldings, the old one, lazy and hard-trotting Toby (unfortunately this is my riding horse), and then a young well-built sorrel by the name of Mat; the latter has not yet been completely broken and is very careless. As to the cattle, we have a few very heavy dark brown work oxen, which have white spots, then we have four milk cows, which were bought one after the other; from them we have two heifers, which started giving milk in the spring, and then there are four heifers, white ones, which are one-and-a-half years old, which will probably all have calves next summer. This year brought us four male calves (two suffered accidents), which run around happily now and are getting fat in the pasture. We have had a great deal of bad luck with hogs, probably because we had no corn earlier with which to keep the young pigs when the weather became unfavorable and partly because during this hard winter we had no warm shelter for them. Thus sixteen little pigs froze to death last winter before our eyes in the nest we had prepared for them in the bushes. At present we have nine older sows and seven two-year-old hogs, which are quite fat and ready for butchering and which weigh an average of at least two hundred pounds. They have not been fed at all. The white oaks have much fruit, and the hogs begin feeding in the woods and continue through the winter, since the black oaks also have many fruits, which fall and are even better after some frost. From last summer only two young sows are left; the drought and the lack of feed caused all the little pigs to die. From last winter sixteen remain, however. Now they are wild and we don't even see them, but they are healthy. Among them are six young sows; the others, if they live, will be butchered next year. The older ones again brought us little ones at a very favorable time, and all the little pigs survived. Twenty-five were brought by the old ones to the house, and all in all there are about sixty to seventy now from the eleven sows. We bought four as a start; two of those died.

And now we come to the geese. But there is nothing to be talked about since we got only one goose in two years. Last spring we had nineteen little ones, but we let them roam freely and thus they fed in the woods and the little ones ate some poisonous weeds and all except one died. And in addition a fox got one old one last year since they always remain in the woods at night. The geese will have to be locked up until they have pretty much grown up. The chickens, the young ones and the old ones, are around a hundred in number. Three cats run in and out of our little house. Bull, an old, lazy dog, B . . ., a young, promising one, and Polly, a little one that can scarcely crawl over the threshold and will probably not grow very much. And then I must not forget our deer. To be sure, we own a young stag that is now a half-year old. For a long time he drank only milk and was quite impetuous when drinking, and now that he is finding the vegetables and the corn very tasty he also drinks water from the branch. He is getting fat, and since next year I will have to take care of the vegetables alone and in addition I would fear that he might be taken for a wild stag, he will soon furnish a beautiful roast. It also annoyed me that he always ate the sandwich for Max. He is already jumping over all the fences.

Bruns will go to Lisletown tomorrow, and therefore I want to conclude this letter and dispatch it; I hope that my rambling will not bore you since I have not written for a long time. I shall write the next two sheets right away since I am in a good mood to write now, and I shall write you everything that I have omitted here. Perhaps both letters will arrive simultaneously and you will be sick and tired of my scribbling for some time. Therefore until then.

Best regards from all of us to the uncles, the aunts, and to all others from your loving sister, Jette.

On 3 March 1839 Bernhard wrote to his Uncle Caspar describing the troubling symptoms of the illness that had brought him to the point of suicide: "I got something which keeps a person in eternal stress, and a man is lucky if he gets out of bed with a healthy mind. He believes he hears a hundred voices which he knows in the wind, in the rustling of the water, which are designed to tease him eternally." Bernhard had come to believe that Jette and Bruns were responsible for the voices, but Father Helias had told him it was the work of the devil.

On 8 April, Franz Geisberg wrote to Heinrich, confessing that he is more used to the plow than the pen, but is happy and healthy in America. "This area has improved considerably. Church and school are now active and there are already seven craftsmen who are living on the church land . . . a carpenter, a shoemaker, a butcher, etc."[35]

35. St. Joseph Church was built on forty acres sold by Franz Geisberg for a token five dollars. Ownership was assumed on 25 June 1838 by the three Jesuit priests, P. J. Verhaegen, Theodore De Theux, and J. B. Smedts, and shortly thereafter by Father Helias. With his superior's approval, Helias, after reserving fourteen acres for himself as a means of support, divided the remaining twenty-six acres into lots, which were sold to artisans and laborers in the German settlement. Thus the town of Westphalia was founded. The first log church, with church and presbytery under one roof, was blessed by Bishop Rosati on his first visit to the Westphalia Settlement on 14 October 1838.

Westphalia
25 April 1839

Dear Heinrich:

On Saturday a letter from you arrived dated Berlin, 12 January. I wanted to write to you earlier, then I changed my mind. I am in receipt of the last letter of 28 July; the note about Bernhard perplexed me: the donkeys? the cattle? (Apparently the geese had been forgotten.) I was not so sensitive about this, and everything was all right with a little white lie (but circumstances prevented me from writing), and I chatted on as usual with just what occurred to me. And then Franz hit upon the unfortunate thought of telling you of our animals. In the letter we have just received our dear brother remarks graciously that exact (even though petty) descriptions can be interesting! This is what I understand at least.

For seven weeks now a Johanna has been resting in my arms, and since that time I have not thought of anything else but to report to you her entrance into this world myself. I have to admit that I am indeed happy to have a little girl now. She is her father's daughter, has little blond hair and seems to resemble Hermann. She is a good child who cries only when she has needs and then really lets us have it. Mother and child were sick for a few weeks, but now everything is better and she is gaining, but she has kept a very pale coloring. —Your notes concerning Bonn reminded Bruns quite vividly of the years of his youth; he told us many things, and he agrees with your opinion that in Berlin real student life is a thing of the past. I am very happy when I hear that my brother is not a wet blanket and tries everything.

Our Johanna occupies me a lot, and for quite some time, since I read your last letter, I have had such a longing to have her with me here that I am often very sad. It is not that I am taking the few remarks in your letter too seriously; however, I can see her situation now with a much clearer view than even you are able to do!! My stay for a year in the same house (under better circumstances, and as a fiancee and the daughter of the brother-in-law who was still living) helps me understand that the young, lively child as I knew her is disgruntled, and in the end, hoping for a good example, she becomes morose and has wishes she cannot hope to see satisfied. Except there might be some people who have just claims to her and would assert themselves! If she were here, I know for sure she would feel freer and happier in our house. Bruns with his enthusiasm says, "She has to come," and the brothers say, "It will be good, let her come." I don't quite know. For I as a careful housewife have to look further, and even if it is possible that Johanna would have a chance to return to Europe, it nevertheless cannot be assumed that she will take that chance. —My position is probably somewhat different from that of a simple farmer's wife. My heart, to be sure, tells me I would be as equally satisfied, but who knows whether I might not be even more satisfied! But Johanna? Will she adjust to circumstances here at the side of a dear husband, as I have the good fortune to have? And then my heart tells me yes again and my wishes confirm it a thousand times. So as not to deceive myself, I have resolved to accept the invitation of the Mallinckrodts, who have many educated German neighbors, in order to become acquainted with their wives and their views. If this visit should turn out as desired, then I would continue to think about it, but then something rests heavily upon my soul. How should Johanna travel here? For quite some time the bold plan of a certain person has remained unmentioned, but some allusions have not been forgotten, and I cannot say anything reasonable even though I am disappointed if our uncle, who has taken care of all needs of the student, remains silent and if the nephew is too modest to want to ask for it. The parental share of the inheritance can be more than necessary for the young assistant, and the little brothers and sisters will find a support in him.

But what are you going to do with Wilhelm? "I do not know" will probably be said by anybody who has a voice for him. Will you make him a packing master, a salesman, at the very best a bookkeeper, who at any rate when he is old will be dependent on the whims of the boss and will play a very devoted role in his kind simplicity? This can make me mad! Wilhelm has to come to us! He can have an education for life, and he can have his farm more easily over here. Even if he would not bring a single dollar with him he can manage, and he will be able to earn more than his needs will be. And it is high time that he come here, highest time, before he is spoiled by the stuffy European air, as Uncle C. says, and becomes incapable of a free active life in this beautiful world. In the case of Wilhelm I advise without hesitation, and urgently stress, that he should come. With God's help we shall do our part, and in the future he will not lack a carefree existence here. What if Wilhelm alone could be Johanna's travel companion? No, no, he is too young, too inexperienced, and Johanna must not travel without a reasonable, reliable person who is an expert in the language here to offer a helping hand. But this can best be done by a brother, and in addition, if she does not share a cabin on the ship with a respectable female, then she can share a cabin with her brother. (Two single beds, or however the case may be.) The reputation of a girl is never smudged more easily than aboard a seagoing ship where boredom and disgust invent many a fairy tale, which unfortunately is often spread and has damaging consequences.

Last year a young girl of sixteen, more to be called a child, came across the ocean with her brother-in-law; she slept in the same bunk with another woman. A young prankster traveling with them later told many an evil thing and many unthinkable things about the young girl. Friends of the family, however, then found out that the maligning stories were invented by *one* originator, and other travelers did not know anything bad. Some casual remarks of the brother-in-law regarding the person concerned and her own timid confession revealed that the young man himself had courted her and that his efforts had been unsuccessful. This had driven him to revenge. Later in Jefferson he had been drinking, had gambled, and finally had run off. The young girl, not knowing of anything, is growing beautifully and becoming very pretty. Several took the opportunity on this occasion to proclaim her innocence. But the great mass of people may perhaps condemn her as guilty in spite of everything; I only hope that her future will not be damaged by this! —Well, here I am speaking so much of the sea voyage, of the dangers, etc., etc., and I don't even know what Johanna herself is thinking of this trip to America. She indicated only very gently her dissatisfaction and did not tell me anything, does not wish anything, and does not even ask for a letter from me, and only reminds the brothers to write and promises that she will write very diligently herself. But the simple seriousness with which she concludes, her remembrance of my stay there, the joy she would have if she could see us and the children again! Enough or I shall become embittered! Yes, she will have to come unless she herself wants to hold back, unless perhaps a rising affection decides her destiny. But I hope that this will not be the case. It would sadden me very much. But I am living so far away and I hear and see nothing. A vivid imagination has to picture everything and has to embroider everything, and thus it happens that I mention the above case. I have written to Johanna, and at the end I merely casually inquired whether the book by Hesse might not have caused her to waver in her earlier intentions. (I'll come back to the book in a minute.) Answer very soon, dear, dear Heinrich, how things are and what I may hope. You know that uncertainty is a gnawing worm, and I say once more that I am longing for Johanna more than is good for me.

And now it occurs to me what C. Mallinckrodt said recently when he visited us. He had heard from the Misses Schimmel in Dortmund (who are continuing his mother-in-law's institute) that the latter is said to have heard in Münster that I was very dissatisfied in America and wished to be back and I don't know what else. The Schimmels formerly lived at the *Domhof* under one roof with the Geisbergs. I wonder if this rumor has come from there? And therefore am I not entitled, especially with reference to Johanna's coming over, to an explanation of the rumors pertaining to me? To be sure I cannot be completely acquitted; I remained silent, and I remember quite well that when bidding farewell to my dear girl friends I replied I would not write if I were dissatisfied. But I've also been a little bit negligent at times; and Marie did not answer my first letter at all, otherwise she would know better by now. This explanation is not to be construed as lacking substance, for in addition, with my weak pen I want to illuminate a few dark sides of Hesse's book. I have to tell you that I cannot take this book into my hand without annoyance, and what strikes me as strange, I even take sides and attack the poor man very severely. Mr. Hesse is really absolutely too unjust concerning this area and this settlement; to be sure, the book may contain many a true thing, but he can distort terribly. Even in his time it had not been like that for a long time, and how much less does his description correspond to the present condition of the area! Many Germans have arrived since Mr. Hesse departed, and they purchased their farms as close to each other as possible. The older settlers improved and enlarged their fields and houses, their cattle increased, and many have sold some of them. The good harvest of the last year, to be sure, caused a lower price for corn because there was no lack of it, but potatoes were a half-dollar per bushel, and pork and other things could be sold very well by those who had them. Tobacco has suddenly risen from four cents per pound to twelve-and-a-half cents, and many Americans begin to raise it because Missouri tobacco has now achieved a reputation that will not cause it to lose its value. —The church land has been occupied on both sides with several houses. The school abuts the church and at times is too small. The Bruns couple sent their firstborn there today on the 8th of June. Oh how old I am getting! In the near future I shall tell you more of the advantages of our town and of the area, which is so well located, where perhaps in the near future Mr. B. Bruns will reside as postmaster of the Potosi route.

Do write to me very, very soon and think about everything carefully, so that we can if possible do what lies so close to our hearts.[36] May it be for the best, by the grace of God!

As always, your sister, Jette

P.S. Do you realize that I take it very much amiss when you do not inform me about things that concern the brothers and sisters? I also must remind you to write the things that are suitable from this letter to Uncle Caspar.

36. In response to Jette's suggestions, Heinrich replied that Johanna as a seventeen-year-old minor would not get the probate court's permission to travel, and besides, there was talk of an impending engagement. Wilhelm, then fifteen years old, was still attending a trade school and his uncle Caspar was trying to get him a position with Gerbaulet in Münster. No member of Jette's immediate family ever visited her in America.

This letter was started in April, and it has already become June. Little Johanna is still very pale but otherwise rather lively. Max is growing every day, a Steffen Glemkiel[37] like his uncle.

On 4 May 1839 Bernhard Geisberg wrote a long letter to Heinrich describing his "little house" and his farm animals and extolling the life of an American farmer. On 5, 6, and 9 June 1839 the Geisberg brothers, Dr. Bruns, and Jette wrote to Caspar Geisberg about their problems with their cousin Heinrich Niedieck, who wanted to withdraw from the business in which he was involved with Dr. Bruns. The brothers offer their farms as collateral if Caspar will pay off the obligations to the Niediecks in Münster; Dr. Bruns assures Caspar that the breakup of the partnership was not his fault (which had apparently been implied) and thanks him for assuming the one thousand dollar mortgage, and Jette expresses her gratitude for her uncle's help. Although the brothers and Dr. Bruns speak glowingly of the increasing value of their farms and the potential of the region, Jette writes of her loneliness and isolation from women of similar background. The following letter to Heinrich was sent as an enclosure with the letters to Caspar Geisberg.

5 June 1839

Dear Heinrich:

I cannot and I do not like to add anything to the enclosed letter, and besides I wish I had more skill to say more in fewer words.

Bernhard is now completely well again and begins to work a little. For the entire summer he was very well, but in a strange fashion. He was terribly lazy and then had very strange views and discussions. Bruns occasionally got to quarreling with him, and Franz did so even more frequently. I wished for the patience of an angel; it would have often been better. And then the nervous fever set in again. It seems to affect him; at least I hope to God that he will not have to live his life as a completely unreasonable person. He likes to speak of his farming. Earlier I could only think with fright of his plan, but now I am gradually getting accustomed to it, and it looks somewhat different. When his strength has returned he will probably go and board with Vennewald, who does not live very far from here.

Franz recently had to go to Mount Sterling to participate in military affairs. It was said that all the Volunteers, to whom he belongs, would have to leave suddenly to wage war on the Mormons, a religious sect. (They live on the border of the state in several counties and had some quarrel with the other Americans; some physical fights developed, and expulsions, etc. Neither party is without guilt, and the Mormons are certainly at a disadvantage.) Volunteers from the entire state marched there, and many Americans had some fun; however, the Germans did not exclude themselves; it is said the Mormons were taken prisoner and approximately sixty were killed in a battle, and now they are to be banned. However, one still does not know anything for sure.[38]

---

37. Steffen Glemkiel is a legendary folk character of gigantic size.

38. For an account of this conflict, see Stephen C. LeSueur, *The 1838 Mormon War in Missouri* (Columbia: University of Missouri Press, 1987). Jette's account here is reasonably accurate, although the rumor she reports of sixty Mormons being killed is exaggerated—twenty Mormons and one Missourian died in military engagements during the affair, and one Mormon was beaten to death by Missourians. Her relatively sympathetic attitude toward the Mormons was shared by many in eastern Missouri, but anti-Mormon sentiment was strong in the western counties. The conflict ended with the Mormons surrendering and being expelled from the state by Gov. Lilburn W. Boggs.

H. Niedieck has been here again for the past week. Four weeks ago he complained that Bruns had blocked his credit with people so that since he did not have any money himself the tavern as well as the store were closed to him. Bruns, who only needed to have an opportunity, erupted and read him the riot act so that, as I had to admit later, it is incomprehensible that Niedieck, with his arrogance, could remain calm. He did not say a word to this; when both of them came into the house, he ran out, came back again, ran out, seemed upset, and finally sat down quietly to breakfast with an excellent appetite. In my opinion this is again a sign of his incorrigibility! What equanimity! Bruns had given him notice to end his stay here, and thus finally two weeks ago he departed for St. Louis after he had Huber fill three bottles for him. He may have been away for two weeks when he wrote back to us from Union that he had spent one night on his trip in the forest and was half frozen, etc., and Bruns should please send him some money so that he could come back. A second letter followed a few days later; in the meantime Bruns had fulfilled his wish, and indeed he came back. All plans, all resolutions to help himself were gone! Now he anticipated Bruns's questions and offered to work on our farm. Where else should we send him at the moment! Now I have to practice patience again. The most annoying thing for me is that he took almost all the clothing he owned along and did not bring anything back. And now I have to worry about that again. Well, enough, I hope Bruns will find a better shelter for him; I wish the winter would be over for him! —Please keep this confidential.

Dear Heinrich, you must certainly draw the conclusion from these two sheets that frequently a sad mood overwhelms me; to be sure I cannot forget unpleasant things as easily as I would like. And then there is many a thing that cannot be trusted to paper. My health has not been completely recovered; even last week I had a fever, a catarrh, etc. If not earlier, then I expect everything by spring, and Bruns is consoling me and putting me off. I have a little Johanna; I hope for new strength; and instead of the old Jenne, a young, more kindly one; and what else? Why should I not imagine the very best?

A postscript: 8 June

We have received your last letter, dear Heinrich, of 11 February, from Berlin. I really felt sorry for you in your imprisonment. It's good that it passed a long time ago. —From my long letter you can see sufficiently well how we are getting along. Instead of the old Jenne there is now a younger, kinder person whom we call Trute, only Max says Tute. Jenne has gone to a Rhinelander about three miles from here where she works, and she also has a love affair. There is no one who can be more foolish than she!

Now Heaven sends us more and more rain; presently the bottom land, which has been flooded, is one big lake. The water flows through the meadows, the split rails are lifted up and float away, the water is still rising—another three or four feet and the entire bottom will be under water, and then everything will be gone and all the toil and work of last spring will have been in vain. As God wishes! —But it would be too hard on us and on most of the settlers on the Maries.

The 10th. It went well after all. The water is gone. We do have to go and get some of the split rails back, and then everything will be in its old condition. The pasture will have a strong fence. —

Bruns is urging, and I have to come to a close. So long, and write soon to your sincerely loving sister, Jette.

August 1839

Dear Heinrich:

Now it is the middle of August, and still I have only your letter of 16 March as the last to arrive here. I am patient enough, but my mood is getting a little strange, and many a day passes without joy when my little ones chase away equanimity.

Brother Heinrich studies, dreams, etc., etc., but the leisure hours for us are very rare! So, from the very beginning I shall write my complaints, and then to something else. H. Niedieck causes us a great deal of concern and unrest as never before. About twelve days ago Bruns and Mr. Meyer prevailed upon him to leave the business. Obligingly he wrote and agreed that it would be better this way. His drinking took preference over everything else. Last Sunday, suddenly Bruns and the pastor were called for again. Niedieck was dangerously ill, the consequence of drinking; morbid convulsions, apoplexy; to be sure a mild case had affected his arm. Bruns got him back in shape, and he was brought here, but he is drinking again and carries out stupid pranks. Bruns took him for further recuperation to a farmer, but he left the house on the second day, rushed to a tavern, and spent all the little pocket money that Bruns had felt necessary for him, drinking. I have to admit that this bothers me. How will it end? With his return to Germany, if God's patience spares his life. I hope it will come to this soon! Bruns has done everything for him that he could. The establishment of the store here in the house was the last and most decisive. Now he has ingratitude, slander, etc. Only when Niedieck believed himself close to death did he act fairly toward Bruns. In the presence of Linnemann, where he was cared for, he made all kinds of confessions without reservation!!! I don't want to write any more of this, but my head is so full that I'm not capable of writing a decent letter to Aunt Boner. For quite some time I have started to write but I cannot finish.

The construction of the storeroom has taken much time. There is no end to the hammering and banging around in the house, the kitchen next, and perhaps the living room, and that will be all. So next year we'll continue! How sick I am of all this! Every day I think how I would have been satisfied to live with my husband and the children and Franz in a little log cabin and be able to do everything myself. I would like to move again, far out into the world!

While reading this you will make a very serious face, brother Heinrich. Well, now I shall see whether I can write a little better. Generalities sound good. Westphalia is coming up in the world, it is a town. Now all who live here seem to get ahead; and there are a carpenter, a cabinetmaker, a blacksmith, a gunsmith, a butcher, a shoemaker, and next week there will be a tailor. Two more houses are being built. And then a family from Hesse, old Menke, Otto, Eck.

It may appear somewhat unseemly if I let the gentlemen priests with their church and school come last. Presently we still hope to get a college here. Gramatica is collecting signatures. A few weeks ago the superior (Verhaegen)[39] was here and stayed with us. Mrs.

39. Peter J. Verhaegen, S.J., like Father Helias, was a native of Belgium. He had come to St. Louis in May 1823 as a novice and was ordained by Bishop Rosati in 1826. Verhaegen became president of St. Louis College in 1832 and obtained a university charter from Gov. Daniel Dunklin on 28 December 1832. In March 1836 he became superior of the Missouri Mission and head of the board of trustees of Saint Louis University.

Bruns did her very best. I shall try to present to you the Right Reverend gentleman. His figure: middle-sized, rather stout, but agile at the same time, his complexion red, brown plain hair, lively blue eyes, a full voice, sometimes somewhat shrill. His character, as I know him, quick, at times too rash, mocking, spouting severe principles, and then, when he wants to be, tolerant and friendly, above all eloquent, with a great dexterity in his speech; he knows how to make himself pleasing to everybody and to put himself into everybody's situation, indeed a fine man of the world! If one would see him without knowing him, see how he attracts everybody in the community with his lively, merry, always kidding and arguing manner, one would think him to be God knows who. And yet one never feels that he lacks for a moment anything that is fitting a Catholic priest. In normal life he has very little dignity. He chats around, he expresses his wonderment at Fr. Bischots's healthy appearance,[40] he corrects Fr. Helias's bad pronunciation, he takes care of the sick, he cooks with the house-wife, he works in the field with the farmer, but the proper moderation is never exceeded, there is never a glass of wine too many drunk, never anything too delicate eaten, and never an argument that is too lively. (Perhaps his joking around with his colleagues could be a little less.) If one now looks at him as an orator, I would maintain I have never heard a better one, and yet I do not understand more than half of what he says because he speaks only English. Kellermann did not have half the skill in language, in position, in gestures. Too bad that the voice of the superior is somewhat harsh. The only thing that occasionally attracts attention is his attitude, which is too serious, the delivery fitting the occasion.

In a short time it will be decided whether the Potosi road will come here; it would do a great deal for the progress of the town. So often in my thoughts I work out scenes from the settlement. So many interesting things happen here, and some people are quite amusing. But my pen lacks the power and the confidence to deliver anything tolerable. Perhaps I shall try it after all.

13 October

In vain I have been waiting week after week for news from you. The letter to Aunt Boner has been lying here for a long time, but I had a feeling that I could not let it go on its way, as if I would have to add something to it. Often the suspicion overcomes me, bad suspicion, that something bad has happened to you or to your letters. —Stupid stuff! Well, soon we shall see. But it's incredible that Johanna does not write at all! I really don't know what you are thinking! It is getting worse and worse from year to year, and in the end a single letter will come once a year, and the letters will then no longer bear the fresh, plucky style, the sym-pathetic style that is so characteristic of youth, but will gradually change into the serious, calculating tone of a philistine. Yet what am I saying; may it never come to this with you, and may the same not be the case with us.

You will easily believe that in spite of many things that are not very pleasant we can still be quite happy. When Father Bruns tells a joke, the housewife laughs with the others, and then the boys and the girl laugh. My Johanna is really a darling child, always friendly, and now she is getting so lively—she scratches and squeaks and plays with her brothers. She still does not have teeth. But her mother will soon be toothless. At the present time she has a swollen cheek again after the disturber of the peace was yanked out. —Now I shall close.

40. Father James Busschots, S.J. (see note 30 above).

Perhaps I shall begin a new method to extort an answer from you, and I will write every four weeks.

Farewell! Write soon where you are, what you are doing, what you will do, and do not forget that your sister in America is thinking of her brothers and sisters every day in painful uncertainty. Many greetings from Bruns and the brothers and your loving sister Jette.

In late 1839 Jette received a letter from her cousin Marie with news of friends and family members in Münster. Marie writes that it is sometimes reported that Jette and her family will soon return to Germany.

Sunday, 17 January 1840

Dear Heinrich:

Yesterday letters arrived from F. Niedieck that had crossed the ocean in twenty days. Quickly, very quickly, good fortune can bring news, but it does not smile on me. There was a note in the margin of Niedieck's letter saying that sister Johanna was in Münster. "Yesterday I found her and her brother Heinrich in a gay circle, a few days earlier at the Cecilia Ball." This sounded very nice. So you are well, you love gay company; that is nice, I do not begrudge it to you, and yet I feel a pang in my heart. You cannot set aside a little time from your leisure at very definite times twice a year to send a letter to us, to me. Have you lost all sympathy for me? Why were you able to write before such loving, open, friendly letters?

Certainly it is extremely irritating to me that you do not let us hear from you; not a thing since the third of June. You do know how much warm affection I have for you. Should the bond of sisterly love be dissolved because the ocean separates us? Or is it perhaps that a letter was lost? But the letters from Niedieck and Uncle Caspar arrived regularly. You have so much to tell us: your leave from Berlin, your trip via Dresden to Münster, and the change that you saw there because of Uncle Adolf's death, concerning which I would have liked so much to hear something more. Did he also speak of us during his illness, was he annoyed or indifferent? The first news of his passing touched me very much. Now, however, I am calm again because I do not feel any guilt toward him, and if he should have misjudged me then, now he will think well of me again. To be sure how I would have loved to have seen a few lines from him. Write me a lot about him from the time of his illness and more. What will happen to our uncles when the house is sold? It's a shame about the beautiful garden. Thereschen and Wilhelm, where will they stay? How are they? Uncle Caspar thought that Thereschen should go to the country because she is so frail.

I still do not know anything definite about Johanna. Uncle Caspar writes of permanent fetters; Marie thought that they were talking of an engagement. Now I would be very much inclined to interfere and make myself important. I have already written to Uncle Caspar, as he has probably told you. I have told him of what I could properly remind him, and perhaps also more. But how could I do it differently, to whom should I turn? Brother Heinrich does not consider it worth the trouble to answer me. I doubt that you will take up my cause in this. I am interested in having Johanna here, but you are probably not. She has written to me and to Bernhard that she would not desire anything more than to be with us, she would consider this her greatest happiness, etc., etc. —Six weeks later she is supposed to have found an entirely different bliss, and at this time Uncle Caspar knows it already! Incredible! Outrageous! Heinrich, you must write me, you must not delay any more. To be sure my hope is almost gone, but do let me know for sure. Johanna must write to me herself. I am thinking of this day and night.

We are now in the process of building a mill and have many workmen here every day. But I am sick of all this unrest, and I've told Franz that he should take a wife so that I could be relieved. The mill business concerns him and Bernhard too. But he is much too dry and stiff and doesn't want to hear of this. If I want to turn to Bernhard, he would more likely follow suggestions. I am so happy that Bernhard is now with Robinson. This place seems just the right one for him. He wants to stay there all summer if the Good Lord keeps him healthy. Zumnorde is nearby, staying with a Loughlin in order to work and to learn English. Zumnorde has purchased land on the Little Maries, approximately four miles from here. He still likes the life of a farmer quite well.

3 February

Finally your and Johanna's letter arrived, dated November 27th, '39. I am almost glad that an earlier one got lost, but no, I still expect it. Well, so it isn't quite as bad as I thought. The letter which just arrived, however, is tremendously diffused, so I have trouble in understanding its meaning. As to Johanna, I am happy that her confidence is still given me, but at the same time I am vexed that I have spoken of this matter to Uncle Caspar, insofar as it has annoyed him. Should he tell you about this, then tell him that I am sorry and I ask his forgiveness. I was deeply hurt, and since Johanna herself wrote, even more so. Why should I hide it from you? Now, however, I am again devoted to my duties. How little I was prepared to suffer with patience the consequence of our estrangement, which happened so late. I shall never, never again see her! —The Good Lord has given me a good, a very good husband. That I realize more and more. I also have to agree again and again that it was to my credit that I yielded to his wish to move here. Our marriage is blessed, and I have to find my peace in the domestic circle. But two of my brothers followed us. They both are to replace the ones who were left behind, to be everything to me! I wish they were not here! But the Lord has done well with everything!

Our situation here is pretty good. As you know, we have made a tremendous mistake by building. To be sure, the medical practice and our farm will gradually remedy the situation again. Bruns and Niedieck wrote of speculations, etc. Our brother is trying to help H. Niedieck again, but this would not work without Bruns. So money arrived, carrying high interest; the money has to earn something, and so a few pieces of property were bought. H. Niedieck did not want to, but Bruns had vouched for it, and O. sends, Uncle Caspar writes, he takes over a lot, and my brothers are partners. Already one good farm has been sold at a good price. What should be done with the other money? Franz and Bernhard do not like to speculate, Mrs. Bruns shakes her head if she hears of this, and Bruns cogitates and thinks about it. In the end they consult each other and decide to leave it with the mill and later start a distillery.

I should remind you that if Franz would have a household and a wife it would be better to have the mill and what follows put on his farm. Niedieck tried to persuade Bruns to begin a store with him. It was the last and only opportunity to be of use to Niedieck, and so Bruns consented. When Niedieck returned from St. Louis with Ferdinand Meyer, he was already drunk every day. Bruns, at my insistence, asked Meyer to step into the business in his stead since he was better acquainted with it. Niedieck kept on squandering, Bruns was still guaranteeing his security, and, as we realized only later, our losses resulted in Niedieck first leaving, and a long time later Bruns was again a partner in the business. The store was existing by itself, and earlier Bruns had told me that if H. Niedieck would do well he intended to withdraw and leave the business to Niedieck alone, since he, Bruns, did not understand anything about it. Now the business is progressing under the name of the firm of "Bruns and Meyer." Meyer has taken over Niedieck's draft, and Bruns is gradually putting in his share. —Thus it has almost happened by itself and without any of our doing that we have become business people.

From the above you will be able to surmise that it was perhaps improper for Franz to participate, which had occurred to me earlier. We will have to leave it in God's hands to see how things develop. Meyer is a man of very good will, and Bruns can help him a great deal since he knows the conditions around here very well. —You wrote you wanted to send us some capital. If it does not pose any particular difficulties, this would be very convenient for Bruns. But it would not be as you thought; instead, you would have to step into place in lieu of Niedieck. Bruns has in mind to transfer everything as soon as possible away from Niedieck. If you were to take a share of this, it would be immensely more agreeable to me and to him since the repayment would not have to take place all at once, and we would like to be free of obligations to Niedieck. Bruns wants to take care of the obligations that are still lying over there, and he himself must indeed write to Uncle Caspar. It has often annoyed me that we have to write for money, but I cannot be convinced that Bruns himself is a great speculator. I hope that he will no longer do things such as buying land etc., etc. The fact that you want to send money and your offer to let us have more lets me assume that you, and who knows who else, do not have the highest opinion of our situation here. That is very embarrassing to me. We could have been quite satisfied even without these money transfers, and I even more so. Believe me that if there were nothing else on my mind, then our situation would be quite good and will grow even better. In addition, one does not need very much here.

The fact that Uncle Caspar is so close to you speaks very much in his favor as far as I am concerned. The good uncle, may he be made happy through you; I hope you will do your part!

But, Heinrich, why this long sermon on "to have to stay there"? It confuses me very much. Have I ever expressed my wish so urgently that you should come over here? I don't believe so, but you write it. Perhaps I have forgotten it. But it seems to me that you criticize a certain comment, that I always have had some doubt that I was hoping, that I was considering something more than you were. To be sure, I have often dreamed of being reunited with you; sometimes here, sometimes there, you came toward me, and I looked at everything with a happier eye when I thought that you would sometime in the future be able to see this too. I no longer know what I wrote about it, but I am certainly not as egotistical as you write. No, dear brother, pursue your career, watch the brothers and sisters, and do not leave us completely without some attention. Write occasionally, and then I shall be satisfied, I will be satisfied. Since, however, you do not want to give this up completely, we shall sometime in the future talk about it again. To be sure Johanna wants to remain there, and Wilhelm should stay there, and thus your trip has no purpose other than to see us. It has been only three years since we last saw each other, and if you would come now it might just be too long for the remainder of our lives!

It hurts me when you write that Johanna pictures being here as too boring and nevertheless wants to come. It exceeds sisterly love; she must have been very much excited when she wrote to me. However, I shall not take it amiss, for she certainly would not want to disappoint me. Will you, please, write to me as soon as possible what you know concerning Johanna? Do it, I ask you. Why do you put Uedinck and Franz Geisberg together? Is nothing else to be said about Marie?

Farewell Heinrich, keep thinking of me in the future. Greetings to all from your loving sister Jette.

P.S. My letter is almost as good as yours, a formal dissertation. Keep it to yourself and forget what is too much in it!

If the letters are to come over here faster, they must not be sent *via* Rotterdam. I, by the way, would like to know whether the postage is cheaper for you. Do write me. Our correct address is: *via* Havre per New York packet, Dr. B. Bruns or Doctoress Bruns, Westphalia, Missouri.

Brother-in-law Hermann wants to marry, and thus I should claim the title of my husband.

In a letter of 11 March 1840, Bernhard wrote Heinrich of his loneliness and his thoughts of the girl he had left in Germany. He offered to loan his younger brother Wilhelm money from his inheritance so he could come to America. In an undated letter apparently written about the same time, he wrote his sister Johanna about his life as a farmer, the abundance of game, and the pleasures of hunting.

April 1840

To write to you a bit more, dear Heinrich, is limited by space. Your letter of September arrived. Right at the beginning the "Beware if your little brother starts to interpret!" scared me tremendously. I wish you could read my soul. I have lost all self-confidence, I don't know how and what it is best to write; to be sure there is often a draft, but then afterward I have to cross out so much. —No, I beg you, do not criticize my letters, that would be a touchy point with me. You know anyway that I do not mean evil; even if some particular word stands out sharply, take it from the good side. I have some things that I cannot quite stand; therefore let your letters be pure enjoyment. I would almost like to hold back the letter lying in front of me if I knew that you would be annoyed by it. Uncle Adolf took it amiss when I wrote him openly, and I can never make this up again. Uncle Caspar perhaps is doing likewise since I now informed him of my intentions. Brother Heinrich can do it also if I send this letter. It is still in my power! —But no, why should you not know what moves me? If all of you become annoyed with me, it would not prevent me from holding to you! —I can still not get over the fact, nor get it into my head, that your sister will be so far away always. Bruns cannot comprehend it quite and says I will have to be calm about it. It will surely work out!

Recently several educated women arrived here, the families Niedecken. They are already in St. Louis. If I were not too dull for everything now, it would be of greatest interest to me to meet them. A young bride is among them. The young people inquired whether they could put up their relatives with us for a few days. Thus we shall see them, as soon as the Missouri is free of ice. —Four weeks ago our big Johann broke a leg in an accident. It so happened that Bruns and I were there when they were felling trees for the mill. The quick aid will, I hope, produce good results. He is now happy and has few pains. Our Franz again recently had fever, and now again an inflammation of his eyes. We have to be concerned that his work does not get into arrears.

This winter was very severe and hard. Most Americans and Germans had many pigs die. That will be very bad for several years! We have been able to save some thirty. Schwarze has lost more than twice as many. Corn is also too scarce. We hear that a steamboat will bring corn down the Osage to Lisle. —Well, good-bye, regards to all from your sister, Jette.

Westphalia, 14 June 1840

Dear Heinrich:

Joseph Meierpeter[41] from the parish of Mastholte, who has a farm near us and is very well liked by us all, took a trip back to Germany on business matters. We used the safe opportunity and packed a box with things that we just happened to have. A few seeds of Bernhard's tobacco, a panther skin, a skin of a wild cat, and I don't know what else. We were in a big hurry. Meyer filled the box with a package to his mother. J. Meierpeter wanted to travel by way of Bremen and there turn the box over to a freight agent to deliver to Uncle Caspar. From Bremen you and Judge Meyer's wife would have had to bear the cost. Later, however, we heard that Meierpeter had gone by ship to England, and this made us worry that he might have some difficulties with the box. An open bill of lading to Uncle Caspar was sent along. We are curious how things went. I, for my part, must tell you that I put into the little box of seeds a medallion for sister Johanna, in the quiet hope that brother Heinrich will hand it to her on her wedding day. It happened too quickly for us to be able to have anything pretty, and in addition, I lacked all assurance; and also the time might become too short with all this writing back and forth for me to be able to write to her myself.

Meierpeter will probably come through Stromberg, Oelde, Münster. We have asked him to call on Hüffers and the Niediecks. He is an exceedingly honest young man. Write Johanna that he has been recommended to you. In addition we have to recommend Mr. Adolph Menges from Mainz. We asked him to visit you if by chance he comes through Münster. He is a friend of Andreas Schmedding, a very fine, solid man who is exceedingly accommodating and whom we have known since we have been here. If the opportunity offers itself, I hope brother Heinrich will be pleasant to him. To be sure, I hope that a letter from you will arrive in the near future; however, I shall not wait for it. We all here are still fine; that is, we are well and have worked diligently, each to his own task.

On our farm the wheat and the rye are flourishing, with heavy heads. Down below the corn, potatoes, etc., are doing well. The pasture furnished for the first time a big heap of beautiful hay, which Bruns himself helped stack until late yesterday. Our garden rewards the good care. This year all plants are just as abundant as they used to be in Germany; beautiful flowers are the joy of the boys. Franz has planted two fields with corn, and a third one with oats and wheat. Bernhard worked last spring with Mr. Robinson, who would have liked to have kept him, but Bernhard wants to work for himself. At the moment he is helping us and Franz wherever help is needed. Bernhard brought a young horse to our house from Robinson. He had to pay only ten reichsthaler.

41. The passenger list of the *Ulysses* includes Joseph Meierpeter from Mastholte, age 27. According to St. Joseph Parish records he was born in 1809 and died in 1887.

Again a few weeks have gone by. Johanna had been sick for two weeks and constantly demanded my care, but now she is improving and begins by being quite ill-humored. Once I sat down at the piano for recreation and found "Easter Morning," the last piece we practiced in the club before Wenner's death. He was already sickly at the time, and it touched me when he sang to me two very appropriate solos. I keep thinking farther back to his first wife, an angel, and the second one, no less one. How they liked us, how we liked them! They are all, all gone! I shall never forget them all the days of my life! —Here, how lonely I am; there is not another congenial female being with whom I could exchange now and then my feelings when I need some relief and would forget the daily worries and cares and set these aside for a short time. —Yet what difference does it make, for I tell Bruns everything and he listens patiently even though he cannot get so deeply involved.

I rarely get to go out of the house. Business does not permit it; if, however, the mill is finished, then I will have to catch up on my visits. The fact that the mill is not yet finished makes us all somewhat annoyed. The Good Lord again sent us another test for our patience and let the mill master, an extremely unpleasant old American, become sick. Now he is better, and so we hope that he will be able to leave us any week now. The workmen are also sick of him, and thus one thing leads to another.

I have spoken with Bruns, who thought it would not be too inconvenient to have some dresses sent by Meierpeter. You will have to inquire by letter whether he would be able to take the little package along and when and where it is to be sent. Joseph Meierpeter, Parish of Mastholte. I would like to have two cotton dresses and one of simple *Merino;* they are to be made to the measure of sister Johanna but about the width of three fingers wider around the waist and not too high at the neck, but they should have a collar, and the cotton should not be too bright. Then I also want a little petticoat with bodice for the two-year-old girl, quite warm. If it should be too difficult for Johanna to buy these things, then Marie could probably do it. If everything works out, I hope that you or Johanna will write me in the first letter what the cost was, and Bruns will transfer it with the proper interest. The dresses, however, will have to be completely finished because that is the point.

One more thing: Brother Franz is recently thinking that he does not want to farm alone anymore. He has made his choice, and even though this is really not too objectionable, Bruns and I nevertheless reminded him of several things I consider important. However, he seems to have overcome all concerns, for Bernhard, with his frivolous mind, laughing all over, reported that they had cut down the trees for his house the last few days, etc. At times his conceit is apparent again, but then it is easy for me to fight that. Franz does not have a very good education. The young girl is not pretty, but as far as I can tell she has a good heart and an even and enduring head.[42] Well, enough of that for now. If he is serious, Franz will not fail to let us know, and I can then add further information.

This summer has not brought as much heat as usual and many cool nights. Because of Hannen's illness and my own little indispositions, my letter has been held here longer than I would have liked, so I fear it will arrive too late for Johanna's wedding; it might also be too late for the dresses I have wanted. But I hope you will try and write quickly. More soon. Hold dear as always your sister, Jette.

42. Gertrude Stiefermann was the daughter of John and Maria Stiefermann (see note 13 above).

P.S. Bernhard seems to want to become very independent, and he is constantly speaking of his becoming of age soon and hopes to begin in earnest for himself then. I am often annoyed at his sloppiness and his clumsiness. He is as if hewn from wood and completely mindless.

Almost every day now we eat melons, a delicious fruit, better than the sun pears from the garden of the Spliethof.

The following letter had been postmarked 15 August and was postmarked again in New York on the 9th of September.

Westphalia
15 February 1841

Dear Heinrich!

First let me report for myself that I once again, in spite of all the fear that I would lose my life, have a stout boy on my lap, who drinks mightily, screams, and sleeps, is named Rudolph, and has blond hair, blue eyes, and a snub nose. My health is returning gradually, and next week I shall again take over the cares of the household.

Two days before my delivery, your letter with enclosures from Roers arrived (it was traveling for three months). I could not get Elise Boner out of my mind, and I sent urgent requests to Heaven to let me continue to stay with my husband and children. —My last letter to you was in August. However, you have already answered that. Since that time we have been rather well. Franz and I had fever occasionally; he suffered longer from the conse-quences. A letter to you is lying half finished, from which I will have to repeat something concerning Franz and his young wife. On 5 November, Franz was married to Trude Stiever-mann. The wedding took place here in the house. Pastor Helias, the parents, uncle, and brother of the bride, the neighbors who live next door, Zumnorde, Meyer, David Bruns, and Hermann Bruns and wife attended. The bridegroom behaved very honorably; he seemed to be very calm, more collected than his sister, who in the beginning in spite of all the activity could not look at him without emotion. Bernhard laughed almost all day long, almost as if to annoy me, as if taking a wife was the easiest and funniest thing in the world. In the evening when the strangers had departed, punch was prepared. We sat around together for several hours until Bernhard and Berndt accompanied the bride and bridegroom, laden down with the most necessary dishes, food, etc., to their house. Since that time they have lived there; the furnishings might have been better, and the house is not yet tight enough. Franz spent the winter making all kinds of new furnishings. His sickness had set him back with his work quite a bit. We had to help from here. Half of his animals have now been taken there. The horses and the cows have already become accustomed to their new place. The butchered hogs are lying in brine; the others, however, are still being fed. His corn is now being dried. He has a good income from this. He has already sold some meat and will still be able to spare more. Franz is very economical and has good cause to be so, for with building and the furnishings the remainder of his money was not only spent, but Bruns had to advance a considerable amount (close to two hundred dollars). Recently Bruns and Franz settled. I did not know the result, but the appearance of the latter made me concerned. Bruns told me, to be sure, that Franz should calculate the lower interest rate that Uncle Caspar gives them, but it is very difficult for a beginner who still lacks necessities and who needs new furnishings. The young woman did not bring anything along; what she has earned she left with her parents and did well in doing so. Franz knew this and has already asked me to take care of some things that otherwise make the beginning of a trousseau. You may keep what I am chattering here to yourself; and otherwise you will agree with Franz that if he can live with his wife beside him that is the best trousseau. She has a good heart and more feeling than one could expect. I also hope that she will do well in the house; at least I will have to believe so after having had a year and a half of experience. I live on very friendly terms with her; however, I want to confess to you that the changed relationship is still somewhat strange to me, and she has probably gotten a very critical relative. But I would be sorry if she notices this in the slightest. She will probably have no cause, for she is always equally modest and friendly and helps wherever it is necessary, asks for advice, etc. Mrs. Bruns likes to help now and again and assists with all kinds of things that they are lacking, and thus I think this will turn into a very beautiful relationship.

Hermann Bruns, who married the oldest Lückenhoff from the parish of Oelde, still lives with David Bruns. I like this young woman very much, too. Thus we are getting more and more relatives, which pleases me mightily. I also believe that it makes me more satisfied. If you visit us soon you will be amazed to see so many little folks dancing around you, little Brunses with still smaller Geisbergs perhaps playing with each other.

So there is probably no doubt anymore that Dr. Roer[43] and his family will be coming over! A few days ago a second letter arrived from him, and Bruns answered immediately. I am always afraid when educated people come over here. Only too often they do not find it as easy and pleasant as they have thought it would be. The Roer family always lived simply, I know, and the wife is supposed to be quite active in the house, but now she is up in years and has no daughters. She knows, I hope, that the wages for a servant girl amount to four dollars a month. Earlier it was hardly possible to get one, but recently we have heard of some who sought service. If the doctor's wife would prefer, as most ladies here do, to head her own household, then milking and washing are two onerous jobs even if the garden is taken care of by her sons. It is also not easy to get a married woman to work. We live too far away, and every woman has enough to do in her own house. Many a person finds it difficult at first to eat cornbread and pork. Vegetables can be gotten more easily now. It is also impossible to get seamstresses to come to one's house. However, a woman lives nearby to whom I can give everything. If you find it appropriate, you can tell Mrs. Roer about this. It would be good to have a strong daughter-in-law come along.

Now to some errands. The good opportunity tempts me. In case Meierpeter has departed too early, then the dresses could probably be sent along. Franz put in a little note, in which he asked his former boss for a piece of gray linen! Would you please look after this and take care of it? Mrs. Bruns also would like to have a piece of strong muslin (to make dresses) for herself and the children; we are not concerned about a pattern. Furthermore, we need thick gray beaver cloth for two petticoats. I am a little bigger than Marie. Trute, who wants the other one, is just my size. Then I would also like to have a pair of nicely knitted woolen stockings and some extra yarn for darning and two pairs of ordinary stockings of blue mixed *sajet*,[44]

43. In her autobiography Jette mentions that Dr. Roer lived on property abutting the garden of the Geisberg family on Neubrückenstrasse in Münster.

44. *Sajet* should probably read *serge*, which is a silk thread.

and an additional two pounds of the same *sajet* but not knitted. Earlier Uncle Hüffer let me have the pound at one reichsthaler and one groschen. Johanna is staying in Ahlen.[45] It is a bother for her to send these things. I think my youngest sister could take the trouble, with the aid of our aunt's advice. I therefore ask Thereschen, when the things have been gotten, to have the stockings knitted and also after the materials have been acquired to have the skirts sewed, since it is just as safe and convenient to send them that way rather than in an unfinished state. If there is still time and if it will not be too much for Therese, then she should add a few dark aprons (gingham aprons) already made. I hope the Roers will be kind enough to cover the expense for all this, and then we would not have to send the money over.

Bruns can find no explanation for his letters not having arrived. Particularly in recent times he has been very punctual in answering the letters to Ferd. Niedieck. Earlier he was at times somewhat slower, but he never completely failed to write. The last letter to Uncle Caspar was mailed toward the end of November. Ferd. Niedieck wrote again and complained about our silence, and therefore the enclosure here follows a letter that had been mailed immediately. Niedieck had given notice for his capital; however, Bruns had anticipated this and had already drawn two drafts and has sent them. The remainder will be sent to him in due time. We will probably give up our share in the store. Dr. Zumnorde's wife seems not to be willing to give her son what he has asked for. It is hard for him since he has nothing to do at the present time and neither can nor wants to continue farming alone. Long illness and fever last year robbed him of his strength and his pleasure in working. Perhaps the opportunity will pass. We should be sorry if he would see himself forced to try his fortune at random somewhere else. He does not want to hear anything about returning.

Bernhard is working hard in the bottom field. Unfortunately the miller, Mr. Ritter, a good, old, strange man, suddenly entered the Jesuit order as a brother in St. Louis, and the deserted mill claims Berndt's entire time. Thus Bernhard is doing the hoeing alone. I believe I wrote already that big Johann died last October on the day of prayer and repentance.[46] He only suffered for three days. Since we had a new girl, I cared for him until Bruns relieved me on the last day. It really affected us very much. He was respected by us all, and rarely was anything done without his advice. Most of our farm work will now stop for the time being. Johann named Bruns as his heir, but he still has relatives in Germany.

I hope that brother Heinrich will now write a long beautiful letter and therefore please Bruns, the brothers, and particularly his loving sister, Jette. Best regards.

P.S. Franz said that he would write to you. Send some little gift as a souvenir for the young sister-in-law; here everything is valued even though it is of no great value otherwise. Perhaps a bow or a little kerchief. However, you must know best.

On 15 March 1841 Franz wrote to his brother Heinrich regarding his marriage. Prior to the wedding he had built a house twelve feet wide and sixteen feet long on his property.

45. A town some twenty miles southeast of Münster, where Johanna's husband, Caspar Offenberg, whom she had married 3 September 1840, was director of the land and municipal court.

46. Johann Brüggink, known as "Big John," died in Westphalia on 15 October 1840. The day was known as *Miserere* on the Church calendar.

28 March 1841

Dear Heinrich:

. . . the house full of children, the barn full of cattle, a billy goat, you just can't imagine what it takes to have the peace to be able to take a pen in hand. For quite some time I had chosen not to have an older girl. However, it did not work. Rudolph was crying about this and that, and the bigger ones had torn everything and wanted to have it patched up again. Bernhard did not have one single pair of pants that was not torn, and so it went.

May 7th

Johanna's letter arrived approximately three weeks ago, and about a week ago yours came. I had longed for a longer letter from you for a long time and for quite some time I even felt a little jealous. —We are all still well except for me. Little Rudolph is growing well; he is a little curly head, which amuses me so much that I don't even like to put a cap on him in the morning after I have washed him. He smiles, is so friendly, and always looks so trusting. I hope he will remain such a dear little son.

Again I had the fever and finally it was almost jaundice. I am still tired and have no appetite. It annoys me that I am sick so frequently. Spring is wet and unhealthy, as in Germany. It sets farming back tremendously. Franz is busy planting corn, and Bernhard is almost finished with his. The fresh green of the forest and the field brings a mild, gay mood. I imagine that I like this year, and I shall not look at flowers and trees anymore as being strange. In the garden everything is growing beautifully. Niedieck gave me two sprigs of roses for planting, and Bruns brought me currant bushes from Jefferson. The fruit trees will follow next fall; at least that is what Bruns promises.

For several days now I have been alone because Bruns has gone to St. Louis. I wish he were back again; I am so worried. Max is also sick and looks miserable. Hermann should really go to school, but we have none. Things are not going well with our pastor anymore. It is sad. One can never go to church without finding some objection to his sermons. He exaggerates horribly and turns everybody against him. Most of them are determined not to contribute any more to his subsistence. He has insulted Bruns several times, but we keep quiet. If only his removal could take place without any further friction. If only we had a good German minister who would be concerned with the well-being of the community! We are strangers to this pastor; he does not do any more than is necessary and at times not even that much. On the other side of the Osage one father had his child baptized by a Protestant preacher after he had waited a very long time. An evil woman is said to be the main cause of this unfriendly relationship with our pastor: his landlady. She is some gossip!

Now farewell! A longer answer to a longer letter. The space for me is somewhat small. I was pleased with your description of Johanna's establishment. She herself is very superficial. However, perhaps she will improve. She would surely do so if she could read my heart. Regards to all from your sister, Jette.

On Ascension Day

I notice that Bernhard had still left one free page and so I shall scribble a little more. On Sunday a letter arrived from Ferdinand Niedieck. You cannot imagine how unpleasant it is for Bruns, and also for me, that a draft was refused. Clarenbach, who usually blames Bruns, has, however, immediately taken care that the money was transferred to somebody else.

However, it is rather annoying for us that it did not get into Uncle Caspar's hands according to his wish. This only by the way. Bruns will write to Ferd. Niedieck.

On Friday, Bruns returned safely and brought a (rich) old gentleman along who had traded for a long time in Surinam, Cuba, Spain, etc.; the latter knew Bitter's and Schimmel's situation. He also knew of a certain Färber, who visited us in Oelde, that he was married to an English lady and living in the vicinity of Cologne. The old gentleman was traveling for pleasure, and he found Formosa[47] situated very pleasantly. The owner has gone bankrupt, and perhaps he will now buy it. How is Marie Geisberg? I would like to know. Once again, farewell! your Jette, in a big hurry.

Westphalia
11 July 1841

Dear Heinrich!

With great impatience we are waiting for Roers and good news. For the time being I shall write you something to entertain you. For approximately two weeks now Zumnorde and Meyer have been in town, where Meyer has purchased a house and is having it changed to a store room. Now our family is limited to Bernhard and one girl, which pleases me immensely. Never before in America have I had such a small household. Now I would be satisfied if I were not so lonely. Foolish soul! Often I think I don't want to write anymore and don't like to think of you all anymore, but that is not possible. You all always stand before me, fresh and alive, and always there is the ocean and the world between us. There can never be hope for a reunion. You are constantly growing deeper into the situation over there and we into the situation here. Do you know anything that could silence the raging emotions? Can no harmony come to my heart? I would think it would work out, but I don't know how to undo the knot no matter how I think about it and brood about it recently. If I were living with the Clarenbachs I would surely become melancholic. The house stands high on top of the hill. The fields lie down the slope and in the valley. The bottom stretches to Lisle and over the Maries. In the far distance the eye sees the steep rocky banks of the Osage. Recently I spent the night there with Rudolph. It made a very strange impression on me in the glow of the moonlight and in the splendor of the rising sun. The far-reaching view! I thought the faraway hills with the forests on top would reveal something precious to me. If longing could have wings and could jump over trees and rivers! But when the sun rose higher I no longer dreamed, but I quietly smiled and asked myself: what do you find there? Desolation, emptiness! No, here in our neighborhood it's better! —I get along very well with Mrs. Clarenbach. Our farm lies quite differently. There one cannot just roam around. A friendly nearness has to be sufficient. Here— meadow, garden, field in the valley. The street winds up around the slope; the clattering of the mill, the hammering in the smithy, the crowds of young fellows, the laughter of a girl! What difference does it make if the rocks from the other side of the bank push back the glance searching into the depths?

47. In 1837 Bernhard Geisberg wrote to his brother Heinrich that "the city of Formosa is being laid out at the mouth of the Osage." The city apparently never developed. However, James's *River Guide*, published by U. P. James in Cincinnati, 1857, positions Formosa nine miles below Jefferson City in Cole County, near the mouth of the Osage River.

From the Autobiography

In St. Louis Bruns was introduced to Senator Benton, who took a liking to him, wanted to keep up the relationship, and invited him whenever they met in St. Louis. And later he even sent his only son to us for a long visit.[48] Hermann, our oldest, took instructions, first with the Clarenbachs' children and then in Westphalia with a Mr. Krone. Later Bruns took him to Jefferson, where he lived in the home of Mr. Kramer, who was a good friend. But when he returned in the fall he was sick and brought along dysentery. In a few days all of our children were sick. Hermann survived the illness, but the little ones! Johanna died on the 13th of September, Max on the 19th of September, and the babe in arms, little Rudolph, followed on the 2d of October. With all of them the last words and the dying glance was "Mother!" And so it is not surprising that I wished I could have gone with them. We were all sick until finally my dear husband exhorted me with all his strength that I still had some duties to tend to. It took us a long time to recover. This was 1841.

3 October

"There rest now, my sweet, my beloved in God; there rest now, in peace, free of all troubles."

And then I stroke the pale cheek and kiss the cold mouth. I want to look once more at little Rudolph. Then they may bed him next to Max and Johanna. —In the house here it is very quiet. Hermann, the only one, is skulking around, still lacking his strength; however, he is almost well now. We have been afflicted by dysentery. My three little angels have been taken away by the Good Lord. Yesterday morning sweet little Rudolph passed away. Since that time his mother has had peace. Peace to nourish her grief, peace to capture resignation.

17 October

Dear Heinrich!

We all had dysentery. Hermann was the first to become sick. On the 8th of September Max and Johanna were afflicted by it. The latter was indescribably sick and died on the 13th of September at 2:30 in the morning. "Mother, mother!" she cried loudly. I still believe I can hear her. On Tuesday Rudolph became sick, then I on Thursday, then Bernhard and Bruns. On Sunday the 19th, at 1:30 during the night, Max died. It was the third night that I had feared his end almost any hour. He quietly fell asleep and passed away. It was God's will to also take Rudolph from me. He died on Sunday, the 2d of October, at 7:30 in the morning. To the very last minute, I had the strength to endure. And then his breath was failing, his eyes closed. He was buried at 5 o'clock on Sunday. All three of them rest side by side now. In the next letter I shall give you a few more details about my angel children. Only when everything was quiet, when everything was over, I began to feel that I also was in need of rest. The little

48. Thomas Hart Benton moved in 1815 from his native Tennessee to St. Louis, where he practiced law and began publication of a newspaper. Elected as one of Missouri's first U.S. senators, he served in that office for the next thirty years. Because of his forthrightness on the subjects of sectionalism and slavery, he was defeated in 1850 when he ran for his sixth term for the Senate. He was elected to the U.S. House of Representatives in 1852 but was defeated two years later because of his opposition to the repeal of the Missouri Compromise. (See William E. Parrish, *A History of Missouri, Volume III: 1860 to 1875* [Columbia: University of Missouri Press, 1973], pp. 48–49.) John Randolph Benton stayed in Westphalia and studied with Dr. Bruns for several months in 1849–1850 (see note 91 below).

one had been with me almost the whole time. Bruns and Bernhard recovered most quickly. Bernhard was tremendously low. The recovery is progressing very slowly for all of us.

15 November

Now all wishes, all striving have been quieted! I even no longer wish to go back to you, to Germany! It is so painful to me. Up there where the angels live and where the Almighty is enthroned, it's probably singularly beautiful. There I will also find you all again! Until then we shall postpone our reunion. There it will be happier. —How I wish I could have said farewell to the world six weeks ago, if only the Good Lord would have considered it my time. I had been provided with the last sacrament. Even though my life, full of sin and weakness, made me fear, yet the hope was strong to find a gracious judge. I believe I could have been able to take leave of my husband and son. It really hit me too hard that I also had to lose little Rudolph. It had been twelve days since his dysentery had been over. I had already tried again to breast-feed him. I could only cry when (I had the little one in my lap) the neighbor entered with Franz's newly born child and announced that I was the godmother and asked me to select a name. The next day Rudolph died. The little one resembled his father and his deceased little sister so much. I myself sewed him his shroud. A lock from his curly head is all that is left of him for me. Oh, how lovely he was, how dear. Johanna always played so nicely with him. She was the pride of her father, an angel on earth. If Bruns had been out and she saw him, she would call, "Mother, Father!" and run quickly to meet him. Max followed a little more clumsily. If Bruns gave her an apple or something like that, she always said, "Hermann, Max!" and brought the gift to them joyfully. Twice she had a little doll (a rarity here), which everybody had to admire, and at night she held her in her arms. She was vain but easy to satisfy. A clean apron, a little kerchief pleased her. If she saw her little red hat she said, "Tute, Franz." She liked to visit there very very much. Max, who was more serious and deliberate, became happier and more confident through her. He always had a few melodies that he repeated again and again, and then she imitated him. The two of them played so well together. They were always marching one after the other, Max in front, Hanna a few steps behind. Max was mother's darling; he shied away from his father until he was led to him this past summer by Johanna. I believe he resembled brother Heinrich. He had such dear, pious eyes. He seemed, as we all thought, to have some talent. He was incredibly good-hearted and shared everything. Usually he was quiet and contemplative but probably short-tempered, therefore a genuine Geisberg. (He even had the two toes that lay above each other when there was no shoe on his foot, like our father and Franz had, but not I.)

You see, dear Heinrich, that I do not tire of talking about the little ones. But you like to hear me pour out my heart.

7 December

It is finally getting time to send this letter off. Little Caspar Geisberg[49] (Grandfather permitted this name at the request of his father) is a lively fellow. He is now two months old and is smiling at the world. His mother confessed to me recently that Franz really was very fond of the little fellow. He is so careful not to let anybody see this. Really, neither I nor

49. Caspar Geisberg, son of Jette's brother Franz and his wife Gertrude, was born in Westphalia 30 September 1841.

Bruns nor Bernhard had noticed that he smiled at his son or that he held him in his arms. Trude told me that when they are alone he often takes him and plays with him. Also during the night he relieves his wife when the little one cries. Is that not nice?

Bernhard had an aversion to his place and was determined to have another. Therefore he came to terms for an old farm with a Rhinelander for $475. Soon thereafter he and Bruns inspected the farm belonging to Johann, who died; it is about four miles up the Maries. There he will settle. We opposed Bernhard for a long time, particularly I. When he left our house the day before yesterday, I accompanied him with a heavy heart a little stretch of the way. Now he has to start over again. Bernhard is still so far from independent. He lacks many qualities of a capable farmer, but he does work industriously and lives moderately.

Franz is not making a great deal of headway with his farm, which worries me considerably. In addition he does not like to take advice. If you think that he has a great deal of persistence, that becomes evident when he quarrels. Bruns and he can never agree, and neither wants to give in. These are hard times for the farmers, and Franz cannot sell anything and has a lot of expenses. But he improvises and saves mightily. However, enough of this! It bothers me very much.

A few weeks ago Bruns and Bernhard bought a few young Indian horses; Bruns bought two for thirteen dollars, Bernhard his for nine dollars. These little horses please Bernhard no end. They are wild and have to be tamed. You will certainly receive some description from him. —Our priest is in a bad way. Some consider him to be imprudent; he does such foolish things. Oh, it is so sad! In this regard, you are so much better provided for. So, I have to picture our good uncle Bernhard in the beyond now. I am always praying for him. Uncle Caspar suffers most. I became quite sad in reading your letter, and I feel deeply that I have to communicate with you. But it takes such a long time for us to exchange our emotions with each other. You think that I am now happily in the circle of my beloved ones—that is over forever. Farewell and pray for me, your sister, Jette.

Heinrich Geisberg to Jette

> *Elegy on the Death of Three Children*
> *in Westphalia, Missouri, 1841*

> There rest now, my sweet
> My beloved in God.
> Rest there from all troubles.
> I caress the pale cheek,
> And kiss the cold mouth.
> One more look. . . . .
> Now lay him with the others.

Ring on, ring on, you are song
To my ears, pure sound, but swelling
You crash over me like the sea
And darkness seizes me.
It is the voice which in dreams of my youth
Whispered to me, whose sound

Fades away in the distance.
Through the brightly glowing forests
It rolls, through the silent valley.
The Maries flood, glistening, breaks
Its waves at the edge of the cliff and ripples round
The greening hill.
There kneels the woman between mounded graves,
Her eye fixed on the grave
Of her darling, her hand
Rests on the sandy mound of the fresh graves.
Woe! I hear the voice,
The cry for help, the voice of my sister
Sister, oh sister, lift the pale
Face, look around you with the clear,
Wide eye. The arm of the husband,
Whose pain and whose love
You are, embraces you;
You lean on the youthful shoulder
Of your first born, who does not know,
Should not learn through you, the pain.
Look to us brothers and sisters
Who love you like our eye
And like the evening star, greet you.
Sister, turn your quiet face toward
Morning, where from the womb of the night
Pure and golden the primeval light pours forth
Drying the tear in our eyes as it dries the pearly dew
In the throat of the flower.
See, the nightly pain flies like a
Vision in a dream before truth;
Our love holds you embraced and we,
With you, stretch our hands toward heaven,
While you pray to the Mother of the Divine Son.
Oh, Mother, Mother of all!
The hand of love
Led me to distant lands
Scarcely had Happiness and Peace smiled on me
In the faraway land,
When to the dust of the earth, into the grave
I laid the children whom you had blessed
So that, blossoming, they grew.
Oh, Mother, when the patron spirit carries
These angels, brothers and sister, closely embraced, to you
Then accept them with love, Oh, Mother.

From the Autobiography

In the following year new hope blossomed, and then on the 19th of September 1842 our
Heinrich came. My brother's son, Caspar, had been born in 1841. In 1842 his daughter

Henriette was born. We helped each other. On 3 May 1844 a little girl, Euphemia, made her appearance at our house, and in 1845 my sister-in-law had a son, Heinrich.

7 May 1842

Dear Heinrich:

Today it occurred to me again that Uncle Adolf did not answer my bad note with one syllable.[50] Since I have been worrying about this, I asked myself, why should I not inquire? In your letter from that time you wrote of "reproaches which were kept for two years" ("do not take this amiss," you added). If Uncle A. was annoyed, then my letter was wrong, for it certainly missed having the intended effect. He misunderstood me, because it was my intention to approach him openly in a friendly way. Even now I sometimes think that it was not wrong to act as I did. I have never misjudged what I owed the uncle and am grateful for the many good things that I owe him. I've always had more affection for him than he probably felt for me. His seriousness restrained me. It is bitter for me that he entered the other world without sending me a kind word. Therefore it was my first thought when I received the news of his death, "Now he knows that I loved him"; —why should I take up something like this again, you think, when it has been such a long time since the death of our good uncle? If my thoughts are turned more frequently than formerly to the departed ones, this should not surprise you. Since I am still alive, perhaps may even live for a long time, it would indeed be pleasant for me to know whether our uncle perhaps intended to answer me. If you know anything about this, then let me know some time. Then I would also like to know some details concerning Tine Osterlinck's illness and end. Perhaps you will see her sister Cathinka, who was always present.[51] I don't think I could really write to her myself.

24 July

A few weeks ago your and Johanna's letter arrived here. I had expected them for quite some time, and yet it upset me tremendously because it seemed to me as if you were sitting before me and saying all that was written, as if you were saying everything right after we no longer had our children. And when I read about Johanna, how she wants to name her little son Max, then I wished I could have the little one here. I had such an indescribable longing to see him and to seek in him my own lost little boy. Softly I whispered Tine Osterlinck's own words: "You have a Max, I no longer have one."

On the 24th of May, Bruns congratulated me on our tenth wedding day; it came as a surprise because I had not thought of it. He added, however, "Today is Johanna's name day." That was too much for me, and in the end I exclaimed, "We shall never have a Johanna again." Our little girl was a child whom we both loved perhaps too much. I remember that when she was still alive, we spoke about this sometimes. Everything, the way she walked, the way she stood, was life and joy and was so pretty, so dainty. She took care so beautifully that the brothers always received their share; she played with Rudolph until he was calm. I loved

---

50. The letter Jette wrote in 1838 to Adolf Geisberg regarding her brothers and sisters has not been preserved. However, in her letter of 23 September 1838 to Heinrich she discusses her uncle's unexpected reaction to the letter.

51. Cathinka Clementine Christine Niedieck (1806–1841) had married Joseph Osterlinck in 1825. Her parents were the banker and landowner Niedieck of Stromberg and Maria Johanna Hüffer Niedieck.

all these children so much, but the girl should not have been taken with them—it was not right. Bruns agreed with me that we shall never want to use the names of the little departed ones again. The three angels are not ever far away; we often think that they still belong to us as before.

Mrs. Bruns lives in new hope and has gradually become accustomed to having wishes and expectations not here during the winter. We scarcely will ever again be as happy as before. Bruns is more serious, and a kind, always gay, wife would be good for him. I scarcely believe that I can follow such resolutions. —As you probably know these are hard times here, particularly for the farmers. But now I am probably less worried about our own existence than about that of the brothers. Bernhard began to work for himself last spring. Since the wages for a hired hand are eight dollars per month, which he cannot afford, he gave up after the land had been tilled and went to Franz. This, however, will probably not last long. What will he begin then? To work one's land, to harvest, and not live there, what will this lead to? He has no doubt that he can stay with us or with Franz and lead a leisurely life. When he has attacks of fever, then he speaks of returning to Germany, where it would be healthier, where even a little tenant farmer could live as well as he here. Such talk hurts me deeply when I have to see that he is not well (I would rather starve myself than be in good circumstances and see the brothers in need). I would like to tell him, "Go back now before you have used up your funds." I don't know what will become of him. You too would certainly find it worrisome to have to advise Bernhard to go back to Germany. Uncle Caspar would find this very strange since Bernhard has now gotten his inheritance through our uncle's efforts. To tell him again "take a wife" does not work either. He is deliberate in this matter since he sees by observing Franz that everything is not always fine, that a wife also has certain claims at times, for which one cannot blame her. A completely uneducated woman would not suit him either, and to choose according to his own liking isn't possible here. Earlier we thought that he would do best to go back to Germany and get himself a wife, but there the costs are too high and one could not count on her dowry, which is not sure when love has to be considered. If you think it right, talk things over with Uncle Caspar.

Franz has his troubles on the farm. It is certain that somebody who has farmed earlier gets ahead twice as fast as he who has not done it before. Caspar, his little son, is a nice child, has very curly hair now, and is beginning to walk. Trute was sickish but is now well again after taking medicine. —Bruns has had a fever for the first time here, but now is quite well again. Mr. Krone has taught school here for five months. His parents live in England. For several years he had been in Münster, where he taught English to H. Meyer. Hermann has done well. Recently we had three little Americans from Jefferson as house companions, so they could learn English and German. It is a shame that the people here do so little for the school. Mr. Krone has been called to Jefferson now, and he has accepted a position there. However, the merchant H. Miller, whose son was here, would have liked to give Hermann room and board again. The Clarenbachs live in Lisle, and Hermann could go there too. Zumnorde wants to open a school next 1 August. But Mrs. Bruns does not like to be without her child, and the father said that we should wait until the time of sickness has passed.

I'm almost ashamed to write something about acquaintances as I just did regarding Zumnorde. Some time ago H. Meyer complained that I had revealed to his family that he no longer lived with us. If that was to be a secret, he should have told us because otherwise our doings are no secret to you and to our good acquaintances. Now, however, it is revealed why this was to be, since Bruns's draft was taken to his mother instead of being sent to us by way of Uncle Caspar. His family doesn't seem to be satisfied. Once again, our store business is annoying us. It is good that everything is cleared up now and that Meyer will not be a low-down cheat even though he could be.

The practice is rather small now, and it would be better if we could give up the farm and the mill. Bruns is wondering if he could not carry on a business on the side. But that may be difficult here in the country. For several weeks now they have been working on the house in order to tighten it up from the outside; it is questionable whether we will get very far with this.

These last few days another letter arrived from St. Louis that asked for money (from Bruns and Meyer). Just imagine, Meyer has managed that the dissolution of the firm was not announced publicly in the newspaper. Once he pretended when he was traveling to St. Louis that he had lost the paper that had been signed for the dissolution of the business, and the second time the editor of the newspaper is supposed to have misplaced it. So several times he bought goods and billed them to the firm, and if Meyer is not good for it Bruns can be held accountable for the payment. Last December a formal settling was scheduled, according to which Meyer had to pay eight hundred Rhenish thaler to Bruns. Since spring Bruns has no longer been a partner in the business, and he let his name stand only as a favor, which I have always objected to. Bruns would like you to ask Judge Meyer's wife to deliver the note of five hundred fifty Rhenish thaler. She will not be able to refuse. Her son has already or will soon dispatch a letter. Zumnorde and Meyer have managed rather negligently this year and had to pay cash for their board, laundry, and everything else. Meyer allowed credit to everybody, no matter how often he had been warned, and he does not like to ask for repayment, and thus the money stays with the people. One is even lazier and more negligent than the other. If this had not been the case with Meyer, then Bruns would not have given up. A store is even now a good business here, and if Bruns is able he will probably start one again, but certainly not with such an unreliable young person. I can be amazingly annoyed at this.

In the near future it will be brother Heinrich's turn to become a godfather. If I knew that you would be pleased and that you would not overlook such an announcement as you did before, which hurt me, who knows what would happen?

I am being urged on, and the sheet is full. You shall hear more in the near future. Greetings to the brothers and sisters and to all and write me as soon as possible. Your loving sister, Jette.

Throughout the summer of 1842 Jette, Franz and Dr. Bruns wrote to Caspar Geisberg about financial problems and loans. Their financial dealings with Germany were becoming increasingly more complicated.

Westphalia
15 October 1842

Dear Heinrich:

Here I have a lot of letters to answer that have arrived before and during the past two months, but the little fellow in the cradle demands a great deal of attention. Two weeks ago Carl Geisberg[52] arrived here in good shape. He had a good trip, no accidents at all, and was

52. Jette's cousin Carl Ludwig Geisberg, the son of Franz Heidenreich Geisberg and Maria Westendorf, was born in Cappenberg in 1817. He is listed by Müller as #960, emigrating in 1842.

always in good spirits and well.

Now let me talk of us first. On the anniversary of the death of little Max (19 September 1842) we were presented with a strong little boy who resembles the departed one insofar as he has dark hair and a little stub nose; therefore he is again a true son of his mother. The following day, the 20th of September, he received the name Heinrich Gottfried Hermann. The second name represents the substitute godfather (Schwarze). Mrs. Hermann Bruns was godmother. It still strikes me as very strange to call the little fellow Heinrich. Quite frequently and unintentionally I call him Rudolph. When calling him, I always think of you. What if he were to grow up and resemble you completely? —He is gaining well. I too am well again.

The teacher Althoff[53] arrived here at the end of July and brought along the dresses, the letters, and the book. I thank you particularly for the letter. Carl brought the remaining things. Many thanks for the trouble you have all had with this. I am glad that everything could be settled immediately. (You probably bought the woven stockings for me?) I do not, however, want to plague you again with details. To be sure, you probably do not know yet that there is neither printed muslin nor gingham to be had here, nor woolen cloth. The women who do not wear their home-woven material dress in cotton (which is not heavy enough for Germans). In the future I will not need any woolen yarn, for I began to spin and dye myself last winter. I enjoy this very much. You will attribute it to the love of the old customs: "the custom of the land is the honor of the land." Mrs. Bruns may dress herself like other women.

In my last letter, which was dispatched at the end of July, I wrote concerning Bernhard and his vacillation. He is still with us and has carried on the work on his farm, but he spoke seriously again of marrying, without knowing whom. These uncertainties do not seem good to me, so I told him recently he should look around among the daughters of the land. He has been out sometimes, but he still has no prospects and has not spoken of any choice, nor has he made any. It is quite difficult because he has little skill in courting. He has come around to believing that he does not want to take the very first one. Earlier we had to hold him back, but now he is slow and deliberate. Since Carl has been here Bernhard has changed; he has become happier, and he almost devours the books that were brought along. This ravenous reading exceeds everything else. We always fear, therefore, that he will become a bad farmer.

If he had a position where he would have to work definite hours and would then be free, that would be the best for him, because thinking for himself is completely foreign to him. In Germany there are many jobs like that. For many reasons I have to wish that he would not continue staying with us, but probably it cannot be helped this winter. If he would stay single for a few more years and look around in the world, that would be good. He does not at all know how to get along with people and leaves immediately when strangers are present. Bruns wants to try to find a job for him somewhere, and he himself agrees. If Carl would find a position in Jefferson, he would be pleased and we too.

The teacher Althoff was well received by us all, and Bruns went with him to see some people so that he could start school during the first week. Since that time he no longer lives with us. It did not work out very well with the school. He did not make any effort, and

53. Friedrich Müller, "Westfälische Auswanderer," lists as #941 for 1842, Gerhard Hermann Althoff from Langenhorst, a candidate for a teacher's position, born in 1810.

therefore the people did not send their children. He is a strange character. His abilities are probably not as good as he thinks, and he probably had figured on staying with us permanently, as a private tutor so to speak, but we do not believe that we need him, particularly since he proved himself during the short time he was in our house to be quite indolent and annoying. Since that time he has changed his boarding house a few times, he kept school for a few more months, and when the former teacher, Mr. Krone, applied for the teaching position, Althoff did not even apply himself and has now gone to Jefferson. The schools are being organized now for this district. Bruns is one of the directors. The school property will be sold so that a fund will be available. Pastor Helias was in favor of Althoff because he is Catholic, and it would certainly be desirable to have the children receive instruction in religion. But what can be done? The pastor does not live here permanently.[54] He has completely lost the confidence of the community, he threatens and scolds as usual, he lies and argues so that one would almost have to assume in his defense that he is not quite right in the head. Oh, how sad it is, it will probably never be good again! What do all the treasures of the world help if one thing is lacking: instruction in religion and participation in religion! The old people, to be sure, hold fast, but what about the youth?

November

My letter has been held for a long time again. Recently Niedieck arrived here. We had not heard from him for three years, and we had not taken the trouble to look for him since he had made such insulting remarks concerning us, which I shall not forget. He visited us several times. At first he did not seem drunk, but later he always was. He showed us a great deal of money. He was dressed [illegible]. He said that he had been sick and he looked miserable. We were supposed to believe his statement that he had not drunk for some time and that he had stayed with a Mr. Lensing in the vicinity of Coutre Island[55] on the Missouri. He remarked to Meyer, and to Bruns when asked, that he had something to settle with Bruns because he had found a miscalculation. But it was perhaps only a pretense, for he departed without waiting for Bruns to return from a visit, and earlier he had not been sober enough and therefore delayed the discussion. He took friendly leave from me and made a few excuses; whether he had lost his money, I don't know. He is supposed to have had some seventy dollars in silver and also some gold, and somebody had seen a note. But why do I write all this? —He cursed the first time mightily against the Jesuits, but he said that a Father Walters[56] in St. Charles had taken the trouble to write a letter to Niedieck's relatives that he had dictated, and other things like this. We guess where the money came from! I would not write this to you, except it might be my duty to write; I wish expressly, though, that nothing be said in letters concerning these remarks. Whether his brother likes it that we still write something concerning Heinrich, I don't know, since Heinrich's name could not be found in

54. Father Helias lived in the presbytery of the church until May 1842, when he moved across the Osage River to Taos, at that time called Haarville, where he had established the Church of St. Francis Xavier. Before leaving Westphalia he attached a Latin distich to the church door: "Why does anyone looking for trouble go to the dusky Indians? Let him come to Westphalia, and he'll find trouble enough!"

55. Probably *Loutre Island*.

56. The official *Mission Catalogue* for 1835 lists Cornelius Walters as one of two newly arrived priest novices. In May 1836 he assumed pastoral duties at St. Peter's Parish at Dardenne in St. Charles County, where he served until his death in 1845.

Ferdinand's letters for quite some time. Even though we don't like to, we still think that we should report this. A few weeks ago we heard that Heinrich Niedieck had spoken to various Americans around here of $10,000 and later of $5,000 that Bruns is supposed to owe his father and of which he is depriving him. He also asked an acquaintance how Bruns was considered by the public. What is all this?!

Bruns is hurt that Carl did not bring the bonds along, at least the one over $4,000. To be sure, Bruns would have liked it better if Uncle Caspar would have been satisfied with a handbill for $1,000. Then the entire sum could be liquidated here. You yourself can see that it is necessary, so that we no longer stand here like this. I wish that Bruns would take up the $800 here and send it separately to Niedieck. Since, however, in about a year a big note owed by an American is due that exceeds this amount, Bruns said we would have to carry it for another year. The interest to Uncle Caspar is covered by a draft. I believe Bruns said that there was a little bit lacking. However, as soon as an opportunity offers itself it will be evened out. Our first worry will be to pay back Uncle Caspar. I believe that there are prospects and that we can comfortably believe that it will be returned to our uncle in various installments. I would have little objection if we could sell the entire farm. Our position is not very advantageous nor pleasant, but we are stuck with it.

Tell Uncle Caspar that we are very grateful for his sending the settlement for Uncle Bernhard's estate. Then I also want to thank you for paying the freight back for the things from Bremen. And in addition, I also want to say thanks to all those who have bought the things I ordered, which fit and pleased me very much. You can imagine your godchild in a little bundle of muslin with a frilly top around it. The boy is getting plump and long, so that he pokes his feet out of his little bundle all the time. He is also always so friendly, and smiles just as Rudolph did.

Things are not going very well with our Bernhard. He causes worry to most of us. One almost would have to fear that he will resemble his uncle who recently died. He himself speaks of this, and he has fantasies again and things of that sort, and he fears that these imaginations or fantasies will never leave him. We are now trying to talk him out of marrying, but he does not want to move to Franz and would not like to stay with us either. He wants to get back to his farm, and yet he cannot begin anything alone. So it is hard to advise. We shall have to prevail upon him to plant tobacco with Franz. Even if he does it, then it is against his will, and he can become quite cross. If one is friendly and kind to him he is easy to get along with, but one must have the patience of an angel; he doesn't adjust to anything, he does not accept any advice or he forgets it, and yet he is said to be a good worker. He knows how to handle an ax. He farms with a passion and wants to do all kinds of experiments, and then sometimes he goes to excess and does dumb things which are not suitable for the rough and simple method from which a farmer can make a profit. I mustn't even think about all of this, but I will have to recommend him to the Highest. But there is still no way out!

I still have to note that your letter to Trute was not delivered. By chance I saw the brotherly "Du" and so on, and thus we read it. It really could not be helped. Bernhard, who also calls her "Sie," agreed. You cannot put yourself in our position. One can be quite well inclined toward a person without the "Du."[57] She is very sensitive and is easily offended. The present

---

57. It is customary to use the familiar *Du* when speaking to children and close relatives as well as to very close friends. The more formal *Sie* is used when addressing adults, including persons above the age of fourteen.

pleased her very much!

Here times are amazingly poor. There is no money at all. Farmers cannot sell anything. They all want to plant tobacco or hemp. Franz had hemp this year, and this will earn him something. Perhaps we too shall plant tobacco. The mill does not bring in anything, since no corn can be sold. We would like to leave it standing there. We are glad that we have no expense. We have our own food and no store bills. —We sold our piano for $150 because I did not play anyway. —Since the beginning of November we had rather severe cold and there are many rather sick people. Bruns himself is also at times a little soft. —Now farewell, write pretty soon, give our regards to the brothers and sisters and to all the others. I shall answer the letters I received beforehand and afterward. I have a lot to do, and so sometimes it doesn't go so fast. Bernhard is also supposed to write. Hold dear as always, your sister, Jette.

The others send their greetings.

We just heard today that Carl is quite satisfied in Jefferson; he is asking for smoking tobacco. The legislators are there now and make the city somewhat livelier. My last letter, as well as the newspaper and the letter to Uncle C. from Bruns, must have arrived a long time ago by way of Bremen.

From Heinrich Geisberg: A Fantasy based on Bernhard's Tale

Münster
26 January 1843

Winter night, the Mary is frozen, silver frost covers the forest.
Ha! Let's go out hunting! Bruno, you lick my hands,
Do you hear the howling of the wolves?
You are pulling at my coat and saying:
Put on your shoes, let's go into the forest.
Lonely companion, you were lying so comfortably
At the fireside in the log cabin
And you want to get out.
Look, the rifle is glistening,
You are happy at the light from the lamp.
Ha, Rifle, you give death and rest!
Who is laughing there?
Ha, you! Sister, you laugh into my realm of the dead,
Do not mock; who is snickering there behind the stool?
Bruno, seize it, howl! Do laugh!

But you should not laugh,
That's evil of you,
And you are pushing the knife so sharply
Into my chest, jeeringly.
What did I do to you?
I am not bad, I meant well,
And it is not I who is to be blamed,
Oh, Oh! I was getting so faint

That I sank back to the bed which I had scarcely left.
Oh, Oh! Yes, Bruno, you are faithful to me,
You are the only one,
You kiss me when I have hurt you,
You do not laugh just to hurt me.

Yes, the morning is breaking,
The rifle is cradled in my arm.
Finally I get out and go over the mountains,
Here it is free; here lives Peace, here lives Freedom!
Bruno, do you scent the wolf?
Look, how he crouches and flees.
Here over the branch the valley opens,
The sun shimmers through the forest
Over the trees covered with snow.
What is that? All glitter!
Over there in the ravine, it glitters like silver
Through the morning dawn.
Look, there is the queen of the elves,
The ruler of the forest. Does my glance meet yours?
Woe, if I would know that face?
Oh if you come down into the wilderness,
If you glide over the ocean, here! Oh!

Bruno, what is it? Woe, you have scared her away.
Where am I? What, so these are only dreams of a demented brain?
The vision has disappeared, and the rifle breaks
Through the ice of the brook.
I did indeed see! There she stood, there she soared.
—All life is a dream, no reality,
No longer truth, whether I live, see, think;
Only illusion! Ha, and Hell is rattling in me!
There up the bluff, there it will be freer!
Even the echo is laughing!
Oh, how tired, how worn-out my limbs are
How desolate are my thoughts
And the people are jeering at me.
Ah, my rifle!

You should save me for the truth!

On 12 April 1843 Jette wrote to Uncle Caspar that her brother Bernhard had decided to return to Germany. The family took the occasion of Bernhard's return to send a packet of letters to their relatives at home.

15 May 1843

Dear Heinrich:

Now last, but not least, a few lines to you! You will have wondered why Bernhard suddenly came to his decision. Even though it upsets me, I am rather pleased that he has done this rather than stay and settle on his farm, I think you will set him straight, so that we will receive him back quite active and social. It is not likely that he will stay with you, and I would not want that to happen.

I am happy that you shall see each other and shall chat with each other cozily. I shall be with you in spirit.

Mrs. Bruns is a very wicked woman (Bernhard also knows that); by the way, I would have liked to cross out the thing concerning the stockings, and it was certainly not meant with any evil intention. But I really thought that the purchase would be left in part to you. This makes me sad and therefore the following. —You certainly know that I have an impetuous and critical nature, but it is not very deep and a single word of opposition would change it.

I hope that I can get a letter as soon as Bernhard has arrived, and until that time I shall be in the most painful unrest, especially since he is somewhat unacquainted with travel. If only I could know that he is there already!

It is not possible for me to write more since I don't know more. I would almost have recommended Bernhard to you. But go easy with him. I only know too well that one doesn't get very far with impetuosity with him. Do everything well with him. But no, the Good Lord will have to do that! Your sister, Jette.

It is so annoying to me that I cannot send you anything, but I know of nothing, absolutely nothing.

Westphalia
9 July 1843

Dear Heinrich:

Tomorrow it will be eight weeks since Bernhard departed. He wrote from New Orleans that he intended to sail on the *Caspar* with Captain Spilker during the same week. This was a great relief to us, and I imagine him to be as safe and as well taken care of as possible. We spoke a few times of the fact that he might be arriving with you any day now. How I wish him well from the bottom of my heart, happy that he has the pleasure of seeing all of you again. He will tell you many things about our life and our activities that cannot be written. If he could retell what I would say, you can't imagine all the things I would chat about with you.

To be sure, first I have a lot to tell him myself, and when I think of his return here I feel strangely oppressed. But he himself knows very well what is expected of him here.

The 29th

Tell him very seriously that he should consider how many difficulties and obstacles he will find here. Particularly in the first years, nothing but trouble and continuous worry is waiting for him, and he will probably never succeed very well compared to the smallest farmer who came here. This perhaps is saying too much, for even if he gets so far that he can expect some profit from his cattle and his produce, then he has far more needs than people who have been long accustomed to living in modest circumstances. It takes an extraordinary amount of contentedness to remain calm and happy.

Also, Bernhard set up many plans and schemes that cannot be realized, or at least will not be rewarding, and then the investments will be lost. One finds only too often that Germans invest their money very poorly. If he could get a position in his home country where he could live independently and without worry for sustenance, then it is my warmest wish that he stay there. Franz agrees with me unquestionably. Bruns says, "He will come back," and then he adds, "but he would do well to stay if he could only find his place." And Carl then remarks, "The boy has more things going for him than he knows." It is certain that whenever he tackles something with enthusiasm he can accomplish a great deal. If, however, it is contrary to his inclinations, then he can also get very, very cross. We shall now recommend him to the Guide in heaven, and we shall await calmly what Bernhard decides. To be sure, we expect him back (until we get different word) and we keep talking about his return. It is reasonable for us to hope for this. The three of us want to hold together then and shall rid ourselves of vain wishes to see all of you again. You too, dear Heinrich, will probably do well not to think too much about coming here. It is too difficult. But after a number of years, if the Good Lord protects us, then I shall send you my Heinrich, and then you shall be good to him and look after him for a few years. This would be a good feeling for me for the rest of my life!

Since you like to hear it, the boy is growing very much; he is built very tall and strong, not too heavy. He has been crawling for several weeks and has six teeth, and he is a wild child, more so than the others. His favorite signs of affection are hitting, biting, and tearing. Hermann contributes a lot to the fact that Heinrich is so wild. He also has a mad little head. He is not exactly handsome, it seems to me, but in many ways he resembles the other children—most of all, however, the girl—in the way his face is formed. The stub nose, however, is that of his mother.

There, Bruns sold Bernhard's farm all of a sudden! At the first moment I was so flabbergasted (we, after all, also have land). But now I believe that he has done very well. It is such a good price that it is hard to expect any better and so much will probably not be offered again. If Bernhard stays with you, then it will be welcome. If he returns, then he can get another place wherever he wishes with the money, and I hope that it will not be very far from us.

I hope you will write soon. We often think that Bernhard would certainly not have thought of writing, but when this letter arrives then I hope that one will be ready to be sent to us.

Here everything is well and unchanged. The tobacco has been pinched out, and far and wide there is none that is better. The trees are being hauled to the house. We are in the process of white-washing. Later the well will be started again. Franz and his wife and child are happy. He now takes good care of himself and is not behind in his work; he has beautiful hay and is still busily selling corn. Meeren is getting one load. Mr. Koch is holding school and renewing the old acquaintance. Huber is also beginning a store. Nacke is sick again. Carl will come here next Sunday, and perhaps we will go to a camp meeting.

Farewell and hold dear your sister, Jette.

I am very pleased that the draft for Uncle Caspar is already on its way.

One more thing: if Bernhard comes back, he should use the money we have given him to bring back some broad linen to make bed sheets, and he may have it cut in the proper size so that it will be less of a burden.

Westphalia
14 January 1844

Dear Heinrich:

It is getting time to answer your letters. Bernhard's behavior causes me some grief. I wonder if he will ever get well? Now I firmly believe that he will have to stay in Germany and that it would be better for him there. But Mrs. Bruns thinks that is bad, and I should not say it; Franz is here, you are there, it will not get better in life; quiet, quiet!

Bruns has been constantly on the go this summer and fall, but now it is gradually decreasing. Is it not foolish to be sad about this? We would become rich people if he would have more of such practice. Gradually the money is coming in, but Bruns usually simply takes IOU's. To be sure there was not a house around here in which there were not sick people. We too were sick, but when it is over one has to forget it. It was the ague and bilious fever. We have an amazingly mild winter. Until now the cattle have been almost without feed, foraging in the forest, particularly the hogs.

Bruns found it advisable to sell a big note of one thousand dollars drawn on a certain Hill. Mr. Hill backed out and there was no prospect for payment, not even for collecting the interest. His brother-in-law was forced to sell his Negroes. Bruns took these and a few other notes, and Mrs. Rheane wandered with her four children into the Bruns house. The family is very happy; they have some virtues and many faults. Gradually they will get accustomed to us. We attempt to get settled and get used to not needing a hired hand, but the mill is still in our way. But gradually things will work out!

Often I do not like the total loneliness in which we live. The educated Germans do not get along. Envy and personal interest are only too frequent. I often wish to live among other people, and it is just this which spoils every investment and makes us indifferent.

Our well is not yet finished. The house is only white on the inside; on the outside we have brushed bricks and new pillars. Carl insists that the banister be painted, also the windows and the doors. Mrs. Bruns has the money in her hands; she only lacks a man to do the work. I have taken in the money for the medicine, and this money is mine. Good chairs have been put in the living room from this. Isn't that very good? We all are well. But Heinrich is teething and is a bother. In exchange for his mother taking care of him, he loves her very much. He is getting more reasonable, but he is a wild fellow, not even a little bit tender. He is heavy and hard to carry. He wants to talk and imitates sounds. In the near future, more. Bruns and Franz and his wife send greetings. Write soon again. Your sister, Jette.

P.S. You do not write how you liked the tobacco. Bruns would like to know at what price a manufacturer would buy similar tobacco and what tax would have to be paid. Bernhard has probably forgotten this. Bartmann's father has already written for more.[58]

Heinrich sends his thanks by way of his parents for the favor of the godfather, and his mother believes that his father ought to pay him.

From the Autobiography

In 1844 the Messrs. Zumnorde, Hofius, and both the Gramaticas went to Oregon. Franz Gramatica died on the plains. The others got there and first settled at Walla Walla, but finally moved to California and found acquaintances there.

58. Müller lists three Bartmann brothers—#679, Franz Joseph; #680, Anton Burchard; and #681, Christoph Franz—from Burgsteinfurt, all tanners, as having emigrated in 1839. Anton Bartmann, born 31 July 1809, age thirty, is listed by Father Helias in his 1839 census of Westphalia. According to the abstract map for Township 43R10W, Christoph Franz Bartmann, the youngest, born 7 July 1811, recorded the purchase of land in the northeast quarter of sec. 22, adjacent to land belonging to Bernhard Geisberg and Henriette Bruns, on 14 December 1841.

Time was passing quickly; if only the terrible illness had not appeared again and again! There was always something new, and there was plenty of work. The climatic fever attacks returned again and again. And then cholera struck. St. Louis was empty of people. And from there the cholera spread even to Westphalia. It spread out quickly. Farmers came for medicine so as to be prepared. The town was isolated, and there were only the doctor there, two resolute clergymen, and two strong men who acted as male nurses and later even had to bury the bodies by themselves. Two thirds of the inhabitants succumbed. It was a difficult time. Bruns and I were not spared. But because of the effective remedies and quick action it passed.

In 1847 my sister-in-law had another son, Matthias.[59] She had been sickly for quite some time, and tuberculosis was developing. Soon thereafter she had to go to bed and then suffered for half a year, suffered terribly. The little son died; she was happy about that, and in a few weeks she followed him. After the first grief had been overcome, we realized that Franz could not continue as he was. The girl had to be let go. He brought Caspar and Jette to us and took Heinrich to the grandparents. He sold his farm and with his brother-in-law, Matthias Stievermann, planned to build a distillery. But they did not have enough money, and so he soon gave up and in the spring joined a wagon train of farmers who, here as everywhere else, followed the lure to go looking for gold in California. My brother-in-law Hermann also went. From Westphalia four wagons went, each one hooked up with three yoke of oxen, with food, clothing, blankets, etc. The men were capable and experienced. After many difficulties they arrived there and worked with more or less luck in the gold regions. Zumnorde then joined them and often introduced them to new connections.

Our oldest son, Hermann, had already been sent to St. Louis to the university, a good academy under the direction of the Jesuits. He was there for four years. We became acquainted with several of the professors, among them Father Superior Van de Velde, Elet, Druyts, de Smet, Horstman, and others.[60]

With the help of the Jesuits, plans were made to build a church in Westphalia. The old one, a solid log house, had been too small for quite some time. My husband was charged with directing the construction. A written document (executed by the superior) authorized him to do this. Afterward he had all kinds of unpleasantness about it, which he could never get over.[61]

59. Matthias Geisberg was born 22 January 1847 in Westphalia and baptized 24 January 1847 with Matthias Stiefermann and Gertrudis Schwarze as godparents. He died in June 1847.

60. The priests, all Jesuits, connected with St. Louis University, were as follows: the vice-provincial of the Society of Jesus in Missouri, James O. Van de Velde, who retired from that office in June 1848 and became bishop of Chicago at his consecration on 11 February 1849; Father John A. Elet, who had served as president of the college since 1836 and succeeded Van de Velde as vice-provincial; John B. Druyts, in St. Louis since 1835, professor and disciplinarian for twelve years, was promoted to president in 1853; Pierre Jean De Smet, one of the original members of the Missouri colony of Jesuits who arrived in St. Louis 31 May 1823, joined the college faculty in 1830 as treasurer and instructor of English. No information on Horstman could be located.

61. A letter of 18 July 1850 to Dr. Bruns from Father John A. Elet, S.J., vice-provincial of the Missouri Mission, preserved in the St. Louis University Archives, indicates the depth of the breach between Dr. Bruns and Jesuit officials. Replying to "Your favour of the 29th inst., if favour it can be called," Father Elet writes that Dr. Bruns has "on more than one point greatly misapprehended my meaning." He advances a six-point argument disputing charges that Dr. Bruns had been cheated: "... whether Fr. Helias swindled you out of [illegible] and Fr. Ehrensberger out of 25 dol. we shall see at my [next] visit, but I feel confident you will blush at the expression when in their presence—They swindle you! No, Doctor, I cannot believe it." He adds, "If Father Helias, as you

Cousin Arnold Boner, who gradually had regained his health, bought a place on the Little Maries, which he worked with two hired hands. He had hoped to raise his children there. I saw him less frequently, and then an illness befell him and quickly took him away. I have sad memories of the year 1847.

We built a horse mill. This and the store in the house made things quite lively for us. Next to the house, in a specially fenced area, we had a garden and a little bleaching meadow. Bruns had the soil treated and spread tanners bark on the walks. He supported my desire for a garden. And thus, favored by the location, we had everything earlier than anyone else. We had pretty flowers, which I exchanged with Mrs. Parberry across the Osage; asparagus seed and other things were sent to me by Senator Benton. Already we were harvesting all kinds of fruits from the many fruit trees. It pleased Bruns tremendously to share some of the pretty peaches with other people. He had built a dam in the river, which made it possible for us to catch a great number of fish after a flood. I had a few other hobbies that I was able to satisfy, such as cooking soap and dyeing things blue. When the wool was a pretty blue it was mixed with white and then interwoven. This yarn, which was spun on a big wheel, was excellent.

In town there was now a family from Hesse—older people. The woman often helped us with our laundry and other work. We got along well together with anything that came up. She was also our only nurse when our children died and when other people were afraid to help. In August 1847 we had a boy, a very delicate, early plant. We wanted to name him Adolf. I was sick, and he died in spite of the anxious care which I devoted to him for over eight days. Thus we had three cases of death in that year, first our sister-in-law, then a cousin, and then a little son.

Bruns took care of his practice as always, but it also happened frequently that he came back feeling sick. He would have fever and an intolerable headache. Often he would lie in a dark room and could not stand the least noise. Then I was very careful, because I knew what to do for him and what to offer him. He was easily satisfied. I only returned the attention to him that he had always given me in the big and small sufferings to which I had been exposed many times. And how good had been the feeling when he brought me some refreshment and sat down beside me on my bed.

Our Louis was born on 17 July 1848. He was a strong boy; however, during the first week he caught a fever and cramps. We would have lost him, but Father's great care saved him. Afterward, however, he was very miserable, and I also.

We received photos from our brothers and sisters, and they wished to have little pictures of us too. There was a studio in Jefferson City, and so we prepared to travel there. It was before the departure of my brother for California and he accompanied us. In the evening we were to visit first in Jefferson City with the Haars, who lived in the bottom. The neighbor Mr. Tergenson had a bear on a chain in front of the house. This startled the horse that Bruns was riding and so he dismounted to quiet it, but in the turmoil that ensued the horse stepped on his foot. The bone was broken. When we arrived at the Walters it was difficult to take off his

say, interferes in politics, he acts wrongly, because contrary to his rules—I will inquire concerning this matter." An earlier letter from Father P. J. De Smet to Dr. Bruns of 26 March 1850 acknowledges receipt of Dr. Bruns's letter to Reverend Elet pertaining to money matters and reports that Father Ehrensberger had been authorized to draw on Father Elet for "the making of pews, sanctuary railing, etc.," promising that as soon as the work was completed Father Ehrensberger's draft would be promptly honored.

boot. We lodged there. All night long I made ice packs after we had put on some dressing. The next day he helped himself with a crutch and went by wagon to the photographer. Bruns's picture turned out well—only a little severe, as brother Heinrich later remarked. My picture was not clear because I had cried all night and was not able to keep my eyes steady. And thus on the picture there may well be a youthful figure, but the features are fuzzy. Brother Franz looked like a Moor. And so we gave up and naturally had to return home by wagon. And now my Lord sat in the house for several months. That was boring. At that time young Randolph Benton came to us, and he was some entertainment to Bruns, who instructed him in various subjects. The young man respected my husband very much and was also very polite to me. It was, however, embarrassing to me to have this guest at the table since it was common custom with us to have the hired hands eat with us. This could not be changed, and the young man's father had expressly requested that our household should not be upset. Young Benton remained for a year and a half, took lessons with the clergyman, and was otherwise unassuming and happy. The stay with us probably would not have harmed him, but at the request of his mother he went to Boonville. He planned to return to us the following year, but he suddenly caught cold and unexpectedly died.

Our children went to the parish school—Heinrich, Effie, Albert, and the two Geisbergs. Bruns frequently had unpleasant dealings with the new priest, and therefore he withdrew as much as possible, but he did not want to yield to the narrow-minded views. The medical practice became too much for him too, and therefore in 1851 he moved to the big farm he owned on the Osage at Shipley's Ferry. Our Hermann, who was still studying for his last year in Columbia,[62] promised to give him active assistance. In the fall Bruns went over there with him and the Negro family while I remained in Westphalia with the little ones because of school and other business that had to be taken care of. We had three rooms while the rest of the house was rented to the Porth family, who had just arrived.[63] Bruns was usually with us on Sundays. Then in the spring we all moved over there. As soon as the weather permitted, the four bigger children again went to school in Westphalia every day, in spite of the ferrying across the Osage, which made it bothersome. Albert studied with me. In the summer he got the fever, and we lost him from a sunstroke on the 24th of August 1851.[64]

25 September 1844

Dear Heinrich:

Bruns is indicating that this page is for me, and so I'll start a new letter. My husband could not get around to writing for a long time, and since you were expecting news from him my little note was not mailed.

It is, I think, somewhat strange that I am writing only now that we have a little girl.[65] She is

62. "Hermann Louis Bruns from Osage County" is listed as a sophomore in *The Ninth Annual Catalogue of the Officers and Students of the University of the State of Missouri for the Year Ending 4 July 1851* (Columbia: Statesman's Office, 1851), p. 10.

63. The widowed Anna Maria Porth with her eight children, ages 8 through 25, arrived in Westphalia late in 1850. The Porth family had acquired large parcels of land in February 1849 and June 1850 and had apparently made arrangements to have a stone house built prior to their arrival in Osage County. The residence is still standing across the highway from Westphalia.

64. Albert Bruns, born 11 December 1845, died 24 August 1851. Jette wrote: "He had forgotten to put on his little hat."

65. Euphemia, called Effie, was born 3 May 1844.

a tiny child. Bruns still maintains that she was probably not any bigger than Heinrich was when he was born. Now, however, she is quite plump and so friendly and good. She seems to wait only for one to look at her to laugh. This was quite useful to me during the last few months when poor Heinrich always wanted to be in his mother's lap. Just imagine, the boy crushed his right index finger; the nail came off once, twice. It continued festering and swelled as big as my thumb. Day and night he had wound fever. Now he is almost completely healed, but the finger is shorter; the part down to his first joint is lost. It worries me that much more since I believe I should have paid more attention to it in the beginning. Bruns says, however, that the bone was probably hurt from the very beginning. I am reluctant to look at him when he has his hand open and I have to look at the little stump.

Bruns has not been very strong this summer. Riding in the heat is hard on him, but his patients do not give him any rest. The fever this year is very bad. Many of the newly arrived people from the area of Borken[66] died. They arrived here too late and probably got the germ of the illness in New Orleans. It is too apparent that the ones who remained are [illegible] and ill and can naturally not expect any harvest and for the next year will have to sell everything they have. Some of them are completely without means.

Franz and family and we are well. Everything is fine on the Mary; it did not flood at all. But we did have backwater up to the branch here, which Bernhard will consider very strange.

Bernhard is not writing at all, and yet we hear that he attended the Pentecost Ball in Stromberg. What is with him? Should he not have enough strength to persist in his subject even if it does not appeal to him at this time? He is too unstable. He goes too far both ways. It is hard on me when our uncle, as well as the Hüffers, maintain that his stay here was detrimental for him. Quite frequently I have wished that both brothers had stayed in Germany. If they would be better off than we I could take it more easily than the other way around.

If I could only satisfy my longing to see you! You write of Huber, etc., and I cannot visualize it at all. Well, we will see each other again! And if another ten years should pass I am not at all troubled by this and I will not give up. But the grim reaper must not come.

When I saw Uncle Adolf last he spoke of seeing us again, and I did not have any doubts.

Zumnorde, Hofius, and Gramatica have really gone now with the great wagon train to the Oregon Territory. Hofius wrote from a fort on the upper Platte River that missionaries were there. Many solid Americans from this area want to go there next year to settle. But we do not. If we would ever want to change our place of residence, we would move to an area that is more populated.

Well, farewell! Give our regards to the uncle and to all the others. Do write me a long, friendly letter and then you shall have an equally long answer from your sister, Jette.

Johanna could really write too sometime; she now has three little children?[67]

66. Borken, a town approximately thirty miles west of Münster.
67. Carl Offenberg, Johanna's second child, born 14 February 1843 in Ahlen, died 4 August 1868 in Münster from the bite of a rabid hunting dog. He was an assistant judge. Johanna's third child, Albert, born 15 July 1844 in Ahlen, died 13 June 1847.

Westphalia
18 April 1845

Dear Heinrich:

I scarcely know what I should write since I would like to consider all of you. First: Mr. Anton Bartmann, the carrier of these letters, will, I hope, visit you personally. He is the brother of our partner and such a very compassionate, good man as there are probably very few over here. He is simple and straight and immensely practical; I ask you to be particularly friendly and courteous to him. He will probably not stay in Germany very long (he seems to need a wife! psst!).

When you give the little letters to the brothers and sisters, do tell them that they will have to answer right away, and then send the notes to Bartmann because he is prompt; therefore do not tarry.

Now to answer your questions: Meyer still does not have a desire to go back to Germany; he lives on a farm, collects whatever he can, lives frugally always by baking buckwheat pancakes and frying bacon. I would think that this would be boring. But he is somewhat outrageous; he has a new coat and a pair of pants at the tailor's (it is his first good clothing since he left home), and it is said that he is doing this in consideration of the Easter season. Do not betray my gossip!

The day after tomorrow our pastor Helias will come, and it is reported that he will stay here for several days so that the pious Christians will have an opportunity to be converted. Our congregation is more numerous than any other, but we have few divine services; to be sure the pastor has a lot of traveling, for he has seven churches to take care of. His headquarters is on the other side of the Osage with his favorite people.[68] There he has had a stone church built. There are not many people there, and in addition to that, there is some dissension. —The people here long very much for regular religious services, but he has given the petition, which is addressed to the bishop, to his superior, and the latter has not answered. Father Helias is quite right when he says that the people will have to side with him, because otherwise he could not help them. However, Mr. Bartmann can tell you more and better about this!

Our Hermann is practicing his English and is even studying Latin in the company of a young man who wants to become a doctor. Thus he will stay another year here at home. Recently he has not learned so well because he has all kinds of foolishness in his head. Niedieck's wife held school here for three months. The boy does not seem to have any great urge to farm, and therefore it is high time that he learns something well! If our children do not want to become farmers, what advantage does country life have for us?

We now have a good hired hand, who helped Bernhard earlier. A black girl is the only

68. See note 54 above. On the front page of the Latin Missal in the church at Rich Fountain, Father Helias wrote a Latin distich dated 3 December 1842: "Flanders begot me; I studied in France; / In Rome, Germany, and Switzerland I sojourned for a time; / After various hardships, and perils on land and sea, / I came to you; on a solid foundation I built Westphalia, / And erected seven temples to the glory of the Most High." The churches he founded were St. Joseph at Westphalia; St. Francis Xavier at Taos, in Cole County; Sacred Heart at Rich Fountain, at that time in Gasconade County; St. Ignatius in Jefferson City; The Church of the Assumption at Cedron, Moniteau County; St. Thomas the Apostle at Indian Bottom, Cole County; and the Church of the Immaculate Conception at Loose Creek in Osage County. Father Helias worked among the immigrant settlers for over thirty-six years. He died at Taos on 11 August 1874.

colored person in the house. We did not like the Negro family, and thus Bruns got rid of them again. The money is safely and securely in the county fund and is only paid back gradually.

It makes me sad when Uncle Caspar thinks that you were surprised that we had some blacks. To be sure, I do not feel very good about it either. The blacks are frequently good for nothing. Our Mary, however, loves the children and is always very cheerful. I would not like to be without her for anything. The white girls are very pretentious and rarely stay very long. Last summer we had a good girl, but after three months she had to marry although she had been hired for a longer period of time. Oh, you people who are not at all capable of helping yourselves, you can easily talk! How often have I said that I would rather preside over the household alone if only I could live alone with my husband and children!

Part of the people from the area of Borken have gone to Wisconsin, and part have moved here. They arrived during the heat of the summer. The water had risen in all the rivers and brooks and tainted many farms. Twice people arrived here. The first ones were doing fairly well; the later ones, however, Heaven only knows why, became ill, and most of them have died. A few orphans have been taken care of nearby. The illness wiped out whole families. The sea voyage seemed to have weakened them considerably. It was horrible! Otherwise there were no cases of death here.

Have you seen the subscription list by Ferd. Wenner, who wanted to publish a newspaper from Borken concerning America and the emigrants? He approached Bruns as a friend of his youth to send him news reports, and he did not seem to doubt at all that he would find subscribers here. I believe that Bruns has too little time to accommodate him. The Germans here do not spend money for newspapers these days. There the undertaking will also find little appeal now, I imagine.

We are still quite well. Bruns now goes every day if possible and drinks a glass of beer, which earlier was hard to come by, and he feels very well doing this. My humble self is afraid of the fever, and I do everything according to the rules in order to prevent any symptoms.

Our Heinrich is growing mightily, but he is still staying strong. For his age he is quite smart. If he continues he can come to something in this world. The little girl is quite fussy and is already hitting Heinrich. She is not as pretty as Johanna, even though she is not ugly. It is, however, good that she is not too much of an angel, for otherwise we might spoil her.

The widow Schwarze saw her Bernhard die of a stroke a little while back. It is too hard! I believe I could not survive such setbacks. It happened on the second anniversary of the death of her husband. All her support is gone now. She has four girls and a three-year-old boy, Wilhelm, who are everything to her. She is, however, a very strong woman and is rather composed again. In the beginning she wanted to return to Germany. I told her that if I were in her place I would do this too, but Bruns said it is better for her and for the children here. Now she has a hired hand, she herself works along with the children, and they do what they can.

We have a young man in the house, Dr. Gibson, who assists Bruns and receives instruction from him, particularly in the practice. Hermann is taking English instruction with Gibson, and both of them together are taking instruction in Latin from Father. Mrs. Bruns has recently made some progress in the English language by reading many English books. This makes it so much easier for me in speaking and understanding that I am amazed. I can already converse rather extensively, and I enjoy doing this. I would never have thought that I would ever get so far with so little trouble and loss of time. Bruns is subscribing to a monthly journal, a so-called "Ladies Book," with pictures, etc., for me.

Now the entire letter is full. In the future I shall write more. If you would follow my example, what, I wonder, could I expect?

Hold dear as always your sister, Jette.

On 14 April 1845 Jette wrote to her brother Bernhard with local news, and throughout the year Dr. Bruns corresponded with the Geisbergs on business matters.

Westphalia
20 February 1846

Dear Heinrich:

Here we have had a New Year again before I ever had a chance to write. Letters via Uedink and a later one from Uncle Caspar arrived here a rather long time ago and have been answered by Bruns. Now we are waiting for letters carried by Bartmann, who has arrived here safely. For the time being we have the assurance that in general you are well. Bartmann has written for his effects. The rivers were too low for the steamboats. He arrived by mail coach with his young wife.

We are particularly anxious for news concerning Bernhard, who was not mentioned by Bartmann. I do not at all know the arrangements in such an institution,[69] and I think it would be easier for me if I knew exactly how he is being treated. My idea of it is to be imprisoned within four walls, to be alone, with iron bars in the windows, with a locked door, etc.—it is hard to be so far away. I often think it might be better if he were still with us, and I could encourage him and do this and that for him. You will have to write exactly how he acts. I hope that you will visit him now and then, and Johanna will have to make up her mind to do the same if the doctor approves. Please do not always leave him so alone! I have compared his condition often with that of Arnold,[70] who was completely off the track and continued to be, even while he was improving, and has not yet completely gotten well. Arnold has suffered tremendously. He was mentally very much affected, which was probably the main cause of this long-lasting illness. He can now usually rise by himself and can also walk without a cane for a short distance, and he has a good appetite and is gaining. He had become so skinny. So far a kind fate has kept his mind hazy; the last events before his departure have completely escaped his memory, and he speaks quite frequently with great love of his children, whom he wants to send for. His circumstances seem to him to be the same old ones. We have remained quiet until now, and do not dare mention anything unpleasant to him. But this cannot last very long. Bruns is waiting for him to offer an opportunity to discuss in detail his plans. I wonder if a good end can be foreseen? Scarcely. He is too spoiled to be able to make it here as a simple farmer. In the beginning this possibility seemed better. He causes us a great deal of concern. When he has progressed a little more, he will surely leave us. Bruns is too serious and too modest a man for him, and when he is alone—we will hope for the best!

69. Bernhard Geisberg had been committed to the State Mental Hospital at Ober-Marsberg, south of Paderborn, where he was to spend the rest of his life.

70. Arnold Boner died on 27 July 1847 after a prolonged illness.

The 11th of December brought us a little boy, who was baptized Albert. He is a small, dainty little fellow with a pointed nose and blond hair. Arnold thought for sure that he would resemble his father most, and I also maintained this. He has already grown and I am well again.

Last year was not good here. We all had to bear our share. I had a light, bilious fever, but afterward I felt fairly good. The children had the same. Little Effie suffered for a long time from the consequences. Now, however, they are quite well and have thick red heads. The same holds true for Franz's children, who never looked so well as they do now. Bruns fared the worst because he had to ride out so frequently. With every new exertion he again attracted some illness, so that he could not ride out this winter except in the most urgent cases. His body seems to have weakened during the last few years, and it can be assumed that he cannot continue his rather arduous practice as extensively as he has. I wish that we could live in a city where he would not have to make so many visitations out of town.

Around Easter, Bruns intends to take our Hermann to St. Louis to the Jesuit College. It costs a good bit, but we have no opportunity closer by, and Bruns insists that he should learn something well, to which I interject that it is so far for a child of his age. I hope that it will go well.

March 5th

Yesterday your and Marie's letter of December arrived. Presumably therefore Bartmann has no letters; he did not know this.

The Missouri is still low. We had deep snow with great cold, down to sixteen degrees. Now the sun has almost melted away the snow, and it is an awful mess.

You probably have received the answers to the various points in your letter by now. On the other hand, you should not be praised for always writing such short little notes and then forgetting the long letter. It often occurs to me that I know so little of you, of what you are doing and what you are thinking, which people you like best, and what occupies you most. It cannot interest me so much, but one likes to hear more about it. If Mrs. Bruns is in a bad mood, then she thinks you will stop writing completely, and then she would also have to stop thinking. This could then, however, cause consumption! When the portraits are here, which do take so long, and Uedink's suitcase arrives, then I shall write again. Uedink is a strange man. Is he a drinker? Or was he really so careless that all his money was stolen? He has nothing but a sack and does not even inquire whether the suitcase has arrived. He is staying with Holtermann and instructs the children, but he will soon have to start something else. He is known for his lies. Now farewell! Do write concerning Bernhard, how he behaves, and what he thinks of himself. The cold was hard on Arnold; otherwise one would think that he would have to gain with all his appetite. But his feet are still swollen. The construction of his house occupies most of his time. He makes drawings, he makes computations, etc., day after day. Then he works with Hermann on his Latin, his essay.

Do not forget your Jette.

Westphalia
20 May 1846

Dear Brother Heinrich:

You will by now have our letter that was written after Bartmann's arrival. Since that time we have received the portraits and the books. At first it touched me tremendously to see you so vividly in front of me; first I stole a glance at the picture of the three of you, and then I had to wait a good while before I could look again. Then, however, I could not tire of it. You are the same, and I would recognize even Wilhelm and Thereschen among hundreds. When I look at your faces like this, I feel that you are related to me and I can chat with you as if I had not been away from you at all, and a soft voice whispers in response to sad longing. So there you are all together, but where is Bernhard? This struck me immediately.

When he saw your portrait, Hermann said, "He looks just like Uncle Franz." Johanna must pretty much resemble me. Your best thanks must be my assurance that the pictures are the dearest thing to me that you could have sent me in all of the world.

Uedink's belongings have still not arrived, and a new tracer has been sent. Franz did not seem to share my joy, for in general he is often somewhat dry, and it annoyed me; later, however, he said he should also have something, and I felt sorry for him then, for I could not give him any one of these and did indeed have the first right to them. But I still had two silhouettes of father and mother that were copied by Schilking[71] and are really the property of Bernhard, and these we put in a little frame and he took them along.

Franz is becoming a regular farmer; he can hardly talk about anything except the fields and his cattle. His wife has him somewhat in control but not always. She is not suited to cheer him up, which he probably needs. Since I am already at it, I will have to tell you that they are not getting along as well as some other people, and I blame his wife for this. She is often moody and always believes herself to be ill.[72] She is not strong, is untidy, which causes many things to get run down, and is conceited. At times I have taken it upon myself to assist them, which Franz accepted without any trouble, but it hurt his better half even though it was so little and was tactfully done. Franz is really plugging away; he is extremely economical and is satisfied with that. But she is not satisfied, and she economizes because she has to. Well, look how black it now looks on paper! But you can share such worries with me, and then it makes me feel better. I will tell you that it embitters my life here. I cannot stand it that Franz is so far behind us.

Bruns does a lot in order to make it as comfortable here as possible. We are as well situated, indeed better situated, as in Oelde; we have furniture, and even some luxuries, such as a carpet, a fine lamp, vases, etc. I have also acquired more dresses, even though, to be sure, compared to those in Germany they are simple. But all of this does not please me. I could give it up without a thought if I could only wish him more comfort. Franz, I believe, would be happy about everything we have, and he knows no envy. But if his wife is not envious, then she nevertheless always has wishes and wants. I would like to live far away from them, and yet I would not like to leave him behind! Nevertheless, I will certainly not deny that she has also many a good quality, and many things have already changed. I am pleased that both of them have an active social relationship with Bruns's brother Hermann, who has a magnificent wife who can be much more effective than I. —You see, dear Heinrich, this is all only for you, and I am already sorry that it is written down.

This spring Bruns took our Hermann to St. Louis. He did not want to put up with

71. Heinrich Schilking (1815–1895), a landscape painter with titles of court painter and professor, was a friend of Heinrich Geisberg. Some of his works are on display in the City Museum of Braunschweig and the *Landesmuseum* in Münster.

72. Franz's wife Gertrude was already seriously ill at this time. She died of consumption in the summer of 1847.

teaching him any longer. Hermann recently wrote and is already more satisfied. We have also written to him already, the first letter to our son! I was pleased that Bruns was so interested, and I could recall so vividly how the letters from my parents had cheered me. I have saved all of them. Hermann lives in the Jesuit College with many other students. There are vacations from July until 1 September. Therefore he will come back in two months, which is quite good for the start.

Arnold Boner's health is not quite as desired. Bruns says he will probably never be quite well. When he had his first walk out, he wanted to rent a room immediately with the Hubers, but we protested, and he agreed right away that he would stay, as we wished, until he was completely recovered. His memory has become very much weakened. For quite some time now he has wanted to return to Germany. We cannot hold him back, and we are very sorry. Even before you wrote I have often thought of our good aunt, and we have made it our duty to practice consideration and patience. His getting settled here has been delayed because of his illness, although he constantly made plans and calculations.

June 2nd

The volunteers from our county are, much to their annoyance (there were already too many troops), back again, but they still hope like many in other counties to receive a call to move to Sante Fe. Everywhere there is a great deal of commotion, and many lies and exaggerations are in circulation. However, serious men also speak of England and Oregon. Bruns thinks that the Mexicans would not be able to hold out long.

Cousin Carl has written and is in good spirits; he praises the city, and even invited Bruns to come there. He has begun a men's clothing store with a G. Brosius. He was going to write to Münster immediately.

Bruns is pretty much immobilized, but his wife is easily stirred up. I do not like farm life at all anymore. I long for peace. It does not bring me anything but a great deal of trouble. However, I have to see that my displeasure does not gain the upper hand, for we have gotten too far here.

Our whole clan is well. Albert is a genuine Bruns and is tall and stout but tremendously lively. Hermann is doing very well in college and has already written three times.

Do write concerning Bernhard and do not delay too long. Hold dear your sister, Jette.

P.S. I will soon answer the sisters and Wilhelm.

Westphalia
6 September 1846

Dear Heinrich:

Our last letters crossed in the mail, and this one might do so again; otherwise it will be so long before we hear from you again. Quite some time ago I had written very diligently to you, but following the advice of Bruns I let it lie for a while. Now I only want to mention a few things from your letter. I was very annoyed at Arnold Boner, and I thought we could not stand it any longer. Now matters have changed so much that he has moved away from us without any ill feeling. He has hired Franz Mertens, Bernhard's former helper, and besides hired a boy to do the cooking. Since Arnold has written quite some time ago to Max[73] that he

---

73. Max Boner, Arnold's brother, born in 1809, became treasurer in Hovestadt.

should take care of the settlement or, as they say, should arrange it, you will probably have been freed of this bothersome business by now. He thinks that he still has a claim to a pension. I think that he must be given a clear account of his situation by Max. Many a thing has disappeared from Arnold's memory. Bruns restrains him from many things; to be sure, that's over now since we are living separately. I wonder if his relatives could not write to him a bit more? Who knows whether he will not need their care at some time?

Our Hermann spent his vacation from the middle of July till September with us. I saw him depart with a heavy heart since he did not really want to go. He is kept very much by himself at this institution. He brought a prize in arithmetic home.[74] —We are all tolerably well except for little Effie, who has had fever for some time. Bruns is also getting stouter and stronger again. We are happy that health conditions in general are good here, otherwise it would perhaps be too much for him again. His assistant, Dr. Gibson,[75] has gone to Sante Fe as a lieutenant.

Uedink's trunk has arrived. The dress lay right in the middle between his old pieces of clothing and was all wrinkled and soiled. The silk kerchiefs of which you write and which he now also mentions were not there. He is also missing all his better clothing. He was very angry at the prank that had been played on him. I hope you will write to August Uedink, for we gave him our complete confidence since we had firm recommendations from him. I do not doubt that his mother or August Uedink will remedy the situation, since their son and brother will no longer be a burden to them and can easily take care of himself. August has to consider that his recommendation could not be ignored by us, or otherwise he should have added a "but." Bruns is quite irritated at this.

18 October

I have waited a good while. In the meantime two letters arrived, from you and from Aunt Boner respectively. While reading her letter Arnold cried very much. For the time being I do not like to write to her. Assure our aunt that we, particularly Bruns, will do what is possible for him. However, there are a few considerations which (among us) we cannot disregard. To flatter him into living again with us? Is this demanded? No more for now!

This past week we had the visit from our bishop[76] that had been promised us for a long time. Since he, as well as the superior, stayed with us, you can understand that we had a great deal on our minds. The bishop confirmed and dedicated the new cemetery. He is a very fine and kind gentleman, Irish by birth, perhaps of high birth, and was called Lordship. Mrs. Bruns participated in the conversation in English, which amazed the gentlemen. Superior van de Velde, a Belgian, did not have the effervescence of his predecessor Verhaegen, but he was otherwise a very lively and dignified man (he is Hermann's superior). A lot is expected

74. The Catalog of the St. Louis Academy for 1847–1848, p. 6, lists Hermann Bruns as the first of five students receiving honorable mention in arithmetic, p. 18.

75. Records in the Adjutant General's office in Jefferson City list William B. Gibson, a sergeant in Capt. Augustus Rainey's company, Osage Volunteers, as having reported at St. Louis 21 May 1846. They were declined for muster in the U.S. service and, after eight days, were sent back. In her letter of 18 April 1845 Jette noted that Dr. Gibson was living in their home and assisting Dr. Bruns.

76. Rev. Peter Richard Kenrick, a native of Ireland, attached to the diocese of Philadelphia, was the pastor of St. Mary's Church. He received the episcopal consecration from Bishop Rosati in Philadelphia on 30 November 1841 and arrived in St. Louis in December to assume the duties of bishop as successor to Bishop Rosati. The latter followed a call to Rome, where he died 25 September 1843.

of the bishop now, and a deputation expressed our very serious desire to have a permanent clergyman here. The gentlemen promised to send one as soon as one could be had who knows how to speak German. He said that they had written to Germany to ask for a clergyman without success, but now they expected two. The bishop declared himself very inclined to let one clergyman come to this community and to leave him here, but he did not want to promise in advance. Now, as always, we live in hope.

We were tolerably well during this fall, and since we had a good frost last night we believe that we have escaped all evil harbingers. The children are growing very well, they are quite lively, and Heinrich is already speaking more reasonably. The little girl begins to chat (late enough) and usually talks a goose Latin. The little rascal is Albert—but when I read your letter over again I almost had to assume that you did not understand who Albert is, for otherwise you would have mentioned him—therefore: on the 11th of December the seventh child of the Bruns couple saw the light of the world. He is a genuine Bruns; his mother is quite proud to see the lost children replaced by such a good boy. Albert is a family name in the Bruns genealogy. The name of our third brother awakened memories that were too sad, and I also did not want to skip over it. Christoph Bartmann is the godfather. The little rascal Albert is a busybody, so lively, so full of energy and quick that we always have to laugh how quickly he can slide from one spot to another; soon he will be able to walk. Mrs. Bruns often has her troubles with the three Pandours;[77] they all want to be served at the same time, and mother is to do it herself with each and every one, which, to be sure, secretly pleases her. When I now go out to the farm or go to Franz's or into the neighborhood, they all go along, and Effie likes to be carried back. They both try to sing. Heinrich is already imitating me. When the bishop was here they had caught a cold, and thus I had to do my best during the night to keep them quiet (they had fever), and during the day there was quite some commotion. Such unaccustomed guests cause all kinds of trouble, as satisfied as they were with simple things. Then we had also asked a few people in for the noon meal every day. On the second day Bruns had to go out and I was getting scared, but he soon came back. I often had to laugh at our help, and often I was annoyed with them at the table. Her husband wished Mrs. Bruns would keep more quiet, but this was not agreed upon. Here in the country such celebrations cost very little extra. We had most of it ourselves—turkey, veal, chicken, etc. The gentlemen drink very little wine.

So your letter pleased me; one cannot always write about things that are significant. I am always afraid to write nonsense, and I often think that we have little to talk about here. You will surely be indulgent now and then if I express things somewhat peculiarly. I am very pleased when you write that you are not quite a stranger to the ladies. Why should you not feel at home in any social surroundings? Your aspirations go only up to us? Oh ho! I should hope so, and wish that you will afford your brothers and sisters who are so far away from you the first place for a few more years. To be sure, you have more of a prospect that you can see us again than we have that we will see all of you there. Just once in our lives again. Well, let's be quiet!

But now it occurs to me—why doesn't the junior barrister Geisberg take his state examination? Do write me about this; it would be better if you would have passed it. However,

77. The Pandours, a Croatian regiment in the eighteenth-century Austrian army, was known for its plundering and cruelty.

you probably have your reasons. But for Heaven's sake do not become too serious and sad! I wish you had my good spirits (however, I should not brag) or that I could chat with you every day. Well, my little brother will have to stop brooding and should not avoid social life. Do look nicely into the faces of the pretty girls and then go on! Aunt Jenny[78] wrote into my album: "If the clouds of melancholy surround you, look up to the stars and raise your sinking courage, etc."

I am glad Thereschen is enjoying her young life. If I could only see her again! I have recently thought that if we would like to visit Germany we must try to do it in about four or five years. And so it is high time that we begin to fatten our purse. Well, let us see! It is curious that I cannot give this up while Franz certainly must have done so. His wife was somewhat sickly, but otherwise things went well recently. Did not Franz put a little note to Uncle Caspar or to you in a letter? I certainly think he did. It is not worth remembering, and so now I have held back this letter. It would do me so much good if Uncle Caspar would think of him; he should rather forget us. I believe I have not written to our uncle for quite some time, and you have to tell him therefore some of the things from this letter. I will soon catch up in order to have the pleasure of getting an answer from him. And now, concerning Bernhard. Before your letter arrived I was already calmer, and Bruns told me about such institutions and that Bernhard would not belong in a bad one. By now you will have visited him, and I hope you will write soon. How he will appreciate it when he sees you! I will certainly also see him again! And now concerning his affairs: the notes you sent I have already received from him, and they have been taken care of with some others that stayed here. Bernhard's horse, with the harness, was sold for $27 by Bruns; the pony is still here (Bruns sold our gelding for $8). There were a few other implements (the owner of the farm did not want to leave the bedstead), and we had left everything standing in case he should return. However, last year we saw no pressing reason to sell, and Bruns also thought that Franz and I might take the things since we had done so much for Bernhard; the trip to New Dortmund to visit Bernhard when he was sick and alone at the Mallinckrodts alone, the expense of which Bruns and Franz shared, amounted to this much. Thus Franz took the bedding and I took the saddle, the ax, etc. If now from the price of the farm, including the interest and the horse, $570 can be gotten (naturally the debts will have to be deducted), then $96 was still to be deducted from the $206. The remainder must have been spent before Bernhard's departure. At any rate Bruns thinks that his computation must be correct, and now you know how it is to be done.

Arnold Boner was here and wanted to go on to St. Louis to make purchases for his establishment here, but a few words from Bruns sufficed to make him give up his trip. At any rate it was too much of a risk because of his poor health. You cannot believe how he has lost his mental powers. Since I last saw him he has not improved; on the contrary, he is duller and does not speak as much as he did when he was with us. If Bruns did not hold him back, he would make strange business deals. It is too sad, for if he were still completely reasonable one could still hope, but as the situation is now, nothing good can be expected. It is good fortune that his Franz[79] takes care of him and also tries to prevent, if possible, his being taken advantage of.

78. Jenny Westendorf Geisberg (1778–1832), wife of Franz Heidenreich Geisberg, lived in Cappenberg near Lünen (Westfalen).

79. Franz Mertens, the hired hand.

Farewell then, dear Heinrich, give our regards to the brothers and sisters and all to whom these regards from me may be welcome. Your loving sister, Jette.

The last issue of the Milwaukee *Banner* contained a pompous announcement of beautiful things available from Geisberg and Brosius. You would laugh if I would repeat them.

Westphalia
20 April 1847

Dear Heinrich:

We expect letters from you, but I will have to take advantage of the opportunity now. Mr. Christoph Bartmann is our new partner, as you know. I do not doubt that you will like him, for he is rather vivacious. And you will not fail to meet him so that he will be able to tell me about it.

Since I last wrote you we have had some news and also had to experience some very sad things. Trute, Franz's wife, had a little boy last January. On the third day she got a fever, and this kept on, was then dispelled, then returned again—in short: she is suffering from consumption and is very low. Already she cannot move a single limb of her body; she has swollen feet and arms, has to be fed, has to lie on her stomach because her back is sore, and she is emaciated to a skeleton. This is really some disease. I feel very sorry for Franz; he is quite patient and usually cares for her himself; they do have a good girl. And that poor little boy! He is thin, has a cough, but is always eating well. I shall probably soon go and get him over here. The poor, sick woman still has a good appetite, but Bruns tells me that some people with consumption eat to the very end. Bruns called this to Franz's attention. When I left yesterday Franz followed me out and complained to me. He had still had some hope. I tried to encourage him and reminded him to do everything that was possible because this would certainly ease his mind somewhat; and in the end—I could not do differently—I still spoke of recovery.

Oh, it will do no harm if he continues to hope to the end! It is always a hard thing for me to go over there, and this has been going on for the past three months. It makes me feel so sad. And she likes it so much when I am there. The soup I cook is the best, and I have to bake this and that for her. Also, my words seem to carry more weight, and she becomes calmer when I try to console her, and she no longer complains so much. On her name-day I gave her a little Madonna as a present. She was as pleased as a child, she shouted with joy, she told everybody and showed it to everybody who came.

And what will happen later? Four little children! I don't know, and I also fear so much for myself. We will have to let our Good Lord take care!

We went to St. Louis for a few days, Bruns and I. It was the first time in ten years I had seen the city; however, nothing was strange to me, neither the people nor the houses nor the traffic and the crowds in the streets. Or am I too dull? One thing touched me tremendously: the music mass in the College Church on Easter morning. Was it the music I had not heard in such a long time, was it the view of a big church and the solemn service I had been doing without, or was it the reunion with our oldest, whom we had just seen shortly before and whom we took along? However, the Mass and the sermon that was inserted lasted too long; in the end it was embarrassing enduring it, and I did not feel well . . .

The end of this letter has been lost.

The following enclosure was written after the death of Franz's wife, Gertrude.

I am not capable of writing to Wilhelm now. It has cost me too much effort to get this far.

I will also write to our uncle later. I hope that you will seal these letters and take care of them by taking them to the post office—naturally only the ones that have to travel farther. Franz cannot write; however, he told me I should send his regards to you. May God assist him!

Once more, farewell, your sister Jette.

The enclosed pocketbooks are for Johanna and Thereschen. We will also think of Wilhelm and of you, but you will have to think of me whenever you use these things.

Arnold Boner died 27 July 1847. His hired hand, Christian, wrote on 10 August that he had made a will and been provided with the last rites. "He had a great farm, bigger than that of any farmer in Germany . . . with three hired hands and a female cook, and we lived in good accord with our master."

Westphalia
11 October 1847

Dear Heinrich:

Several weeks ago your letter with the enclosure for Carl arrived. The latter was forwarded to him. The notice of Marie's death[80] did not come unexpectedly, since one has to be prepared for everything, but nevertheless I believe remembering her will make me feel very sad, and I often think that the Good Lord should have taken me rather than her. If I should ever again come to see you, you will have a great deal to do to keep me happy. If it continues like this, then there is no use in a trip.

Here we have settled down a little bit, that is, we are well. It makes me feel good to see that Franz is also getting a little more cheerful. The smallest of the children, Heinrich,[81] is staying with the grandparents; the other two, Caspar and Jette, are with Franz. The girl is keeping house for the time being. You cannot believe how his deceased wife suffered; what a misery this was! Franz was incredibly patient and composed, and it took a great deal to tolerate her ill humor. She was terribly excitable and was very inconsolate and despondent with little tolerance. (I wonder if anyone would not be the same in her situation? I would think not, but may God help us!) We are still happy that she had all possible care, and Bruns says that there was not another sick person in the settlement who could have had the same care. It cost Franz a great deal, and it cost me a little trouble. But this is nothing—I frequently had scruples that I did not always do it with love, but she probably did not notice that. These were hard trips for me, but she always was happy when I arrived. Her strong appetite and the many sores prolonged her suffering. Franz said a few days ago that it was after all good that it had come to an end; she had often expressed the fear that even if she recovered she would not be able to take care of herself. I wonder if I have mentioned earlier her irritability; it had no boundaries. At the slightest cause, she had heart palpitations, etc. She was often blind with fear when Franz was hitching the horses, and she followed him and was completely out of her

80. Marie Geisberg, Jette's cousin and friend in her youth, daughter of Franz Heidenreich Geisberg, died in Münster 27 June 1847 at age thirty-five. She never married.

81. Matthias Geisberg, the youngest child, had died.

mind, as she herself said. I tried to persuade her to have courage, to tell her that it was her duty to be somewhat more composed as the wife of a farmer, and I told Franz that he would have to assert himself so that she would not lose her mind. During her illness she maintained that she had had the sickness for a long time in her body, that she had once been frightened at the sight of a snake. May God give her eternal rest!

We are anxiously awaiting the arrival of Bartmann. In case there should be some change in the business, we wonder whether Franz might not perhaps join us. To be sure, he does not show much desire for this and fears his lack of knowledge, but he at least takes our advice to wait until the decision is made, especially in view of his weak health. In that case he ought to move to our house! This is just between us!

December

In your last letter you said that I should by all means tell you everyday things. Oh, Heinrich, this moves me tremendously! Why do you wish this? Your sister is a person who is often at odds with the entire world. Our position, Franz, the priest, the whole settlement! All of these things fill my head, and I cannot make anything good out of anything. I often tell Bruns that we ought to move away. You can imagine how little he likes that, and yet I cannot overcome it. If I were alone with him, then it would not matter, but the children! For days and hours on end I make plans, but I do not enjoy it, I have no courage and often wish that our Good Lord would give me peace and quiet in my heart! It's been like this for a long time!

Our children are now quite well and are getting so rambunctious that we have taken your godchild to school.[82] He is already tired of it and now always has to be taken there, but he will have to have a bit more play time. Caspar is learning well. Heinrich is just as tall as he is. Effie is a dear little mother and already cares so much and pays attention to everything. She still speaks somewhat indistinctly, and is quite plump and heavy. The little rascal Albert is quite jolly again and is claiming the rights of the baby (of which they frequently talk when he is brought to the church.) He lets himself be rocked in his cradle, sleeps in his mother's arms, and likes to be carried. He has grown well but is still a little light and peaked. He will certainly become quite a rascal, for he has innate qualifications; he cannot be quiet for one minute. This is probably a distraction for me, but it also tires me out at times.

I do have to confess that the events of the summer still occupy me frequently. Arnold Boner's death is not the least among these. It makes me so sad to think of it, and I just cannot help it. I wish that no one else would come here under similar circumstances.

10 February

Christoph Bartmann finally arrived here on the 20th of January. We were extremely anxious, and his brothers too were becoming nervous; Anton became sick. Christoph was well and comfortable on the trip. He was at sea for seventy-four days. The last part of the trip, here in the country, has, it seems, caused him to catch a cold. Perhaps it is something else too. He is not well, hardly eats anything, and seems to be ill-humored. However, it has become a little better during these last few days. We were very sorry that he did not find his true love. For many years he had been engaged to a girl in Amsterdam, an only daughter, rich, supposedly having eighty thousand guilders (Protestant); her father died last year, and

---

82. Heinrich Bruns was five years old at this time.

the mother had been dead for some time. She died last spring, and he did not know it until he got to her residence. This certainly has affected him very deeply. This is a *secret* here; at least we consider it so since his family does not talk about it.

We have received your letters. Soon I shall write more; Bartmann's belongings are still in St. Louis. For the time being, thanks for the books. Hermann writes that he has kept the one that was for him, since his name was written in it. He asked me to thank you, but I think he should express his thanks personally in the near future.

In my last letter there was a great deal of talk of business. It almost repulses me, and I wish it would finally be settled and done with. If only I could be Bruns for a while! Well, I have to have patience and you will, I hope, soon send the missing paper. Be considerate if at times I do not express myself particularly well. I still think about Bernhard's belongings. At this moment it cannot conveniently be taken care of, and it is indeed just a small thing. We thought he would surely return, and then we could give him back his things or equivalent value for it. (Now only for you: It is very good that our settlement is being taken care of. If my share has been estimated too high, then Bruns thinks that it should be given back.)

Ferdinand Meyer is preparing for his departure. He seems to be quite serious about it. And then I shall write further although so many things are urging themselves upon me now. Yours and Johanna's letter are, I think, somewhat serious and have not been written in a good humor. Do not speak of embarrassment and similar things. Be of good spirits and make everything easy for yourself! When I hear something like this, I always think I should be there on the spot, for I have the confidence that I could remedy everything for you. Now as to Bernhard, it certainly will come to pass that we will see him again!

There is an interruption again, as there has been for several weeks. Well farewell! Soon more. Regards to all and thanks for the letters and for everything.

Hold dear your sister, Jette.

P.S. Aunt Therese will get a good letter. You probably did not know that I returned from St. Louis quite ill and that the other letters were ready earlier, before we went there. This should not be blamed on any intention or any carelessness.

On 10 February 1848 Jette wrote a long letter to Aunt Therese describing her life in Westphalia, reporting on the gardens and orchards that Dr. Bruns "enjoys so much," but dwelling on her loneliness. In April she wrote to Uncle Caspar, expressing her concern for Bruns's health and the future of their children in the isolated Westphalia Settlement and asking him in confidence to urge Bruns not to jeopardize his health with his widespread practice.

Westphalia
25 December 1848

Dear Heinrich:

It has been a long time since I have chatted with you, that is, since I have put it down on paper. Quite some time ago I wrote to Johanna, whom you have not mentioned for a long time and to whom I owed a letter. I wanted to fill the sheet, and so I wrote all kinds of dumb stuff. Copying is against my habit, and thus I have not yet finished it.

Today on Christmas Day I have been thinking of you especially, and so I got to daydreaming. We just live from day to day now. We were, God be thanked, not sick. Yet let's not talk about it! Bruns recently wrote you, and when I inquired I learned that he had forgotten the most important thing while discussing other matters. Namely, that little Ludwig was born on the 17th of July! This deserves a reprimand. The little fellow has already caused me much alarm, he had *Treminen* etc.[83] Now he is rather plump and seems well. But his mother takes care of him and pampers him as if he were the first instead of the ninth child. Both of Franz's children are here; and so there is lots of childish play going on. It is almost too much. During the summer we got along fine, but now that I have them inside it is almost getting too much for me. They had been anxiously looking forward to Christmas, and I did my best to fulfill their expectations. Franz and Mathias Stiefermann were also here and helped me decorate the tree. Bruns had to keep the children quiet until I finally called. You should have seen them! And then everything had to be shown to mother. There was jubilation without end!

Franz was in St. Louis during the summer and in Marthasville, where Wenker, our former traveling companion, still lives. Franz had decided to go into the distillery business, and he is starting with his brother-in-law Mathias as a partner. Mathias is a good young man who previously helped his father with cabinet work and in general has a great deal of practical knowledge. They live on the Osage, on a nicely situated place which Bruns bought and let them occupy. Well, it is Franz's decision, and I hope he will succeed in it! I had hoped that he would start something in St. Louis so that he would not have to strain himself so much physically.

I am quite happy that we are still getting something in the division and that Bruns will leave the money there so the transfer of money can come to an end. Bruns still has money available and has spoken of writing Uncle Caspar. I was very sorry to have written something to the uncle that I should have spared him. I wonder if he's now back on the old track? I hope that you endeavor to replace for him the ones he lost.[84] I can picture quite vividly how I too would have to do everything for his sake if I were with you. Do write us soon concerning the influence the continuing unrest had on you and on the area around there. I wonder how things will turn out in the end?

You have to tell Thereschen that she will get a proper letter because hers has really given me a lift. Give her my regards and also sincere regards to Uncle Caspar and Aunt Therese. How few you are now! Also do not forget to give Phina[85] my regards. Soon more! Franz has written me unexpectedly and thus I have to end quickly. Should there not soon be a letter for us?

Your sister, Jette.

P.S. Meyer is a real gossip. We would not like to continue writing him.

Westphalia
16 February 1849

Dear Heinrich:

Your letter arrived by mail by way of Meyer; he himself will probably soon follow. When I saw the thick letter I felt so good, but I now feel very sorry since I have read it. And when I

---

83. *Treminen* is an obsolete name for a childhood disease that is characterized by rigors.
84. Ursula Boner, Caspar Geisberg's only sister, died in Münster on 13 March 1848.
85. Phina Boner, the daughter of Ursula Boner, was born 29 May 1817 in Münster.

read it anew, I think I don't know what to do, I don't know what to think. What is it that oppresses you? Is it physical illness or a bad mood? Certainly it must be both! Oh you dear, dear brother! You must not suffer! May God keep you!

I hope that I can hear more in the near future so that I can be calm again. If you do not make good progress in the examination quickly, then it must go slowly in Heaven's name. When you have conquered it, then you will feel more free. Why brood about it before taking the exams? That is probably not good. What does our uncle say about this? He is perhaps himself the biggest obstacle. Even we have heard of his amazement that you are procrastinating, and what should I then say? If I pushed you, I would regret it a hundred times before you got my letter. You know best. When you have a firm position, how nice it will be then. You will be close to our old, good uncle, our caring aunt, our sisters, you will have the close relationships with friends, a free nature where every flower, every straw, every bush represents an acquaintance of your youth that will bud anew again and again. Familiar situations, even though changed, cannot upset or reverse everything. You cannot imagine how hard it is to become accustomed to things here. The customs, the morals, the language, people without feeling, everything is foreign and cold. At home I could take pleasure in the outdoors, and I became happy as a child after a walk. Here it makes me melancholy to see the wild, desolate abundance of plants and trees. The disadvantages make walking disagreeable, the ticks, all kinds of hindrances such as burrs, the lack of well-built roads.

We are making a little garden next to the house as our paradise. Besides the useful, Mrs. Bruns has some flowers and such bushes as can be had here. Papa is now planting grapes and trees where there is space, and he lays it out, which he did not do before. And then naturally I have a lot to do, but when I take my hat the little folks are there, and then I have to help look at many things first. If I go and get something, they all want to come and carry it, and so it goes.

I'm sick of the eternally long winter, and I can scarcely wait until spring comes. Bruns cannot stand noise very well, and so I now sit all day long in the storeroom, which, to be sure, is quite cramped with four little doctors, two Geisbergs, and the junior Hermann Bruns. The children probably feel it even more to be locked up, and then when the three boys return from school I let them play until they get too wild. It has never been so cold for such a long time since we have been here; there is always ice on the road. The animals suffered very much; our beautiful meadows protect us from a shortage of feed, and thus our stock is in good condition while other farmers have lost either a lot or some animals.

24th of May

Today for the seventeenth time the day has returned in which I stepped to the altar with my most beloved one. We talked recently of our silver wedding anniversary and, if it pleases our Good Lord, then I will invite you to come over. You know that today is also a day of mourning for me, and when in quiet memory I think of the celebrations of our mother's name-day, of my wedding, and of our sister, now and then a tear comes to my eye and I cannot forget the dear child.[86] Then the joy is over.

86. Jette's daughter Johanna, who had died 13 September 1841 at age two, was named in memory of Jette's mother, Johanna Hüffer Geisberg.

27th

Now a letter from you to Franz and me has arrived. I had expected it, only I wished that you could dispel my sad doubts. It makes me indescribably restless, and yet you must not be silent. You owe it to me to let me know exactly what concerns you, even if it is hard. But Heinrich, how do you come to have such serious, dark thoughts? Without reason surely! But I shall tell you that it would be better for you to give up studying for a while, and you probably have now done this already and are probably marching against the Danes.[87] It surprised me in your letter; the newspapers are so large here that I always let them lie. Bruns says it doesn't mean anything, for the Danes are too insignificant, and thus it would mean only a small change. In Germany, at least with you, it will surely remain calm. You will comply and do as you are told, and it will work out for the best, at least I hope so. And Bruns also said there would hardly be any emergency with you in Westphalia.

Would it be possible to select some other field so that the eternal study could come to an end if you wanted to use your qualifications and find a suitable, even though moderate, existence? Our father had a good income. In Münster surely there must be some prospects. What kind of doubts are these that you are voicing with regard to Offenberg? I have no doubt that if he is transferred he will nevertheless find a position equally good![88] A fourth Bartmann recently arrived here, coming by steamboat across the ocean in sixteen days. Suddenly it occurred to me that in four months we could be over to see you and back here again. The little ones could go for this time to Hermann Bruns. Our Papa agreed; he will fill the purse for next year. We talked back and forth; it would really work. I could not sleep during the night. On the following morning I had the feeling that I no longer loved the children at all, at least I loved you more. A few days later I gave it all up. This was several weeks ago, and now yesterday Bruns started it again. These are hard struggles, for I cannot go without the smallest ones. And Bruns said, "It is better alone!" But don't say anything of this, for these are probably castles in the air!

The children are well. Caspar is the first to show off; he is more reasonable than the rest, and yet yesterday he fell backwards from a fence while he was balancing and hit his head on a stone. But it is already healing. Heinrich is probably not quite as well behaved as his uncle was when he was a child. He worries me a great deal because of his bad manners, his disorderliness and laziness. I have much too little time for the children, especially since we have no teacher for the summer and I have to instruct them myself. However, Heinrich is not malicious; it is only that he puts everything off when he plays. Flowers and birds occupy him most. Jette is already learning. She probably has a little of the irritability of her mother; yesterday we went out for a ride, and the horses started running. She was screaming, while Effie sat very calmly, which pleased me very much. —You should see Albert. Such a smart, funny little fellow. And Louis, oh, he is so fat, so beautiful and well behaved! We are so proud when people say that I have had no child that looked as healthy. Bruns said he would

87. War between Denmark and Schleswig-Holstein broke out 3 March 1848, when Denmark declared that the Duchy of Schleswig was inseparably linked to the Danish crown and proceeded to enforce annexation. The Frankfurt Parliament decided to intervene and commissioned Prussia to send federal troops. The Armistice of Malmö, concluded 28 August 1848, provided for the evacuation of both Danish and Prussian troops from the duchies and an eventual peace treaty, which was signed 2 June 1850.

88. Caspar Offenberg, who had been director of the municipal court at Warendorf, became a member of the county court in Münster in October 1849.

resemble me. He has my eyes and a turned-up little nose. We are anxious for Hermann's arrival in the middle of July. He is supposed to be so tall. The teachers are very satisfied with him. Bruns thought that Hermann would have to decide whether he wants to pursue a learned subject; if not, he will have to try something else. He will *finally* share my next letter. His mother is to be blamed that he was silent last year. The sheet is full. Quite certainly you will have to write me again immediately, and something very nice. If it is the will of our Lord that you will continue to suffer, then you will write about it, and we shall come and I shall talk to you and make it better. Your sister, Jette.

P.S. A week ago Franz was here. He will probably write with Bruns in the near future. He was well; he is in general in high spirits since he has forgotten the old troubles a little bit. A few weeks ago I wrote to Johanna and Therese.

Westphalia
17 October 1849

Dear Heinrich:

Your letter of last March is lying in front of me. I suspect that one from us will have arrived for you during the summer. Since that time there have been a lot of things going on with you, and we have nothing except news from the newspapers. I don't like to look at them at all anymore. This argumentation and scolding! Particularly with reference to the Prussians, false rumors of defeats, etc., etc. Bruns always kept saying, however, that it didn't mean anything, and indeed this seems to be true. Did you have to march out with them? In the newspaper there was some reference to the battalion from Warendorf. It often made me quite nervous. Every mail day I am hoping for a letter.

We have experienced something too this summer. Early on I had the bilious fever. After I had recovered somewhat, we proceeded with the necessary repair work on our house, and we had several workmen boarding with us. And then the cholera broke out in St. Louis. The news became worse and worse. And Hermann was still there. We urged him to be careful, but we did not really know how we could get him home, until suddenly at the beginning of July he appeared in our room. It seems that the professors were satisfied to be rid of their worries. Nobody got sick at the college, and they seemed very inclined to attribute this to the Mother of God. By the way, the students had been kept from going into town. Cleanliness, diet, everything was in order. To be sure, six ministers from among them were always with the sick in the city day and night. It is believed that approximately ten thousand people died. Half of the inhabitants fled into the country, and thus the cholera frequently was brought into the interior. In this manner it also came here, and the residents of our town were neighborly and did not pay attention to admonitions until it was too late. Thirteen people died (among them the older Bartmann, Franz); this was approximately one-third of the inhabitants.

Bruns naturally had to fulfill his duty, but he himself was always a little sickly, so he found it a bit difficult, and once he also had cramps. However, medicine and precautions helped him get through it. He has managed to make it through to the end, but it did take a long time until he was well again. For a period of about two months he could not eat anything except soup. He worried me very much. His wife fared about the same, only some bilious fever developed from it. With every excitement the cramps returned. The children and the servants, however, were spared. It was an ugly time. All around us were similar cases of illness, and everybody came to get medicine at least as a precautionary measure. Westphalia, to be sure, was in ill repute. We had our minister,[89] but on Sundays no church was held. The farmers found other ways to get to the doctor. Nobody went out except for an emergency. Now, God be praised, things are almost normal again and back on the old track. We in our house are well. Bruns and I have such tremendous appetites that we will soon have regained our usual weight. Hermann had a long vacation. The boy can be useful in many ways and make himself pleasant. He did not want to declare himself definitely for a scholarly subject. Now Bruns wants to see whether he can get him a job somewhere. Last Sunday the superior from St. Louis came and Father de Smet arrived here. There were some disagreements concerning the building of the church, which now have fortunately been resolved. After they had left us on Tuesday, father and son rode to Linn (the county seat) in order to hear Senator Benton, who had asked them to come, which pleased our Papa very much since Mr. Benton is really said to be a very important person. In the meeting that followed, Bruns accepted the position of delegate to St. Louis (because of the big railroad story, a railroad is planned to California). Thus the suitcase was packed and both father and son left the next day. Now it is clear why I have peace here to write you a long letter.

During the time of the cholera our workmen ran off, and thus only yesterday the painter was finished. The house received a stone foundation, the basement was enlarged, and on the north side of the house a portico was attached. It cost us a good bit of money, and it annoyed me so much because the carpenter was so slow.

The 28th

Today is my birthday, and Bruns wished for me and for himself that the thirty-six years may be doubled. That may not be our Good Lord's will. What would I yet have to experience during this long time? It is exactly twenty years now since I met Bruns. He knew better than I when I saw him first. Our dear father explained to me on Sunday morning that I would have to go visiting (I had returned on Friday from Münster), and he accompanied me in person and introduced me to his acquaintances as a grown young girl. On the long street Volmer came toward us, accompanied by Bruns, who said to him, "There is Geisberg with his daughter; that is a woman for you!" It is so good to be able to remember the kindness of one's parents. But today it makes me sad to be so alone. What will brighten my life's evening? Frequently I am too lonely to be able to be happy! To be sure, our little family is getting bigger and bigger, and I can already see with Hermann that even the many troubles are rewarded by joy. Bruns found a position for Hermann in a big apothecary business: Schütz and Eggers.[90] It seems that Hermann has no inclination to more serious study. Well,

89. Father Andrew Ehrensberger, a native of Bavaria, arrived in Westphalia on 17 November 1848 and stayed until 17 September 1851, when he assumed the duties of professor at St. Xavier College in Cincinnati. During his stay in Osage County he worked to improve the parish of the neighboring Rich Fountain, where many Bavarians had settled.

90. Schütze and Eggers was a pharmaceutical firm in St. Louis. *The St. Louis Directory* for 1848 lists Gottfried Schuetze as a wholesale and retail druggist at 169 N. First St. Edward Eggers is listed as a partner of Angelrodt, Eggers & Barth, "Importers and Dealers in Groceries, Liquors, Wines and Segars," in business at 167 N. First St., thus next door to the druggist and presumably having an interest in the apothecary shop. Charles F. Eggers is listed in the 1845 *Directory* as a druggist at the corner of Morgan and Third St. *The Missouri Gazetteer* for 1860 lists Schuetze & Eggers, wholesale drugs, chemicals, etc. at 151 N. Main.

we'll have to see! Now he doesn't cost us anymore, and so Bruns leaves it up to him what he wants to do. In the college he cost approximately three hundred dollars. Hermann is so tall! Last year he studied so well that the professors would have liked to keep him. He had very little communication with others, and he is therefore quite naturally not acquainted with the vices of the world. If only he would remain this way! However, it often seems to me that he has inherited from his father some equanimity and cannot be moved by momentary impulses. At the first opportunity he will dedicate a few lines to you too, and then you will have to answer him. Heinrich is somewhat lazy, but he is getting along very nicely. Effie is always active, and I hope the best for her. The little rascal Albert causes a great deal of unrest because of his liveliness. Louis was ill and still cannot walk, and he is getting quite heavy. Since the time of the cholera Franz has his little ones back with him. He wants to bring us Jette again; Caspar is going to school. He himself is well. They are making very little progress with their installations. The workmen were sick. Franz comes often, which cheers both of us. Some time ago Wilhelm sent us a very good but mostly political letter. He probably will have visited you by now.

If you are waiting for this letter then answer quickly, but I hope that we will receive one before that time. Greetings to all and do not forget your sister Jette.

P.S. How is your health? Are you feeling better mentally? Do write me about this and otherwise be of good spirits! We shall see each other again! If I'm not quite well, I sometimes feel I have to complain to you. It is good that I'm often prevented from doing this. You write, I believe, nothing of everyday affairs, and yet I would like to read such very much.

Mathias Bartmann will return next spring, and I'll send more with him! This is probably a very topsy-turvy letter, but I just hate to copy it again.

Westphalia
9 January 1850

Dear Heinrich:

Today your third letter, of 26 November, arrived here, and seeing it made me quite uncomfortable. You can see how little I am used to waiting patiently. However, it has pleased me very much that you seem to be so much happier and in good health. You will now be able to look toward your future life happily and with strength. It is strange, but against my usual custom I have imagined this time a blessed New Year. How it will develop we will have to see!

We have forgotten the cholera, and we feel vigorous and healthy and strong enough, perhaps better than in years. To be sure, Bruns had a not insignificant accident. About two months ago his horse shied; he was holding it by its reins, and it jumped onto his foot and the first bone was broken. Now he is almost to the point that he can put aside his crutches.

California frequently occupies us. Bruns declared a year ago that he would go there if he did not have a family. A young fellow who was working for us was listening intently and became anxious to go. Bruns assisted him with pleasure, and upon his recommendation Martin, that's his name, was able to join a wagon train leaving Jefferson. On Sunday his brother arrived with his first letter from California. Martin does not say what he is earning, but he wants to send a thousand dollars in the course of a year. And then he promises his brother one hundred dollars annually if he will stay with his mother. The news is amazing; many acquaintances of ours have already gone there, and we are anxious for their reports. What do you think, Heinrich? Should we not also try our fortune? Bruns wonders and looks at me so strangely when I speak of this. Recently he said he would have to go there with Hermann and Heinrich, and his wife and the little ones should go to Germany. Well, enough of that! Aren't we getting rich without going to California? Look, the big railroad is being built from St. Louis to Independence on the south side of the Missouri. A straight line would bring it approximately one-half mile from our place. The best ferry across the Osage to Jefferson City is Shipley's Ferry, which Bruns bought last year along with a big farm for fifteen hundred dollars. If we are modest, even in the worst case the railroad cannot be more than twenty miles away. That is good enough to get us back into communication with the world. Therefore, we will have to wait to see what the spring will bring.

Here in the house there is unusual activity. Last fall Colonel Benton asked Bruns whether he could send his son to us, and we thought it was empty talk, particularly since I was somewhat afraid of this. We had almost completely forgotten it until three weeks ago when the young gentleman suddenly appeared. He is to learn German and also French, etc. The gentlemen of the cloth are also in the midst of it and are able to help. Bruns wrote to Hermann's boss, and since there is little to be done during the winter he arrived a few days ago and now participates in the instruction. In the course of the winter Hermann will probably also decide what he wants to do. If he wants to continue his studies, his father believes it would be best if he were to go to Germany for a few years. What do you say to that? I wonder whether he would be welcome with you? Naturally you would have to take care of all the arrangements, and if he cannot stay in the house then you would have to find a room for him nearby. However, Johanna too is now with you in Münster, so we would not have to be embarrassed in case Aunt Therese should be afraid of the trouble it would cause. However, I do not yet like to think about this; it is, after all, too far and would also be rather costly. Do talk about this from the distance.

Mathias Bartmann is threatening to depart soon, and then we will give him as many letters as I am able to write. Therefore you will have to put off Thereschen until that time.

You have not written concerning Bernhard for a long time. If we come to Germany, we will have to bring him back with us. At least I always dream about this, when I am awake and when I am asleep. —Wilhelm must still get an answer from us. What do you think of his position? Will he come closer to independence there? He did not seem to think so. Bruns wants to end the letter. So, for now farewell! When I am in a more cheerful mood then I shall start another letter for you.

Regards to all and think frequently of your sister, Jette.

The 13th

Bruns wanted to complete this letter but he delayed until this morning and then of course he was called out. It is his first excursion in two months, and his foot is still so swollen that he could not put on a boot. But he will write later on. He looked over the calculations yesterday with Franz, and they agree. Franz needs a lot of money, especially since his brother-in-law cannot add anything to this. Their work is progressing too slowly. The father-in-law, who directs the whole thing, cannot move. I have never liked it, but it could not be helped. If they would only start distilling, there would be some definite income, and Franz would be rid of the other hard work.

Bruns is just returning. Soon more and some better news. Your sister, Jette.

On 16 January 1850 Jette wrote to Aunt Therese, reporting that the family was doing well and inquiring about the possibility of sending Hermann to Germany. In a letter of 16 February, Dr. Bruns wrote to Uncle Caspar that Franz had decided to go to California with Hermann Bruns. On 19 February he wrote to Heinrich that "The treasures which are so easily obtained in California amaze and excite everybody here," adding that Jette also wanted to go and seek her fortune there, but he had persuaded her to wait for a year.

Spring 1850

Dear Heinrich:

Now I scarcely have any time or any news for you. We are all in good spirits, only in a great deal of commotion. Bruns has tremendously much to take care of and to put in order in his fashion. Franz's departure causes me to have to think, to advise, and to help. Then besides very ordinary business comes the almost late spring. What do you think about Franz's resolution? We are rather collected. He is in good company, in good health; his children are taken care of without him and are just as much orphaned with him. It is cruel to say. Caspar is also returning now. I hope to God that they will stay in my care and will grow up together with our children and do well. Franz is such a solid person and certainly not lazy. When he has survived the trip, he cannot fail to earn a good income. Then he can do whatever he wants to do, without a partner and perhaps without a store. We have a great idea to attract a young person over: now is the time for it, and from this point of view, having survived the tour over the prairies, being a citizen of these states, why not take the spade in hand? You will have to write immediately whether you wish to hear more concerning California. If more is not necessary, then support Wilhelm to your best ability with our uncle. And in case in a year or two some gold should have gotten into our hands, then we will be spending it freely for a reunion!

Well, now take good care of yourself. Do go once more to the baths during the summer so you can finish what you have begun. And when your head is fresh and free again, then try anew to brave the storms of life. Just as we do!

A thousand greetings to the uncle. I hope that one of the poor little pictures will please him. Then he could use it as a book mark. And every time he began or stopped with his book, he would think of me.

Bruns wants to write with the mail; he as well as Franz will write to Oesterlinck. Your sincerely loving sister, Jette.

P.S. The portraits are meant for Thereschen. We send only that of Bruns and me. The one of all three of us is so dark that we decided to keep it.

Westphalia
12 June 1850

Dear Heinrich:

A few days ago we received your letter, and since I had expected one I want to reply to it immediately. M. Bartmann has by now handed you a package of letters from me, while

Bruns and Franz did not want to trust this opportunity. I hope that I have done everything correctly. At any rate it was my intention, although I was somewhat confused at times.

Brother Franz left us in April. Before this he had been with us for several months. In this way he avoided the constantly increasing arguments with his brother-in-law [Mathias Stiefermann], who really treated him somewhat rudely and whom Franz could not oppose. It annoyed me tremendously that Franz did not show the courage to fight his way through, and in the end Bruns had to settle this matter entirely without him. Without Bruns's interference he would have had his last penny taken from him without thinking of the children as his primary interest. I've often said that he can never be independent! Well, keep this to yourself, you have to bear it with me!

Earlier I had told Franz what was in my heart, and I thought, "Now it will be easy to take leave." But I could not utter a single syllable. He said, "Farewell Jette," he shook, he kissed me, and he also remained silent when he faced Bruns! I hope that I shall see him again—he is, after all, the only one!

It is strange that he never once said, "Do look after the children," or any such thing. To be sure, it is understood, and as long as I live they will not be deserted.

We received a letter from Franz from the vicinity of Independence dated the 13th of May in which he said that so far they had done very well. They had five yoke of oxen and two cows and a saddle horse with their wagon. From here, their quarters have been under the open sky. They immediately began to bake and to cook. They had to buy only a little additional grain for the animals since the pasture was sufficient. Hageböck wrote on the 21st that they had already passed the Kansas River and were a hundred miles beyond. They all were in good spirits, and the cows give a lot of milk. There are seven wagons with people whom they know, but they will have to join a larger group now. They passed the Indian mission. Perhaps there will be an opportunity for another letter. If they remain well, everything will turn out well. They have the necessary medicine with them. People who stop in at the cities and those who go by way of the sea encounter more danger than the most seasoned travelers over land; the trip across the prairie almost tempts me, for it might strengthen my health and shake off the eternal fever and bouts with bilious fever. However, Bruns and his wife are no longer wild adventurers, and in addition they have a house full of children. The news must be very challenging or we will stay put.

And Wilhelm may by all means remain a clerk with his six hundred reichsthaler if he is not drawn over here of his own free will. We have sent letters to him by way of Rotterdam. To be sure, he would have to put up with hardship and deprivations. But the hundreds who have to sacrifice their lives, how do they do it? The greed for gold lets them think of nothing else but digging in the ground. Right from the start, as soon as they arrive, they begin. They sleep in tents, just as before, and eat nothing but bread and meat. Everything is expensive. When the rainy period begins, it can be endured for a while; they keep on washing, they become sick, they have no nursing care, no food. An American acquaintance wrote to Bruns, "If the people in Missouri would live as most of them do here, then no one would survive."

When they arrive at the mines, they select a place. Each one stakes off a square where he wants to begin, and this is untouchable. There are hardly any preparations made; a hoe, shovel, sieves, pans, food, wood, boards, and clothing is all, and consequently prices fell significantly. There is no stealing at all, which amazes us. But there is something behind that; lynch law is well established. Well enough! However, I still have to say that in the cities the greatest trash of the world gathers, and in the mines there is room for all of America to dig for the next hundred years (so they write).

We are all in good spirits. The children go to the pastor to school every day. Heinrich is easygoing beyond compare. He can daydream and enjoy and be happy about any little flower. If he has to study, he whiles away the time. If, however, it means something, then he can make up his mind and get to work helter-skelter and be finished in two minutes. Caspar gets ahead more with persistence and is much more orderly, but his head does not bend very easily. Jette learns well and in general is much more stable than Effie, but on the other hand also more timid. Effie and Albert are now spelling and are doing well. Thus I am all alone in the morning with Louis, who is now quite lively and wants to chat a lot. I can still not say anything definite concerning Hermann. He seems to prefer not to continue his studies. Well, in Heaven's name! It has been offered to him. However, I am often worried about him. We don't know at this moment where we could place him suitably. Randolph Benton is with his sister in Boonville, where his mother also came for a visit. We are quite embarrassed by him. I wish he would not come back. He is such a wild fellow![91]

Wilhelm certainly must answer now so that we can have peace of mind. And then, how can you talk of *taking leave again* since the trip there gives my only assurance of seeing you again? Don't you believe that longing to see you drives me to put up with a few years of hardship, etc.? I have one concern: the children! Otherwise, I can assure you that I would prefer the trip to California to any other prospect here in the vicinity, and so you now know how things are, and Bruns and I will certainly never separate again. Farewell, dear Heinrich, do write to me and do not scold your inconstant sister Jette.

P.S. In Jefferson the surveyors are in the process of surveying for the railroad.

Westphalia
25 August 1850

Dear Heinrich:

Your letter of the end of June arrived here a short time ago. To be sure, I wrote you recently, but since unexpected news arrived from Franz on Wednesday, I feel compelled to relay this information and in addition I wanted to say something concerning myself. On 14 July, Franz was in the South Pass between snow and ice on the summit of the Rocky Mountains. Two fellows belonging to another wagon were sick, but had nevertheless caught up with them. The prairie had been very dry, and at times they suffered from lack of water, which caused them to have to drive more slowly. Now in the colder region their progress was

---

91. John Randolph Benton, son of U.S. senator Thomas Hart Benton, was chosen to deliver the welcoming address on the occasion of Louis Kossuth's visit to St. Louis on 9 March 1852. Senator Benton wrote his daughter, Jessie, who was in London with her husband, Charles Frémont, that "Ran" had delivered the speech in German with such eloquence as to call forth "general press comment" (Catherine Coffin Phillips, *Jessie Benton Fremont: A Woman Who Made History* [San Francisco: John Henry Nash, 1935], p. 186). A few days later, twenty-two-year-old Randolph was seized with a malarial infection. He was visited at his father's Walnut Street house by his friend Father Pierre Jean de Smet, and on the night of 16 March he declared his desire to be taken into the Catholic Church. At sunrise the next morning, he died.

better, they were in good spirits, and there were no mosquitoes and no dust. For the remainder of the trip they will have hard roads with lots of snow and steep hills to climb and go down. According to their information they hope to be in California at the beginning of September. That presupposes a good deal of luck. Last year the people from Jefferson and many others did not arrive until the middle of October, but a few wagons from Osage County arrived earlier. Two men from the latter group are already back and have told us a great deal. They had worked for three months; one has had a yield of three thousand dollars and the other two thousand.

It is quite all right that Wilhelm will stay there, and even without his coming Franz can realize his hopes if he is lucky. They, both of them, may stay with you if God wishes it, and in saying this I am blinking my eyes. As far as we are concerned, it is still almost a year until next May, as you say. I am sorry that the people from Oelde, or rather the ones from Stromberg, have taken my letters so seriously. Perhaps Mrs. Bruns has expressed herself too frivolously, too boldly. Well, I have a mind for it, but there are many castles in the air. It will be difficult to get our things in order and leave everything behind, and to start from scratch again seems too hard and too daring. Besides, it is also not any small matter to travel with so many children. (Franz and brother-in-law Hermann must definitely be a part of it, or otherwise nothing will come of it.) You can therefore tell people this or answer them this way.

If Johanna is longing to show me her little ones, should I then stand there without any children, as if I did not have any? This is Bruns's opinion, to be sure. And if I come to visit you, nothing should oppress me. Therefore practice more patience! Until—it is too late! But I would want to work and work hard in order to teach the children and be able to tell them everything and promise them something.

"Patience, patience, even though your heart is breaking, do not quarrel with God in Heaven!"[92]

You did me wrong when you said I had not sat still, and I also wrote Thereschen about this. Bruns had broken his foot, he was in ill humor, and he said all kinds of things; the day was one of the unhappiest days of my life, and I had been serious for many years to please you.

Here I include a little sketch of the front of the house as it is now. The gate at the fence is missing, but otherwise it is pretty accurate. The picture of Franz is for you in case he is not able to send a new one. I believe it was sent before; however, it is better this way.

With the exception of Heinrich our children have the whooping-cough. Caspar and Louis are suffering most; and it has been going on for a long time. Roer[93] is supposed to arrive here soon, and then there will be letters, also some from our sister. What else, I no longer know.

Hermann must soon be more involved in activities, and you might have spoken a bit more kindly to me. We see, however, that it will be acceptable, and if we can ever decide, it

92. Quoted from Gottfried August Bürger (1747–1794), part of the last stanza of his ballad "Lenore": "Geduld! Geduld! Wenn's Herz auch bricht! / Mit Gott im Himmel hadre nicht! / Des Leibes bist du ledig; / Gott sei der Seele gnädig!"

93. Franz Roer, whose family was known to Dr. Bruns and the Geisbergs in Münster, was born in 1810 and emigrated in 1850 (see Müller, #3849) to Westphalia, living at first with Friedrich A. Meyer in a log cabin; he later moved to Jefferson City, where he established the city's first tannery and became a successful agent with the Germania Insurance Company of New York. See also letter of 15 February 1841 and note 43.

may be that Bruns will pursue the matter quickly. I would indeed be happy from the bottom of my heart. Hermann certainly has many faults, but after all he would make himself pleasant, and in the end he would be educated quite well.

Regards to everybody and particularly to our uncle. We hope that we will soon hear from all of you, and do write concerning Bernhard. Around Christmastime we may expect letters from California. Please, dear Heinrich, be of good spirits again! We will see Franz again in a year and a half if God wills it, and whatever there may be in store for us in the future, I hope that I may look forward to it calmly and cheerfully.

Hold dear your sister, Jette.

Bruns also sends his regards.

> Westphalia
> December 1850

Dear Heinrich:

Roer has been here since the beginning of November and has delivered everything. We send our sincere thanks, and ask you to convey thanks also to our uncle and sisters. It was a special relief to me that Aunt Therese had taken the trouble to put in a little note. We have seen Roer several times here already, and his natural, simple reports are very pleasant for us. He has also seen you more and has spoken more to you than I thought. He does not seem to like it too well here yet. Meyer's manner of living, the dirt in this bachelor establishment, etc., are indeed extraordinary. I wonder why he did not bring a wife along?

Together with your letters and presents, guests also arrived. As I wrote you already, we have rented our house and farm to the Porth family. They arrived here with Roer. It was a restless time and a strange feeling for me that you took care of the beautification of our rooms just as we will soon be leaving this shelter. I thought that your letters arrived at the most opportune time, and I have read them over slowly from the beginning to the end when I was in a bad mood or was tired. We have kept only three rooms in the house besides the kitchen and the other auxiliary houses. However, we are comfortably and warmly situated now and still have a large and suitable place. Now, let Mrs. Johanna do this also! One learns things like this only here in this country! The Porth family is large, mother and eight children, most of them grown, and still some other people. It will not work well to stay together. In about two months we shall sell our cattle and anything else superfluous. We will by that time have decided on a new place of residence. We have had to discard a trip to Europe, of which we were thinking first, but there were several reasons for it, and it would be inopportune to travel until the return of Franz and brother-in-law Hermann.

A letter arrived from California a week ago from a young man who went in the caravan from here. He reports that they made the trip in good health and have settled for the time being sixty miles above Sacramento and will try their luck there. He reported that Bruns's brother-in-law from the parish of Oelde, and Marcony (from Stromberg),[94] were preparing

---

94. Heinrich Marconi is listed by Müller, #330, as a thirty-three-year-old day-laborer from Stromberg who emigrated in 1836 with his wife and two children, ages eleven and four months.

to travel to Sacramento to get provisions and everything that was needed, and he quickly seized this opportunity to send word to his relatives. No other letter arrived the week thereafter. We can hope for another letter next Wednesday. So we know that they arrived safely, but we wonder where the letters are.

Frequently people from California come back and usually have with them between two thousand and three thousand dollars. This is a modest gain and we can hardly expect any more for our people. Hofius and Zumnorde with several others from this area are expected back about Christmas time. I shall write again when Franz has written, since I have to assume that you are just as anxious to hear of the outcome as we are.

I wanted to tell you that Bruns cannot transmit the money before the end of January, when the money from the sale of the Rienermann farm will be sent to Vonnegut. Bruns said that he hoped that our uncle will not take it amiss since it would only make a few weeks' difference; however, I did not want to fail to notify you.

Our son Hermann has been at the state university in Columbia since last fall and is very satisfied with it. His studies seem to be carried on somewhat better there. We are gradually getting ready to let him go to Münster after all.

Our little clan is well off and is going to school with the pastor every day. Albert also goes. Our pastor recently wanted to make the entire community saintly all at once with the aid of a missionary. The good man preached for nine days, he gave instructions, he heard confessions, etc., etc., and promoted brotherhood. On the third day my husband ran off, and his poor wife then had to decide for herself what to do. So every day I went to church and suffered humbly when he heckled the sinners who were not ready to confess, and I tried to carry home at least something that was good. But it was so repulsive to me, and in my innermost soul there was a voice that whispered, "You have not been cast out even if your service to God is of a different kind." And the Mother of God looked down on me so quietly and so peaceably as if she agreed with me and did not approve of all this commotion. I wonder whether you have had a similar experience?

Greetings to all from Bruns and your loving sister, Jette.

28 December 1850

Dear Heinrich:

It seems the unrest will soon be over, and so we are anxious to hear how you are getting along and whether you did take your position as a lieutenant. It gave us some serious moments. When this letter reaches you, I hope that you are back with your studies. Hermann Bruns has finally written, rather lengthily. He described the trip as arduous; they had to suffer so much because of the dust and the stench of the cattle that had died. It was reported that eighty thousand people had traveled over the prairie to California, and brother-in-law Hermann writes that the people lost approximately twenty thousand oxen. Our people were successful in getting their cattle there, but because of their generosity they almost had to starve themselves. They roamed around for three weeks and have now settled at the Wolf Creek Diggings,[95] seven miles above the mouth of Bear Creek. They found Zumnorde, who immediately joined them. So there are now Hermann Bruns, Franz, two

95. *Diggings* is a term commonly used for a site where mining has taken place.

Lückenhoffs, Marconi, Höcker, and a farmer Fick from here in the group. The others are about a mile away from them. They were in the process of building a house. Two of them had gone to Sacramento, about sixty miles away, to get supplies for the winter, and the others were digging for gold. The gold nuggets were very small; however, he thought they were earning about four to five dollars a day per person. Groceries are not high, and it is much healthier there than here. Heckemeyer, from Franz's wagon, did not like to dig and therefore took a job with a farmer for one hundred dollars per month. An American from here is herding cows for seventy-five dollars. Times therefore are not so bad as we feared, but also no longer as good as they were. Franz, I hope, will soon write himself.

I am happy that he stayed with brother-in-law Hermann, and our concern that he might perhaps be drawn into the whirlpool of the cities because of Zumnorde has therefore not materialized. As soon as we hear more I shall write more. We are healthy; however, I do not want to say that we are in merry spirits before we definitely decide what to do.

I hope that you are well and please think often of your loving sister Jette.

P.S. Bruns sends his regards with mine.

Spring 1852

Two fellows from the group with Franz have returned with a piece of gold for us, and they thought that he would stay there until fall. This winter, times have been miserable in California and the food is tremendously costly. I am glad that he is in a more southerly location. Some wrote that in the northern mines there was snow to a depth of eight feet.

Now farewell and see that our little sister remains in good spirits. You stand for more than merely a paternal authority.

Sincere greeting to our uncle! If all of you are now at peace, then he will soon receive a friendly and happy letter from us. Please give our greetings to Johanna as well as to her husband and to Wilhelm. Your sister, Jette.

Shipleys Ferry
9 January 1853

Dear Heinrich!

There! I had written the salutation before I could think about it, and therefore our sister will have to wait. To be sure, she really could have written a long time ago, and it almost seems as if I am testing her. I sent a letter to you at the time we sent the power of attorney, and afterward I was happy I had done so since a rather serious eye infection incapacitated me for some time and prevented me from any further communication. Even now I cannot see clearly, and I must not strain my eyes, so that I always have to concentrate on what is most urgent at any given moment.

My letter was a repetition of an earlier one that Bruns had forgotten to send with his long letter to our uncle. I found it next to his books. This second letter, I wonder where it is? You do have the power of attorney. I had informed you of Albert's death and don't like to write about it again. Johanna has also again lost a little boy.[96] I had asked for more information

---

96. Ernst Offenberg, born 10 September 1847, died 22 February 1852.

concerning our financial status with you in my last letter. I thought that Bruns had paid off the entire sum to our uncle as well as to you. Think about it, he himself thinks so too, and yet this does not seem to be the case. Franz is on a separate account, isn't he? Bruns says he has always left it up to you, and frequent changes had to be made. Since it is my most ardent wish not to have any debts, please write soon how things are. Franz has executed a note that our uncle must still have.

Roer arrived here in the middle of December and soon visited us. My sincere thanks for the book, the collar, and the ribbon. You probably have sent the book, and I shall use it a lot. Roer asked me openly what I have written to you concerning him. I still remember vaguely. Mrs. Offenberg had talked about it when she was at Lena Honthumb's, and the latter then mentioned it to her brother, and Mathias says: "Caspar should not give him any money." Although my remark concerning Roer was not as sharp at that time, I still did not want to warn anybody, and Mrs. Bruns as well as Mrs. Offenberg would have done better to keep quiet. Roer is a gossip, by the way. He has told you that we would visit you next summer, and he had not been requested to do that. It seems as if people enjoy teasing me about this; it is being talked about here too. And then the impossibility of it all! It is bitter. In recent times it seemed to me I could not wait any longer. I constantly feel driven and torn apart. When Franz returns, I wonder if it will not then be too late?

Why do I imagine that my presence would be so pleasant for you? As if I were capable of relieving you, of banishing your suffering forever just by speaking strongly and taking care of you. By my sudden appearance a bright light will shine into Bernhard's confused darkness! He will recognize us again, he will live in the present again, and he will travel back quietly and happily with us. And my sisters! What a pleasure for them, whom I had to leave when they were still children, and for me to become acquainted with them as mothers and housewives. And then our uncle, the only one of the old ones, he would welcome us because we also belong to him and we stand closer to him in years and experience than all of you! Oh, what dreams!

But what am I now? You would be disappointed in me, and you would have only sad memories when I had left you again. There is none of the youthful freshness left, but instead a stiff, sad, indifferent figure, without manners, without interest, with aged features, a mouth without teeth.[97] For you I would only be somebody to pay attention to because of the love I hold for you, which has never weakened! It would almost be better if we would stay here and not touch the old wounds that are now covered with scabs!

At any rate, it seems to me best that we come over to you if the opportunity offers itself. I am giving you notice of this so that we both will be prepared and will be able to really savor the few days in peace and quiet joy.

Carl's stories were too harsh. He has not let us hear from him. Roer's father wrote extensively concerning this.

Now farewell, greetings to all. I am expecting a letter from Therese any day now. Bruns sends his regards too. All winter long he has been away quite frequently because he has many sick people.

Your sister, Jette.

97. Jette was thirty-nine when this letter was written.

The Geisberg family to Jette

Franz v. Hatzfeld, County Judge

and

Therese v. Hatzfeld, née Geisberg

herewith respectfully announce

their wedding

Lüdinghausen and Münster, 12 May 1853

Dear Sister:

Look! There it is on paper that our youngest sister has taken a new name, and, I would say, has removed herself; for the time being they are soaring in the distance like a specter in the fog. Enough, I don't even like to think of her anymore or of the last days that have just passed. I try to live from one day to the next, and I occupy myself with my activities as a municipal judge. It is good that Wilhelm is here, or the difference for our uncle and for me would be too radical. The Offenbergs invited us for the noon meal yesterday, and we in turn invited them today, on Pentecost Monday. The weather is very pretty after a long cold wet spell, and it is good for the travelers. Wilhelm will start on a little trip to the Rhine tomorrow since he has not yet gotten beyond Cologne.

I wrote to you a few weeks ago and in particular worked out a business statement for you. Now God be with you!

Your brother, Heinrich

I also join the brothers and sisters in sending you, dear sister, as well as all of your family, greetings from Münster, where I have led our youngest sister to the altar. For the time being, I will stay with my position in Hamburg, where I am quite well off; even though I am not exactly brilliant there, I enjoy the greatest possible freedom, at any rate as a dependent person, which I am still. From here I am thinking of taking a little tour along the Rhine, which I hardly know at all, planning to return in about two weeks by way of Frankfurt, Cassel, and then back to the customary work.

Once more sincere greetings for everybody, and I remain as always your faithful brother,

Wilhelm.

So, dear Jette, greetings from all your relatives and from all the brothers and sisters who are gathered here in response to the announcement which is on the other side and which I forward to you with joy as the oldest person present on this solemn occasion.

It was a beautiful day, this wedding day on which only you, Bruns, and Franz were missing, whom, however, we remembered with fond thoughts. The day was somewhat dimmed by sadness because of the seriousness of the parting, since Therese has lived with us for more than twenty years and we have gotten very fond of her. But it had to be so. She now has a good and honest husband with whom she can be domestically happy and satisfied. Heinrich, Johanna, and Offenberg and children are still with us to console me in my old and sick age and to assist me. Farewell, dear Jette! Soon more. Give my regards to Bruns. Your uncle Caspar.

Heinrich has handed me this little letter, so that I can add a few friendly words. Therese has departed with her husband, and we hope they will be happy. The young people are excellently suited to each other, and Therese had changed so much during the period of her engagement; she was much happier and had become much calmer, so that she will become a very good-natured housewife. However, Heinrich will indeed miss her, and so it is good for him now that he will have a lot of work in his new office. Uncle Caspar will have to become accustomed to my noisy house, which I am sure will work out. Yes, just imagine, on Therese's wedding day when we were all here in the evening and the girls were downstairs, he went upstairs to the sleeping children and covered them, since they had thrown off their covers. Was that not touching? In the near future I shall write more. If you write soon again, I hope to receive a few words from you too. You cannot imagine how it would please me, and you need only write something of your children. Hold dear your brother-in-law, Offenberg.

From the Autobiography

On the 23rd of April a delicate little baby girl was born at Shipley's Ferry, our Ottilie. We were content on this beautiful farm even though it was not yet as comfortable as our house in Westphalia. But we had the fever again, and we had a lot of work. In order to make it easier for the children, Bruns took a teacher into the house, Heinrich Uedink, the brother-in-law of my cousin, Johanna Geisberg. The latter was very busy either as a teacher or hunter and even took care of the ferry whenever he was needed. Beside the black people we had two hired hands and a girl. Frequently we also had to lodge strangers. This, and the income from ferrying people across, made the servants worthwhile. We were able to sell our entire harvest on the spot to people who were driving cattle by. Whole trains of donkeys, cattle, and pigs passed us and were ferried across. Our oldest son did not like this rough life for long, and after a year he went to Jefferson. And Bruns frequently had to make the old tour to Westphalia and the surrounding country in spite of the fact that the priests had sent for a new, pious doctor.

After an absence of four years my brother Franz returned from California. He never tired of talking about it, but he became grouchy when he was afflicted by the fever.

Shipleys Ferry
7 September 1853

Dear Heinrich:

Franz has gotten back to us safely. He traveled during August through the southern regions right through the yellow fever. He looks well and is strong and free of any care. We did not expect him until winter, and when he speaks of the treasures he left, which, to be sure, are still hidden, then I am still not quite comfortable that he let himself be persuaded by my last letter to return. However, there is no end to the gold, and it was necessary to tear himself away. He tells of many amazing finds that he witnessed, but it never happened to him or to his travel companions. When the cost of the first trip and the equipment is added to the cost of the trip home, there is only a moderate gain left to him, and now he needs everything and has not yet begun a new project. For the time being he will stay with us, partly in order to rest up completely, and in addition to have an opportunity to contemplate his future activities. If only he would stay with us forever! He is really not fit to be a housefather, even though his children would be able to assist him in a few years.

We have received all of your letters, dear Heinrich, and the more proof of your love I received through them, the more I was unable to reciprocate. I waited in vain for Franz last spring. I surely believed we would be with you in May. The simple-minded Roer raised some hope in you concerning this, but then I became ill, probably because of this, and later could not overcome my pain, and then I could not confide my feelings to anyone. So, you see, I had to fight all this out with myself, and that was difficult. The prospect was close at hand, Bruns had deposited the money, and then how far away it was! Would it not be better for me to give up the scheme of seeing you, and particularly our uncle, once more? I have new hope, but I am sick a lot, and then speak of dying, which makes Bruns very impatient. It is really not reasonable of me.

This summer we had a great deal of activity, which was probably very good. Bruns had many patients and there was a lot of traffic here and a lot of commotion and good income from all sides. At times we thought it might be too much, but then we got through after all, and now that I am less able to handle it, it is getting calmer. Bruns was quite vigorous and managed to hold out quite well against his opponents. But we really do not enjoy our farm here, and we will perhaps make it a bit more comfortable for ourselves and move back to Westphalia if nothing else is offered to us.

Our Hermann is still in Jefferson and is satisfied with his position. We still have the pleasure of his visits every few weeks on Sundays. He is young and seems to enjoy seeing more of the world. What he will do later we shall probably leave to him and to whatever opportunity offers itself.

We were very happy to hear that you have finished your examinations. You can rest at ease now and take what is offered and educate yourself in more practical matters. How nicely this has worked out that the Offenbergs are living downstairs in the house, particularly in cases of illness, for Johanna will be on the spot and it will not be necessary to call in strangers. It could not have been planned better and could not be more comfortable for our uncle. Since we have been frustrated in our plans, I still have one wish that rises again and again. To be sure, we have a very good portrait of the uncle, but from his younger years. Perhaps almost fifty years have elapsed since that time. It would probably not be too bothersome for Uncle to sit down a few minutes for us so that we could have a better likeness and see him as he is now. It would make me so happy. Will you tell him this? Then he would find an occasion to have it made.

It is high time that I write you that we would like to have a piano and that one was suggested to us. A certain schoolteacher by the name of Meyer who came here with Roer wants to have an instrument brought here through an acquaintance if his brother, the vicar in Ostenfelde, can get it for him. He is personally acquainted with the instrument builder Niemann in Münster, and we would like to have you inquire of the vicar whether his brother here had given him the order; we would be inclined to take a second piano. You might perhaps look into it yourself and have the builder furnish us a good piano and then you will only have to pay the cost. The shipment to Meyer in Alverskirchen, packing, etc., would be taken care of without your involvement, since he himself has promised to import both instruments and we are known to him. Then I would also like to have a few new pieces of music and songs for a beginner, which you could include. The old ones make me sad. This amount should be taken from the estate of our aunt. The money you will still have in hand should be credited by way of Arnold Boner's estate and changed over to our possession, as Bruns says he has also written you. A small part of the farm has not yet been sold.

Now farewell! Hold dear as always your sister Jette.

On the margin: A thousand greetings to the young married couple, to our uncle, and the Offenbergs. Bruns will inform you as soon as he has arranged for the sale and will send you what can be gotten. Franz has written to you.

2
The Years in Jefferson City, 1853–1868

Our Heinrich is gone. The handsome, good boy, full of life, the pride of his father, the quiet worry
and joy of his mother. He fell in battle at Iuka, Mississippi, shot through the chest . . . on 7 July 1863.

Jette Bruns to Heinrich
August 1863

From the Autobiography

In November 1853 Wilhelm was born.

About that time old man Brenneke liked our farm so much he offered Bruns four thousand dollars for it. Hermann came and advised selling, as did my brother, and so Bruns
accepted. But where should we go now? Finally we settled on Jefferson. Mr. Uedink and our
hired hands went to California with Governor Edwards,[1] and the black people chose a new
master. Hay, oats, and corn were taken by boat to the railroad. Some things were shipped to
Jefferson for our use, an auction was held, and finally we were sent for. At first we lived in a
little house that belonged to Colonel Fulkerson. This was at the suggestion of Mr. Walther
and was close to his place, but was probably a mistake! Bruns, who, after all, had many
acquaintances, did not socialize much with them, and frequently dispensed with the daily
riding and walking. We were pretty isolated, which he felt very much, and this made him
disgruntled. My brother was with us, and he also had nothing to do. Jürgen and Betty, who
had moved with us, stayed in a house nearby, and he soon had work. Wilhelm was only a few
months old, Ottilie was a sickly child, and Louis was sick with fever. I had my hands full—
however, the worst was that Bruns was so depressed that he hardly talked any more, and he
would not go out. It was difficult for me to remain unaffected. It was the worst time of my
life. What would become of us?

And then my husband became ill. He contracted pneumonia. When he realized that, he
sent first for Doctor Krause, who prescribed some medicine. But my husband would not
take it. When I showed it to him, he made me throw it away. This went on, and he finally
became delirious. I was scared, and my brother and Hermann agreed to send for Doctor
Edwards, whom Father respected very much. And then Doctor Snodgrass, Doctor Wells,
Doctor Dorries, and Doctor Fiedering[2] from Westphalia were consulted. He was usually
delirious, but in clear moments he would say that he was going to die, and then he would
take only whatever my brother handed him. We were in a real emergency. The crisis passed
and he felt a little better, but he still did not want to take any medicine, only Seidlitz powder[3]
and ice. Later he said that it was this alone that cured him. The recovery came very slowly,
but with it his old energy returned. Gradually he began to go out again, and then he bought

1. John S. Edwards (1804–1888), a lawyer born in Kentucky, served as governor of Missouri from 1844 to 1848.
In 1849 he moved to Stockton, California, where he was elected mayor in 1851. He subsequently became successful
in law, real estate, and ranching.

2. The physicians Edwards, Snodgrass, Dorriss, and Wells are listed as practicing in Jefferson City in the 1860
Missouri State Gazetteer. A Dr. Ludwig H. A. Krause died 11 April 1862, and his gravestone is in the City Cemetery in
Jefferson City. No information could be located on Dr. Fiedering of Westphalia. Osage County records, how-
ever, show transfers of deeds from an August Fiederling to Henry Doehrhoff, Bernhard Hollermann, and H.
Rennekemeyer in October 1862 and January 1863.

3. *Seidlitzpulver,* or *pulvis aerophorus lascans,* was a commonly used purgative.

two lots on High Street[4] and began to build, to make plans, to order materials, to hire workmen, and so there was a great deal to be done. Work began immediately. In January we were able to move in. Down below there were two big stores, and after one place was rented, Bruns said we could just as well start a business of our own. Hermann had been employed for quite some time in Cordell's store, and he did not really want to join our business. My brother was a businessman, and he quickly worked himself in. His son Caspar and Anton Baurdick became his assistants. Hermann proved to be capable and had a great deal of practical insight in buying, and my brother assisted him solidly, and so the business flourished. They saw to it that payments for goods were made promptly, which raised their credit rating. So this went on successfully for several years.

Jefferson City
12 September 1854

Dear Heinrich:

We moved in here at the beginning of February. We were just loading the ferry when your last letter arrived. My chest of drawers was already gone, and so Bruns had to keep the letter. And now it is completely misplaced! There was something in it about a sour face, which hurt me at the time. Perhaps it wasn't quite so bad. With such constant distraction I don't express myself in my letters well enough—if only I could have read the letter over again. Since that time, however, I have not been writing you as I used to. (Or you have not received as much in writing as I have told you in my thoughts.) Particularly when I had pain or worries, I did not like to think of you, and I sought to swallow it. And look! Since all kinds of things happened here, I do forget much more now than formerly. It is not pleasant, but this is how things are!

Our moving here was, I believe, only a giving-in on the part of Bruns. I considered it better for the children, but otherwise I remained undecided. Franz and Hermann voted in favor. We have a residence half a mile from the crowded part of the city. Bruns did not do anything to make himself known—well, he is no longer young—Franz went out even less. We were advised against starting a business, and so there we sat! Bruns became somewhat desperate; his wife had worries enough but did her best not to let it be known. She chatted, she inquired. Franz usually said his normal yes, and Bruns, if he could help it, usually didn't say anything, and then put on such a frosty face! And then he got a fever, which did not want to end. On the third day I had to go and get medicine, and since he did not improve he agreed that I could send somebody for a doctor, but he did not take the medicine except for what had been prepared by his wife, according to his instructions, in the absence of a doctor. He spoke in a delirious manner and we were in great distress. He was always very contrary, but we consulted two more doctors, and he let himself be persuaded to take the medicine.

On Good Friday he explained he would have to put his affairs in order because he could not endure much longer. He thought I should return to Westphalia. And then he said I should return to you. What satisfaction there was for me in this proposal! But I denied it firmly! We used force to persuade him to rest. On Easter Sunday a crisis occurred, and then

4. Three deeds executed 20 April, 9 May, and 23 May 1854 indicate that Dr. Bernhard Bruns purchased several parcels or lots designated as lots 336 and 344 on the north side of High Street between Jefferson and Monroe streets. Bruns later bought additional property and built a large home at the corner of High and Washington streets. See note 12 below.

he became better. The doctors could not agree, and he was mostly against the medicine, which made it extremely difficult for us. He did not take half as much as he should have taken; however, he got so much calomel that it caused all his teeth to become loose. He had a very painful after-treatment. He still maintains that he helped himself by using ice water with Seidlitz powder. The illness was pneumonia. Now, God be thanked, he has been well and strong again for some time, and since then has taken many a ride into the area around us because he let himself be persuaded to run as a Democratic candidate for the House of Representatives for this county. You will probably be acquainted with the result; it happened to him as to his higher predecessor, Colonel Benton—he did not receive enough votes.[5] The Germans defended themselves bravely. Some, however, let themselves be persuaded to stay at home. Then the anti-Benton Democrats, as they usually do in the state, went over to the side of the Whigs. Since the August elections, one party, which is called the Know-Nothings, is more in favor with the Americans.[6] These are native Americans who deny the immigrants and Catholics many of their rights. Here too there are said to be very many of them, and they hold secret meetings. Bruns thought the nativists would not have any more significance now than earlier.

10 October

The construction of our house is progressing slowly. Everything is incredibly high. The wages for a carpenter are $2 per day, for an ordinary day laborer $1. All groceries are high, and potatoes are almost not available—they cost one and a half dollars a bushel where they cost twenty-five cents before. —Next winter we will move into our new home. This house represents a capital well invested. Rent is terribly high. If we do not like it after a winter in the house or in the city, then the world is still open to us.

Franz cannot decide on anything, and his sister is almost bitter about this; perhaps I shall tell him some time. And there are his children. What is he doing for them? If he is not doing well, I cannot be satisfied.

5. In a letter of 25 February 1854 in the *Jefferson Inquirer*, Dr. Bruns was called upon to become a candidate of the "true Democracy" for a seat in the Missouri legislature as a representative from Cole County. Signed by about one hundred fifty "Democratic Fellow Citizens," the letter pointed out that "the Democracy will support no man who is not favorable to the re-election of T. H. Benton to the U.S. Senate and in favor of the repeal of the . . . so-called Jackson resolutions." Dr. Bruns replied on 8 March 1854 that although he had not sought office he accepted the invitation because of his support for Senator Benton, whom he wished to see restored to his seat in the U.S. Senate, and his opposition to the Jackson resolutions, "to which I have ever been opposed; believing them . . . to be pernicious both in principle and intent; and designed for the purpose of commencing a mischievous slavery agitation and binding the state of Missouri to go blindfolded with the nullifiers and seceders of some of the Southern States in a mad attempt to resist the laws of the United States or effect a severance of the Union." The "so-called" Jackson resolutions had been introduced before the Missouri General Assembly on 15 January 1849 by Claiborne Fox Jackson, representative from Saline County (see Perry McCandless, *A History of Missouri, Volume II: 1820 to 1860* [Columbia: University of Missouri Press, 1972], pp. 247–52). The official results of the election, published in the *Jefferson Inquirer* on 12 August 1854, showed that the anti-Benton candidate, G. C. Medley, won the seat from Cole, defeating B. Bruns by a vote of 477 to 426.

6. The nativist movement of the 1840s was revived on a national scale after the election of 1852. Officially called the American party, it was popularly known as the Know-Nothing party because of the password "I don't know" used by members of the secret lodges active in nearly every state. The party called for exclusion of Catholics and foreigners from public office and advocated a twenty-one-year residence requirement for obtaining American citizenship.

1 November

I always told Bruns that he should urge Franz on and leave me out of it. But it remained as it was. Franz said, "I don't know," and Bruns said, "You have to think it over." And so then I said a few harsh words to him, and it was all over. He said he wanted to go to St. Louis, and he would return if he could not find a job there, otherwise he would write—and now he's gone. Now three weeks have elapsed and we still have no news. Bruns says, "You have made him obstinate," and I reply defiantly, "I have the right." But I am sorry. I shall probably bear it! In the meantime I don't get ahead with anything, I don't sleep any more, etc.

Should I let this letter be mailed?

From the Ferry I wrote a letter to Wilhelm. It was addressed to you by Bruns. Now the little boy is almost one year old.[7] His uncle, however, has not given any indication that he is the godfather. He *must* love the little fellow, what does he think!

We are still very pleased that he has this name, and we meant it from the bottom of our hearts when we named him thus!

Do you all want to hurt me! I scarcely believe that you will ever write me a real letter again. To be sure I cannot write anything except what I feel, and how I feel, only the heavens know.

Give our best regards to everybody, more in a few weeks.

Your sister, Jette.

8 February 1855

Franz has been back for a long time, and he is still with us; he occupies himself as well as he can. Since the 7th of December we have lived here in the new house. Even though not everything was finished, we are quite well settled and we are almost finished. Rent is terrifically high, and we have already rented several rooms. During the session of the legislature I rented a room to four gentlemen for several weeks for $16 a week. It is quite lively here; however, we see little of this and live our own way. The children go to school except for the youngest ones. Little Willaemken was quite good and quiet during the first year of his life. Now that he can walk, he is becoming spirited. He plays and laughs and we all have to love him very much. I surely believe that he will resemble brother Wilhelm.

Your letter to me arrived, and I am happy about it. There was also one from v. Hatzfeld and Johanna. I hope that in the very near future I shall become eager to write again so that I can answer these letters with good humor. Otherwise I find it very difficult.

Farewell, dear Heinrich, and may God bless you! Regards to Uncle and to the Offenbergs and write in my place to the Hatzfelds and to Wilhelm until I can report in myself again.

From the heart, your sister Jette.

Bruns will probably set up a store, and Hermann is supposed to stay home, and Franz will also take part. However, we are not yet that far!

In January 1856 Franz wrote a long letter to Uncle Caspar, reporting on the success of his business, a store stocking groceries and also, "according to the custom here," manufactured goods such as papers, books, porcelain, glass, hats, shoes, etc. Farm produce was purchased to sell in St. Louis.

7. Wilhelm Bruns was born 24 November 1853 and was named for Jette's younger brother in Germany.

From the Autobiography

Bruns now told me that if I wanted to we could take a trip to Europe. Once before I had declined because he had made the condition that the children could not go. I thought about it awhile and then agreed. It really went quite well. We took Heinrich and Louis to the Bartmanns in Westphalia. Brother Franz and Hermann had two good girls, the household got along, and except for Wilhelm the little ones were sent to school. After the receipt of the first letter in Münster I was very satisfied that the children had stayed at home. We soon recovered from the sea voyage and first went to Lohne. Bruns's brother was dead. A young man had come into the household, and the deaf and dumb brother was still alive and was happy to get a map of the country from Bruns. In Drievorden things had gotten on well; the brother, sister-in-law, and three grown children welcomed us. In the forest on the heath, which had been planted earlier, trees as high as houses could be seen. They took us to Drensteinfurt by way of Bentheim, where we visited the Bartmanns. A younger son of the family drove us to Münster, where we were expected. In the old home that had formerly belonged to our grandparents, Uncle Caspar lived upstairs with my brother Heinrich; my sister Johanna, who had been married for quite some time to the mayor, Caspar Offenberg, lived below with her family. They had seven boys and one daughter. Uncle Bernhard, Uncle Adolf, and Aunt Therese were no longer living. Sister Therese, who had been married for quite some time to our cousin, Franz von Hatzfeld of Lüdinghausen, welcomed us, as did brother Wilhelm from Hamburg. It was a moving reunion after twenty years. Half-grown children had become stately adults. And now there followed for me a doubly pleasant time because I had missed it so long. Most of the time we spent in Münster; however, we went back to our former home in Oelde and Stromberg. In Oelde the only close people were the Wesemanns. The Oosterlings were both dead, but there were still dear acquaintances. In Stromberg there were Uncle and Aunt Hüffer. At the Niediecks' Grandfather and Iwan were missing. I was not ready yet to talk about the Hüffers, although he was my mother's only brother and because of that I had frequently spent rather long times with them in my early years. We had never liked to be there as much as we liked to be with the Niediecks. Both of the Hüffers were probably very good people, but they were petty and sour, and everything in their lives went like clockwork. We did not feel like talking freely. With Grandfather one was always very welcome, and there was always a great deal of social activity, especially on Sundays, when the families from Münster were there.

Freedom, lively company, and a very varied social life were provided at the Niediecks, and we belonged to them when we were able to get away. But we were received with lots of love at the Hüffers. Both our uncle and aunt were very cordial, which I enjoyed very much. Clara, their daughter, was there, and Wilhelm. The three older sons had established themselves in Saxony and near Leipzig.

In Wadersloh we visited the pastor, Bruns's older brother, whom I had seen only when he married us. He was a capable man in his profession and a blessing for the area. After we had returned to Münster, I went to visit my sister in Lüdinghausen, and Bruns went back to his home. In Münster I stayed at home most of the time. It was touching for me to see that my uncle took it as a matter of course that I was there, and in the afternoon he considered himself part of the company. We took all kinds of short excursions, once again to Oelde, to

Stromberg, to Wadersloh. The time went very fast. We paid one visit that moved us very much: we traveled with Heinrich and Johanna to Obermarsberg, where our unhappy brother Bernhard had been in an asylum for many long years. It was considered advisable that only Bruns go in to see him. We looked over the wall as the two of them walked back and forth in the garden. I never saw my husband so agitated as he was afterward. I was completely beside myself, and we arrived in Paderborn late at night, sick.

Bremen
6 May 1856

Dear, dear Heinrich:

Here we are! We have survived the sea voyage happily and arrived a few hours ago. Everything seems so strange to me and yet so familiar; it makes me sad. I would almost like to turn around and go back to Missouri to my children. You will have to make an effort to cheer me up.

We are closest to my husband's relatives, and therefore we intend to visit them first. It will take a good week before we can be in Münster. We hope that we will find all of you in good health. Naturally we would like to stay with you in our grandparents' house again as long as we are here. If, however, Johanna has no room for us, please take a private room for us as close as possible.

Regards to our uncle, Johanna, and Offenberg: so, only a few days until we finally see each other again. Your sister, Jette.

Lüdinghausen
Thursday,
28 May 1856

Dear Heinrich:

It has surprised us to receive a letter immediately even though it is "only" from you! If you would only write more when I am back home again. Perhaps you would succeed if you would try; at any rate, I am becoming much more rambling, and with God's help, I shall begin to try to write when we have returned.

By the way, I am quite well in Lüdinghausen and am enjoying the rest a bit more, and I think it will be best to stay here and wait for the return of my husband. I have figured out that he will not return before Saturday evening, and then perhaps will return only to Münster. I regret missing the *Send* in Münster.[8] However, I can spend that Sunday better here in the company of Therese and her husband, since Johanna will probably go out there with Offenberg. Only I would seriously wish for some good weather so that our uncle could perhaps be persuaded to come here with you!? Then we would all go back to Münster on Monday, and nothing would have been lost. You will know what you can do; I won't leave here without some kind of a special incentive, only I would really very much like to go walking with our uncle every day.

When Bruns has returned he can open the suitcase, but there is no rush until I get there. Should I not arrive by Monday morning, then Johanna will have to take over and just have

---

8. The *Send* is the annual fair in Münster.

Anna write up the laundry, including Bruns's, since it will have to be called for with the understanding that I will send more as soon as I come to Münster.

Now, I hope you are well. I hope you will come with our uncle on Saturday evening and that my husband will come on Sunday. It would indeed be very nice, also for Therese. And then everything will be over so quickly. Friendly greetings to our uncle and to the Offenbergs. Your sister, Jette.

A postscript: Therese to Heinrich

Dear Heinrich:

Think it over well and leave Jette to me as long as possible, at least until the definite return trip on Monday. If you want to stay longer and are able to, it will be all right with me, and I would be very pleased to see you here on Sunday. Otherwise postpone it a little bit. She is not impatient yet, and is well and happy. Are you sure that Johanna is not able to come here? We three sisters really should be together more. Farewell, and don't take it amiss that I overslept on the day of your departure.

Your Therese.

Oelde
12 July 1856

Dear Heinrich:

On the way we have thought over the trip. Tomorrow afternoon we will go on to Hovestadt.9 The day after tomorrow we will go on to Wadersloh, in the evening on to Stromberg, and then can be found either here or there in Oelde until Thursday afternoon, when we shall arrive with our baggage at the railroad station (about the same time as we arrived here today). Farewell until then, greetings to Uncle and to all. Your sister, Jette.

Jette to Wilhelm

Liverpool
26 July 1856

Dear Wilhelm!

Our trip to Hull was unfriendly and stormy. Sophie immediately became seasick the other morning, and soon afterward most of the ten passengers. Another gentleman and— Bruns walked away from the noon table. Just imagine! There I sat alone with the captain. I am really proud of myself!

On Tuesday morning we arrived in Hull, and by about 11 o'clock we were at the railroad station. Mr. Glover promised to dispatch our baggage to Liverpool before 9 o'clock on Wednesday morning. Thus we traveled quickly straight across England. The sea voyage was indeed a hard trip. We arrived here about 5:30. The next morning Bruns went to the agent here, Mr. Durant, who immediately doubted that the baggage would arrive. There was still space for us on the *Atlantic*. Our things did not arrive, and thus we have had to stay here until now. Mr. Durant immediately said we would have done better to expose ourselves to a

9. In Hovestadt, Jette was to visit her cousin, the tax collector Max Boner, brother of Arnold Boner, who had died in Westphalia in 1847, and his wife, Marie.

search on the *Rob Roy,* where things went more easily. Then we could have kept everything with us.

Mr. Glover also neglected to tell us that our baggage went as passenger luggage, and thus Bruns had to go yesterday from one customs office to another. I am quite mad at this Jew!

The effects are here, as Bruns had assured himself yesterday, and they are safely aboard the boat *Asia,* and at 1:00 o'clock a steamboat will take us there. So in God's name we will go on!

We were so happy that Heinrich stayed behind. The trip through England would be very pleasant if one would not have to rush.

Greetings to the brothers and sisters and to our uncle, and farewell. Now I belong again to my own family! If it could be arranged to live with you and with them! You were all so good to me, and I love all of you so very much. God bless you!

Your sister, Jette.

Bruns also sends his sincerest regards.

On 8 August 1856 Bruns wrote Heinrich of their safe arrival in New York after a voyage of eleven days, reporting that among those on board only he and Jette were not seasick on the trip from Hamburg to Hull. On 4 November 1856 Franz wrote Heinrich, asking for help for the education of his children from the Geisberg-Hüffer educational fund. On 12 March 1857 he wrote to Caspar and Johanna Offenberg with the same request, attaching a statement regarding the fund.[10] *On 13 May he wrote to Uncle Caspar, apologizing that he had offended his uncle and brother, who had been "deeply hurt" by his letter to the Offenbergs. Since Heinrich had indicated there was no hope of receiving help from the family foundation, Franz withdrew his request.*

From the Autobiography

In August 1856 we were back home again. We found everybody well. It had been decided earlier that we would have a residence away from the business. The land was bought, and we began to build. It was going well. On the 24th of May 1857 we celebrated our silver wedding anniversary. Many people, including friends from St. Louis, came. Jette Geisberg was in the convent of the Ursulines, and Effie went there a year later. Heinrich attended the university

10. The following was attached to the letter of 12 March 1857 to the Offenbergs: "My father told me when I was still studying in Münster of a fund that had been created by the Geisbergs and Hüffers, and he said that he would try to see if we might not be able to claim the same for our education. Later, however, I heard that he had been put off with empty excuses. And thus the whole matter was left, and I have never again heard anything of this except recently from Bruns. As I have learned, others from the family took the matter into their own hands and arbitrarily used this fund, created primarily for the education of children, for their own use. People who really don't need it at all have claimed the fund, which would have been of use to many of the family . . . . However, enough of this. Our parents as well as the uncles considered others were equally just . . . as they were themselves and were not inclined to investigate seriously and thoroughly a matter that is of the greatest importance to the family. I would not utter a word for my own self, but as a father of a family I feel obligated to investigate the matter if in this way I could make it possible for my children to enjoy a proper practical education, which in case I fail would not be possible because of my lack of means. I am giving you herewith unlimited authority to act in this matter and to get to the bottom of this business. Please speak with Heinrich concerning this, and please claim a right to which you yourself as well as I am entitled, and please do not be put off by flimsy reasons. You will excuse me that I am burdening you with such a request. I am ready to reciprocate in your service any time. I respectfully sign Fr. Geisberg."

with the Jesuits. My brother wanted to found his own business and built a house at the corner of Broadway and High Street and moved there with his three children. This was very good for me. It was a great relief that he had finally, after so many years, acquired a position, although we missed him. The last time he was with us, he told me how magnificently his business was developing, but then he caught cold and a critical situation developed, and after a few days the end came. I stayed there and helped Jette and did everything I could. When he became weaker, he gazed at me for a long time. And I gazed at him. This was enough for both of us. As before, his children came to us. That was the 18th of October 1858.[11]

Jefferson City
20 April 1857

Dear Heinrich:

What should I say as an excuse that I am just now writing? I am not at all satisfied with myself, but it has been on my mind for a long time. I have tried to write to our uncle four times already, but when I was in the midst of the letter I suddenly could not go on. This is my third attempt for you. Is this not strange?

We were all well except for Louis and Ottilie, who have the so-called mumps, and I tell them how patient Wilhelm and Richard Offenberg were. At first after we returned I had sick servants and had to work hard to get everything back on its old track. Then Jette was outfitted and taken to St. Louis. Before Christmas we had to furnish two rooms with dressers and beds so that they could be rented out for the legislative session. During the winter months it is quite lively here. Even my good husband let himself be drawn into this confusion more than once. Now the gentlemen are gone, and since we can expect spring to return soon we have spread out. But it is still cold, and for the past month the buds have not been swelling any more. Mrs. Bruns had started the garden early in order to compensate for the lost year, but her forwardness was punished, and my German plants are ruined. Now the earth has been entrusted with new kernels, and it is bubbling and brewing, so in the end everything will be all right. Bruns and I often quarrel about the garden. He does not want me to invest anything in it because he maintains we may not stay here, but I believe one should use the present time and enjoy it.

The foundation and the basement for the new house are ready, and the windows and the doors are being worked on.[12] Now our gentlemen have a lot to think about and to order. Perhaps Bruns will go to Chicago to purchase wood more reasonably there, and I hope he will then travel to Milwaukee. A lady from here was there and told us that Carl is in bad health. He is said to have fallen off a lot. As soon as the weather permitted he wanted to travel to a resort.

Mill and business are doing well, not so much in volume, but nevertheless respectable and

---

11. Jette is in error here. According to her letter of 29 November 1858, Franz had died the previous day, 28 November.

12. On 31 March 1856 Dr. Bruns, his son, and his brother-in-law bought property recorded on the Jefferson City plat map as lot #460 at the corner of High and Washington streets for $1,306. The deed shows that Joseph O. Boggs sold the lot to Bernhard Bruns, Herman L. Bruns, and Francis Geisberg except for a strip forty-two feet wide on the east side that had been sold to Mathias Wallendorf. The large house built on this lot faced the Capitol and provided a front-row view of events of the war years. After Dr. Bruns's death in 1864 left her destitute with four children to support, Jette boarded German legislators in the home.

sufficient. It will probably stay this way until changes are forced upon us. Caspar will have to stay here until a prospect opens up somewhere else and we can get along without him here. Heinrich too is still with us. We will have to think about what is going to happen next school year. We have a good German school and a capable teacher of both languages. Now, however, the pastor wants to form a Catholic school and has written for a teacher who would work with Roer. Then a female academy will be built, a plan in which Bruns also is participating.[13] In general, a great deal of building is going on and seems to make the city more active than we had expected. Building lots are enormously high, all wages are equally high, and the food, particularly meat, has risen significantly. This winter smallpox was around (and indeed still is), and so there was a good deal of inoculation to be done.

Recently we wanted to have pictures taken for brother Wilhelm. Well! We got dressed and went there. But at that point he did not want to take us on two plates. Father and Mother and Hermann were taken first and I did not like that, but it was done anyway. My husband maintained that I should open my mouth a little bit, to make a more friendly face. To be sure, I wanted that, and so I did. The artist opened the window after we had been arranged and it became quite cold. It took only a short time, but I could not help it that my teeth were rattling in my mouth. Bruns had a great deal to do, and he was getting impatient, and that settled it. The face of his wife looks pitiful; it is, to be sure, that of an old woman. Heinrich, Effie, and Louis got their turn then, and this was passable. Ottilie and Wilhelm next. The girl could not sit still. It was getting late and we arranged to come back.

A nice long letter arrived from my dear little sister. It pleased me so much that I sat down immediately to answer her, but I am still not finished. You will have to tell her immediately. We are proud to have a mayor of Münster in our family.[14] May the young people enjoy the office in health and prosperity!

And you will write a whole letter to Bruns, and who should answer? Therefore do think a little bit of me too, and when I am better at it I shall write a great deal and very nicely and not as leathern as now.

What it is, I really don't know, I am always so uncomfortable and dissatisfied. And then I have too much to do, and the young people are so ill-mannered. I always have such an inner turmoil, and I would like to do better.

Give my regards to our uncle, and a thousand greetings to all the others, and do not forget your sister, Jette.

Now I remember that the Schapers from Portland were here and wished that Bruns would be a warrantor for him for the purchase of a farm, but my husband declined since we had not known him before, although we had invited them. And then we heard some detrimental things concerning his character. If you consider it fitting, you can tell his relatives about this. Otherwise, he looked quite decent.

13. The *Jefferson City Inquirer* of 11 April 1857 reported on the election of city officers. Jefferson T. Rogers was elected as mayor. Those elected as aldermen were B. Bruns, 114 votes, C. P. Anderson, 100, A. Fulkerson, 75, E. B. Cordell, 67, W. A. Curry, 76, Chris Gundelfinger, 92, and C. L. Meredith, 81.
14. Caspar Offenberg was first elected mayor of Münster in 1856 for a twelve-year term; in 1868 he was reelected for another term of twelve years. On 24 November 1856 he was appointed a life member of the House of Lords.

[c. September 1857]

Dear Brother:

I believe we owe you letters; at least, I have not heard from you, and I believe that for quite some time Bruns has also not written to you. I always wanted to report that we are not only in good spirits but also quite active.

We are pretty far into the old year, and I wanted to send some family greetings for Christmas. May our wishes reach you, and if you have gotten together, may the memory of us be dear to you all.

We still are together except for our two, Heinrich and Effie. The men, father, brother, and son, are very busy. The legislative sessions have come to an end this year, and I would like to, if I could, send you things from our newspaper occasionally. The political parties in Missouri are very strongly represented. Bruns is occupying a not insignificant place there.

Our city seems to grow significantly, and in the near future there will be a university and various [illegible] will develop. Five gentlemen who call themselves the Jefferson City Land Company[15] have plotted the city extensively and have purchased land and invite immigrants from the east to come and settle here. There have been a considerable number of articles in the newspapers concerning this. Even though I had some apprehensions in the beginning, it is not insignificant, and who knows how things will develop? Our city cannot remain as small as it seemed it would.

Brother Franz is building a house for himself and will start a business as soon as possible. It seemed to us that it would be best for the children on both sides to separate. The location of Franz's house is beautiful, and since he has begun building, a hundred different opportunities have offered themselves. If only he would show some confidence in himself! We think it cannot go wrong and that he will do well. The other building is therefore entirely the concern of the Bruns family now. And they have built it somewhat high, with three stories. In a short time we will occupy one of the three apartments.[16] Bruns believes, however, that we will not like it, and he is always speaking of the bluff and has had fruit trees planted there. But his wife does not want to move there for at least five years, and then demands a coach and coachman.

We have all been well. The boys, Heinrich Geisberg particularly, are learning wonder-

15. According to the *Jefferson City Inquirer* of 4 July 1857, the organization of the Jefferson City Land Company was undertaken by a group of civic-minded and enterprising citizens: Judge Robert W. Wells, of the U.S. District Court, Gen. Thomas L. Price, Mr. James B. Gardenhire, former attorney general, Dr. Bernhard Bruns, Dr. William A. Carrey, and Mr. James W. Bouta of New York. On 18 July 1857 the *Inquirer* carried a lengthy article on the Jefferson City Land Company and an advertisement that offered the sale of shares as well as lots for either investment purposes or for settlement, designating them as Class 1 or Class 2 at $500 or $350 a share respectively. Apparently hostility to the enterprise developed because of the political stance of the board. In a letter to the editor dated 7 November 1857, five board members presented their objectives. The major objective was to establish a first-rate university by donating $70,000 for that purpose and erecting appropriate buildings for not less than $80,000. The letter further declared that there would be no discrimination on the basis of political convictions or affiliation and that all democratic principles would be in effect. The proposed university was to emphasize Bentonian principles. The death of Senator Benton in 1858 and tensions relating to the approaching war led to the abandonment of the project.

16. In a letter of 21 September 1858 Dr. Bruns wrote to Caspar Geisberg that the house he had built across from the Capitol on High Street had three separate apartments of nine rooms each. There was a basement under the entire building, and side buildings in the courtyard contained the kitchen and laundry. A half-acre in the back provided a garden for Jette. The family occupied one floor of the house and rented out the other two for one thousand dollars annually.

fully. Only he is still bashful and awkward. Caspar is again going to evening school in order to catch up on the things he has missed. He is a good hand in the store. Jette is also at home now, and her aunt is very busy endeavoring to instruct her in managing a household. Wilhelm is at home alone but would also like to fly the coop.

And what are you up to now? Do you have rheumatism again? Are you still taking a walk with uncle on your arm? And at noon, how many are sitting in your lap at the end of the table? Do write again how our uncle is getting along!

I hope you are well and hope the Christ Child will present you with something pretty and the New Year will bring lots of blessings and fresh hopes. Hold dear as always, your sister Jette.

Bruns also sends his best regards.

Jefferson City
8 September 1858

Dear Heinrich:

There, your letter and Johanna's arrived today, and I really wonder now why I have not written for such a long time so that even Johanna is ahead of me. Quite some time ago I also received a letter from Thereschen, which I had been looking forward to for so long that I did not dare inquire for worry, and I wanted to answer the letter from Uncle first.

For the time being, according to the old custom, I shall turn to you and tell you things as they occur to me. We are all well. Vacation began in St. Louis at the beginning of July (the 4th to the 12th), and since that time we have had all the children at home again. Both Heinrich and Effie had good reports, but Heinrich was otherwise not so satisfied, so that Bruns decided to send him to the recently built high school here for the next session, which suited him very well. Effie, on the other hand, wanted very much to return to the Sisters. Now Father is taking her there again, and at the same time he will be visiting the exhibition in St. Louis,[17] which pleases him very much. Bruns is in need of some inspiration to get out of here, and I am curious to hear his report on it. Your sister is really still alert and would like to associate more with the world and with people if her husband would only set an example! However, we withdraw, carry on our business, read newspapers, and wish for a bit more social activity. It cannot be completely attributed to the lack of educated Germans.

So, we have not written concerning the change in our dwelling? I believe I was still worrying about Franz and wanted first to see how he was getting along in the beginning. It dragged along with his house, and he did not urge them on and did not discuss it. The boy has given me many a worrisome hour. Now his business is going quite well, and the boys assist him, as does Jette. If he handles everything right he will get along very well, but I think he communicates less, and Hermann is to be blamed for that, since he thought he would supervise him, which Franz was not supposed to notice. He has more trust in Bruns, and rightly so. We have to hope for the best, and I really do not know why I should be afraid since there is no reason for it. It pleases me very much to see how all the children, including ours, always stick together. It is very pleasant for me to go there. Franz has, by the way, made a very good

17. The third annual fair of the Agricultural and Mechanical Association of St. Louis took place in September 1858.

purchase. His property is now valuable, and the house brings in good rent. And then his simple household does not cost much since he gets a lot from the store.

We now occupy one-third of our newly built house and have, all in all, nine rooms. They are now building an office for Bruns next door. The space behind the house is narrow, but then abuts directly with half an acre of land, of which one part is a garden and the greater part is pasture for a calf. From the second and third story one has a pretty view from both sides; from the first story, however, the houses that are built block the view more and more.

I was very sorry that Bartmann left us so suddenly, and afterward I knew much better what I should have done. That's how things are! He will probably come soon. Bruns and I have visited his wife. It is good that you have kept the money there. When Bruns is back again we shall write in greater detail. Above all, greetings to our uncle and to the sisters and to all the others. I would very much like to hear something concerning Bernhard.

Hold dear as always your sister, Jette.

In a letter of 21 September 1858 to Caspar Geisberg, Dr. Bruns reported enthusiastically on the new home "on the best street," directly across from the Capitol. His business, located in the old place, is run by two clerks who board with the Bruns family. The steam mill is doing a good business, but the Jefferson City Land Company, of which he is vice-president, had not made the anticipated progress because of the 1857 economic collapse. However, Jefferson City is constantly growing, and over a hundred houses have been built during the summer.

Jefferson City
29 November 1858

Dear Heinrich:

I had recently planned to mail a letter to our uncle and to all of you with a very happy and joyful message for Christmas and the New Year's Festival, but I waited. Franz was ill. We nursed him, but now our Good Lord has called him. He died yesterday afternoon, on the 28th, at 4 o'clock.

It is still so new to me, and my head is still so upset. Yet I shall report to you. Approximately two months ago he experienced pain in his abdomen with bowel movements. He complained that he could not stand, and therefore sat in an easy chair, asked for medicine, and gradually became well again. He believed it was a cold.

And then he went out again, and one evening he got very cold feet and the complaint returned. It very quickly grew worse, and he began hemorrhaging. On Thursday a week ago he went to bed. He did not have much pain. He had complete care and all the medicines. On Friday, the 26th, he felt a little better; however, he was still talking deliriously, but on Saturday he became calmer. At that point we believed we had won. Then, however, once again there was bleeding. His body was exhausted. I stayed there on Saturday night, and he was visibly getting weaker, so that I often became very worried. However, I endured until morning. When Bruns arrived, he also became concerned, and we called for a priest. He answered only when asked, did not make any comments, showed no concern, no hope. Only once I told him, "Soon you will be well." And then he looked at me with such a serious and profound look that both of us were satisfied. This was his farewell. He remained calm, drank a little, and was refreshed a little. His end was short, and I stayed with him and held the hands that were getting cold until his breath stopped. I would like to die in this manner!

The children are hit hard, but they are accustomed to keeping close to us. Bruns and Hermann will help me with what is to be done. The business had been going for about six months and went very well. Franz was probably never, as long as he has been here, so satisfied and so full of hope. And just now, as he had the best prospects for himself and for his children, he had to leave them.

Can the business be kept? Hardly! Caspar is still too young. We shall take it over with them. Bruns thought we ought to be able to arrange it so that the children could keep the house and the yard. The rent should bring in more than the capital that Franz has invested in the business, and the children, except for Heinrich, are capable of helping themselves without financial assistance. Heinrich will also be old enough in a year or two. This afternoon Franz was buried. Many came to the funeral. The priest delivered a short sermon, and the singers sang a farewell to him. So this is the first in a row of brothers and sisters!

Farewell, dear brother, I have thought of you a lot. Regards to our uncle and to all. You have to tell them. We shall write to all of you later. With sincere love, your sister Jette.

In January 1859 seventeen-year-old Caspar Geisberg wrote to his great-uncle Caspar about his father's death and inquired if the five hundred dollars Franz owed could be "left a while longer" if the yearly interest were paid. If this was not satisfactory and Caspar preferred "to call the loan back earlier, our uncle {Dr. Bruns} will not object to transmitting it."

On 24 June 1860 Dr. Bruns wrote to Uncle Caspar reporting that in May he had been "sent to Chicago in Illinois as a delegate of the Republican party in Missouri in order to nominate suitable men as candidates for president and vice-president. This mandate was of great importance, the consequences of which can perhaps not be estimated. The delegation was complete from the slave-holding state of Missouri, that is, eighteen regular delegates were there. The German sector of Missouri was represented by five delegates. No state in the Union could muster an equal number of German delegates." He added that if Heinrich should "still have money for me in his hands . . . he should pay himself back interest" and "pay the debts which Franz Geisberg may have with you."

End of 1860

Dear Heinrich:

I have to admit that I no longer know when I last saw a line from you. You have forgotten me entirely. Have you been well all this time? The sisters do not write about this.

With us things are proceeding in the usual humdrum fashion. Bruns reads the newspapers, smokes, visits the sick people, or sits at home, particularly since the elections are over and it has become quiet here. I am often sorry that he has to sit alone since I always have to be upstairs with Wilhelm. The little one bears his cross patiently if he is entertained with books, with pictures, with stories. Telling stories is a difficult task for me, and when I let my imagination run freely, Effie asks naively, "But mother, is that really true?" And then Tillie comes and sits down quietly beside him and chats in her own way, and that is really funny. On Sundays Caspar and the clerks have to pay their respects. If you could see your nephews and nieces, you would not know which way to turn. Caspar is the tallest one, then Heinrich, then Hermann, who is taller than his father. Jette has a figure like Thereschen; Effie is just as tall as I am. Only Effie is so fragile and weak now she can no longer walk. Heinrich has been socializing with the apothecary and has been studying botany, but he will soon take a job in the store.

Things look very bad in the state of Missouri. I don't know that we have ever had such a money-poor time. The crop failure crowns all the misfortune. It is really depressing. I am also at times somewhat depressed when Bruns and Hermann discuss it, and we cannot hope that it will soon improve.

The election of Mr. Lincoln to the presidency has caused a great uproar in our slave party, and one can hear all kinds of threats. Here in the city a German newspaper was suppressed because it belonged to the Republican party. The editor had to leave the city.[18] Bruns has always favored this party, as has General Gardenhire,[19] who is an orator of unmatched ability. He has now departed to join the new president. This winter there will be a new legislative session, and all kinds of preparations are already being made. For two years a number of penitentiary inmates have been working in the immediate vicinity of the State House. Now it is already beginning to look very beautiful. The ground has been leveled into terraces, and there are all kinds of flower beds bordered by grass, and bushes have been set. The armory is located in one corner, and it has beautiful building blocks, and all around it is a heavy solid wall with an iron fence.[20] The whole thing cost the state over fifty thousand dollars. A German, Mr. Vogt, supervises and directs the whole thing. Since we live so close, it serves as a beautiful walk for us.

Now farewell and just imagine, dear brother, that when you receive this letter my sick people will be well again and we will all be in good spirits. If it were not so close to Christmas I would have preferred to wait until then. I hope that you are well and that many a wish that would please you will be fulfilled. Do write soon and tell us how Uncle Caspar is, and what you are all doing, and what you are up to as a lawyer, and whether you still suffer from headaches. Your loving Jette.

Yesterday we looked at the birth register written by Grandfather. Uncle Caspar was seventy-eight years old on the 29th of September.

Jefferson City
26 April 1861

Dear Brother:

For months now I have been waiting for the better times that Bruns believes will come so as not to alarm you. If Missouri goes with the South, then it is possible that the mail connection will be interrupted. Thus it is safer to report to you the best that is happening, and this is what we are doing.

18. The *Jefferson City Demokrat* had been established in June 1853 and was edited and published by A. Meyer. See Karl J. Arndt and May E. Olson, *German-American Newspapers and Periodicals, 1732–1955* (Heidelberg: Quelle and Meyer, 1961), p. 242.

19. James B. Gardenhire (1821–1862), born in Davidson County, Tennessee, was appointed attorney general by Gov. Austin A. King in September 1851 after the death of William A. Robards. He was elected to the office for a full term in August 1852. Nominated for governor by the Republicans in 1860, he ran last in the election, after Claiborne Jackson, Sample Orr, and Hancock Jackson.

20. Soon after moving from St. Joseph to Jefferson City in October 1857, Gov. Robert M. Stewart, a bachelor, obtained special appropriations of five hundred dollars for repairs to the governor's residence and upkeep of the grounds. In 1858 he obtained another appropriation of one thousand dollars to continue the work. In two of his major addresses to the legislature, Governor Stewart appealed for a "new and substantial edifice." At that time the Governor's Mansion occupied a site in the same block as the Capitol.

Since Christmastime Wilhelm's arm has healed completely, but it is still stiff, and I often look at him with serious concern, which, however, no one notices or understands. Bruns had a mild chest fever, he was quite low, but he is now much better and is smoking, etc. Sometimes he thinks perhaps he can not tolerate wine, and beer even less. So then I have to talk him out of this, and I refer him to Uncle Caspar.

I was tremendously pleased to receive a letter from Johanna, and we have also received a letter from Phina from Trier.[21] Bruns has just gone to Westphalia to comply with their request, and he will write to them and says he will also write you. I hope he will be able to make it possible to be more than straight with you.[22] We are living in very stirring times. The new governor[23] is a great secessionist; he is unpopular but he has the power. The legislature is usually on his side. There are capable men in the legislature, and we may expect nothing but good from them. The legislature has been called up for an extra session for 2 May. The state's militia has been called, and in the city as well as in the country young people are preparing for military service, naturally to carry out the governor's intentions. The Union people in the country are keeping extremely quiet. The captain who is in charge of Hermann's militia yesterday demanded his release, etc. The St. Louis Unionists will now have enlisted the four regiments in the city that the governor declined to send to comply with the request of President Lincoln. The Arsenal is full of troops, and new ones are sworn in daily. It was reported that the militia would move toward St. Louis, and then again that an order for the arrest of the governor had been issued by the president. Here the public peace has not been disturbed; only it has been necessary recently to tolerate a tremendously large secessionist flag that has been flying. I wonder whether Missouri can stay neutral? We doubt it! And I fear that we shall side with the South. That party is prone to use power and cause public unrest, and, what is even worse, it sneaks around in the dark. In almost every county vigilante committees have been formed, and they direct their anger against Republicans and *foreigners*. To begin with, a few northern people here received notice to leave the state within ten days. We are not afraid although we are both Republican and foreigners. As long as volunteers still come forth it does not affect us; I only hope that the boys will not get into any kind of a position against the Union! Well, what should we do?

We have been experiencing a favorable spring and now have good prospects for the harvest. If we do not have a war in Missouri, it seems we will be able to recover. At present almost no business is carried on. At our place we sell only for cash, and consequently business is not worth mentioning. We are limiting ourselves because we cannot collect any more. The people have no money. One has to wait and not use anything.

9 May

The gentlemen from the Senate have already been here for over a week, but since they have secret sessions we are not well informed. It is reported that it is a question of finding the means to raise two million dollars in the state in order to organize the military. With every

21. Phina Boner was the sister of Arnold Boner, who had emigrated to Westphalia and died there 27 July 1847.

22. This sentence is very ambiguous in German: "er wird es möglich machen können, mit Dir mehr wie grade zu sein." Jette has now been in Missouri for twenty-five years, and her German retains its regional characteristics while showing the influence of her American environment.

23. Claiborne Fox Jackson took the oath of office as governor on 3 January 1861. He died 7 December 1862 in a boardinghouse in Camden, Arkansas.

day we come closer to the South. Today a flag was hoisted in front of the governor's house. A significant amount of powder (26,000 [pounds]) has arrived here with approximately one hundred soldiers to guard it. A man made the remark that if Blair and Börnstein[24] would come from St. Louis with their regiments, they could easily capture the governor and both houses. That spread like wildfire. Suddenly everybody was armed. General Gardenhire from here, an excellent speaker and a lawyer and friend of Bruns, has been called to Washington by the president to accept a position there. We are looking toward future events with composure. There is probably no personal danger involved for Bruns. And thus you will not have to worry too much. Perhaps my letter is not for everybody. Bruns has the principal on our residence entered. It is impossible to pay it off at the moment although I would prefer it.

Now, may God keep you, let us hope for the best. All, including Bruns, send their regards, and of course your sister, Jette.

(I, and Bruns also, will soon write more; however, your newspapers will also inform you.)

From the Autobiography

One often hears different views regarding the events of the Civil War. I too want to report about the war and how we were affected by it. At this time the Southern element was very noticeable. Governor Jackson gathered people in the city and country, who then organized. In the Arsenal in St. Louis General Lyon took command. Fort Jackson[25] was taken, and

---

24. Francis Preston Blair, Jr. (1821–1875), was born in Lexington, Kentucky, and educated at the University of North Carolina, Princeton, and Transylvania University. In 1843 he began practicing law in St. Louis, where he founded and led the Free-Soil party and established and edited the *Barnburner,* a Free-Soil paper. He was elected to the State House of Representatives, where he served from 1852 to 1856, and to the U.S. House of Representatives, serving there from 1856 to 1858 and from 1860 to 1862. Prior to the outbreak of the Civil War, he organized new German immigrants, who were strongly antislavery, into Wide-Awake clubs to counteract secessionist efforts in Missouri. Ultimately reorganized into Home Guards, the German units participated in the capture of the St. Louis Arsenal and other military actions by Capt. Nathaniel Lyon. Blair raised several regiments for the Union and entered military service in 1861 as a colonel commanding the First Missouri Volunteers.

Heinrich Börnstein (1805–1892), one of the most problematical and controversial of the St. Louis German radicals, was born in Hamburg, Germany, the son of a Catholic Austrian actor and a Protestant mother. During the last years of the Napoleonic War, his father took the family to his home in Galicia, where Heinrich had to attend a Catholic school, much against his will, an experience that was to result in an implacable anticlericalism. Börnstein emigrated to America in late 1848 to join his friend Karl Ludwig Bernays in St. Louis. In 1849 he published a virulent anti-Jesuit novel, *Die Geheimnisse von St. Louis,* translated in 1852 by Dr. H. W. Gempp as *The Mysteries of St. Louis, or, The Jesuits on the Prairie de Noyers.* In 1851 Börnstein took over the editorship of the *Anzeiger des Westens,* which became progressively more controversial under his leadership. Although he was active in the cultural, economic, and political life of the city, founding a theater in 1859, investing in many business enterprises, and supporting Benton and Blair in their political campaigns, it was as a journalist that Börnstein had the most widespread influence, as the *Anzeiger des Westens* gained circulation in Missouri, Illinois, Indiana, Iowa, and other western states. In May 1861 he participated with his regiment of compatriots in the Camp Jackson affair. In June he traveled with General Lyon to Jefferson City, where he was left in charge as Lyon proceeded to Boonville, where Jackson had retreated.

25. Camp Jackson was located in Lindell Grove, in what was then the outskirts of St. Louis, approximately where St. Louis University stands today. Early in May 1861 Brig. Gen. Daniel F. Frost had assembled about nine hundred militia there, which Governor Jackson and Frost planned to use to capture the U.S. Arsenal at St. Louis. Confederate flags were openly displayed, and camp streets bore such names as "Beauregard" and "Jeff Davis." On 10 May Capt. Nathaniel Lyon, with several hundred regulars from the Arsenal and four regiments of Missouri Volunteers commanded by Colonels Blair, Boernstein, Nicholas Schuettner, and Franz Sigel, surrounded the camp. After forcing the surrender of General Frost, the men marched from the camp onto Olive Street, where

people shot at the returning troops in the streets. St. Louis secretly sent for weapons. Here, people from the North were expelled. My husband received threats, but they were then withdrawn. The unrest became very noticeable, and we waited quietly and anxiously. Many young people removed themselves. The Osage bridge was threatened. And Bruns said one morning at the breakfast table, "If I were young, I would now go." By noon three in our house were missing: Caspar Geisberg, Anton Baurdieck, and our Heinrich. They went individually to the depot and got away. In St. Louis they were immediately accepted at the Arsenal, and after a few days they were in the service. Unfortunately, they did not stay together. Through recommendations Heinrich got into the Third Infantry Regiment, commanded by General Sigel.[26] Since that regiment was then at full strength, Anton and Caspar enlisted in the Eighth Illinois Regiment, the Zouaves. Soon thereafter my husband went with Gen. Tom Price[27] and Captain Murphy of Linn Creek to St. Louis to see what was happening. He saw the boys. The Osage bridge[28] was burned behind them, and it took longer for them to get back from the city of Hermann on Captain Murphy's boat. The rumor was already circulating that General Lyon was coming up the river with troops. The governor went into hiding every night. The mounted troops were riding madly out of town every night.

Across from our house a company of soldiers, people from Clark Township, were camped, and they were cooking there and were noisy, but otherwise were not bothersome. One morning they were lined up; there was something going on. We became uneasy since they all looked toward our house. Finally the officers rode forward, and Bruns went out and was told to treat one man who had been shot by mistake while on patrol.

---

they waited for further orders. A crowd had gathered, and taunts and rocks were hurled at the soldiers. When Capt. F. C. Blandowski of the Missouri Volunteers was wounded by a bullet, some of the soldiers fired into the crowd, which included women and children. Twenty-eight persons were killed and many more were wounded. Conflicting reports regarding the "Camp Jackson affair" persisted for many years, and in the popular mind blame for the "massacre" was generally placed on the German soldiers. See Steven Rowan and James Neal Primm, eds., *Germans for a Free Missouri: Translations from the St. Louis Radical Press, 1857–1862* (Columbia: University of Missouri Press, 1983), pp. 16–19, 205–17.

26. Franz Sigel (1824–1902) was born in Sinsheim, Baden, Germany, and graduated from the *gymnasium* at Bruchsal. He entered the military academy at Karlsruhe, from which he graduated in 1843 to become a lieutenant in the service of the grand duke. Having resigned from the service in 1847, he led four thousand revolutionaries against the government in 1848, but was defeated and had to flee to Switzerland. Recalled to Baden as minister of war, he again took to the field against the Prussian army sent to restore the old order, but his inferior force was overpowered, forcing Sigel into exile in Switzerland again. After spending 1851–1852 in England, he emigrated to New York, where he gained the rank of major in the 5th Regiment of the New York militia. In 1857 he accepted an instructorship in mathematics and history in the German-American Institute of St. Louis. When the Civil War broke out, he organized the 3rd Missouri Infantry, and on 4 May 1861 was elected colonel. Soon assigned to command the 2nd Missouri Brigade, he was promoted to brigadier general and participated in the actions in southwest Missouri at Carthage and Wilson's Creek and in the Battle of Pea Ridge, Arkansas, 7–8 March 1862.

27. Thomas Lawson Price (1809–1870), born in Virginia, came to Missouri in 1831 and settled in Jefferson City, where he became a successful businessman. In 1838 he established the first stage line between Jefferson City and St. Louis. He was elected the first mayor of the city in 1839 and served two terms. In 1847 he was commissioned brevet major general of Missouri militia. Elected representative from Cole County to the state legislature, he served in the stormy session under Gov. Claiborne Fox Jackson. A personal and political friend of Thomas Hart Benton and a loyal Unionist, he was commissioned brigadier general by President Lincoln.

28. The Osage River bridge was first burned on 11 May 1861. After Governor Jackson reported to the legislature on the Camp Jackson affair and forced it into a night session to pass measures giving the governor emergency powers, he dispatched a detachment to guard the bridge. However, alarmed by rumors of an impending attack, the guards set the western span of the bridge on fire. The damage was repaired the next day.

They marched toward Boonville. Gen. Sterling Price[29] had taken command. Their head-quarters was opposite us. The general was acquainted with my husband and was friendly toward us and came to our house. When the young men on guard made ugly remarks to Bruns, the general advised him to make an official report. Suddenly, some light showed in this cloud, and they began to pack up and move out. In a few hours they were gone. The next day three steamboats with Union people arrived.[30] General Lyon was in command. That was a relief. After a short time, however, they went on to Boonville, where they had a clash with the Rebels.[31]

Frequently we had news from Heinrich, who remained in Missouri. We had less news from the other two, who were stationed in Paducah. In Jefferson and surrounding areas, the Home Guard was organized under Col. A. P. Richardson. Bruns and Hermann belonged to it. Many troops came and went, but only Union soldiers. Soon wounded and sick people were sent to us. The battles of Wilson's Creek and Pea Ridge were fought.[32] Heinrich partici-pated. In the latter battle he captured a horse, a rifle, and a heavy knife. When he was galloping on his adversary's horse back to his own lines, the general came toward him and ordered him to go back to direct friends who were possibly lost. Soon they had to leave Springfield, and in this retreat they even lost their baggage. His tent buddies and several others had been taken prisoner. Mr. Flach was among them. They had a hard time and had hardly anything to eat, but were released on orders as they passed Jefferson. We soon saw Heinrich again. He had been sent by the general to be a recruiting officer.

The regiment then went way up to Forsyth over the Arkansas line into an area which is

29. Sterling Price (1809–1867) was born in Prince Edward County, Virginia. After attending Hampden-Sidney College for a year to study law, he migrated with his parents to the new state of Missouri. In 1833 he married Martha Head, also a native of Virginia, and settled on a farm near Keytesville in Chariton County, where he grew tobacco and owned several dozen slaves. In 1840 he was elected to the state legislature and in 1844 to the U.S. House of Representatives. At the outbreak of the Mexican War in August 1846 he resigned to become a colonel of a regiment of Missouri volunteers. In 1853 he was elected governor by the anti-Benton faction in Missouri. Retiring from political office in 1857, he returned to his plantation, Val Verde, and was active in promoting the railroads. In May 1861 he accepted Governor Jackson's appointment as commander of the state military forces. See Albert Castel, *General Sterling Price and the Civil War in the West* (Baton Rouge: Louisiana State University Press, 1968), for an account of Price's military career.

30. General Lyon arrived in Jefferson City aboard the *Iatan* with about two thousand men on 15 June 1861. He was welcomed by Thomas L. Price and some hastily organized Home Guard units. Finding Jefferson City aban-doned by the governor and state troops, Lyon remained in the city for only a day before embarking for Boonville with his troops.

31. The battle of Boonville, on 17 June 1861, was the first Civil War engagement in Missouri. Lyon quickly routed the poorly organized and untrained troops led by Col. John Sappington Marmaduke and his uncle, Governor Jackson. Sterling Price, suffering from recurrent ailments contracted during the Mexican War, was unable to take to the field.

32. The Battle of Wilson's Creek took place on 10 August 1861. General Lyon and his weary and hungry troops had entered Greene County almost a month earlier, on 13 July. Ordering the troops to camp at Pond Springs, he rode into Springfield in hope of finding the supplies he had requested. Taking charge of all Federal troops in the area, a total of approximately six thousand, which included, however, nearly fifteen hundred who expected to be discharged because their three-month enlistment was ending, Lyon had to choose between withdrawal to Rolla or attacking the Southern forces gathering along the Arkansas-Missouri border. He chose the offensive and, count-ing on the element of surprise, attacked a much larger Confederate force, led by Price and Gen. Benjamin McCulloch of Arkansas, that was camped at Wilson's Creek southwest of Springfield. During the battle General Lyon was killed on "Bloody Hill" while leading Iowa and Kansas troops. Both sides suffered almost equally high casualties. When the Confederates withdrew to regroup at midday, Maj. Samuel D. Sturgis, who had succeeded Lyon, ordered a retreat to Springfield. However, the Battle of Pea Ridge, Arkansas, 7–8 March 1862, resulted in a decisive victory for the Union forces.

pretty rough, and suffered all kinds of hardships. Heinrich stepped onto a nail while cross-ing a river. Since he could not walk, he rode on a donkey, which threw him when it made a sudden jump, and he broke his collarbone. He was bandaged, and when they arrived in Helena, Arkansas, he was given a leave. The leave was set to be for two weeks, but when Father interceded, Dr. Hammer obtained two more weeks for him. Thus we had him over a month, and we were so happy to have him with us again. His recovery was good under Father's care.

Jefferson City
Undated
[c. June 1861]

Dear Brother:

Yesterday your letter arrived, and I hasten to answer you at the particular request of my husband. I assume that you have by now received a letter (mailed before May 20th) in which I informed you of the beginning of the unrest. I am pleased that you now ask me for more information, and I shall try to comply with your request if the mail gets through.

So you know that General Lyon requested General Frost[33] to surrender his camp outside St. Louis. The latter complied, very much to the dissatisfaction of his soldiers, who followed the victors grumblingly and with threats; however, they had to yield. They were escorted by the Home Guards, who were fired upon from the crowd of onlookers. The Guards then reciprocated and several people from the mob fell, including some women! Whereupon some newspapers really set up a howl. Then President Lincoln sent the commander-in-chief of the western division of the army, General Harney,[34] to St. Louis. As a native of the South he sympathized with them, and he hesitated and saw Gen. Sterling Price, who had been appointed by Governor Jackson, and made a treaty to do nothing against anybody. He passively watched the arming of the secessionists (who, by the way, drove many Union people from their farms and homes and mistreated them, etc.). It finally got so bad that Unionists who were higher up turned to the president, who recalled the brave old warrior, General Harney, who was unfortunately no diplomat, and consequently General Lyon was appointed again to the highest rank and the chief command. Then in St. Louis they recruited and drilled for the Union. Here it was really lively. Opposite us was the Headquarters Com-pany. From the counties above us everybody came to the State Fair near the State House. The city was crowded with troops, approximately fifteen hundred, who let themselves be sworn in against the Union and thus were issued weapons.

33. Daniel M. Frost (1823–1900) was a native of Schenectady County, New York. He graduated from West Point and served in the Mexican War, in Indian scouting, and in Europe before resigning from the army in 1853. A Southern sympathizer, he settled in St. Louis, where he served in the state legislature and as a general in the state militia. In 1860 he commanded the militia of the First Military District on what was known as the "South-west Expedition" against the Jayhawkers on the western border of Missouri. As commander of the militia at Camp Jackson he was taken prisoner by Captain Lyon on 10 May 1861. Exchanged, he led his Missouri brigade at Pea Ridge in Arkansas and subsequently was promoted to brigadier general in the Confederate army.

34. Gen. William S. Harney was commander of the Department of the West, with headquarters in St. Louis, during the critical months before the outbreak of the war. At the request of Frank Blair, Jr., President Lincoln agreed to relieve Harney on the grounds he was playing into the hands of the secessionists. The order dismissing him was sent to Blair to be delivered only if necessary. On 30 May, Harney was relieved, and Capt. Nathaniel Lyon was promoted to brigadier general and took command of the Department of the West until he was replaced by Gen. John C. Frémont on 3 July 1861.

The officers however were not prepared, they had no provisions, etc. In short, many of the soldiers became dissatisfied [the corner of the letter has been torn and approximately four sentences are missing here].

The governor dismissed most of them, and they then proceeded to make better preparations here. Powder, lead, rifles, blankets, material to make uniforms, and food were brought in. Twice there was a false alarm—it was reported that troops were coming from St. Louis, and the governor, the officers, the common soldiers, and the secessionists' families rode, drove, and ran away. And then on orders from the governor the Osage bridge was burned (partly); thus things were developing here, and we were perhaps a little alarmed, but we tried to keep as calm as possible and hoped every day that the Union would intercede somehow. Until finally on Sunday, a week ago, Bruns said, "I am going to St. Louis." I was in agreement with him. Two hours later he was gone. On Monday the governor attempted to have a meeting with General Lyon. A deputation arrived with an extra train, assured them safe passage, and thus the governor and General Price departed.[35] The governor demanded from General Lyon the dissolution of the Home Guard regiments, the surrender of their weapons, and the assurance that no United States troops would stay in Missouri or would pass through except those who were already stationed there. For his part he agreed to dissolve the state militia and take care of all citizens no matter which side they favored.

General Lyon did not want to hear any of this, and thus they separated after the governor had given the president of the Pacific Railroad his word of honor that the railroad would be left in good condition. During the night both gentlemen arrived here again. The train waited for half an hour, and then a company of soldiers went down and, on his orders, burned the Gasconade and the Osage bridges. On Wednesday afternoon he issued a proclamation and ordered fifty thousand soldiers to report.

Well, in the beginning I thought, "Bruns is gone, Hermann is a soldier, and what should we do?" [The upper edge of the sheet is missing.] Caspar and Heinrich had gone to St. Louis and enlisted on the 20th of May with the approval of Father. Since that time they have written that Heinrich received a vacant position in Colonel Sigel's Third Regiment through recommendations. Caspar and Anton went to the American Zouaves. Instead of enlisting, everybody [in Jefferson City] prepared to leave, no one knew to where. The entire depot became empty, and they all left by railroad, by steamboat, or by wagon. On Friday everybody was gone. In the morning Bruns returned. He told us that Gen. Tom Price, a respected gentleman, our neighbor, and another gentleman went with him to General Lyon and Colonel Blair and asked whether the Union could not do something, that impatience had driven them from their homes. They inquired about everything in great detail and explained that they were ready to go back. Well, the news of the destruction of the bridges inflamed citizens and troops, friend and foe alike. Bruns accepted a commission from General Lyon to form the Citizens' Guard to enlist members in Cole County and the neighboring counties.

On Saturday afternoon five steamboats arrived with troops, and General Lyon took pos-

35. Governor Jackson, accompanied by Gen. Sterling Price, met with General Lyon and Col. Francis Blair at the Planter's House in St. Louis on 11 June 1861. Instead of yielding to the demands made by Jackson, Lyon declared open war on the state government headed by Jackson and offered to escort the negotiators through his lines. They hastily departed for Jefferson City, burning the bridges over the Gasconade and Osage after their train had crossed.

session of the Capitol. On Sunday he went with Colonel Blair to Boonville, forty-five miles from here, where the secessionists had their quarters. The Second Regiment arrived, and Colonel Börnstein was named commander in charge here. On Tuesday there was a skirmish below Boonville. Two Union men and forty-two state troops were killed. Then all supplies, powder, rifles, etc., fell into the hands of their enemies. The governor is gone, and Gen. Sterling Price is sick. The State's Guards fired only once, and then ran and threw away their rifles. Today it is reported that they are reassembling, and we are constantly consulted. Only four hundred men are stationed here; two companies of Home Guards have already formed, and everywhere in the country the same is taking place [the upper edge of the sheet is missing]. Bruns believes that it will not last long and that we will stay with the Union, but there will certainly be many a small bloody fight taking place.

It is sure that if the Union troops leave the city we cannot stay one minute longer. Heinrich has gone to the southwest with his regiment, to Rolla on the way to Springfield.[36] He is in good spirits. The others are still at the Arsenal. Yesterday evening there was a rumor that the remainder of the State's Guard was approaching the city, approximately eighteen hundred men. Here only four hundred men were left. I began to pack again, and suddenly the drums were heard, and from the river a whole regiment of St. Louis Home Guards came marching up. They reconnoitered, and no enemy was found within twenty miles. Bruns thinks that in a short time everything will be settled. But he also has such rigid views, and he says that great severity should be exercised, and sometimes I begin to be frightened because of this. The only good is that the Germans become aware of their strength and their predominance. Now the Americans fear them, and later they will probably respect them more.

Hermann is now also a lieutenant in the Second Home Guards. Bruns is everywhere. Colonel Börnstein is constantly consulting him. All around there are people who think differently, yet they are few, and we stay on friendly terms with them. —We are all well, although we do lack some rest at night.

Farewell, dear Heinrich, give our regards to our uncle and to all. We will soon write again. (The mail goes by steamboat until the bridges can be repaired again.) You will also have to let us hear from you. Later I shall answer the letters from Uncle and also from the sisters. Bruns sends his best regards and joins your sister, Jette.

A few weeks ago Bruns wrote a long letter to his brother, the pastor, and, by the way, asked him to pay you the $87.20 that we advanced to Holtermann's niece. The pastor and her relatives guaranteed us at the time that repayment of any expense we might have would be made.

Jefferson City
14 August 1861

Dear Brother:

I do want to apologize to you very much that I have not had anybody write earlier. The events here are so extraordinary that they capture our entire attention, so that we are quite numb. I believe I indicated in my last letter in June that General Lyon arrived here. After

36. Springfield was occupied by Union forces on 23 June 1861.

him, the Second Regiment of Volunteers under Colonel Börnstein arrived, and General Lyon and Colonel Blair went by steamboat to Boonville, which is about forty-five miles by land, where they defeated the State's Guards, who then fled to the southwest near the Arkansas line. Well, down there stood Colonel Sigel with the Third Regiment of Volunteers, with whom our Heinrich is, in Company K. He used to write frequently, and then wrote twice after the battle of Carthage, on the 5th of July, where Colonel Sigel won a glorious victory.[37] They had only one wounded in Heinrich's company. He was full of courage and did not complain about anything (and often the soldiers suffer very much).

The Second Regiment was stationed here, and the citizens and soldiers were in general quite satisfied. Bruns was very much occupied every day. The colonel always had to consult with him, the secessionists needed him as a negotiator, the Home Guards needed him to organize things. Batteries were positioned all around the State House. Then other regiments passed through here, going to all areas of the state. And whenever the soldiers were sent elsewhere because of unrest, then suddenly it was reported that on that night the secessionists would come. Hermann frequently had to accompany these convoys with his company.

The Convention[38] was summoned here for the 2nd of July, and in spite of difficulties most gentlemen succeeded in getting here. There was a quorum. Governor Jackson was declared unfit for his office, and until the new election in November, when a new governor can be elected, Mr. Gamble from St. Louis is to serve. So far so good, but the latter, an old, rather timid gentleman, sent a message to the people, admonishing them to keep the peace at a time when we are living in war. All newspapers are full of it and are reproaching him mightily. The Rebels are tricky and drive away the Union people, murder them, and rob wherever they can. If they are pursued they disappear completely. The Union people take prisoners, bring them to their headquarters according to orders, where they are fed for a few days, and then they have to swear an oath to the Union and are politely discharged. The oath is immediately disregarded since it was forced upon them, and then the Rebels are playing their game anew. The Union soldiers are threatened and demoralized by this. It is a miserable time!

For three weeks I had to be in bed, and I wanted Effie to write for me and to make daily notes.

General Fremont[39] is now the general in charge of the western army, and since he is here

37. The information from Heinrich Bruns that Sigel had been victorious at Carthage was also announced in St. Louis by the *Anzeiger des Westens* on 11 December 1861. Actually Sigel had attempted to block the southern advance of Governor Jackson's forces, but, outnumbered four to one, succeeded only briefly on 5 July and then retreated to Springfield.

38. At the State Convention at Jefferson City on 22 July, there was an 80 percent attendance, with most of the Southern sympathizers absent. The delegates declared the governor's seat vacant and elected Hamilton R. Gamble and Williard P. Hall to the posts of governor and lieutenant governor, respectively. Gamble served until his death on 31 January 1864, whereupon Hall succeeded him in office.

39. John Charles Frémont (1813–1890), a native of Savannah, Georgia, educated at Charleston, South Carolina, worked as a surveyor before being commissioned in the U.S. Army. In 1841 he married Jessie Benton, daughter of Sen. Thomas Hart Benton of Missouri. During the Mexican War he participated in the occupation of Monterey, San Francisco, and Sonoma. A quarrel with Gen. Stephen Kearney led to a court-martial in 1847–1848, which found him guilty of mutiny and disobedience. Resigning from the army, he returned to California, where he was elected senator from the new state but served only one year. In 1856 he was named presidential candidate on an antislavery platform by the newly formed Republican party, but was defeated by James Buchanan. At the out-

things are going differently. He is a man full of energy and without prejudice against the Germans. Caspar and Anton are stationed in Cape Girardeau; they are well and have already marched once to the northwest, without participating in a skirmish, however. And now since yesterday there are telegrams that Lyon has been killed, that eight hundred Union people are dead or wounded and five thousand rebels are dead, among them Gen. Sterling Price and General McCulloch,[40] that their army has been dispersed, and that all supplies have been burned. Sigel spent the night on the battlefield, and on the next day, Sunday the 11th of August, after he had assembled everybody he moved back to Springfield and still farther back to Rolla, which is the last railroad station. He had to fear being cut off by General Hardee.[41] The army of the Rebels was greater than they had thought: Texans, men from Louisiana, from Arkansas, and even Indians, twenty-three thousand; against them there were eight thousand Union men.[42]

For quite some time the newspapers have been lamenting the fact that Lyon and Sigel were getting so little help. The distance between Rolla and Springfield is 125 miles, a wearisome trip since the Union families had joined them and all horses and wagons had long before become the booty of the Rebels. By Saturday already, three thousand volunteers had moved from Rolla toward them, and further regiments had left St. Louis. We hope that all of this help does not get there too late, and God knows how many days we will have to spend without news. At the present time we have only a few companies of Irish here and a regiment of Home Guards, who are from this and the surrounding counties and do not like to leave their wives and children alone. I wonder whether we still have to fear? It is unsafe. It is certain that the great majority in the state is for the Union.

We shall write to you in a few weeks again. We hope our uncle and all of you are well and we send our best regards. Your sister, Jette.

I wish you had our maps with miles indicated. Do write soon.

From the Autobiography

In Jefferson there was always commotion. Troops came and went. It was at this time that Lieutenant Pinhart, with whom we became friends through Father, was there. While marching to Frankfurt, Missouri, he was shot and killed by guerrillas.[43]

---

break of the Civil War he was appointed major general of Volunteers and commander of the Western Department in St. Louis, but his brief term was marked by authoritarian policies and disputes with subordinate officers. President Lincoln relieved him of his post in November after only one hundred days. He was then placed in command of the Mountain Department of Virginia, Tennessee, and Kentucky, where he served two years.

40. In spite of a painful wound, Gen. Sterling Price led his men throughout the battle at Wilson's Creek and even advocated immediate pursuit of the retreating Union forces; he was dissuaded from this by General McCulloch, who argued that the Confederate troops were exhausted, disorganized, and short of ammunition. Neither Price nor McCulloch was killed at Wilson's Creek. McCulloch suffered a fatal wound at the Battle of Pea Ridge on 7 March 1862.

41. Brig. Gen. William Joseph Hardee had organized an Arkansas Confederate brigade early in the war and had then been transferred to Kentucky, from where his forces posed a serious threat to the Union operations in Missouri.

42. The figures estimated by General Lyon and by newspapers were often highly exaggerated. Intelligence and communication were poor, preventing commanders in the field from making accurate estimates.

43. The Report of the Adjutant General notes that First Lt. Julius Pinhard, Company E, Ninth Cavalry Regiment, Missouri State Militia, was killed by guerrillas near Cambridge in Saline County on 26 September 1862.

The 10th Regiment of Cavalry was organized. Colonel Cornyn[44] in St. Louis was in charge. Mr. N. Lusk was a recruiting captain here and took Heinrich as his lieutenant. Since, however, his company soon filled up, the men elected Heinrich to be their captain for Company G, the 10th Missouri Cavalry Volunteers. They were mostly people from here, and then some men from Westphalia were added. Thus he did not get back into the 3rd Infantry Regiment.

We had to part. The whole city participated. They were very solemn. I could barely say more than the few words that were necessary. Both Hubers[45] went along. Wilhelm, the younger one, was constantly laughing. He went gladly. Not so, however, Joseph. Bruns and Hermann walked them to the depot, and many from the city went along. At the end, Heinrich gave his father an envelope with the request, "Give this to Mother." He had given me a lock of his hair. We never saw him alive again. This was in August. It took a while until the regiment was filled, and then they went toward the South.

Now and then we heard from Caspar until he received marching orders to go to Fort Donelson.[46] He participated in the battle and was hit by a shell, which smashed his left arm. He also received a deep wound in his leg. Anton and Tom Sullivan dragged him back to a nearby log house. But probably a lot of fellows had been brought there, and he soon lost consciousness. His feet and his right hand were affected overnight by the frost. On the third day he was taken to Dover, and his arm was amputated. Then he was taken to Mound City, Illinois, and put into the hospital. We found his name on the list of the wounded. Father immediately got ready to travel. Then a letter from him arrived, saying, "If only I could be at home!" At the hospital he immediately received permission to be moved, but travel was slow and troublesome. He was very weak. From Cairo they traveled by steamer. In St. Louis they had a rest. Here, the Turners[47] carried him into our house. We cried when we saw him. But he smiled, saying, "I am happy that I am here." After four days his suffering was over. He had a hard fight with death. I alone was with him. It was the 18th of March 1862.

Frankfurt, later called New Frankfort, had been founded in 1850 by German settlers. By the summer of 1862, increased terrorist activity in the state by armed bands or bushwhackers prompted Brig. Gen. John M. Schofield to order his men to shoot armed marauders on sight. For every Union soldier or citizen killed by guerrillas, "rebels and rebel sympathizers" would be required to forfeit five thousand dollars, the money to be paid to the victim's family.

44. Florence M. Cornyn, son of an Irish immigrant, settled in St. Louis in 1852 and was appointed physician at the City Hospital. At the outbreak of the war he became surgeon of the First Missouri Infantry Regiment, commanded by Col. Frank P. Blair, and participated in the battles of Boonville and Wilson's Creek. In 1862 he resigned the surgeonship of the First Missouri Infantry to raise the Tenth Missouri Cavalry Regiment. This regiment had many engagements with Gen. Nathan B. Forrest in Tennessee and Mississippi. Cornyn was killed by one of his own officers in a personal dispute on 10 August 1863.

45. Joseph and Wilhelm Huber were from Westphalia in Osage County. First Sgt. Joseph C. Huber appeared on the rolls of Company G, 10th Cavalry. According to records in the Adjutant General's office, Joseph died 5 May 1864 at Vicksburg.

46. Fort Donelson, near Dover on the Cumberland River in Tennessee, was taken by Gen. Ulysses S. Grant on 16 February 1862, and the stage was set to split the Confederacy with a drive down the Mississippi to Vicksburg.

47. The Jefferson City *Turnerbund* was reported in an article in the *Jefferson City Inquirer* of 6 June 1857 to be a gymnastic society and not a "political organization" as "a majority of people suppose." Following the precepts of Friedrich Ludwig Jahn (1778–1852), Turner organizations began to spring up in Germany about 1810. With the motto *mens sana in corpore sano* (a healthy mind in a healthy body) from Juvenal, the Turner societies became very popular. The physical training served as preparation for military service for youths ready to fight against French occupation. German immigrants, particularly the 1848 revolutionaries, brought the idea to America and founded *Turnvereine* in almost all cities with large German populations. In St. Louis the first *Turnverein* was founded in May 1850, and at the outbreak of the war it had over five hundred members. The groups were in fact often highly politicized, and the St. Louis Turners provided entire companies of the Missouri Volunteers. See William Hyde and Howard L. Conard, *Encyclopedia of the History of St. Louis*, vol. 5 (1899), 2314–18.

His funeral was very moving. Several regiments were there, all the troops stationed here, also the artillery. When the procession arrived at the cemetery, the last were still at the house. The band played Körner's "Vater Ich Rufe Dich"[48] at the grave.

Jefferson City
3 April 1862

Dear Heinrich:

Frequently I have thought that I would have to write you, and then yesterday your and our uncle's letter arrived. I would have liked to let a letter go off to the "Archivist C. Geisberg," but I think that I should write to you again at this time. I believed earlier it would be most fitting for you to be informed of these rough and miserable times first, and I wanted to spare our uncle. For I do not doubt that the death of his nephew, his godchild, and his last name-sake will hit him harder, and consequently I shall turn to him somewhat later.

When Bruns arrived with him [Caspar] on the 13th of March we all hoped for the best. He himself was so happy and content, and he spoke with his usual strength and was not at all as miserable as I had anticipated. In order not to disturb him we let him spend the first night on his cot, the bed of suffering on which he had been lying during the entire trip. The next day we took him upstairs to his bed, which fatigued him very much. We made it as comfortable for him as we could, and he was so satisfied and did not complain about anything. However, he did not want to be bothered with food. And then we could not stop his awful diarrhea. And so it went on, and at times he had very severe attacks, followed by fever. On Monday morning he was retching for a long time, and afterward he became very sick. I laid my hand on his head and then he said, "You need not fear, everything will be over now." He was conscious, he prayed with the priest till the evening, and at times his thoughts wandered away. Jette and Hermann stayed with him until I arrived at two o'clock and relieved Jette. As it went on he became fearful, and he shouted, "Mother, Mother, I am so afraid!" I said then, "Caspar, in Heaven it will be better!" "Yes, I believe that," he answered, and his voice was as firm and deep as that of his grandfather and his father. Then he mostly dozed, the phlegm rose higher, there was some twitching, and it was all over. Bruns had been there half an hour earlier and had said, "He will not see the evening." God bless him!

He was a good boy. We would have liked to have kept him in spite of his cramps and his lost arm. He has probably been spared many a hard hour! His funeral was so pompous, arranged by the military. It is said there had never been so many people there, civilians also. He is resting beside his father.

A few days ago two letters arrived from Heinrich; he is well; he wrote immediately after the Battle at Pea Ridge[49] on the 10th of March; they had not been very much involved. The entire hospital here has been dissolved, the sick people have been sent to St. Louis, and the sisters and doctors will be going back. Attendants, cooks, and everybody else are looking for other occupations. We are glad that Bruns has been relieved early. He was offered a position

48. "Vater, ich rufe dich!" is the first line of the song "Prayer During the Battle," composed by Karl Theodor Körner (1791–1813) in 1813 and set to music by F. H. Himmel.

49. The Battle of Pea Ridge took place in northwest Arkansas on 7–8 March 1862. About 17,000 Confederate troops under the command of Gen. Earl Van Dorn and Gen. Albert Pike were decisively defeated by Gen. Samuel Curtis's Union forces, which totaled about 11,300. After that battle, Missouri was not seriously threatened by a large Confederate force until Gen. Sterling Price led a raid through the state in September and October 1864.

in General Grant's army in Tennessee, which he declined because of his health. We shall get more rest here it seems. If only peace would come! Hermann will again continue his business. Bruns and everybody else sends regards. Soon more!

Your sister, Jette

From the Autobiography

In 1862 Hermann brought his young wife, Netty Holtschneider, to us. A year afterward, a daughter, Jenny, was born to them. In June 1863 I took Effie to Springfield, Illinois, where she was to stay for a year with the Higis. On the 7th of July I returned and was met at the depot by Bruns and both boys. A day later the news arrived that Heinrich had been killed on the battlefield. And afterward dozens of letters reported that he had been shot at Iuka, Mississippi. Then the news came that Colonel Cornyn had ordered that the body be brought home. Several telegrams followed, and finally on 18 July the train arrived. Father and Hermann went to the depot, and many others too. Lieutenant Rice stepped forward and handed Father the saber of the fallen one, which he then laid on the coffin. Silently, the Turners again took over their duties. They carried the body into the house. Because of his large size, a second coffin had to be sent for from Memphis, and because of the long delay and the southern climate we were hardly able to recognize him. It was a great shock for me. The commandant of the post, Colonel Pound, took care of the funeral. All troops stationed here, several regiments, and many, many citizens took part. It was a long procession, as it had been when Caspar was buried.

The skirmish at Iuka was not a big battle.[50] The Rebels had held a protected position on a hill among trees. When the company under Heinrich was ordered to advance, they dismounted from their horses, and he remained at the point, as he was accustomed to do, saying, "Come on, boys!" He and three of the fellows close to him were hit. Then the enemy withdrew. On the orders of the colonel, Heinrich was carried to an ambulance, to which he first objected. Wm. Huber climbed in with him and held him. He died of internal bleeding. The shot had gone through his lung. "Poor Father, poor Mother," were the last words he said. They withdrew to Corinth, where they stayed for a few days.

Jefferson City
August 1863

Dear Heinrich! Dear Brother!

Our Heinrich is gone. The handsome, good boy, full of life, the pride of his father, the quiet worry and joy of his mother. He fell in battle at Iuka, Mississippi, shot through the chest. He suffered for only one and a half hours and was conscious most of the time. Even now it often seems impossible. (He fell on 7 July 1863.) And it hit us so unexpectedly, like a thunderbolt. It is too hard! Our Lord gave us the strength to suffer the first pain calmly, and

50. The skirmish at Iuka, Mississippi, in which Heinrich Bruns lost his life took place on 7 July 1863. A detailed report by Colonel Cornyn dispatched from Corinth on 9 July describes the encounter, which was one-and-a-half miles from Iuka: "Capt. H. G. Bruns of the Tenth Missouri, a young and dashing and as brave a soldier as ever wielded a sword, fell at this point, pierced through the lungs by a musket-ball, in advance of his men and cheering them on to victory. Two of his own men and one of Company E, Tenth Missouri Cavalry, were killed at this place and almost at the same time." See *The War of the Rebellion*, ser. 1, vol. 24, pt. 2 (Washington: Government Printing Office, 1889), pp. 663–65.

so it will probably go on. But the whole war, and the whole miserable world—one gets so tired of it!

Since all the newspapers had picked it up[51] and since in general there was so much sympathy shown, I can include a few printed articles. We received the first news of his death on Wednesday, the 15th, and the next day a telegram arrived from Lieutenant Rice, in which he reported that he was bringing the body to St. Louis on the *Belle of Memphis*. The boat was delayed by a day. On Saturday, the 18th, in the afternoon, the train arrived with the caisson. Bruns and Hermann went to meet it. And there the first company of the local militia had been lined up. When the coffin was carried onto the platform by friends, Lieutenant Rice stepped forward and handed Father the sword and sash of his son. The soldiers all stood at attention and saluted. The body was placed into the hearse. Bruns placed the saber on the coffin. With the company in front, then Father, friends, and onlookers following, he was brought home. It seemed to me that I would expire, and I sat in the room next door until I could see him alone. The first view frightened me tremendously. Afterward I was so resigned. It was after all beautiful that they sent the body home. Lieutenant Rice, the first lieutenant under Heinrich, lived with him in the tent. When they returned with the dead and wounded into the camp near Corinth, Mississippi, they sent for a metal coffin from Memphis. When it arrived it was too small, and so they left the body in a wooden coffin until they could get another one in Memphis. The upper part is made of glass so that his face and chest could be seen without having to open it, which was no longer possible. On Sunday morning, 19 July, he was buried with military honors. Peace be to his ashes! —He is lying next to Caspar, then there is brother Franz. What touched me most was the fact that the common soldiers from here and Westphalia wrote to their relatives and expressed their regrets. Thus one of them wrote to his father:

> During the third charge we went forward, our cannons began to thunder, the branches were flying from the trees as if they had been mowed down. Then the Rebels charged no more but fled everywhere as quickly as they could and left several dead and wounded on the field. Our company suffered heavy losses, we lost our Captain, a Corporal and Nic S., all of whom are dead now, and today, this afternoon at five, we buried them here in Corinth. Our Colonel had tears in his eyes when he spoke. We are very sorry for our Captain, he was the best in the Regiment and was respected by everybody in the Regiment. Our company is just as if lost, for he was so good to us, and we shall not very quickly forget the day on which he fell. The Corporal was a young man, he leaves a wife and two small children. Our Captain and he were the men next to me. I saw him fall, our Captain fell at the same time, but I did not see him for they shouted "Forward" and we advanced. I soon saw that our Captain was not among us and I also did not see our Lieutenant, but he was farther to the right with another part of the company.
>
> I went with the first platoon a little more to the left until we were called back, and there I found out that our Captain had been shot and also that N. S. is severely wounded. The Rebels were 1200 men strong on the right wing where we were, and on the left 800. They could not charge the cannons for we did not give them time for that. All in all we were 1,000 men and a few companies were not under fire. We had our little cannons with us. We stood in the cross fire for a while and the Rebels wanted to surround us, but we lay down on the ground behind trees and thus we held

51. The *Missouri State Times* in Jefferson City carried articles on "Captain Henry Bruns" on 18 July, 21 July, and 25 July 1863, with extensive quotes from the military report cited in the previous note.

them so that they could not drive us back. We were not more than 60–70 feet from each other. I thought we would get involved in hand-to-hand combat. If they had come a little closer we would have used our revolvers and then they would have suffered. Our Captain will be sent to Jefferson. I think that we will not get such a good Captain again. Otherwise all the fellows are well. Peter and L. were not involved this time, and John held the horses on the battlefield, and there it was not dangerous and I came away lucky for which I thank God. Your son, G. Baill.

This is a good letter, so simple and natural that I thought you would like to read it too. — And then there are two good friends of ours in the company, the Huber brothers, the younger one, Wilhelm, stayed with Heinrich from the beginning until his suffering was over. Joseph, the older one, wrote to me. I shall give it to you in his own words:[52]

The fatal day your son Henry was killed will always be remembered by his companions and fellow soldiers. He died about one and a half hours after he was wounded, fully conscious of his approaching death. He did not speak much and when questioned he did not reply. He told my brother William that he was suffocating with blood. Col. Cornyn, hearing of his wound, went to see him immediately and examined him. He saw that earthly help was impossible. Henry was placed in the ambulance. He tried to hear our shout of victory, after which I went to him, but he was not conscious any more and Col. Cornyn then gave him ease. He died before we began to move back to Corinth. —He was beloved by all soldiers, as well as officers, and he was the special favorite of Col. Cornyn. His company was the best. —My brother intended to come up with his body but was ordered back from Memphis. Signed Jos. Huber.

An orderly from the company is here now on leave. Hermann sent him back to me. The man saw him at the time; Heinrich sat down on the ground after being shot. And then he fell backward, he suffered great pain and did not want to get into the ambulance, etc.

A short time before this battle Heinrich had written to all the children. In his last letter to us he sent his picture and wrote, "This is how I look now!" He sent his picture to Effie and Jette last. Effie was to send him books.

Five weeks ago I was in Illinois and took Effie to an acquaintance. The girl wanted to have a change. It disturbed me very much that she was not at home; however, so far she has been very satisfied and intends to spend a few more months there. She was very much attached to Heinrich. Bruns is still very busy as a surgeon for the army and mustering soldiers for Missouri. I wonder whether it will come to this? Perhaps not! And then I hope that he will go into retirement. The discontent is great; I wonder what will happen? The Radical party[53] has a very bad reputation. The governor is criticized very much, but he has the power, and the

---

52. Joseph Huber's letter was written in English.

53. The Radical party was a faction of extremists who advocated immediate emancipation and a punitive policy toward the South after the surrender. The "Platform and Declaration for the Organization of the German Radicals," established by a "Convention of their Delegates" held at Cleveland on 20 October 1863, renounced all party allegiance and called for adherence to eleven principles, including the "Integrity of the Union and subordination of the several States under the sovereignty of the People of the United States," the unconditional suppression of the rebellion, the abolition of slavery in the entire territory of the United States "in the shortest way," and "treatment of the re-conquered rebel States as territories for the purpose of re-construction." It advocated confiscation of lands and settlement of the slaves on such lands, mass education of the Negroes, and support of revolution in Europe. The declaration resolved that "the Convention take most strongly the part of the brave emancipationists of Missouri, so cruelly persecuted under connivance of the Administration" (University of Kentucky Archives, German Broadsides 48 M 53). Dr. Bruns was a member of the German Radicals.

Copperheads[54] are satisfied with him. Everywhere meetings are announced. I almost wish that Bruns and Hermann would not be so active. I no longer have any courage for anything. I am constantly afraid.

Missouri is a beautiful country, and yet if we cannot find peace here I would like to move away. Heinrich always said, "I shall not remain in Missouri!" —Great expectations have been carried to the grave with him!

Regards to our uncle and to the sisters from Bruns and your sister, Jette.

Jefferson City
17 October 1863

Dear Heinrich:

A few days ago your and Uncle's letter arrived. I had expected them, and it was so comforting for me to hear from you.

5th December

I did not find time to continue writing to you, but in the meantime I have answered our uncle. —Last week a letter arrived from Carl Boner[55] from Philadelphia with a letter from his father as a recommendation. The young man seems to have been ill-advised by a certain Pape, and he asked Bruns for fifteen dollars to buy clothing. Bruns sent him the money, which you may report to his father, Max Boner. He is, he said, employed in a pharmacy, where he is only getting his board. To write to his parents, he says, would take too much time, since he is in need of clothing. We have helped him, since there were no other acquaintances to whom we could turn, and now he will have to fend for himself if he does not want to come here. But here positions are also very scarce. Why did you not write earlier concerning this?

We see and hear nothing but politics. Since you are getting newspapers regularly from Carl [Geisberg], I hope that you will look particularly for Missouri. We have also often wanted to send you newspapers as we were sending you mail during the summer, which, as Bruns says, might be appropriate now.

Tremendous things are happening here now. The enlistment of Negroes into the regiments will, if the order is not rescinded, bring a quick end to slavery. The poor governor, they attack him constantly, and if he resigns, the lieutenant governor is not any better. I wonder whether the president will finally realize that he is being kept in the dark concerning Missouri?

More in the near future. Hold dear your sister Jette.

From the Autobiography

Bruns was appointed assistant surgeon in the hospital by Gen. Tom Price. He had a lot to do, and many sick people were sent to him there. In the beginning the rations were very inade-

54. *Copperheads* was the name applied to those Northern Democrats who opposed the Union's war policy and favored a negotiated peace. President Lincoln exercised strong executive measures in suppressing them, including arrests, suppression of the press, and censorship.

55. Carl Boner (1845–1878) was the son of Jette's cousin Max Boner, who was treasurer in Hovestadt. Carl later became a physician in Brooklyn.

quate and unsatisfactory, so that at the request of Bruns several ladies and I attempted to do something for the sick. Later the Sisters of Mercy from Chicago arrived. For my husband this was a blessed activity. He was untiringly busy. Finally, he became a surgeon with the Board of Enrollment.[56] He had his office in Mrs. Lusk's house, but he complained about the location. On the 10th of January 1864, he became ill of the nervous fever. After a few weeks he was lucid again, and then said that he would die. He suffered and was miserable for a long time. Doctor Follenius,[57] who treated him, paid a great deal of attention to him. He lived with us. And at night he sat up and kept watch. At the request of the sick one, we also consulted Doctor Richardson, who was with the staff of General Brown. Bruns knew him well. It caused me great consternation when the legislature adjourned at the beginning of March and Doctor Richardson also had to leave. Both doctors discussed the matter in detail with Doctor de Wyl,[58] who wanted to come twice a week. I constantly exchanged reports with Doctor Follenius. And then, in addition, we also consulted Doctor Winston.[59] A swelling under Bruns's right kneecap had formed and was very painful. He suffered so much, and we despaired, but we hoped! He became weak. On 1 April he died. It seemed to me he was breathing more easily, but then sweat appeared. I went downstairs to tell the girl to wait with the soup for him, and I looked after the boys, who were splitting wood. When I returned he had quietly gone to sleep. Tillie, who was sitting there, had not noticed anything.

Jefferson City
5 March 1864

Dear Heinrich:

It is finally getting time for me to turn to you. I had intended to do this earlier, but partly hope prevented me, partly the nightly vigils, the constant care and worries. Today, Sunday, it has been eight weeks that Bruns has been severely ill. He was afflicted by a rheumatic nerve fever. After a few hard weeks the nervous symptoms decreased, and an inflammation of the knee in his left leg developed, which is very persistent. At present it is not quite so painful if he lies quietly, but he has constant fever from it so that he is tremendously weak and he is again talking deliriously.

Just imagine, in the beginning I missed brother Franz constantly; I felt so deserted. Now I have become accustomed to consider the children my first help, but they are not experienced enough, even Hermann. During the first days we had good medical care. The first doctor, a member of the legislature, lived with us. He was there every moment and gave us complete

56. Under the provision of the Law of Congress, approved 3 March 1863, Boards of Enrolment [*sic*] in each congressional district were appointed, and on 20 November 1863 a progress report was submitted listing "Bernard" Bruns, surgeon, as a member of the board in the Fifth District. Within a few months over 9,938 men in the district had been processed and were determined to be ready for enlistment. See *Annual Report of the Adjutant General of the State of Missouri for the Year 1863* (St. Louis, 1864), pp. 52–53. William H. Lusk was clerk of the Cole County Circuit Court.

57. Dr. Wilhelm Follenius was the oldest son of Paul Follenius, cofounder with Friedrich Münch of the Giessen Emigration Society. He was five years old when the Follenius family arrived in New Orleans on 2 June 1834 on the *Olbers* with the first contingent of the society. He became a physician and wine grower in Augusta and was elected to the Missouri House of Representatives in 1862 and the Missouri Senate in 1871 and 1873.

58. Dr. DeWyl was not listed in Jefferson City in the 1860 *Gazetteer.* Nicholas DeWyl was listed as a druggist in Jefferson City, residing at 213 High Street, in the 1876–1877 *Missouri Gazetteer.*

59. The 1860 *Gazetteer* listed a physicians' office of Drs. Wells and Winston in Jefferson City. Separately G. B. Winston was listed as a druggist.

confidence. And then, at Bruns's request, a very well-known regimental surgeon met with him frequently. But the latter had to go to Warrensburg a few weeks ago with General Brown, and the former left us when the session ended. I then hoped that the worst time was over, and I thanked God that it had been willed in such a manner, but now it is not yet better, on the contrary. His strength decreased every day, and there was constant fever, pain, deliriousness; and if for a few days a little calm occurred, then suddenly he became so ill that we believed he could not stand it any longer. He admitted this and made all kinds of arrangements. Thereupon he gradually became quiet and calm again, began to eat some soup and things of that sort. We were waiting upstairs. Yesterday he got higher fever, he had spent a bad night, and he is now deathly weak. The leg is swollen even more. The doctors disagree among themselves; one wants to have the knee opened, the other does not. I am corresponding with our first doctor, Follenius, and he also advised us to treat it only with cold poultices. Bruns himself would be satisfied if an incision would be made immediately; Hermann likewise. I, however, am definitely against it because it is said to be very dangerous, particularly in the case of severe weakness at his age. There are no indications that there is pus. —I still fear that he will not survive unless it soon gets better. The children, particularly the bigger ones, are assisting me very well. This constant vacillation between fear and hope numbs me; I am getting so lethargic. Fortunately my strength suffices since I am treated with great consideration, particularly during the night. During the daytime I am always there. During the night for quite some time I did not even get undressed; I slept like a log, but then I could jump up any minute. I have written to my brother-in-law, the pastor, and have tried to explain to him, with the approval of Bruns, how he had vouched for the money for Helle. Since Bruns was so poorly, I asked him to inform us of further developments.

Besides the fact that Bruns is so sick, I have many difficult hours when I hear and think about our situation. And it pains me indescribably that we are in arrears with our interest payments. But of course I must not be angry with the poor man. Perhaps if he remains alive, he will know how to take care of it. In the meantime, what do you have in hand? Is everything in order? Will you have to send the power of attorney here so that you will be at the top of the list? Bruns has made a last will, in which I am designated as a guardian and everything becomes my property. Should it turn out to be, in case Bruns is torn away from me, that nothing is left or only a fortune that is too small, then I will not stay here with the children.

Well, you see that I am desperate; perhaps it is not all that bad, and it does not concern anybody over there except you alone, you know that. But it is surely hard to bear since he lies there so miserable and helpless and I do not know whether I shall ever see him again, and then he is so ill that I can change little in our style of life and I am sitting here completely tied down.

Here in the city there is a little more lively life; all houses are full, and the rents are going up. Hermann is building a not very big but very livable house for himself. I wish we had it. Ours is almost too big now. The news of the war indicates an impending end. May God grant it! However, we are no longer so involved, and even though I cannot deny some feeling I am still quite dull and think only of our boys. Only now I realize that I had worried about them a great deal. I was so restless day and night during the entire time. Now everything is over! Bruns and I thought we should go into the new year quite confidently, participating more in everything than during the last half year. And now—!

You must not believe that I am despondent; there is a strength in me that lifts me above all misfortunes and makes me capable of subjecting myself and bearing that to which I am destined. Let us hope that it will remain this way!

The children, Hermann and his wife, are all quite well. Now do write how our uncle and you are getting along. And particularly I often think of brother Bernhard, of whose welfare I have been left in ignorance for several years.

To be sure, I shall continue writing or have somebody write to you. Your loving sister, Jette.

P.S. Greetings from all.

Jefferson City
4 April 1864

Dear Heinrich:

On Friday, 1 April, my beloved husband died. He suffered much, and yet it hit me so suddenly; I had believed he could endure for a long time yet. He had been noticeably poorer for a few days, so that I thought I would have to give up, and yet ——. On the last morning he took a few eggs and drank some milk; the bedding was changed in his bed with the help of Hermann and another man; he was probably quite weak, but still answered when he was asked. When the doctor came, Bruns still told us what was to be done during the day. He pulled up the blanket and I asked him whether he was cold, to which he replied he was. When he had been covered more warmly, perspiration appeared on his forehead, the phlegm was loose, and I relieved him of it several times when he was coughing. When I gave him something to drink he had to cough. I was sitting with Ottilie in the room and writing, but then I often quickly jumped over to him; he did not like it when I bothered him too much. When the letter was finished I stood by him, dried his forehead, and felt his hands, and then I went downstairs and outside to the two boys. After about two minutes I was back upstairs again, and his life had escaped. Ottilie had not noticed anything. I was terribly upset, and I could not get over it at first that I had spent day and night for these past twelve weeks with him and had failed him just during his last moment. How easy his end was! God be thanked for that! I had thought that it would be so hard! —He had always been so patient and good, and he was never so composed as now when he was suffering greatest pain.

I have still not quite come to my senses yet. He was buried on Saturday beside brother Franz with the two boys in front of them. My brother-in-law H. Bruns arrived in time. Bruns was still the mayor of the city, so city officials followed the casket, and also, without my having wanted it, the military, which was present, had been ordered to fire the military salute at the cemetery. —I do not yet know how I can continue living. I have told the children that I will merely be there for them, but sometimes such a deadly lonesomeness takes hold of me. I was not at all accustomed to act independently, and I wonder what is ahead for me?

My brother-in-law has calmed me very much. I wish he were living here. Hermann is still too inexperienced; however, he will be and wants to be a support for me. As they say, a great deal of worry has been spared me because of Bruns's last will. You must quickly send in your claims. How much, together with the interest! —I will have to report to the court within sixty days. —Well, enough of this; inform Therese and the members of her household, and wherever else it is fitting. Hermann will write to his uncle, the pastor, and to Wilhelm.

I thought you had probably already answered my first letter. I hope you are all well! Your sister, Jette.

On 28 April 1864 Heinrich wrote Jette that a Requiem Mass was to be held for Dr. Bruns in Münster on the "30th day of his death." Relatives in Lüdinghausen and Stromberg had been notified. He reported he had recently been in Greven: "Our parting there always comes back to my mind. Hermann unconcerned, wandering around in the chickenyard, and we others, quiet and inconsolable. Almost a human life span has passed since then, and we have almost become old during this time . . . ." He urged her to return to Germany. "Land and people over there . . . seem to be really so cold, so egotistical in their uncouth contrast between thinking and feeling. There is no harmonious education that binds them together." As she had requested, he listed Dr. Bruns's debts. The last payment of interest on the promissory note of 29 December 1838 for eight hundred dollars had been made 14 January 1846.

Jefferson City
11 June 1864

Dear Heinrich:

Your letter arrived a week ago. I had expected it longingly. I felt quite deserted and tried to convince myself that you were so far away that I must not really count on your sympathy. However, I really only asked for a few lines from your hands, a few loving words, and these have arrived for me; I also received word from the sisters, as well as from Bruns's brother, Hermeling, and from the parental home in Lohne, where the lady of the house, my niece, has also died. Only no word has come yet from his brother, the pastor, and also none from brother Wilhelm, but he probably hasn't had time yet. I wrote to the pastor myself, since a wedding certificate was asked for, which made me laugh. I am outwardly already rather composed and am not so deeply sad as I was at Heinrich's early death. But I cannot help it that I feel so hopeless; for me there is nothing any more but to follow him. But that is not so bad and is quite in order; if a couple has spent thirty-odd years together, as we have, and particularly if the last years were inclined to make us feel serious and reserved, then one is composed and looks toward a reunion with longing.

God be thanked that I am physically strong again so that I can begin to fulfill my duties to the children and to the estate. I only feel a haze in my head, I am so dull, and I forget things. I should have somebody whom I could ask, who would do everything for me—and Hermann is not adequate any more. Should I have a lawyer? That would cost a lot, and I don't trust anyone here. Recently the inventory was taken and taxed. Then I wanted to ask somebody to collect the debts that are on the books, and I thought I wanted to have the things in the house auctioned off (I would keep the more necessary things out because of the tax value), and thus be fair to the creditors. Perhaps the latter is not exactly necessary, but there are many things we could do without, and the smaller we keep our household the better it will be.

It has been published in the newspaper that I would be the executrix and that those who have claims on me should report them to me. I shall then know whether I can accept your claims and witness to the correctness of them. Surely everything will be covered, it seems to me. Only I have no insight into the store business, and only the future will reveal that. — Whether there will be anything left for us to live from after a year I do not yet know. At present this does not even worry me very much. I would only wish that my dear husband's creditors be treated fairly and that his memory remain respected. Whenever I am encouraged a little bit and place the credits opposite the debts, then Hermann appears again and lists sums of which I have never heard. Then for days I am so upset that I do not know what I should do, and I have no one who could give me an encouraging word, and I cannot understand how Bruns has managed. Even in Germany Bruns could not be brought to the point of demanding his fees. Even then I did not write out any bills. Here, he was very active in his profession, but whoever did not come by himself was not asked to pay. In the country our needs were not great. Here, however, where we have to buy everything, where many projects had to be carried out, the business could not take care of everything. Our brother Franz once said, "But Bruns is not writing down anything at all in his account book"—it was really so. Several years are almost completely blank in the book. Finally I got him to the point that he would tell me in the evening what had to be noted. But then it was already too late. The store was going backwards, and bad times were upon us. Suddenly I was told not to spend any more, and in this regard I have had quite a bad time. Thus I am more hardened, and even though it does not look good I will hear the truth in one or two years. I am now constantly studying in what way I might be able to earn something. My strength is giving out, I work a lot in the garden and the house, but often the hardest work pays least. Now that I hardly leave the house at all, the garden is somewhat of a diversion. The girls take care of a lot in the house, but what about outside? Well, we live in a slave state where it is only gradually becoming different. The little ones are already helping, but not seriously and they are still going to school.

Earlier Bruns would have liked to build a house on a place he owned where he had planted fruit trees that are already bearing. He often spoke of that during his illness. But now where should we get the money for building? I shall first turn to his brother, as he asked me to. And if there is no money at all left for me, then an empty house is also no life. We will have to earn money. Formerly I thought that I would rather go somewhere else than stay here, where we occupied an important position. It is bad for the girls!

Why do I write all of this to you? I have to talk to someone. Only you must not take it hard. I was supposed to cheer you up. You have had so much hard luck in life, and when you write that you are so preoccupied I get scared. When our uncle cares for you, then you do not have to worry so much about your livelihood. Is it the old rheumatism? I recently thought that I was similarly affected. I cannot enjoy anything any more, and I also do not feel as deeply any more. Give thanks to God for that! I would otherwise be quite miserable. There are still many things that depress me!

Therese is quite upset about her husband's transfer. Well, now it is over, but I feel for you. "And although the cloud hides it, the sun remains in the Heavens." Bruns always wanted to hear that. In the next letter I will write more definite details. The girls would like to add a few lines, but then I become jealous. Later, if nothing important is to be reported. After reading over the letter, I would almost like to keep it here. I will let it go, but you have to be careful even when you discuss matters with our sisters.

Do write to me soon again how you are getting along. It is after all a physical illness; the spirit soon recovers and seizes new hope. Your sister, Jette

From the Autobiography

Now I had to struggle by myself to look after the children. Our financial situation was very sad. I took over the administration of the estate, and with that a great deal of unpleasantness. This was made easier for me through the active assistance of U.S. Judge Arnold Krekel.[60] As winter approached we prepared to take boarders. Friends of Father who had a position in the legislature appeared. Heinrich Geisberg and Louis were already earning something. Wilhelm became a page in the Senate. The gentlemen were Sen. Friedrich Münch, his son Hugo, who was a page, then Sen. Friedrich Kayser, Senator Goebel, Doctor Dugge, Colonel Dallmeyer, Mr. Klauss, Mr. Ernst Decker II, Mr. Finkelnburg and his wife, Mr. Kellermann and his wife, Sen. Theodore Bruere (and before him his brother Gustav Bruere), and Mr. Huhn.[61] Judge Krekel, who was often seated downstairs in the lounge, called our house "the

60. Arnold Krekel (1815–1888), born at Langenfeld near Düsseldorf, emigrated to Missouri with his parents in 1832 and settled with them on a farm in St. Charles County. He was admitted to the bar in 1844 and founded the *St. Charles Demokrat* on 1 January 1852. In that year he was elected to the Missouri House of Representatives, and in 1860 he was a member of the Missouri delegation to the national convention that nominated Abraham Lincoln. During the war, Krekel served as a colonel with the Missouri Home Guards, and in 1864 he was elected a delegate to the Missouri Constitutional Convention of 1865. Chosen president of this body on 11 January 1865, he signed the emancipation ordinance abolishing slavery in Missouri. President Lincoln appointed him federal judge for the Western District of Missouri in 1865. He helped found Lincoln Institute, now Lincoln University, in Jefferson City and was elected president of the board in 1883.

61. Friedrich Münch (1799–1881) was cofounder with Paul Follenius of the Giessen Emigration Society. After the collapse of the society in 1834, Münch settled near Follenius in Warren County, where he farmed and wrote extensively for German and German-American newspapers and journals. He was elected state senator to represent Warren, St. Charles, and Montgomery counties in 1862. As a leader of the radicals or "charcoals" he was affectionately referred to as "Papa Muench" by his friends, but his zealous advocacy of speedy emancipation of the slaves brought him into conflict with some of his colleagues. He lost his bid for reelection to the senate, but in 1865 Gov. Thomas C. Fletcher appointed him to the State Board of Immigration, on which he served for many years.

Hugo Muench (1851–1936) was the youngest son of Friedrich Münch and Louise Fritz. For the 1864 session of the legislature he accompanied his father to Jefferson City and served as one of the pages in the Senate. Hugo remembered the "boarding place" where he and his father took their meals: "Usually, the discussions upon burning questions waxed so warm and interesting that the wants and desires of the small boy at the foot [of the table] were quite forgotten, and not daring to disturb the flow of conversation by impertinent requests, he not infrequently left the dining table filled with more information than food." See William G. Bek, "The Followers of Duden," article no. 18, *Missouri Historical Review* 19 (January 1925): 349–50.

Friedrich Kayser and Gert Goebel had been elected to the Missouri Senate in 1864, representing the 29th and 21st districts, respectively. Another newly elected representative at this session was John Dugge of Franklin County. Representing St. Louis County were Col. W. Q. Dallmeyer, Ernest W. Decker II, who later married Effie Bruns, and Gustav Finkelnburg.

Gert Goebel (1816–1896) was the son of Professor David Goebel, a tutor to the Court of Saxe-Coburg who emigrated with the Giessen Society in 1834. The family settled on a farm at Newport, near the present site of Dundee, west of Washington. Goebel participated in organizing the Missouri Reserve Guards and was elected to the state legislature in 1862 to represent the counties of Franklin, Gasconade, and Osage. He served in the State Senate in 1864 and again in 1866. In 1877 he wrote *Länger als ein Menschenleben in Missouri [Longer Than a Lifetime in Missouri]*, which was published by C. Witter in St. Louis in 1877.

Ernest William Decker II (1838–1871) was born at "Waldeck" farm, St. Clair County, Illinois, the son of Ernst Wilhelm Decker and his wife Caroline Engelmann. After graduating from the Cincinnati Law School, he joined the St. Louis law firm of Finkelnburg and Decker. He served as a lieutenant in Company A of Colonel Frank Blair's First Missouri Infantry Regiment and later as a captain in the 43rd Illinois Regiment. He returned to St. Louis to continue his law practice with the firm of Krum, Harding, and Decker and was elected to the Missouri House of Representatives in 1864. He was a member of the radicals meeting at the Bruns home, and on 24 May 1866 he married Euphemia Bruns in Jefferson City. When he died in 1871 he was serving as prosecuting attorney in St. Louis. The couple had three sons, the youngest born two weeks after Decker's death.

radical corner." Thus we managed for several years.

Through an advance from my brother Heinrich and a widow's pension from the Land Company, which was obtained by Judge Krekel for me, I was almost able to pay for the house in which we had lived for a long time.

Jefferson City
14 August 1864

Dear Heinrich:

Your letter by way of H. Dietrichs arrived here by mail, but I have not heard from him personally yet. I wanted to have your claim registered through a lawyer, but he said you would have to send a notarized copy of the note. And then I have to inform you that I can pay this note only with the current local money here. As he said, I "could reimburse you later if I wanted to, but I am not obligated." I would indeed want to compensate you, but I wonder if anything is left to do this? Then you would lose a lot. Do search your soul concerning this. If it could be arranged that your debt could be put in current money, this would suit me fine. Money stands usually at 150 premium.[62] It is enormous. [Bruns's] brother, the pastor in Wadersloh, writes me now that he hopes to get something from Holtermann. You may take that, because I do not want to hear anything about it. Also the $15 from Carl Boner, which at that time stood at approximately 75 premium. Later when I have settled everything, we can, if at all possible, settle further among ourselves.

Bruns's estate would suffice to cover the debts if the store would do justice by him. Since Hermann has not made a complete inventory I cannot judge that yet, but he already says that because of the war he has lost great sums of money. We will have to fall back on our property. There are a few acres that Bruns had designated for our residence, but he has given his brother a promissory note for that. If I can get it free, I would try to get money to build a little house on this property. We could live much more cheaply there. The children are very much in favor of this. Our place here brings a high rent. But the garden is not worth much, and there is nothing sure. I really will have serious worries until everything can be straightened out. This uncertainty really wears me out, and I have no firm support. Bruns answered me, in reply to my questions, that he did not know anybody whom I could trust (except for a person in a high position who is not here very much).[63] However, he had requested Hermann to assist me, and he, to be sure, wants to help but is not capable. And you cannot help me, and I am not yet capable of helping myself get along. If only I could live near you.

Theodore Bruere, a descendant of French Huguenots, was born in 1831 in Cologne. He emigrated to America in 1850 and worked in New York as a civil engineer before moving to St. Louis and Warren County, where he worked as a manual laborer and night watchman in a mill. In 1852 he was employed to teach Latin and other subjects in a private school, but soon resigned to accept a position on the *St. Charles Demokrat*, published and edited by Arnold Krekel. He subsequently entered the law office of Krekel and in 1855 began practicing law in St. Charles. He was elected to the State Senate in 1866.

J. V. Gustav Bruere, Theodore's brother, born in 1832 in Cologne, emigrated to America in 1852 and moved to St. Charles, where he bought the printing office of the *St. Charles Demokrat* from Krekel on credit. In 1864 he was elected to the State Senate. In 1872 he became business manager of the *Anzeiger des Westens* in St. Louis, but in 1873 he returned to St. Charles and purchased the *St. Charles Zeitung*.

Heinrich Huhn, editor and publisher of the Washington, Missouri, newspaper *Die Freie Presse* from 1865 to 1868, apparently covered the events in the capital for the paper.

62. This reflects the ratio of gold to paper money in the United States, which had been driven off the gold standard.

63. Jette found in Judge Krekel and Hermann Bruns, her husband's brother, sympathetic advisers.

I am happy that you had a vacation. If one can get away from the old humdrum of everyday life, he can return much refreshed. And you will rise again if you really want to. You are still together, and is that not a lot? Tell our brothers and sisters and Uncle that their letters brought consolation to me and I had longed for them all. But I cannot yet answer them; I will when I am no longer so tense. In many respects I am better off here than in Europe; many things are open to me to establish a new existence for myself—at least I hope that this is so.

The war is still going on. Soon they will draft more soldiers here. Hermann is subject to the draft. It is very unsafe in the state, and on both sides robberies and murders are committed. The city is full; there is not an apartment free. Also, particularly recently, there have been five to six hundred items declared contraband, which the citizens do not like, and since they have little means, they often take refuge in stealing. There are few military personnel here now. Give regards to our uncle and to all others from the children and from your sister Jette.

P.S. One of our sisters might like to have the little picture. Therese must send me one, too. I wonder if Uncle and Aunt Hüffer would have one for me? I was so sorry to see that brother Wilhelm looks so old; the picture must have turned out very poorly. In November there will again be a county court session. I would like to have the things I asked for before that time. You cannot believe how high the prices are here now. People limit themselves severely, and then there are still the high taxes! I wonder how I will get through? —However, cheer up! If only we were not so alone here. If for no other reason than because of the children, we will have to associate more with people.

4 January 1865

Dear Heinrich:

My letter to sister Johanna will have been received by you. We are living on and are healthy. On the advice of Hermann, and because Bruns had always permitted it with some special friends, I have put up ten gentlemen during the session of the legislature. It is, to be sure, entirely against my inclination, but it is a way to earn something in a decent manner. Thus for a few months we really have to stir about. —The lawyer told me that you would have to send a sworn note (he could have said this immediately). The copy that you have sent was personally handed by me to the court and was notarized there. Here then is his statement. I hope that you will quickly find your way through it. At the beginning of May the first "settlement" will be demanded of me. Then I will probably know a bit more about how many debts the store has. I am quite discouraged about that.

I had thought that I would be entitled to Heinrich's army pay, but now it is to go to the estate. We are living in a terribly expensive time, and one still cannot see any change. On Monday the inauguration of the governor[64] took place. He is a very radical man. Too bad that Bruns did not live to see this! The members of both houses are also mostly radicals. A big difference compared to the former legislature! Missouri will soon be free. Politics is the main thing here now. There are few soldiers here, but it is still unsafe in the country. Again

64. Thomas C. Fletcher, a native Missourian and the first Republican to be elected governor, was inaugurated on 2 January 1865. On 11 January he signed an emancipation proclamation declaring that "henceforth and forever, no person within the limits of the State shall . . . know any master but God," making Missouri the first slave state to renounce slavery.

volunteers have departed from here. A close young friend has been captured in Memphis. Another one, Wilhelm Huber, was wounded in the side up here near Fort Setle.[65] After the bullet had been cut out of his back, he received leave and brought the smallpox home with him. Nothing but misery!

I have begun the new year quite sadly. I kept thinking how Bruns and I had firmly resolved last year to face coming events with new courage. Can I now do this alone? Of course not! However, the present makes constant urgent demands on my attention, and thus I stumble onward, striving to live up to my situation.

Yesterday your letter arrived. I was happy that you wrote about our uncle since you had not done so earlier and I had been so concerned about him. And I was so confounded when you mentioned the outstanding debt of brother Franz. To be sure I knew that; however, I had forgotten it, but his children had not. Now Franz has been dead for six years, and our uncle's claim has not been handed in to the court. By chance, no final settlement has been made, for Bruns delayed because of the war, but otherwise, according to the law, it has to be done within three years or else claims become void. Franz's house was still there on a one-acre lot. The public administrator sold it recently at a public sale—to my chagrin, for there was still no estimate of the reparations due since the soldiers, etc., who had been in possession of the property for years, had completely ruined it. The entire estate is in a mess, and although we thought in the beginning that after the deduction of the debts something would be left, it now turns out that the interest that has been compounded consumes more than there is. And our uncle's claim will surely be lost. My dear husband had assumed that Uncle had given the sum as a present. Since, however, no appraisal of the damages had been made, I very much wish that you would send me Uncle's notarized note, or a copy with yours, and I shall try to see whether it cannot be put together with the other claims. It would be foolish not to try it, and I shall do whatever can be done. To be sure, it annoys me when I think that the public administrator beat me to it. I wanted the estate to be settled in order to save expenses and to preserve our good name. My head is getting so confused; may God save me!

I still have some right to concern myself about brother Franz's estate since nephew Heinrich had me appointed by the court as his guardian, and my niece, who is of age, would be delighted to let me take care of things. To be sure, I do not know whether you will be concerned that you have to give a sworn affidavit; Bruns accepted 6 percent, and whatever other creditors took you are certainly entitled to also. By all means take Prussian money at the current rate of exchange in gold. But I know that you know how to arrange this. I still want to mention that it is all right with me that the percentage rate may be lower on your note, but since many demands here are set higher, I ask that you leave it at the former rate and compute your note at 8 percent and thus figure the outstanding debts accordingly. On the original note that had been handed in, 8 percent was listed, and the court has not yet discussed the outstanding interest. It is only fair. And then you also do not yet know how high the American dollar will be figured compared to Prussian currency. —Once the status of the estate has been decided, I can, as far as I can see, not pay all of the debts, but I shall, after the property and the houses have been sold, come to some agreement with the creditors

65. *Fort Setle* is evidently an error in spelling or transcribing. It should probably read *Fort Scott.* Records show that William Huber's Tenth Cavalry participated in actions on the Big Blue River and in the battle of Westport 23 October 1864.

and give away whatever there is, and then, if my strength will still allow it, I will work together with the children and then—think of me. Perhaps Bruns's brother, the pastor, might be willing to do something for us, since my dear husband always acted very helpfully during his good days in favor of his brothers, just as he did for mine. We have never told him that. We are all in debt to him! His brother, the pastor, wrote me that I should let him know what the situation was with the estate, and I have referred him to you.

My children will soon be grown. Louis is already in a store and receives ten dollars a month for the time being. My brother-in-law Hermann in Westphalia and another old, dear friend say I have to keep up appearances, because of the girls at least, and thus I have let myself be persuaded to stay here in the house and to take care of other people.

Here I am running out of paper. In the near future I shall write to our uncle and to you in more detail. I love to listen when you chat with me, and I shall study your letter again and again in special hours. But when you say that you are lacking something, I become concerned as I never am with the others. Listen, I will take care of you again, but not there! Thoughts!

Effie, who likes to write, is supposed to write to you concerning politics. She is a happy person, but to be sure is sometimes a little catty. Her character is getting more stable and substantial. She will fill her place in the world well.

All the children send their best regards to you with me. Hold dear your sister, Jette.

Jefferson City
11 January 1865

Dear Heinrich:

I now have to send a few words to you! Missouri is a free state! The State's Convention in St. Louis has declared it unanimously, and a dispatch is reporting it to the legislature. The governor delivered a very enthusiastic speech to the thundering enthusiasm of the members, and then they went home to invite the ladies and all who are interested to gather with them this evening again. Now everybody has gone there: the gentlemen, with Effie and the children, Heinrich Geisberg, the girl, and the boy. I am sitting alone in the house, and at times I look at the brightly lit State House and think, "I wish our father could still have seen this." It brings Missouri a promising future! If God wills it! Still years will pass before laws and extermination will drive away the murdering bands. But let us hope! It excites me and I have hope for my children!

4 April

Before anything else I will report one other important event: the fall of Richmond.[66] Yesterday, telegrams arrived constantly, officially addressed to the governor. In no time the entire city was bedecked with flags. The cannons announced it to the area around us. I cannot be joyful about anything any more, and I only say, "If only our men were still alive, then we could participate more."

I have had a hard time to live through. On 8 March I had a public sale, and then I repurchased what I believed I could not do without. Since that time we have tried to get

66. Gen. Robert E. Lee began withdrawing his lines in front of Richmond on 2 April 1865. A week later, on 9 April, he surrendered to General Grant at Appomattox Court House.

settled again, and this means vacating as many rooms as possible in order to rent them out. Our bedroom was the first—the most beautiful, the most airy room in the city. In the beginning I was constantly shaking my head and did not know where to begin. Then I wanted to be strong and I attacked it, and then I suddenly got to crying until I was quite dull, and then it worked. Now I have been almost completely settled in my living room for the past two weeks, but since that time I have had a cold and fever, etc. And now during the most beautiful spring weather I have to stay inside. And there is the garden to take care of, and making soap, and the girls can't do anything. If I want to hire a man to help me, that costs two dollars per day. Well, I'll practice patience.

I am looking forward to a letter from you with great impatience; I am waiting for the answer to my January letter that should be here by now, in which you were to send me information concerning your loan, with outstanding interest, and forward the sworn affidavit required here. By all means, ask for it in Prussian currency according to the current status of gold. I shall ask for a copy of the form from the lawyer. He should have thought of that in the very beginning when he had a copy of the document sent to you. In May there will be another court session, and by then I ought to have it.

I calculate and figure often that if I realized the note against the store that was for $8,000 at 8 percent, taken out in 1860, then the debts could be more than covered. Hermann, however, says that this is not the case. The remaining assets will hardly cover more than half the debts. I shall then file for permission to sell the house and lots in order not to let the interest mount any more. Hermann thought he would like to repurchase for me the part of the house I occupy so that I would have a home. That may well be correctly thought through; however, it does bother me. In the first place, I will have to pay interest on a rather big sum, and I cannot live here as modestly as somewhere else, and I would have to rent out rooms and also give board.

(My own opinion of my situation is this: that I really am not suited for anything like this, but could do much better in any other kind of work, even the most menial.) My strength often surprised me recently, and the children will also be more capable in a few years. Thus I will probably have to follow Hermann's advice. My brother-in-law also said that I would have to try to keep up appearances, if at all possible. It is good, however, that one can help oneself better here than over there where you are.

There is still one hard nut to crack. I went to the public administrator to inquire about the status of brother Franz's estate. I wanted to submit our uncle's claims, but I was told it was useless. He will possibly get half of what is owed and will be able to pay the other debts. Later creditors will come into another category, but he did not have anything else to take in. Bruns probably believed that Uncle had given the sum to Franz as a gift because there was no more talk about it. This is the only possible explanation that the debt was not listed with the other debts. The public administrator frightens me by saying that he considers Bruns's estate responsible for bills that have not been collected.

Since the first of April I have begun to keep house on my own account. I wonder if it is that alone, or whether it is the anniversary of the death with all the other memories, or just my being sick? I have been feeling quite unstrung, I have no mainstay any more, and have still not earned anything. I wanted to give lessons in music and German, and then I can probably sell something from the garden, milk, etc. —I shall probably take the Supreme

Court Judge Krekel as a boarder, I very much want to, so that he can give me some legal advice; he is more like an old acquaintance of Bruns's and mine. Until now I always had to be so considerate of Hermann and had let myself be pushed before I would speak. I know that he does not act in accordance with the law, I have felt for the longest time that I should step in, but I still do not know how I stand with reference to the store. Oh, I have to tell you, he drinks. For quite some time I have received reproaches from friends, and I warn him and his wife. His father did the same without success and despaired. His reason is gone, he constantly talks such nonsense, I had to let many a harsh and inconsiderate word pass, and it seems indeed that I am dependent on him. At least he acts so, which in turn cuts me to the heart. His friends say straight out that this will end quickly. I suggested to him that he resign his job in order to begin somewhere else. It is not his wife's fault (she, to be sure, has such a cold, superficial nature), but he is attached to her, is a tender father. She is patient enough, perhaps too much so. Now that I have written this I would like to take it back again.

Do send me what I ask for quickly, and my next letter will sound better, that I am sure. The young people are well and face life cheerfully. All send their greetings together with your sister, Jette.

P.S. Attempts are being made to take the Geisberg children away from me. It is foolish. They can help themselves better, and my Heinrich pays his board, and during the winter Jette has learned to make clothes and is already earning money.

I wish that Effie would be skilled in some kind of line. It is only in music that she could succeed, and practice always takes so much time. It was rather hard on me recently when she refused to take the offer of a good man. If I had only the three little ones to look out for, then this whole matter would be different. Jette was going to go to an acquaintance in Quincy, which I declined for the time being, however, as did Heinrich. I could not bring myself to let her go.

I did write, didn't I, that I had received the fifteen dollars and thank you? But you must not deprive yourself of anything. If only you were a Croesus! But we'll manage all right.

Jefferson City
May 1865

Dear Heinrich:

I was prevented from writing by all kinds of business, and I had thought I would have something better to report as I indicated in my last letter. And now your letter just arrived; before opening it, I thought immediately that it would contain something good or bad.

It touches me deeply that the good, dear boy is gone[67] —in his best years, just when I believed that he had settled down and could soon look forward to a carefree future. It happened just as it happened with brother Franz, and with him I could not at all get over it at first. He had worried and struggled so much in his life. Who knows whether Wilhelm had not worried about his future? But he had after all seen better days than the oldest brother, and with his charming character he must have had good, dear friends who took the place, to some degree at least, of his nearest relatives. I have often thought that I knew so little of him

---

67. Wilhelm Geisberg, Jette's youngest brother, born in 1824, died 19 April 1865 in Hamburg following surgery for appendicitis.

and was hearing less and that we were almost strangers to each other and yet so close. Every sign of life from him was comforting to me for a long time. How good that he had not suffered long! But both of you had to put up with so much! If you could at least have been able to close his eyes for him, just as I caught Franz's dying gaze. Earlier I often thought that Wilhelm could visit us sometime, and even recently I often thought that if somebody from my family would come, how comforting this would be for me. But all of you have crosses to bear in life, and I shall endeavor not to be so discouraged any more. I imagine that in a few years things will be much better.

On the 8th of May, this house was publicly auctioned off, on Hermann's advice. He as well as many friends advised me to remain here, and since nobody fought for possession of the property, the house and garden was sold to me for the small price of $2,225. I had figured on $4,000 or $5,000. But in spite of the fact that apartments are very much sought after now and that it was put on the open market, nobody wanted to expel the widow. Hermann paid for the purchase and will try to acquire the money for me. Now I have rented out several rooms, and if this continues through the summer the interest will already be covered and I shall live free for the second half of the year.

The girls, Effie and Jette, are making themselves independent, Jette by making dresses and Effie by giving language instruction. At times I give piano lessons, and many things from the garden go to the market. This is not a bad beginning. Louis is earning twelve dollars a month. Heinrich Geisberg pays his board, and so now there are only the two little ones who still cost a little bit. Also these past few days a certain official [part of the sentence is missing].

To be sure it will only amount to some twenty dollars per month, but it would be something secure. But I have been disappointed so many times that I can scarcely hope to receive other help than from my own strength, and as you see we do not sit around and wait.

The governor has reappointed civil service officials for the entire state. Hermann was confirmed as sheriff. The court has not yet been reconvened, but this will happen in a few weeks, and I will then submit your papers. Certainly this cannot be postponed, so that your claim can remain among the first ones. Hermann admits that he wants to transfer the settlement of the store to somebody else, and I also would like to see this done. I have too much worry about it, and I am often not capable of doing anything else when new annoyances occur. There still will be new claims. I cannot give an accounting before the August date, and it is not until then that I can file for the sale of the lots.

As far as we are concerned, we are well. The troops are mostly being discharged. But I have no one for whom I can wait, and this always lies heavily on my mind. If only our boys were still here! Our father would take me in his arms if he were still alive! This was his quiet way, and this always told me more than many words. Effie is sitting beside me and crying, and the others are doing a little bit more for me than usual and are more quiet.

God bless you and all of you! The children send their regards to all of you with your sister, Jette.

P.S. Hermann is well-meaning; I see that in recent times he keeps better company. And so then he remains more proper, and his wife comes frequently and asks all kinds of things and seems to like to hide behind me. The little girl, Johanna, called Jenni, is cute!

Jefferson City
July 1865

Dear Heinrich:

A few days ago I received your letter, and I was wicked enough to laugh out loud, that is to laugh to myself, for are we not all nothing but candlemas![68] Now this has long gone by, and I feel bitterly that Uncle and you are so affected. Poor Wilhelm certainly was also concerned about that, and always thought Lady Luck would smile on him and that he would be in a position to make everything right again. I hate his boss, and I have hated him for quite some time. Why did he not treat a clerk who had served his business faithfully for so many years better? He really let him dangle, he threw out some bait for him, knew how to make him well-disposed so that he began to like him and could no longer tear himself away from the circle of friends—thus he spent his best years without any hope for independence until just at the very end when he no longer could see it realized.

It seems that most of us brothers and sisters are not endowed with great good fortune. However, earlier I would not have complained, and this I should remember. For have I not spent many long satisfied years with Bruns and lived without worry? How many women exist who can say this! But now it is doubly hard that he has left me and I have to struggle with the greatest worry to provide food. I would rather have suffered pain if I could have been free of care. Last year in order to deaden my pain I seized on work courageously, but now I have become hopeless and so dull that I fear for myself. But this won't do—the children will have to begin to act for me.

Judge Krekel made his appearance, and I was able to talk to him to my heart's content. He got busy immediately, he saw Hermann, and I have every prospect that our cause will be taken care of. He will help me as a friend even though in his present high position he no longer practices as a lawyer. Until this time I had not been able to learn from Hermann how the store was doing, and I hoped that everything could at least be paid off. Krekel now tells me that it will be less than half. That was a hard blow! And it is also one for you! It makes me dizzy!

Hermann is not doing right by me; I hope he will change. In August I shall submit the bill; even though I do not hope to get anything for myself, I shall at least gradually have peace of mind. It affects my reason, this eternal pulling and suffering.

The power of attorney has now been executed. I wish you could be spared this! You can inform me sometime soon of your new title[69] so that I can address you correctly.

A short time ago we became acquainted with a Mr. Florenz Settemeyer at Hermann's place, and Roer found out that he was related to us due to the fact that Andreas Hellweg is his uncle.[70] We see him frequently, and the girls enjoy calling him cousin. However, I like to converse with him too.

Yesterday Wilhelm Huber and Anton Baurdieck returned from the army with many others. They are still exuberant. The 4th of July will be celebrated magnificently. And the

68. Candlemas is an ecclesiastical festival celebrated on 2 February with lighted candles in remembrance of the presentation of the infant Jesus in the Temple and the purification of the Virgin Mary. Jette seems to be comparing the transiency of human life with that of a lighted candle.

69. Heinrich Geisberg had been appointed treasurer and secretary of the Academy in Münster.

70. The relationship was by way of Heinrich Andreas Hüffer, mayor of Stromberg from 1770 to 1808, who married Elisabeth Hellweg. They were the parents of Jette's mother, Johanna.

children will have fun. The new [Missouri] Constitution has been adopted, a severe blow for the Rebels, who for the time being have been deprived of their right to vote.

I have recently sent a letter to our uncle, and you too should send the letters without prepayment of postage.

I shall write later how things are, and I am looking forward with great anticipation to the next months.

Regards to everybody, particularly to the sisters, and do write again to your sister, Jette.

Jefferson City
16 March 1866

Dear Heinrich:

I always think that I have to delay a little longer, and now several months have already passed since your and Uncle's letter arrived here. Since I last wrote to Johanna we have been very busy and still are, three senators and eight gentlemen of the House of Representatives, besides Judge Krekel and son and Judge Rombauer, are here. Next Monday they will leave for home. It has been a long session. I must say that I have had my fill of cooking. Recently it became quite a burden for me, and yet I have to be glad it lasted this long. I am still undecided how I shall carry on.

It causes me a great deal of concern that Effie will be leaving the parental home in the near future. She became engaged at New Year's to young Ernst Decker, and since there was no serious reason to prevent it, the wedding will soon take place. He comes from a respected family. The mother is an Engelmann, the sister of the wife of Governor Körner,[71] who recently became ambassador to Spain.

He himself already has a good position as a lawyer, and he is such a good man that I can hope for the best for Effie. But I always have to wonder how this could have happened; she has not distinguished herself at all in any way, and we have kept quite modest and even withdrawn.

This winter I have earned something, and Effie is still going to the Seminary[72] and giving German instruction, so that we are able to buy the most necessary things. Ernst will take care of household effects in St. Louis, as this is the custom in America. I must say that he and his mother[73] and sister have been extremely considerate. After the death of his father he inher-

71. Gustav P. Koerner (1809–1896) participated in the Frankfurt uprising of 1833 and had to flee to France. From there he emigrated to America. Arriving in St. Louis and finding slavery still prevailing in Missouri, he and his party decided to settle in St. Clair County, Illinois, where several friends and relatives had already purchased land. This colony, often referred to as the Latin Settlement, soon became an influential intellectual and political center. Koerner practiced law in Belleville, Illinois, served on the Illinois Supreme Court from 1845 to 1850, and was lieutenant governor of the state from 1852 to 1856. He was appointed minister to Spain in 1862 to succeed Carl Schurz. Koerner wrote *Das deutsche Element in den Vereinigten Staaten von Nordamerika* (1880) and an autobiography, *Memoirs of Gustave [sic] Koerner, 1809–1896,* edited by Thomas J. McCormack and published posthumously in 1909.

72. After attending the Ursuline Convent School in St. Louis, Effie returned to Jefferson City to continue her schooling in the Young Ladies Seminary.

73. Caroline Engelmann (1806–1872) was one of thirteen children of a prominent Frankfurt family who emigrated to Belleville, Illinois, in the early 1830s. She married Ernst Wilhelm Decker (1809–1847) in 1836. After the death of her husband in 1847, she maintained a boarding house in St. Louis, where she raised her two children, Ernest William II and Lena, who later married Theodore Hildenbrandt. Her brother, Dr. Georg Engelmann (1809–1884), had come to the Belleville–St. Louis area in early 1833. A physician and botanist, he became one of the most active members of the St. Louis scientific community.

ited no fortune, and the mother has kept boarders for ten years just as I do, etc., until Ernst began earning money, and now they seem to be well off. He was born here, and he says that he had often heard people mention Bruns as an excellent German. And we also knew that the Engelmanns belonged to the Latin Settlement. Bruns knew several members of it. The young people are very well versed in the English language; they endeavor, however, to speak German as well. Particularly when I am present, only German is spoken.

My son Hermann is causing me trouble. He is presently without a position and is not always sober—well, he often does not have bad intentions. It did not work out as it was supposed to, and now he has finally handed over the administration [of the estate] to a lawyer, who will now take the remainder. It appears to me that I will have to lose the entire amount Bruns had invested in the store. Then there will be hardly anything to cover our private debts, and my good, dear husband will be stigmatized. It is good that he is no longer living because I truly could not bear that! I thank you for the offer to spare me the interest. In August I think I will be able to see how much can be distributed. There are still several suits pending. Judge Krekel seems really sent by Heaven, and with him even the lawyers show respect. My ownership of this house is being contested because of Hermann's debt. To be sure I have to pay interest on the money, and I have already paid a good bit.

If I win this suit, then the invested money will not be lost. I will have to borrow the remainder, but Krekel says that I would most likely be able to live free because of the settlement of the estate and my part in various pieces of land that will bring a profit.

Well, we shall live on and we shall continue to work! If we get ahead, then I probably will not have so many troubles in the future.

Now farewell, Effie is putting in a note. Soon more. Your sister, Jette.

Regards to all.

Effie Bruns to Heinrich

March 1866

Dear Uncle Heinrich:

It seems that I have so little time to write, and I am now sorry that I did not quite finish my Christmas letter to you. Since that time a great change has taken place in my life. I have become betrothed. The 24th of May, which falls on a Thursday this year, will be our wedding day, just as it was with Mother and Father.

I wish that I could come with Ernst to visit you and to present ourselves to you. But I will have to send you our pictures. I hope that you will enjoy having them. We had planned to have a better, a bigger one for you to slip into the envelope.

I ask you to give this information to our closest relatives. Do write me a few lines and hold dear your niece, Effie.

From the Autobiography

My oldest daughter, Effie, became the wife of the lawyer Ernst Decker of St. Louis on the 24th of May 1866. A year later on the 2nd of May 1867 my niece, Henriette Geisberg, married Henry Nitchy.[74] Ottilie wanted to prepare herself to become a teacher and was persuaded to live with the Deckers in order to enjoy more advanced instruction.

74. Henry C. Nitchy was a clerk in the U.S. Post Office in Jefferson City.

26 May 1866

Dear Heinrich:

My Effie is gone!

On the 24th of May, our wedding day, she was married here. An hour later she followed her husband, accompanied by his sister and a few close friends, and left for St. Louis. In the beginning it was so quiet and empty here. But we begin to recover. During the last few days I was very excited, and I am glad it is all over. Since the young man is not Catholic, this gave rise to some offense. However, I am at peace with myself, and I do not have the least doubt that the young people will fare just as well. I have missed my husband very much on this occasion, and therefore I have to decide by myself what I have to do.

However, there was no lack of sympathetic friends. They were a beautiful couple and there was a merry company, which will be a pleasant memory to the young couple. Ottilie was bridesmaid.

And now turn the page.

I cannot keep it from you that your claim is almost completely lost. Of the $20,000 debts perhaps $1,000, or $2,000 can be distributed. I probably need not tell you how I feel about this. In August I shall be able to find out more. In the meantime I already know that Bruns's investment cannot be retrieved from the store, nothing, almost nothing. Some creditors have made their claims to the firm and transferred this to the private estate so that the sum amounts to twice as much.

I myself need not give up my dower, and for quite some time I have tried to make a living for myself and the children. But this will always be an eternal thorn, and I would like to get away—God knows where to! It hurts me so much when Bruns is judged so harshly; he does not deserve this at all.

Farewell, soon more! Do finally also write to your sister, Jette.

There! Johanna's letter arrived and has pleased me very much. And the dear pictures! For years I have been waiting for pictures of Therese and her family. Do ask her again for them. And she must write me.

Jefferson City
28 May 1866

Dear Heinrich:

Yesterday your letter arrived. All day long I have been studying it, and it occurs to me that I can just as well answer it now as later. A letter was sent last week to our uncle with an enclosure for you. —I have forwarded your letter and the draft, which was a present for Effie, to the young people. In St. Louis as well as here they have been given many presents, so that I consider it better that they can select a remembrance from you themselves. I know that Effie does not expect this courtesy, and she will be doubly happy. She always complained that she was so far away from her relatives.

The wedding took place on the 24th of May. Mr. Decker brought his sister Mrs. Finkelnburg (who lodged with us during the winter with her husband) and three friends. Here also some of our closer acquaintances attended. The wedding ceremony proceeded quite seriously, but afterward everybody was merry; they all seemed to feel with me that the young people were suited to each other and would enter their future united in spirit with a firm and easy courage. I did not take the leave-taking an hour later so hard because I know that she is well taken care of. —But now I shall not hold back. I had wished that the wedding would be different. Decker comes from a Protestant family. Upon my inquiry he told me he would not put any obstacles in the way of Effie in regard to her religion, but he asked me not to demand any promises in advance. Effie did not want to hear of anything. And thus the Catholic priest did not want to perform the ceremony.

In the morning she went to church to attend to her devotions. At 10:00 o'clock, at their mutual request, Judge Krekel tied the knot. He gave a short but beautiful speech and mentioned that the couple had chosen the wedding day of their parents for their own.———Judge Krekel spoke with emotion, and his resemblance to my husband made me look very closely at him. But the uproar when he concluded did not let me dream on. —As I have said, I would have preferred a Catholic wedding, and the bridal pair had agreed to this. To you this civil act will appear more strange. Here it is quite common.

You believe that I am a sorely tried woman, and you are probably right. I had to experience all kinds of things after the death of Bruns that you cannot imagine. If I could have had you or perhaps my brother-in-law, Pastor Bruns, to talk to at times, this would have been a great relief and blessing for me. But I had to go my way alone, and had to set an example for the children, and had to act according to the will of my dear husband. At times I have gotten into conflict with the priests, but in the meantime I am getting calmer. My Wilhelm will soon go and take his first communion, and then the church education of the children will be finished. Our priests here are not like those back home.

Our dead are resting in the general cemetery (a big stumbling block). In fairness to the young people, I want to say that in view of Decker's serious character a good rapport will certainly remain if the priests do not act so brusquely. Things like this have occurred previously in the family.

And now I should write you some more details concerning my situation; on the enclosed little note I have already told you that your claim is mostly lost. Many times I told Bruns he should send back your money, and he had always wanted to do it. But this is over now, and I am the third of the sisters with whom you must lose. Bruns was too good and too careless; he always had the best intention. If his plans had been executed as he expected and as he himself would have done, he would have been a merchant and we would be well enough off. As long as brother Franz was in the business it went well (as Bruns often said later), and then when Hermann was the principal it no longer remained as solid. And then the war turned everything upside down.

In June 1864 I took over the administration [of the estate]. The next deadline will be in August, when an accounting will take place. The third and final settlement will then take place, and the administration will be finished. The private debts and the store debts that were transferred to private property amount to over $20,000, according to Krekel. It seems that I am not getting anything from the store; on the contrary, the debts from the store will be debited to me. In the end 10 percent on the dollar will be paid. However, I am only guessing. It is miserable!

Earlier I thought that I wanted to move into a new area with the little ones where no one knows us and where we could earn an income and pay the debts. But Judge Krekel explained quite soberly that I should not even think of that, that I should not pay the debts of my husband because that would not be expected. I was amazed at that, but he is so strictly legal. To be sure, it will indeed be difficult for me to earn my living if I stay here. Hermann has played a stupid prank on me with the house. I had the intention of bidding for myself. We got it for $2,000. I was so happy and immediately gave Hermann $600. He wanted to advance the remainder. When I later wanted to see the deed, he said he had it made out to his wife and I could live free as long as I lived. This infuriated me, but I couldn't do anything. Krekel said it was acceptable but low-minded. Now the St. Louis merchants have gotten wind of it and filed a suit declaring the sale a swindle since the woman had no fortune and his fortune had been forfeited to the store. Thereupon a complete document was made out by both of them, and I would be the rightful owner if it were not for the suit, which might easily cost me $300. During the winter I gave Hermann $400, for which Krekel reproached me very much. I could lose this. A widow has one-third of the income from real estate as long as she lives. The property was probably very heavily mortgaged, but they cannot take away my legal right to it. And it is possible that this would amount to $100 a year for me.

Since I had to take care of our living arrangements immediately (erroneously I believed that the first year would be free), I have come back. The few months military pay of my husband and our poor Heinrich, to which I was personally entitled did not by any means suffice since I had to buy furniture and household implements again. This winter I saved somewhat. But now Effie! After all, I could not let her go without some clothing.

You are again willing to sacrifice your money. Let it be, dear, good brother! If I could get the capital for you, I would ask you to lend it to me for the house, and I would pay interest punctually. If I live until the children are grown, I shall go to one of them. I am always good for my keep, and there will always be something for clothing. It seems to me that I will have a few hard years until both boys can become independent. I now let Louis go to the commercial college in the evening; this costs forty dollars. And next year Tillie should have some higher instruction, as should Wilhelm.

Hermann thought that we should move in with him; he is not so bad, but he made such a bad mistake. And he often drinks very heavily. I am often frightened that this might come to a bad end. Keep all this to yourself. I don't like it at all that I have written this to you.

Jette is still with me and does whatever she can. It seems to me that she would rather stay here, and her brother also wishes it. We shall see whether we can get along together. If we could make some claim on the Stevermann Foundation for Jette or my children, I might well accept that. But no! Now that I read your letter over I see that you are getting some money for Bernhard, and so I will be glad to step back. I will manage all right. Well or badly.

When the suit is over in August, I shall inform you immediately how things went. I have the greatest fear that it will not come to an end yet. This eternal uncertainty tortures me, and often makes me quite confused. The house will, as Krekel figures it for me, cost two hundred dollars annually in taxes, insurance, and repair. It would bring four hundred dollars in rent. Now I have rented out three rooms. Only two gentlemen are boarding with me; this is not enough. Well! At some other time it will probably be better.

Now the letter is almost finished, and it is already the second one, and I would almost like to copy it over. For what good would it do that you know the story? It might perhaps be better if you would think that we no longer existed! Well, that is bitter again!

I have had some hope for quite some time that I would receive a pension, but this is over now and has affected me probably without my knowing it. I am still quite upset about this. Later I shall be more collected again and be indifferent. Judge Krekel is here again and will move here next week for good. I don't know what I would do without him.

And how are things with you? The Prussian troops have crossed the border.[75] I ask you to tell me very soon how you are affected by this all. Our sister Therese has not written to me for some time, and I have been waiting even longer for a little picture from them. Johanna's family is so nicely depicted. I threatened that we should also have pictures taken, but this would not amount to much, and Effie is now gone.

Earlier I wrote of a Florenz Settemeyer, whom we call cousin; he is related to the Lagemanns (Hellwegs, Dr. Krone, privy councilor Lesemann). We have gotten to love the young man very much. He too felt quite at home with us. During the winter he lived in St. Louis again, but before his departure for home, he came by to bid us farewell. I sent a few lines to you with him, but he did not know whether he would get to Münster from the Rhine, where his parents live. I loved him like a son.

20 June

Since it has taken so long, I have to tell you that the young people write diligently, and then I always answer right away. Effie is threatening with an impending visit when the courts have come to their decision. I am beginning to love the young man very much. (Earlier I was somewhat more reserved because of some other person.) He really shows himself so loving toward me and toward all in the house that I could not wish it any better. Judge Krekel maintains that Decker will make a political career (and he has already been nominated president of the radical committee as I see from an article in the paper), and this would take him away from the family. Often when I am ill-humored I take out a picture of them both, and looking at them does me good. Even before the wedding both of them spoke of the little ones, that Tillie could go to school there. —Now this letter may sail off. You will have to overlook the fact that I have expressed myself in such a black mood. The next letter shall be better. As you say, one can more easily get adjusted to present situations than one can endure the dark visions of fear of the future.

Again and again I try to pick myself up, and then I get depressed again. This must come to an end some time, and then I know what I will have to do, and we can help ourselves. I shall manage quite well with the little ones. Our poor uncle, give him our regards, and also all the others

from your sister Jette

Jefferson City
2 September 1866

Dear Heinrich:

I should have written to you a long time ago, and it was just your letter that I have delayed the longest. To be sure, I had a great deal of business to attend to, I had to think a lot, and in

---

75. Otto von Bismarck had maneuvered Austria into a confrontation over the Schleswig-Holstein problem. Prussia declared on 3 June that Austria had breached the Gastein Agreement of 14 August 1865 and sent troops to occupy Holstein.

addition I had to write a lot, and then I had seriously thought of having a picture taken with the children, but there was always something lacking to carry this through. Thus September is already here. —At first, then, my sincere thanks! You are much too good. To be sure it suits me very well. In a few years, if I live that long, it must certainly go better with us. And it's quite unfair of me when I become impatient or disheartened. For quite some time I had a family from St. Louis rooming and boarding with me, and then of course we ate with them, even though the girls and I always have things to do. I would so much like to have something secure coming in every month, and when there are a few rooms empty I immediately become so worried that I cannot stand it. The house that we lived in last has finally been signed over to me for the third time because of the settlement. Last week I paid the court costs, the lawyer, and $300 for the settlement of the claim on it. The papers are in my hands, and thus for the time being I can live in peace. I have had to pay $800 on it, and the $1,400 that was in my hands but belonged to the estate. After a year I will have to take up this debt. But there will be several more hundred dollars available for me then. If only I can manage to arrange my life with this house! To be sure, things will work out gradually.

I would so much like to send the little ones, Ottilie and Wilhelm, to school this year. But then I would lose Ottilie's help in the house; the girl is really growing up too fast for me, but it is high time. She is almost grown up, and is not exactly ugly, but she still has to study. If she would attend high school here this year and then go to the Deckers later, that would be the right way. The school fee amounts to about $30. That to be sure is not so much. Wilhelm will need less. Louis is already earning something, but it is not enough for his board and clothing. Hermann is remorseful that he accepted the advice of his friend against his mother. He will pay the $300 if he is only able to. He is not really so bad, and usually he means well by me, if only he would stop this miserable drinking. I hope that he will follow me and will tear himself away here and accept any kind of active position. He has promised me this.

My married daughter is in good spirits. I really don't know whether I already told you that Effie and Decker were here for the 4th of July and spent several days, and I had every reason to be happy concerning the young couple. They have spent some time with his mother in the country in Illinois, since the cholera appeared more severe in St. Louis and the girl was naive enough to be afraid. I tried to talk her out of it several times, but when she was among all the new relatives on a beautiful farm where they did not have to fear any illness, she always said that *we* could get·the cholera. She wrote every day, and when I was slow to answer, her husband would come and ask me to write her. I have done this diligently, and it was not too difficult. Yesterday she reported that they would come back to St. Louis. Health conditions there are said to be much better. Now, however, they both think that I will have to visit them, and I was weak enough to accept this invitation. There will be half-price at fair time, although I would rather be with them when it is quiet. I often have scruples, but I would like to do it. Now they are threatening to come and get me. Jette has begun to put my wardrobe in order, and thus the trip will probably take place in four weeks.

Judge Krekel, who for the time being has rented in our neighborhood, is getting dizzy spells, and this seems to be very dangerous. He is fairly well recovered again; however, I fear a relapse. I had to take care of the second annual accounting at the court by myself since Judge Krekel was not able to be there. I am getting quite brave in negotiating with the gentlemen, and in another year I shall feel much easier, for then the final settlement will be taken care of. And my children and I will manage quite well.

We have followed the news concerning the campaign of the Prussians and would like to know more about the troops that are known to participate. Mr. Roelmann claimed to know that the Westphalians were not involved in the fight. It is really funny how all Germans here take sides for their home provinces. At times it is said that they even come to blows. And now peace has been concluded.[76] I am very curious whether troops have returned or whether they are still stationed somewhere else. I hope that Carl Offenberg will come back home unharmed.

What things we have had to endure without talking much about it! It is a constant torture to know that the children are participating in these fearful events.

The 24th

We have been so occupied that I was not able to have our picture taken. And then I also had fever again, but I nursed myself gradually back to health. Now we have the fair here, and my name is being mentioned again with the ladies' committees, and when the prizes are awarded I will have to go and let my voice be heard. If I had cultivated flowers as I used to do, I would send a bunch of them.

If I did not have so many things to think about, I would participate, for I like these fairs very much. —Effie is already becoming impatient to see me. Nettie and Hermann will also go along. Yesterday little Jennie demanded to go to see her grandmother. She already talks quite well. My children are really a very important source of support.

Today I received a long letter from Carl Zumnorde from California. It seems that he is giving in to the wish of his sister and wants to return home. I hope that he will do this, for he lives such a lonely life in California.

12 October

I did not get around to sending this letter; I went to St. Louis, and Johanna's letter was forwarded to me there. Niedieck's bankruptcy is still very much on my mind.

We are well. Soon more. The letter is full. Best regards to all from my children and from your sister, Jette.

P.S. As I read over the letter I fear that you will think that I am complaining and that I am in need. If that is so, I would rather not write any more concerning myself!

Jefferson City
28 January 1867

Dear Heinrich:

There was so much that prevented me from writing that I offered my wishes for Christmas and New Year's silently. I hope that you will acknowledge them. I was in the mood to give up the Christmas tree because I was so busy. But then it occurred to me that Bruns would never have done without it, and in addition it was his birthday, and after all the children must have a holiday. But it doesn't really come from the heart any more. When Effie arrived in the evening on Christmas Day, I had them all together again. She was happy, and we had

76. The "Seven Weeks' War," culminating in the Austrian defeat at Königgrätz in Bohemia, ended with the Treaty of Prague on 23 August 1866, in which Austria relinquished claims on Schleswig, Lauenburg, and Holstein, establishing Prussia as the uncontested leader in German affairs and resulting in the creation of the North German Confederation, with the king of Prussia assuming the presidency.

enjoyable hours. She is really much more sensible than earlier, and it seems to me that in time she will make a good housewife. On the last Sunday of the year Decker also came. As I said before, he is such a dear man that one has to be nice to him because he is so good. I only wish I could see them more often; it would do me so much good and be so comforting. But it is a costly trip. I have received your draft. Many thanks! I shall try to keep the money for a while until the settlement can be taken care of, for I will have to make up a lot. Ernst took the draft along and sent me $91.

The arrival of the legislators and the preparations for them made it somewhat less peace-ful for both of them than I would have liked it to be. It could not be helped. Ernst slept at the hotel during the last days, and Effie slept on the sofa as I did. I have rented out the parlor this year along with the rooms, and that brings in $72 more per month. The session does not last long, and I have to consider a few more things. I had to pay over $100 in tax. This will probably be reduced later. I was quite incensed at this; however, what could be done? If I had managed the household it would be cheaper. —It is too bad that I cannot overcome a reluctance to lodge strange gentlemen. But we are making headway! I have several new ones: Lieutenant Governor Smith, Senator Winters, Senator Bruere, Mr. Huber, Mr. Weinrich. I have some older acquaintances: Mr. Nolle, Senator Goebel, Mr. Finkelnburg, and Mrs. and Col. Dallmeier.[77] Again, I had to look after the party a little bit, and I have only Radical members.

There is still a lot of trash in politics. However, people believe that quite honorable people represent the state. I often wonder how such important matters are treated so very simply. We miss Senator Münch. It is embarrassing that St. Charles County voted him out.[78]

I shall report to you later concerning your claim on Bruns. At any rate, it will take its place among those of the other creditors. In August of this year the settlement should be finished. During these past days I have obtained authorization from the county court to sell six shares [of stock] privately. However, I still have to settle with the Land Company. Whether this will turn into a suit I do not yet know. I asked Judge Krekel several times to inquire about this. It does not proceed very quickly. If I cannot get everything done and conclude everything, then I cannot pay on a pro rata basis. I would feel much better, however, if I had settled this and would have to worry only about our livelihood. Do you think I could stay here if I would have to meet people every day who had gotten the short end from us?

Nephew Heinrich has given up his position with the post office; he was really working so hard there that it affected his health. He is talking of Leavenworth! I wonder what will happen with us in the next years. I often urge both Heinrich and Hermann to aim higher and threaten that I would follow them. The girls, that is Jette and Effie, fear these new areas. But I had already conceded to Bruns that we wanted to begin anew, and as soon as the boys no

77. Some of the recently elected or reelected state officials boarding with Jette Bruns at that time were Lt. Gov. George Smith from Caldwell County, Sen. Jacob R. Winters representing the 13th District, Sen. Theodore Bruere and Rep. Conrad Weinrich of St. Charles, Sen. Gert Goebel from Franklin County, Rep. Gustav A. Finkelnburg from St. Louis, and Rep. William Q. Dallmeyer from Gasconade County. Neither Huber nor Nolle is listed as being in the state legislature at the time.

78. Friedrich Muench was highly regarded by his German neighbors, but there was some criticism that he never returned to the ministry after arriving in Missouri, and his unwavering advocacy of immediate emancipa-tion had offended some of his constituents. Even today in Warren County, some of the descendants of the German immigrants regard him as a free-thinker and radical.

longer have to study it would be possible. But this is probably just an idea, and I will probably have to stay in the house, and will have to rent out, and will have to cook until the children are able to plan differently concerning my future.

During these last years my health has been better on the whole, and I am getting stronger than ever. I am amazed about this. Jette, I believe, would rather stay in Missouri than go back to Quincy where she could accept a good position again. I often wish that some of our expectations would have turned out differently; however, let us trust to higher guidance!

[The rest of the letter is missing.]

Jefferson City

23 June 1867

Dear Heinrich:

For some weeks now I have resolved every day to write you, but then I lack the time or the mood, and then the heat is so enervating. In the evening I would have most peace, but then I like to sit down outside with the young people to enjoy the fresh air. Then my head feels more free and I breathe easily, even though the perspiration is quietly and unnoticeably running down.

I would have liked so much to hear from our sister Therese, and I want to ask you to tell her to let me know as soon as possible how she is getting along with her little ones. I would also like to have a good picture of the parents and the children (in duplicate for the album). You said that the memory of Hamburg is painful to you. With me it is more than that; it evokes a bitterness against the boss, who should have been more fair to him [Wilhelm]; if only he would have been more honest. But I am glad that he, after all, had many a pleasure— how little I really know about him.

Three families are now living in my house. Since last fall the family Grollak from Posen,[79] very fine, dear people, then the Nitchys and—Hermann with his wife and child. I was advised against taking in Hermann, and you advised against it too. Well, there were reasons that led me to agree to it. His wife has probably suffered a lot, and her influence on his behavior is less than mine in my position. By his coming here, every one will see that I want to respect him as my son, and I have also told him that he could ruin me. —To be sure, I will have many a worry because of this, but I shall attempt it in God's name. —At any rate, later my situation will change, and I am only trying to do the best for the three little ones. I am glad that I am strong enough to make my life now on my own.

The Nitchys will begin setting up their own household toward winter, and [Jette] implored her mother to spend a few weeks with them. Ottilie will also be with them during the next school year and will attend a free school (which is said to be very good) for older girls.

There will soon have to be a change for Louis, who will be nineteen next month. It is just too petty in the store here. I am waiting for an opportunity to get him into some other job. Wilhelm passed his examination in school during the last few days and is happy to be permitted to visit his uncle.

---

79. Posen, a city in a province of the same name, was located east of the province of Brandenburg, halfway between Berlin and Warsaw, Poland.

In August I would like to arrive at a settlement and will pay the money I have in my hands to the creditors. The final settlement cannot yet be made because of the store. It would only be fair if you would send a power of attorney, perhaps to your nephew since I am the executor of the estate. Then you will be able to dispose of it any way you wish, and if you think that you would want to leave it with me I will be grateful to you. It is quite embarrassing and humiliating for me. I shall be able to pay only ten cents on the dollar. It often makes me so confused. You can probably imagine that I am often questioned, and that I also have to hear some rather harsh remarks. I do not know how I shall be able to stand it if the people receive so little for the money they had lent.

If only I had an opportunity to earn money. There are quite a few people who do become rich!

This is a favorable year for the farmers, and we hope that the price of grain will be reduced. Yard goods are already down. The city is growing very much. There is a great deal of construction going on and beautification and planting. It's a real competition among the citizens.

Best regards to our uncle and the brothers and sisters. The two young women want to write themselves. Hold dear as always, your sister, Jette.

P.S. Do write how Bernhard is getting along. Recently at the Rodmanns I saw a picture, a scene in an insane asylum. I wasn't able to look at it at all. Nephew Heinrich felt very embarrassed that you have set aside something for his picture. He is generous, and he also believes that I should put stamps on the letters. You can also let it go as you did earlier. Hermann got a job as a clerk in the registrar's office. I believe I have mentioned to you with thanks that I have received the draft.

Jefferson City
31 May 1868

Dear Heinrich:

It has surely been half a year since I wrote you last. First, my sincere thanks! Can you really spare it? I wish that I could become more well off and could reciprocate somehow. For this reason I am dissatisfied with my present occupation. Heaven only knows that even though I manage very frugally I still do not have anything left. To be sure, I have to keep a good table. This winter I again had gentlemen from the Senate and House, as I did last year, the same group, half Germans, half Americans; upstairs I had the lieutenant governor. They are very respectable people, nothing but "Radicals." I could otherwise have taken a few more, but I did not want to take anybody from the other party. —There were a few setbacks, as often cannot be avoided. Now since they are gone I have, besides Hermann's family, only one other, a Presbyterian minister.

In a short time I expect both daughters. Effie with her little son[80] is to spend the summer here. Louis has a job in a big store in St. Louis and still sleeps at the Deckers, and Tillie has her vacation. On 15 April a little Effie Nitchy[81] made her appearance. Both mother and child

---

80. Harry B. Decker, born 28 August 1867 in St. Louis, is nine months old at this time.
81. Euphemia Nitchy, called Effie, was born in Jefferson City 15 April 1868 to Henriette Geisberg and Henry Nitchy.

are doing well. Jette is quite concerned, but her husband is so attentive and practical that she can depend entirely on him.

In the spring I caught a head cold, and I am still somewhat sickly, so that I had to have a doctor. But now it is getting better, and I can be up and around most of the time. There is a liver problem at the bottom of it, which caused such a weakness that I had no courage at all.

The settlement of the estate cannot be brought to a conclusion because of the suit. It will go before the district court for a further appeal. I am getting so impatient; I would like to have peace, and then I could be able to see better what I can do. Effie and her husband are thinking of St. Louis. I would not like to move away from here, but I also would like to have something more tangible so that I would not have to fear from one week to another that I will get the short end. The children will soon be grown and will not cost me any more, at least the boys. Well, we'll see how things develop! I am firmly convinced that better times will soon come!

In the political world there has been a great deal of excitement since the impeachment of the president.[82] If often seems to me that the high officials are really proceeding very clumsily.

Our city offers a quiet life. There is much building going on, and many strangers are settling here, Germans as well as people from the east. The latter are not as pleasant and are more inclined to bigotry.

Hermann, like many others, has used the bankruptcy laws in order to get back into business. In the near future he will hear the decision, and I look forward to this with great impatience. I firmly believe that he will then endeavor to get some job somewhere else. His wife is acting very bravely during these bad times, and on the whole I believe it was better that I took them in so that they were able to maintain their respect as far as public opinion was concerned. He is so weak and indecisive. It is difficult to bring him out. His wife says that she wants to go to her parents, and I will then keep Jennie.

With respect to our European trip, I often regret that I was not able to spend some time in Oelde in peace, recall old memories, look for many a playmate from my youth, enter into their spheres of activity, and associate with all the people as we used to. I believe that it is a gift of mine to achieve a certain happy spirit easily and to see the rosy side. If only fate did not play so severely with one!

I am eager to hear from you again, from the older ones, headed by our uncle, and also from the younger ones. Otherwise I won't know at all how to find my way around in the family. In the near future I shall write to sister Therese. My regards to our uncle, to you, the sisters, the brothers-in-law, and to all the others from my children and your sister, Jette.

P.S. Ottilie has passed the examinations well. She also had to recite "Die Bürgschaft."[83] I learned this from the newspaper; and now only one more examination for the high school, and then they will come home.

---

82. Andrew Johnson was impeached on eleven charges, including alleged violations of the Tenure of Office Act and Command of the Army Act, but the impeachment proceedings, culminating in the Senate vote on 10 May 1868, fell one vote short of the two-thirds necessary for conviction.

83. "Die Bürgschaft," or "The Pledge," is a lengthy ballad written in 1798 by Friedrich Schiller. The theme is the undying loyalty between friends.

Jefferson City
30 July 1868

Dear Heinrich:

So it has happened, that which I feared for such a long time. Uncle Caspar too has left us.[84] Except for Uncle and Aunt Hüffer *we* are now the old people. At first when I received your letter it hit me quite hard, and then I thought and thought until I was comforted, for I myself have no more pleasure in living. Perhaps if I could be close to you it might be different, but here only young people are around me, and I figure that I belong to a generation which has been. And my happy and eventful days are irrevocably interwoven with those who have passed away. My dear brothers and sisters, you are so far away I almost count you with the others.

It must be quite lonely for you. For such a long time you had to take care of our uncle. How good that both sisters are living close by. You must not live alone, but must move to one of them, and they will hold you dear and take care of you as you would like. If I were in Europe I would claim that prerogative, and how rewarding that would be for me. But I must not continue thinking along these lines. When our uncle charged the close relatives to a mutual love, then it happened, I believe, for the longest time and was probably always so. You must include us. My children also are on the best terms with the Geisbergs, just like one family. I see this now quite well with the adults.

For approximately six weeks now my daughter Effie with her little son have been with us. Her husband was here twice for several days, and the family is then big, especially when the Nitchys with their little daughter also come. I am very happy that they can get together here. If only Bruns could have experienced this!

As to our uncle's estate, I believe that you are really entitled to everything. You consider yourself rich, and yet there is after all so little income except for what you earn during the year. And what if you should get sick or incapacitated some time? When I informed Jette and Heinrich Geisberg of this and told them by the way that I wanted to renounce everything, they did not want to comment, which embarrassed me, and I have not spoken about it since that time. You have suffered enough because of us, and when I mentioned this, Jette commented immediately that our father was also to be blamed. If I were not so sick of everything because of the long years (when we were in your debt and could not repay you because of carelessness and also often did not even pay the interest), I might accept it as a loan. What is the interest rate? Here generally it is 10 percent, and at the bank I receive 6 percent.

You know that when I make a final settlement I will have to take out a loan. At present there is still one suit pending, which has won in the lower court but was appealed by the creditor, so that I still have money in my possession from the estate. It seems to me therefore that if you wanted to trust me again it would be best if I would borrow four hundred dollars from you and you would set the rate of interest and hold that back immediately to the first of January 1870. You could then send the remainder by way of Angelrodt and Barth of St. Louis,[85] who would pay it to my son-in-law E. W. Decker, attorney at law.

84. Caspar Geisberg died 28 May 1868 in Münster. He was eighty-five years old and the last of the Geisberg brothers.
85. Ernst Karl Angelrodt (1799–1869), a native of the Mühlhausen area of Thuringia, was a liberal member of

As to the brothers and sisters Geisberg, you will have to decide what is best yourself. They would both be quite satisfied if you would not pay attention to the uncle's wish. It is not my affair. In case you would want to send the sum he had set aside for them, then send it also to Decker.

Can you not take a vacation some time? Would it not be worth the trouble to take a trip to us? Would it cost too much? It seems to me it would be beneficial to you, such a sea voyage! And then we would see each other again! And you would become acquainted with my children! One can travel quite well second-class cabin, and it is not high. If I could hope for this, it would be such happiness for me!

My life is the same. I have a few families boarding. I can stand it, but I have to stretch myself from one month to the next. If my children were taken care of, I would not have to worry so much. There is Louis, who is now in a good business in St. Louis through the kind offices of Mr. Decker, and he is still staying in the house with them. He sees only good company, and Ernst watches over him. If he does not spoil it himself, he will be able to make his way.

Ottilie has now graduated from the first class.[86] She was learning well and passed the examinations for the high and also the normal school before her departure. She told me that she would like to study to be a teacher. I do not know what I should do. Then she would always have something secure. I wonder if it will be necessary for her? I don't like to be without my children. Should I move to St. Louis as Effie suggested? Should I take in boarders there too, and should I make available to the two of them the use of the excellent free schools? Or should I stay here and take care of their material needs for them? It will have to be decided before the first of September, and it causes me so much concern that I cannot rest. I have no one with whom I could discuss this and get advice, and I cannot decide anything by myself. I shall never be able to be satisfied there, and they will have lost their home if I move away. But where is their real home?

We have been living in constant heat and drought for six weeks. It is quite unheard of. But one has to put up with it! On 16 July a big State Convention took place here. I had the whole house full, and there was so much commotion. The old Lieutenant Governor Smith was not nominated for governor. On the other hand, two of the gentlemen staying here were nominated, one for state treasurer and one for state attorney.[87] Henry Nitchy's boss has not been nominated again for state auditor, so that Jette's husband will probably have to look for another position. Heinrich is still working at copying, and it will be that way for some time.

the House of Representatives in Saxony when he joined the Thuringian Emigration Society, which, like others, broke up soon after its arrival in America in 1833. Arriving in St. Louis, Angelrodt settled about thirty miles west of the city but moved back to St. Louis in 1836. In 1845 he was appointed consul for Prussia in St. Louis and over the years represented Saxony, Bavaria, Württemberg, Baden, Hesse, Braunschweig, and Austria. Because of his extensive import-export trade relations, he handled many financial transactions with the home country for German immigrants.

86. Ottilie Bruns was seventeen at that time. The *first class* was a designation used in Germany for the highest class of a secondary school.

87. The following candidates won office in the November 1868 election: William Q. Dallmeyer from Gasconade County was elected treasurer; Horace B. Johnson from Cole County replaced Robert F. Wingate as attorney general; Daniel M. Draper from Montgomery County succeeded retiring state auditor Alonzo Thompson; George Smith from Caldwell County was elected lieutenant governor to succeed Edwin O. Standard of St. Louis; and Joseph Washington McClurg from Camden County was elected governor to succeed Thomas C. Fletcher.

He has no energy to find anything elsewhere. I wish I could put him and Hermann somewhere else, and then they would surely work.

At present, times are quite bad, and one hopes for the fall. The harvest was good, but now the corn and the later crops are drying out. Here in the city there is again a great deal of building going on. Probably in the near future a second train stop will begin operation. And an Osage railroad is projected. Jefferson seems to be improving a great deal.

I would like very much to hear soon how you are getting along and what you may have decided. But a new thought occurs to me—what would instruction cost for Ottilie and Wilhelm for a year over there? Would $400 for instruction, clothing, and contributions to the household suffice? I would then keep your household and would rent my house here for approximately $500. I would manage the trip from [selling] furniture, etc., and other things. Really I believe I could manage it. Do write by return mail, and I shall also continue thinking about it and will bring my affairs to a close. I could then stay for two years.

[This paragraph was crossed out by a heavy line.]

3 August.

I have now thought it over, and I see that it is impossible. Nothing would be gained to further the careers of the two children. The travel expenses would be lost and would amount to twice as much as I had thought in the beginning. And I would probably have more expenses than money and would be dependent upon you, and that at least I will not abuse. Pardon me for letting it stand there, but I don't like to start over again. The plan to move to St. Louis will probably be realized in the end. First I want to wait for information from the Deckers before I inquire here how I can dispose of my house and possessions. I spoke with Judge Krekel, and he thought that I could not do better than to use everything for the further education of the two youngest children. I could certainly leave here without endangering the settlement if everything had been taken care of except the last accounting. I could board strangers as I have been doing here and could make my life secure. He assured me again of his further assistance in case something should happen. This has made me somewhat calmer. Effie, to be sure, thinks I would have to have something secure before I could burn my bridges here. And certainly this will be very difficult for me. Let us therefore wait for the answer from Ernst, and then may God guide us as is best!

I am still probably physically quite strong, but I cannot think through things as clearly, and I have to concentrate to muster some interest in the things I have to face. If my little ones are taken care of, then I would like to have a little more rest, but God knows what will happen to them. Hermann seems to me to have a sad future; he is so frivolous and has no occupation. Well, perhaps they will soon be better off than I think. His wife is holding him somewhat on the straight and narrow.

I shall write in the near future to sister Therese. I wonder whether you will now take a vacation trip. I hope so. Who is with you? I find it hard to think that our dear uncle is no longer there. How good he was, how noble. I often tell my children this. You have repaid him most of all, and now you step into his position. Just now I would like best of all to be with you.

Give regards to our sisters, brothers-in-law, and everybody else. My children and the Geisbergs send sincere regards. In expectation that you will immediately give me your decision, I remain with all my heart, as always, your sister.

3
The Restless Years, 1868–1899

With everything that has happened to me in my life, with hard trials, heavy losses, I have always found strength and courage at the right time and was never completely discouraged.

Jette Bruns to Auguste Geisberg
15 November 1883

From the Autobiography[1]

Heinrich Geisberg got a position with Mr. Hickmann in the U.S. Circuit Court,[2] and Louis got a job in Mr. Stinde's shoe store,[3] leaving only Wilhelm with me. I rented the house and moved to St. Louis in September 1868.

Heinrich, Louis, Ottilie, and Wilhelm lived with me. Later Hermann and his family followed us, and he obtained a position in the assessor's office under Col. Robert Rombauer.[4]

St. Louis
29 November 1868

Dear Heinrich:

So you don't want it any differently and have sent me the money from our uncle's estate. It seems that we are all rich people. I shall not touch this money for the time being; it has been deposited in the savings bank. I will have to see whether I cannot invest it at 10 percent interest. I would like to add whatever I earn now and then.

As you have probably heard from Johanna, I have moved to St. Louis. My Ottilie was begging to continue her studies at the Normal School, and I did not want to leave her alone any more. Effie continued to advise me to move. I don't know myself how I was able to decide. An acquaintance of ours rented my house and wanted to have it right away. Well, I let her move in and naturally then had to sell my furniture, and finally I rushed my departure so that Tillie and Wilhelm would be here when school started. Parting from Jette was hard on me, but sisters and brothers were still together.

Effie with her child and Wilhelm went to Westphalia to say farewell to my brother-in-law.[5] Tillie had gone ahead. Toward the end of August, on the 29th, we arrived here at 8 o'clock in the morning in a downpour. Decker and Louis awaited us. We stayed for a few weeks with

---

1. Jette Bruns's autobiography, apparently written in 1868, ends with this segment.

2. Benjamin F. Hickman, listed as a clerk, U.S. Circuit Court, resided at 307 S. 8th St., St. Louis. See Richard Edwards, ed., *Edwards Twelfth Annual Directory* . . . (City of St. Louis, 1870).

3. The 1864 St. Louis *Directory* lists C. R. Stinde & Co., a wholesale boot and shoe company, operated by Conrad R. and Herman F. Stinde, at 15 N. Main Street, St. Louis.

4. Robert J. Rombauer was listed as president of the Board of Assessors for St. Louis County in *Edwards Twelfth Annual Directory*, 1870. He is probably a younger brother of Judge Roderick E. Rombauer, a native of Hungary, who, with his parents, was exiled in 1849 and emigrated to the United States in 1851. See *Encyclopedia of the History of St. Louis* (New York, Louisville, St. Louis: Southern History Co, 1899), vol. 4.

5. An interesting correspondence between Jette and her brother-in-law Hermann was made available to the editors through the generosity of Mrs. Ted Borgmeyer and Mrs. Joseph Dubbert of Martinsburg in Montgomery County, Missouri. Five letters written between 28 October 1865 and 5 August 1868 demonstrate Jette's involvement in managing her own affairs and those of her brother-in-law. The letters primarily discuss renting property, collecting rent, and dealing with tenants' requests for improvements.

the Deckers until I found a suitable apartment, had my things sent by way of Heinrich Geisberg, gradually purchased things that were lacking, and began our household. A few weeks later Heinrich joined us and, with the aid of Mr. Decker, obtained a job as clerk of the U.S. Circuit Court. Thus the five of us are together again. The two older ones, Louis and Heinrich, pay me for their board. I add to this whatever is left from my rent and try to manage. I would like to give some piano lessons, but I am still a stranger here and nothing could be arranged so far. I have also not been able to take other people as boarders for the time being because of the expense for furniture, etc. Initially I lived from the profits of the sale. It is not quite sufficient, but it seems to me after some thought that not much is lacking. Up to this time I have had every reason to approve of our moving here.

Ottilie has passed her examinations well. She probably has to study a lot, but she does not mind and is unassuming and quiet at home. I often feel sorry for her, but she indeed wanted it this way. Wilhelm is going to school diligently, but he does not yet take it seriously, although he had his fifteenth birthday and is a collector of rare things, which he can do very little here. Since other minerals are lacking here, he sometimes enjoys coals. However, he will get along better, and he is beginning to read a lot and understand it. He is always the best boy and surely resembles his dear uncle in figure and character, which often strikes me when I think of the departed one.

Louis still has a job in the same store. His wages have been raised to thirty-five dollars. He registered here with the free evening school, where he goes four times a week. This makes him very proud, and he is carrying on his schooling with pleasure. It will be of great use to him.

Hermann and family soon followed us here. They lived with us in the beginning until they found an apartment not far from us. He is temporarily employed at the city assessor's and is participating in the census. They seem to be satisfied now and are happy to have torn themselves away. The Deckers live on this street, and I often see Effie and the little one, although it is pretty far up the street. His father is at his office during the day. The old mother is not satisfied if I do not let myself be seen every few days; she is a very intelligent, magnificent woman, only too awkward to be able to get out of the house. When the young people are gone all day long (the three older ones cannot come home for lunch), I do become a little pensive. I often look at the picture of our uncle with longing. If only he were still with you, our dear, good, kind uncle!

Why does the thought make me so sad? We have lived and loved. Why should we not want to follow them? Certainly, since Bruns is dead, I cannot attain much pleasure from life, and therefore I try to find pleasure in the well-being of my children, and this gives me great satisfaction. If only all grow up decently. It seems to me I will have to keep them together here and must not continue to think that I should be back united with you. I have constantly longed for you during all these long years. How grateful I was and am still to my dear husband that he took me back to my home country. That satisfied me as far as could be expected. My children must not have to endure this. With the quick and easy travel conditions now I wish we were rich so that the distance did not matter. Well, then!

In two years, if everything goes well, Ottilie can hope to figure on earning six hundred dollars or more a year if she stays with me. Wilhelm could even now earn his living, and if he continues to go to the free school for a few more years, then many a prospect where his arm is no handicap will be open to him.[6] I will certainly be able to carry them and myself through for a few years if, as now, the bigger ones help me. Should it not go well, then I can start some kind of a store (a remark which annoyed the young Mrs. Decker very much). I will certainly do something. —I would not like to sell the house right away. Who knows whether we will not want to go back soon, although I hardly believe it. However, it does depress me that I cannot live well there because not everything has been paid. Judge Krekel, Decker, and others say, to be sure, that the wife is not obligated and should not suffer if her husband leaves debts, but it constantly tortures me. I wish I could earn money, even if the work were hard. And how relieved I would be if everybody could be satisfied. But interest eats up interest, and I am wearing out. Well, let us seek to spend our lives in some good manner! Let the children look for a decent position in the world, and then my task will be finished. For myself I will certainly have sufficient means because of the income from the house and the amount I have received from you.

Jette will write for herself. I always have to encourage her. They seem to miss us very much. But I do feel very sorry that when I sent the draft I made the condition that part of it would have to be used for a trip to visit us.

Soon Christmas will be coming and then the New Year. I will have to hurry so that my letter will not arrive late. If I were among you, I would spread balm on the wounds in a gentle and loving manner so that it might not be felt so much that two dear members of the family are missing.

God protect and save all of you. So let us begin the New Year with renewed hope and courage enough to accomplish again what is asked of us and to fill with dignity the place that has been assigned to us. Give regards to our dear sisters, brothers-in-law, and children. I'll write to Therese soon. As always with love, your sister, Jette.

P.S. Our nephew is not doing so well with his German, although he speaks it here constantly.[7] Therefore for the time being I send in his behalf his grateful acknowledgment. They are both very much surprised that they had been remembered. I do not know whether you require a formal receipt, and therefore we include one herewith. Heinrich will write to you later. J.B.

Letters to Hermann Bruns of 26 September 1869, 7 May 1870, and 3 January 1871 from the Borgmeyer-Dubbert collection indicate that Jette had financial difficulties in St. Louis. She moved to a three-story house at 1312 Poplar Street and began taking in boarders in 1869. Most of the rooms were rented at first. Among her boarders were Hugo Münch[8] and another student, Mr. Görling. In 1870 she wrote that she frequently had empty rooms in her boarding house and was therefore giving notice to the landlord. Her son Louis had gone to Kansas, and Wilhelm wanted to quit school. However, Hermann seemed to be doing well. By 1871 she had moved to Buena Vista Street, near Effie.

6. The correspondence available to the editors does not reveal the cause of Wilhelm's infirmity, although an accident apparently occurred in the fall of 1860. See letters dated "End of 1860" and 26 April 1861.
7. Although the generation of the Bruns and Geisberg families born in America spoke German in their homes, they did not write the language easily, even though most of them had German instruction.
8. Hugo Muench had boarded with Jette in Jefferson City while his father served in the legislature. He was preparing to enter the St. Louis Law School.

St. Louis
10 April 1871

Dear Heinrich:

Now, finally, peace has returned to you.[9] Jubilation and victory celebrations greeted the hardened warriors. May they be happy again in their home country! My warm sympathy goes to those who stood—just as I once did—behind the curtains with tearful eyes looking sadly after the returning soldiers marching to the Capitol, where they were received with great festivities and flags waving a welcome. Their leader was missing. Even now when I meet one or the other of the fellows, they greet me, and I think that they, just as I, experience a shock of remembrance. In February I was in Jefferson City for a few days.

I hope our two nephews have returned safely.[10] I can vividly imagine that you were in constant turmoil. Now this will have calmed down a bit. With those who have to mourn their losses, the first pain is over now, and they will attempt to push forward in their lives without their dear ones, for better or for worse. —I do not like to hear how the emperor is being insulted, that is, in private letters. The newspapers show respect for the Prussians, who have certainly earned it. Naturally, things may have happened that do not please everyone. —And where is the victor who is not somewhat intoxicated by his glory? —Here, too, victory festivals were celebrated, and the Germans were very enthusiastic. The Americans admire the victory over the French. They had not thought the Prussians were so powerful, but to some degree they will give them their due recognition. All in all there is a great deal of sympathy for France, but the press is very much practicing moderation.

Winter did not pass so easily for us, for when we moved here in December, Wilhelm was already suffering from a swollen knee. The doctor prescribed rest for him. But this was not possible until after the move was completed. I was tolerably well and, as I thought, perfectly capable of taking care of the household, of shopping, etc. Everything went very well until before Christmas when we got deep snow and severe cold weather. And then I became somewhat ill-disposed, and it dragged on until the doctor asked why had I not sent for him earlier? He diagnosed it as an infection of the liver and the spleen and thought it would take a long time to get rid of it. Thus I have had to take medicine up to now. I have very little pain, but I am short of breath and cannot exert myself.

I shall continue to take the medicine, and perhaps it will get better after all. Wilhelm is well now but far behind in school because of his absence, which lasted several months. By his own wish he had been with a gardener for some time, but he was not able to continue there. He wants to become a farmer and keeps torturing me about it. It seems to me that he is getting as simpleminded as Max Steinbicker, if not even worse. His sisters are nagging him with their advice, and this makes him cross. I would like to move to a new area with him and try to make our way. But the others do not want to hear of this, and I will have to yield because I am not well.

9. The general armistice concluded 18 January 1871 ended the Franco-Prussian War ten days after Wilhelm I, king of Prussia, was proclaimed German emperor at Versailles. The final peace treaty was signed at Frankfurt/Main on 10 May 1871.
10. The nephews are Adolf and Heinrich Offenberg, sons of Jette's sister Johanna.

I went to Jefferson and finally made the last accounting, the final settlement with the court, and it does not turn out as well as I had expected earlier. I am in debt to the estate for six hundred dollars, which I will have to take care of later. This cannot be changed, and it is quite correct. It is also all right with me that the court did not approve of more for the administration and upkeep. There will be a time when I can sell the house. It annoys me, however, that the taxes are so high and that two feet were taken away for the sidewalk and that new steps had to be built, etc. Since the beginning of November I have not received any more rent. This is quite another sad story. But it does not affect me so much any more. If only I were well, if I could find a permanent occupation for Wilhelm, and if Louis could persist and could get ahead, then it would be easy for me. Ottilie is a conscientious teacher. She is not quite so strong in German, although she passed her examination. She studies and reads in the evening with Mr. and Mrs. Decker, his sister, the widow Hildenbrandt, also a teacher, a Mrs. Bindernagel, who lives with us, and nephew Heinrich. On two evenings, German writers; two evenings, English; and two evenings, Heinrich and Ottilie take French lessons. If they could only continue during the summer. Mrs. Bindernagel is a capable lady, not young any more, who had been teaching in England for eleven years and received a position here immediately. It is not quite so pleasant to have a stranger among us, but she also brightens up the circle here when the others are more quiet and would remain more simple.

Ernst was sickly a lot, and since he has some heart trouble he is often very depressed. His wife is also not strong. And the same goes for Heinrich, who has received a better position because of the death of his boss. He is indispensable to the new clerk. Judge Krekel told me that Heinrich is very capable and will have a good career. If only he would not be so very timid! But he has daily contact with the best lawyers, and we often receive interesting information through him.

Our new apartment is wonderful during the summer, and now flowers and trees are already in blossom all around us. And yet I would like to have something for myself again.

Recently in Jefferson things looked desolate, and I did not even go into the house because Jette advised against it. And how could I survive if I had to live there by myself? —But now we shall wait and hope until I am sixty years of age. Judge Krekel, who will probably take my garden, said I would have to keep the house as a home for myself. I do not understand him. For he himself still wants change and wants to wander—last winter Mrs. Krekel died. —I will have to use the money from the garden for the debts I have incurred here. I had to support Louis, etc.

You can already imagine that I am willing to accept your tempting proposition, one hundred dollars, and will not decline it if it is still available. If only I could put the sum to some use for income for myself! But since this seems to have come again from you, could I perhaps not take some from the Stevermann Foundation just as Phina did? Well, I mention it only in passing. You already know who has to be given preference. I can use it, but my Ottilie and Heinrich Geisberg are already doing what they can and what is necessary. But I would feel so good if I could manage by myself. I am always making new plans.

Soon I shall write to sister Therese. But I would like to have news very soon about how deeply you were involved in the war. I am still quite troubled and therefore ask you to relieve me of my worries.

On the occasion of Hüffers' golden wedding anniversary I wanted to present myself to the venerable old people with my children and grandchildren. And I have already expressed my wish to them. Is it not on 10 May?[11] The time is getting close.

Well, farewell, dear brother, give regards to all and greetings to you from the young people and from your sister, Jette.

P.S. I would very much like to hear how Pastor Bruns is getting along. A few years ago I wrote to him, but I did not receive an answer. It was after all his way. He is a little older than my husband was. I wonder whether he is still strong? I will have to write to one of his younger brothers . . . .

For a period of almost four years, from 18 April 1871 to 24 January 1875, no letters from Jette to Heinrich have been located. Ernest Decker, Jette's son-in-law, died 6 December 1871, leaving Effie with two small boys. A third son was born two weeks after his father's death. Hermann, Jette's oldest son, the one for whom she had been persuaded to seek a better life in America, died 22 June 1872, leaving one daughter. He was thirty-eight years old.

Heinrich Geisberg married Auguste Josephine Boner on 4 April 1872 in Trier, and many of the letters Jette wrote after his marriage are addressed to Auguste.

Jefferson City
24 January 1875

Dear Auguste:

My silence is really getting to be too long! For a while I consoled myself that I had a letter in the mail for both sisters. But now it seems so long since I have heard anything from you that God only knows what may have happened in the meantime. Frequently an uneasiness seizes me and I have to reproach myself vigorously: "In the final analysis it is you who upsets yourself." According to our natural relationship, you ought to send news to me, but how can I expect letters if I do not write any myself? I fear that my letter at Christmas time was not very festive. Often I am so dull.

For the holidays I had lots of visitors: Louis, Ottilie, Heinrich Geisberg, Jr., and Gustav Decker. Since the schools do not close in St. Louis until Christmas Eve, they traveled during the night and arrived here at two o'clock in the morning. Heinrich spent the first night here, but later he had to go to his sister's. I felt very comfortable having them here again, and they liked it very much at my place. The little one, usually a dull little fellow, acted as if he had always been with his grandmother. So this year we had a happy eight days, and I have started the new year in a joyous mood. I shall try once more to master my uneasiness and worries. — One thing after another worked out well, and then afterward there was a great void. Now we are accustomed to it again, and I try to keep myself busy and to forget. —Since I have some extra space here, I shall furnish one room to rent during the session of the legislature. But there is no demand for it.

On the 29th

The day after I had written the above, your letters arrived. I was relieved. So you have already had some very difficult experiences.[12] Since it was my destiny to lose seven children,

11. The golden wedding anniversary of Heinrich Jacob Hüffer and Elisabeth Rubens occurred on 22 May 1871.

12. The first child born to Heinrich and Auguste Geisberg was Johanna Maria Josephine, called Maria, who was born in Münster on 11 April 1873. They lost their second child, born 21 September 1874, after only a few hours. She was listed in the family records as Johanna Amalia Maria.

big and small, I perhaps know more how to sympathize than others. But even now in the death of relatives, it grieves me most when they are children. I never completely get over it. Since I have read here in the newspaper the news of the death of my brother-in-law[13] I have thought a great deal about dying. And why not? You report several cases to me. Max Boner, his wife and son.[14] Are the other children already grown? Mr. Martigni had told me that your sister had become a widow.[15] I had thought that if my brother-in-law did not want to pass us over I would inherit something; however, there are two other sisters-in-law whom he did not mention. He has held very strictly to his brothers and their descendants. The last will and testament was very carefully thought out, just as one would have expected of him. I wished for a little souvenir when a farmer from this area sent me a newspaper from Beckum in which the inventory of the estate was announced for sale.

And now, belatedly, I will have to wish you special happiness and blessings for the New Year. May your own wishes and expectations be fulfilled! You are after all not so immodest as to ask for anything unusual. —And the little one! Do you still not see any resemblance? She surely must be talking now and going out with you. Jette's little daughter, somewhat younger, runs around and makes the house lively.[16]

Everybody in St. Louis is well. Recently Decker's cousin got married in Illinois, and Effie's sister-in-law persuaded Effie to go to the wedding. She had to spend a night away from home, and Heinrich was amazed at the many instructions and admonitions she left for him, Louis, Ottilie, and the girls in case the children should be visited during these twenty-four hours by an attack of angina. He writes very beautiful letters and such long ones. To be sure I have to be satisfied that he writes in English; however, he speaks good German.

I read very detailed news from Westphalia in a St. Louis newspaper. It was very interesting to me. Perhaps it also sounded worse than you would consider it. However, it seems to me that Offenberg has a difficult position. I saw his name mentioned several times in connection with criticisms. Your uncle in Trier has hopefully not been molested. We are anxious to see how this confusion will be settled. After all, it cannot continue.[17]

Now dear Auguste, farewell! I hope to hear some good news from you soon. When? My Wilhelm and Jenni send their regards to their distant aunt. Hold dear, just as your sister holds you, Jette.

P.S. The relatives from St. Louis report to me that a cousin of yours, Alexander Bernay,[18] had

13. The Reverend Hermann Bruns died 14 November 1874.

14. Max Boner, treasurer at Hovestadt, married Maria Bischopink 23 September 1841 in Stromberg. Their son Franz was born 17 May 1844. Max died 13 December 1873, Franz died in July 1874, and Maria died 20 December 1874 of tuberculosis.

15. Amalie Kochs, born 19 December 1836 at Herten, daughter of Jette's cousin Franz Arnold Boner, lost her husband, Dr. Ferdinand Kochs, on 10 April 1874 from the effects of the War of 1870–1871.

16. Ida Nitchy, the daughter of Jette's niece and namesake Maria Henriette Geisberg, was born in 1873.

17. The term *Kulturkampf,* meaning "struggle for culture," was applied to the struggle between the Catholic Church and the state, particularly Prussia, beginning in 1872. The clergy opposed the so-called "May laws" of 1873, which stipulated that the clergy was to be regulated as to their education, employment, and disciplinary proceedings, for which a special court for church affairs was created. Other "May laws" in 1874 and 1875 provided for expatriation of clergy and prohibited all church orders and similar organizations except those involved in caring for the sick. Negotiations and discussions between Prussia and Pope Leo XIII were begun in 1879 and eventually, in 1886, resulted in a peaceful settlement and gradual revocation of the "May laws."

18. Alexander was the son of Dr. Karl Bernay and his wife, Marie, née Hammer. The Bernays were neighbors of the Geisbergs in Münster and related through the Hammer and Boner families.

visited them. What a shame that he did not know that I was here. I would have liked so much to see him. He passed through here. However, I am glad that he has seen the young people. It seems that they liked him very much and that he has told them a great deal. Effie praised him as being very open-minded. Well, I hope that he is well-situated now and will be able to enjoy the fruits of his work. I wish it would happen more frequently that young people from here and over there could become acquainted with one another. Then they could become closer, if for no other reason than for the sake of the parents. —Cousin Auguste was described with a great deal of praise. I wish I could have been there.

On 26 January 1875 Jette wrote Effie that she had been able to rent rooms to the legislature for committees and had to provide tables, chairs, and spittoons and move upstairs "without any warning." Since she had let "the girl" go to school and thus did not pay her wages, she had to do most of the work herself.

Jefferson City
26 April 1876

Dear Heinrich:

I had thought that I might get the letter from you that you mentioned in your letter to Louis. Since it has not come, I don't want to delay any longer. First, I would like to express my thanks to you for the $31 you have sent. They come very opportunely for me since I am saving for the interest payment that is due in June ($90). I cannot pay less than 10 percent. But perhaps in due time this will change, at least I hope so, so that there will be an opportunity to sell. At present, everything is still down. It is useless to worry a great deal; one just has to bear it and get along as well as possible. And since my young people do not let me starve I have no cause to worry.

My children accepted Jennie, Herman's daughter, as an equal heir as you had suggested.[19] And then Ottilie increased Mrs. Decker's share to $100 (otherwise $63) and gave her mother an extra $25. This all has pleased me very much. The girl is very frugal for herself and does not buy anything that is unnecessary but nevertheless likes social contacts and appears in public as is fitting. Louis is a much poorer manager of his money. He is probably quite respectable, he likes to dress up, he smokes, he spends money here and there until it is all gone. And then he complains that he hasn't saved anything. —Wilhelm is clerking now in Heinrich's office. He, on the other hand, is very frugal and would like above all to give me everything. I now attempt to make him understand that he will have to take care of himself as if I were no longer here.

Nephew Heinrich Geisberg has been married since the 10th of February.[20] It was a very quiet affair. Louis and Ottilie came, a few more friends, the Nitchys, and we. The young couple went to Chicago for a few days. Now they have their own household and are elegantly

19. In her letter of 26 January 1875 to her daughter Effie, Jette reported that the last will of Pastor Bruns provided for a division of the estate among five heirs or groups of heirs: "1. His brother, Hermeling, 2. Uncle Herman [his brother Gerhard Hermann], 3. the seven children of his niece in the parental home [in Lohne, Parish of Schepsdorf], 4. the children, still living, of his brother, Dr. B. Bruns, 5. the brother J. Heinrich Bruns (deaf and dumb)." A copy of the last will, given at Wadersloh on 6 November 1874 and publicly read five days after the pastor's death on 14 November, verifies Jette's report. Jennie, born 23 January 1863 and baptized Johanna Henriette, was the only child of Jette's oldest son Hermann, who had died 22 June 1872. It is interesting to note that Jette here spells her brother-in-law Herman's name in the Americanized version, with only one *n*.

20. Heinrich Geisberg, the son of Jette's brother Franz Geisberg, and Amelie J. Guyot, daughter of the Jefferson City jeweler Julian Guyot, were married on 10 February 1876.

installed. My only concern is that Emma (Amelie) is very delicate, and even though she has the best intentions, she should not exert herself. Johanna reported the same to me about her Heinrich.[21] It is getting empty at the Offenbergs.

How does it happen that I hear nothing at all from sister Therese? I was the last one to write. It has made me uneasy for quite some time. It is just as if this family is no longer in this world. I am just waiting for a few pictures and will then write to her.

I see from the local newspaper that the bishop of Münster has been removed from his office.[22] Do you also have to fear the loss of your position in the convention of canons at the cathedral? I am getting worried. And that will probably not change very soon. I can imagine that people will have to suffer all kinds of hateful things. Do tell me how things are affecting you. Or are you personally at all troubled? I hope that you will let me have some news in the course of the summer.

As always, with sincere love, your sister Jette.

P.S. I am really very happy about Max.[23] I hope that he becomes such a sensible, gentle boy as mine was, and as is the manner of the Geisbergs. I firmly hope that later as a man he will find a calling that will give him more satisfaction than the state of priesthood can afford him. Do tell me sometime where the Fürstenberg monument is standing.[24] Perhaps there are some small photographs.

Jefferson City
12 July 1878

Dear Heinrich:

I thought that I could postpone my next letter for a more convenient time. We have approximately 30 degrees Reaumur daily and feel this very much, particularly since Ottilie and I have just returned from a trip to the north that took us on a tour, partly on the Mississippi and partly by railroad, and afforded us a great deal of enjoyment. We chose the railroad route for the return trip particularly to visit cousin Carl, as well as some other acquaintances in Chicago.

I wrote to Carl from Dubuque on the Mississippi and received an answer by return mail. He was just in the process of leaving for Europe. His ticket had already been booked; otherwise he might have postponed it. I was very sorry, but our trip had already been arranged, and a close friend of ours, who had heard through Carl of our plans, urged us to let him know of our arrival. We spent several very pleasant days there and also visited Mrs. Anneke, Mathilde Giesler,[25] who has made a special career, as you perhaps already know. It

21. Heinrich Offenberg, born in Ahlen on 13 December 1845, married Ludmilla Windhorst on 12 August 1875. He is the author of the *Offenberg Family Chronicle* of 1891 as well as a two-volume history of the city of Münster.
22. The bishop of Münster, Johann Heinrich Brinkmann (1813–1899), was exiled to Holland from 1875 to 1884, a victim of the *Kulturkampf.*
23. Max Geisberg was born in Münster on 9 October 1875.
24. Franz Freiherr von Fürstenberg (1729–1810) is credited with founding the University of Münster in 1780. A monument honoring the founder stands on the *Domplatz* near the university.
25. Mathilde Giesler Anneke (1817–1884), who played a significant role in the women's suffrage movement in the United States, was well known to the Geisbergs in Münster. Married in 1836 at the age of nineteen, divorced a year later, she engaged in a long custody battle for her daughter. Although she won, she later wrote that she "became a victim of Prussian Justice in the divorce proceedings" (letter, Milwaukee, 26 April 1877, published in

was very pleasant that she recalled with such warmth her stay at the Geisbergs, and we were able to remember dear people and mutual friends. I found her extremely kind, as did Ottilie. We did not get around to discussing her social opinions in great detail because time was so short. She is a very gifted woman. If we had stayed longer, we probably would have found some points of disagreement. Our paths had after all been so different, and consequently also our points of view.

I did not hear anything particular concerning Carl. Our host, Carl's former partner, ventured the opinion, in answer to my question as to why Carl had left the partnership, that he had not participated in the business for quite some time and that he was so indolent. Mr. N. has three sons in the firm. It is carried on with great energy. My private view was always that Mr. N. was far more practical, while Carl had furnished the capital. It may be that everything went all right, which one could conclude since both of them remained to the end very good friends. Much special attention was paid to us, which we, to be sure, had shown them in Westphalia a long time ago.

We returned to St. Louis on 8 July. There it was very uncomfortable and even warmer than it is here, so Effie had a difficult day. She was packing jackets, pants, stockings, etc., by the dozens, and on Wednesday we were on the road again with her three fellows. She let them travel with us in order to have some rest for her impending English examination. It has been proposed that the German language be stricken from the curriculum in the public schools.[26] Perhaps it will not take place for a long time. However, they were advised to plan for it.

Yesterday I received another letter from Carl, which immediately puts me back to work. He says in it that he is not living very happily with his wife and that they have therefore resolved to live separately. They continue writing each other constantly. Naturally their son is the connecting link between them.[27] This separation should explain all kinds of things to

---

Journal of German American Studies 12, 2 [1977]: 35). No longer socially acceptable in her upper-middle-class circles in Germany, she began to write to support herself and her child. She married Fritz Anneke, a former Prussian army officer who had been discharged in 1845 for subversive activities, and accompanied him to battle in the unsuccessful 1849 revolution in Baden, in which he served as lieutenant colonel of the revolutionary Palatinate army, with Carl Schurz as his adjutant. After the failure of the Baden-Palatinate campaign, the Annekes were expelled from Germany and settled in Milwaukee in 1850. In 1852 Mathilde Anneke began the first women's newspaper in the United States, *Deutsche Frauenzeitung.* Following a lecture tour, the Annekes resettled in Newark, New Jersey, and continued the paper, but after the death from smallpox of two of their children in 1858, they returned to Milwaukee. A year later Fritz Anneke went to Italy to report on the Italian struggle for liberation, and in 1860 Mathilde joined him. Although her husband returned when the Civil War broke out to join the Union army, Mathilde remained in Europe until 1865, writing antislavery tracts and fiction. Returning to Milwaukee, she established a school for girls based on the German model, the *Milwaukee Töchterschule,* which provided her with a meager income for the rest of her life. She continued to be active in suffrage and other social reform causes and served as vice-president of the National Woman Suffrage Association.

26. During the superintendency of William T. Harris (1868–1880), the St. Louis public school system experienced great expansion and transformation, which are reflected in his *Annual Reports.* German-language instruction was introduced in September 1864 as an "experiment," and during the next decade spread through nearly the entire system, reaching over fifteen thousand students, or 47 percent of the elementary school enrollment. In March 1878 strong objections, particularly from the Irish, threatened the continuance of German instruction, and a petition to add Gaelic to the curriculum was presented. The German community countered with a petition, signed by forty thousand people, submitted prior to the election of school directors, and despite objections the school board upheld the established system. See Selwyn K. Troen, *The Public and the Schools* (Columbia: University of Missouri Press, 1975), pp. 61–73.

27. Leo Geisberg (1867–1921), born in Milwaukee, later became professor of music in Munich.

his sister.[28] He said that he has often tried to write of this but has not been able to bring himself to do it. I am now the first one with whom he has shared this information except for a few very intimate friends in Milwaukee. (This must be the case because I received no indication in M.) He urgently pleads with me to tell his and my brothers and sisters about it so that his path will be a little bit prepared. (I wonder whether this was a very difficult task for him?)

From all of this I have to conclude that he suffered very much in this situation, and it seems to me it would be very natural if the brothers and sisters would again become very close to each other.

A niece of Mrs. Anneke's was in Münster, as I was told in Milwaukee, and there she was immediately asked whether Leo had been baptized and was Catholic. I choose you as the recipient of this news, and you will know whether you yourself or one of the sisters should take this information to the two widows. I can not say anything further since I hope that I will hear later that for all concerned there was a satisfactory reunion and he will stay there. He wanted, I believe, to go to sea on the sixth; therefore this letter will leave later than he because of our trip and our sojourn there.

Farewell, dear brother, best regards to Auguste and the sisters from your sister Jette.

Jefferson City
6 February 1879

Dear Auguste:

Your dear letter surprised me in St. Louis, where it was forwarded to me. My daughters had insisted that Mother would have to spend the holidays with them for a change, and so I obediently packed my *Lebkuchen* and *Pfeffernüsse* and departed in spite of snow and ice. Louis, Ottilie, and Gustav were on hand that evening at the railroad station; we then took the streetcar, and soon were home. For the entire two weeks we had ice and snow, and most of the time we stayed at home, which suited me quite well. Christmas evening was peaceful and enjoyable for all. The young people were happy and enjoyed themselves while they were feasting, talking, and trying the new games until late into the night. One thing struck me: Decker's sister's daughter and our grandchild, both Jennies, decorated the tree and put the presents in order—so there we are, another generation.

What are you doing? Certainly the little candles on the green tree were shining for your two little ones, and you probably joined in their excitement and jubilation. May the New Year bring you many nice and good things! Kind thanks for the beautiful gift from your hand. We were very astonished at the contents of the packet, and I immediately showed the delicate work to my girls.

I am sorry that you had to move, and now I no longer know where you are.[29] Can you tell me where the new place is? Perhaps I would know by chance where it is. Would it not be nice to live in the circle of the sisters? I have a nice room free, and you are quite welcome to it. The

---

28. Carl Geisberg's sisters were Mrs. Johanna Uedink and Mrs. Antonie Petri. Carl, who had emigrated to America in 1842 and after a stay in Missouri settled in Milwaukee, returned to Germany and died in Boppard on the Rhine 4 June 1883.

29. In 1878 Heinrich Geisberg moved from Domhof 24, the old Chamber of the Seals, to Hörsterstrasse 25. This western half of a duplex remained in the family until 1924.

traveling could also be done on your part for a change. Always, the shabby money is lacking; otherwise I would quickly come over again before my great journey. I am strong enough, and there is nothing else to prevent me. I would then stay for a whole year and would go around quite at ease, only visiting my most beloved ones and a few old people, the few old ones who are still left there.

You were in Trier, and yet you do not specifically mention your uncle and the aunt.[30] And what about your sister? How did she die?[31] And how many children did she leave behind? I am not clear about this. —What has become of young Bernay? I did not see him myself, but was told a great deal about him. At that time he was really quite a whirlwind.

Here they're still complaining about the bad times. But we have to keep on hoping! At present the legislature is in session again, and therefore there are many strangers here. The great majority are Democrats, and I believe that there are many former Rebels among them. The lieutenant governor is a German, Brockmeyer,[32] and in addition a fellow countryman, from near Minden. We have known him a long time.

The United States Court, Western District, has been divided by Congress and, with the approval of the president, has been moved to Kansas City. For the time being, nephew Heinrich Geisberg has sent his deputy. We do not want to think that the entire company will have to move. That would affect him and also Wilhelm.

A little daughter arrived last December at the Geisberg's house.[33] The Nitchys are satisfied with their row of children, who are all good and smart.[34]

The winter is unusually severe for here, and there was a great deal of snow and sledding. At a sledding party Wilhelm hit his feet so hard that he hurt his ankles and had to rest for two weeks. However, since nothing was broken, he now tries to walk again.

Farewell, dear Auguste, kiss your children and Heinrich for me, and you will have to tell them about me, just as I tell my children about you. Hold dear, as always, your Jette.

I shall soon write to you, dear brother. Greetings and kisses for the New Year.

As always, your sister
Jette

30. Auguste Geisberg's uncle, Franz Boner (1801–1883), the dean of the cathedral at Trier, lived with his sister Josephine (1817–1891) in the little street *Sieh-um-dich* ("Look-around").

31. Antonia Sträter (1838–1878), née Boner, died in Amsterdam while giving birth to her sixth child.

32. Henry C. Brockmeyer (which he sometimes spelled *Brokmeier*) (1828–1906) was born near Minden, Prussia. At age sixteen he embarked for New York, where he worked for a while as a bootblack and currier, learned the tanning and shoemaking craft, and then traveled through Ohio and Indiana to St. Louis. He spent some time in Memphis, Tennessee, where he established a combined tanning, currying, and shoemaking business. In 1850 he entered the preparatory department of Georgetown College, Kentucky, but transferred to Brown University at Providence, Rhode Island, to finish his studies. In 1854 he came back to Missouri and settled in an abandoned cabin in Warren County, where he lived as a recluse for two years, devoting himself to the study of philosophy and making a literal translation into English of Friedrich Hegel's *Science of Logic*. He worked for a while as an iron-molder in the Excelsior Stove Works in St. Louis, but during the Civil War he enrolled in the militia, where he soon rose to lieutenant colonel, and was authorized to raise a regiment. In 1862 he was elected to represent Warren County in the state legislature, but at the end of his term moved to St. Louis and began the practice of law. In 1870 he was elected state senator, was reelected in 1872, and in 1876 was elected lieutenant governor. He served as acting governor in 1877 during the illness of Governor Phelps.

33. Ada Geisberg, born 15 December 1878, died 12 July 1879.

34. The Nitchy children: Effie, born 15 April 1868; Walter Henry, born 25 April 1870; Hattie Gertrude, born 31 October 1871; Ida, born 1 July 1873; Hilda Stella, born 26 June 1876; and Frank Frederick, born 25 May 1881.

Jefferson City
18 March 1879

My dear brother:

Letter and check have been received, and I thank you most sincerely. Our letters crossed, and therefore I hope that Auguste received mine a long time ago and that my seeming tardiness has been remedied.

I have been back home again since Christmas. Nettie, who was managing my household while I was gone, stayed here to try to obtain a position as a clerk in the senate during the session of the legislature. The gentlemen legislators are now tackling a revision of the bills for several sessions, so she will probably have work for months.

Nettie, who is very precise in everything, informed herself quickly about the procedures and is now busy for several hours every morning in a separate room writing and calculating, for which she receives five dollars, just like the gentlemen themselves, and therefore earns thirty-five dollars a week. A magnificent position! Her daughter Jennie is still in St. Louis with the aunts Effie and Ottilie; she is attending high school but is supposed to stop in the summer in order to help her mother or herself in some fashion.

Recently Louis reported that he has become engaged,[35] and I am happy at this. He is getting to be thirty years old. Wilhelm, who was never very pleased to be working in Heinrich's office, has rebelled again, for he would like to get out into the world. And then Heinrich tells him that he will have to care for his mother, who is grieving herself to death about him, etc., and then he says again that he will stay. Now, however, Mother says she wishes that he would go and become a man, that he should work and try to stand on his own feet and should not be tempted to spend his money. —Now both of us are agreed and that is good. I would not like to have it any differently. However things work out, I will have to bear it.

At the request of Heinrich I wrote to Louis to inquire whether he wants to come here, and he consented. And so I will only have to exchange the two sons.

There's still a great deal of complaining concerning the bad times. Here property is very low. Many houses are standing empty. I have to lower the rent and will have to take new renters again in the spring. I did not succeed in renting any rooms upstairs. The check and the rent are to be used to pay the interest. I still cannot manage to pay less then 10 percent interest. Food and clothing are cheap, and as I do not need much, I am satisfied. It is very lonely for me, but I am accustomed to that. I could repay Effie so much if I could be with her. And the boys love me. Probably they will all come up here again during the summer.

I am very happy that you have your own house, and I know approximately where it is. The dimensions on the outside are smaller than our house here, and I have to imagine frequently how much less it is. Here is a sketch of our magnificent building.

There is a twenty-three-foot frontage, and both downstairs rooms are sixteen by eighteen feet. There is a hall of six feet; in the yard there are long flowerbeds on both sides, and the footpaths have been paved with brick. Behind Bruns' office there is a little gate, and in the middle a cistern with a pump, then a round flower bed in the middle of the lawn, and a smokehouse, etc.

35. Louis David Bruns married Emily Louise Sander on 3 September 1879. Born in Massachusetts on 6 October 1861, she died at Mercer Island, Washington, 1 January 1912.

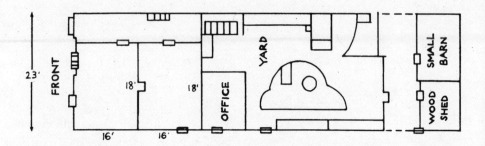

Uncle Hüffer has become quite old,[36] and our dear mother had to die so early! August Boner's death surprised me.[37] Offenberg's condition upsets me very much because he has been suffering for such a long time.[38] Last fall Hermeling, Bruns's brother near Steinfurt, died.[39] They all go, and I wonder when I will follow?

Has Wesemann remained in Münster?[40] I have not heard anything about Bernhard for a long time. You could let me know some time how he is getting along. Is the doctor still there? Your friend?

You said that a longer walk would be good for you, and that I believe. Only there won't be time to take walks. The moving around in the house is good for me too, and running up and down the stairs is not difficult for me at all. However, now and then I would not like to do it if I could get along without it. When should I write again? You probably have many more subjects to discuss. I wish one of you would come some time so that the land and the people here would not be so foreign to you.

Best regards to Auguste and to all. With sincere love as always,

Your sister, Jette

Jefferson City
29 October 1879

Dear Auguste:

Yesterday my birthday letter arrived—and now there are five letters lying here that require an answer. Of my children there were two sons here and a new daughter, who has been called Frau Bruns since 3 September.

This summer was eventful. Since Wilhelm did not want to stay, Louis agreed to accept the position in Heinrich Geisberg's office. He arrived, and Wilhelm went to Colorado on 24 May.

36. Heinrich Jacob Hüffer died 7 December 1878. He was eighty-one.
37. Jette's cousin August Boner died at Salzkotten 4 January 1879.
38. Lord Mayor Caspar Offenberg died in Münster on 3 March 1879.
39. Bernard Hermann Bruns, called Hermeling, died at Drievorden near Emsbüren 4 January 1878. Although Pastor Bruns in his last will referred to his brother as "Bernard Heinrich Bruns, genannt Hermeling," parish records at Schepsdorf list him as Bernard Hermann.
40. The Offenbergs' only daughter, Agathe, married Clemens Wesemann 24 May 1873. In 1879 Wesemann became counselor of the district court in Hamm, and in 1880 was appointed judge at the imperial court of Emperor Wilhelm I in Leipzig. In 1887 he became privy counselor in Münster.

In the meantime we had accepted the invitation of a friend who owns a nice property outside the city, mainly because of the boys, whom I expected for the vacation with their mother and aunt.[41] I had also invited the young bride and Jennie. They all arrived in June. We had a nice time here in the country. The garden stretches far down to the river. The fence adjoins the railroad, which runs below. It is a magnificent place, with beautiful terraces, winding paths, trees, and a spring surrounded by rocks. The owner came back because of some business for several weeks. And thus the house was completely full.

Emily's brother, with whom she lived, indicated that he would follow a call to California, and we decided that she should therefore join her chosen one immediately. She went back to St. Louis and took care of her affairs. Effie had gone home a few weeks earlier, and at the end of the vacation Tillie and Louis also went. Then a quiet, joyful wedding took place and they came here. The young couple is now living with me. We stayed here this winter as we had promised Mr. Hess. It is a little far for Louis, but it is good for him to commute. He is already quite settled, and the job pleases him. He will soon have worked himself in, and in addition he studies so that he can fill the position permanently. His wife is eighteen years old and still somewhat naive, but everything she does becomes her, and she will probably make a good housewife in due time. She is capable with the needle and also has a well-trained musical talent, which gives us much enjoyment. Since she lost her mother, she tends to cling to me quite a bit. I shall enclose her pictures. I wanted to wait for another one of Emily. I don't like this one. She is small and delicate, and the pretty eyes do not show up very favorably.

I hope that Heinrich will make our Christmas happy by writing a letter. How do you like it in the new apartment since you have been there for quite some time? It is somewhat different, but one feels safer than in a strange house. It seems that I will not have my home back immediately. Perhaps never! For the time being I have rented out the downstairs. But my belongings are mostly out here in the country.

Since winter is coming it is now very lonely here. We still frequently see the brother and sister Geisberg with their families. However, they also wish that I would go back with them. And I console myself that perhaps next winter! However, who knows!

Everybody in St. Louis is well. They have to work hard, and I don't know how Effie can manage. We would very much like to have one of the sons here. Perhaps she will make up her mind.

Sincere greetings to your husband and children. Your Jette.

Jefferson City
11 November 1879

Dear Heinrich:

There, I have written to your wife, and just as I was going to address the letter I could not think of a title. I simply wrote "Frau Auguste Geisberg." And then I thought—should I add her maiden name? And as I noticed too late, I went back a whole generation. I wrote "née Hammer," and you have to attribute this error to my hastiness. I hope, however, that the letter will arrive all right. Otherwise you will have to call for it.

---

41. The property seemingly belonged to Carl E. Hess (1839–1904). Born in Hannover, Hess was educated at St. Charles, Missouri, took a law degree from Harvard, and served with the Union army in the Civil War.

Now I ask you to report to me with what title you want to be addressed. Here there are several other Bruns, so I continue to call myself, as do others, "Frau Dr. Bruns,"[42] and I like to hear this best of all.

Now we are not very far from the Christmas holidays and the end of the year. I wish you good fortune from the bottom of my heart for both holidays. May you celebrate them happily, and may you be happy, and may you make people happy! The children are old enough to understand and respect the event, and therefore the pleasure of their parents will be that much greater. For so many years we also experienced this. Bruns insisted so much on the celebration of the Christmas evening. In health and in sickness the children had to be thought of, even during the war when the bigger ones were missing and we really were in constant turmoil and worry. We always postponed the celebration of his birthday, which fell one day earlier. For years afterward this made Christmas rather sad for me. But now I am over everything and enjoy the present time and do not spoil anybody's joy with my quiet sorrow.

The younger generation enjoys what is given to them. Effie particularly was haunted early in life by hard blows of fate. I probably reported earlier that since her youngest one was in school she had accepted a teaching position. Even though no great income, this was still something constant and always a little contribution to the household, although it did result in a great deal of work and commotion for her before and after school. Now, however, they are contemplating abolishing the German language in the public schools in St. Louis, and the German teachers were dismissed, Effie among them. Now she studies for the English exam. Since she has enjoyed instruction in this language, it will not be so difficult for her, but all the things that one forgets she now will have to pass well. And in addition she has too much modesty, or really not sufficient self-confidence, pertaining to her capabilities. We have always judged her very highly. I fear, however, that it is quite difficult for her. Tillie, in addition to her work, still has three classes in German, which she took over for Effie so that her sister would have more free time for studying. A part of the examination is coming up.

For some time I thought that I would ask you whether you could be instrumental in getting additional financial support for Effie and her studies. Is this possible? Is she entitled to this? Or is it still too early? If I am right, the Boners and you, too, have received a stipend from the Stevermann fund.

Harry Decker, her oldest, is now twelve years old, and I must say that Effie (and also Decker's sister) have spent much for the education of the children. What they don't get in school is practiced at home, and private instruction is given. Think about it and write me sometime soon. —And now I have written a lot. How many things we could talk about if one could delve more into detail with daily things! Writing is getting difficult for me because I am living in foreign circles. But gradually the family circle is enlarged. The nephews stir. This summer, life was rather exciting here. Besides the Deckers, Walter Nitchy was here a lot, and the boys played so well together. Jette came frequently with her girls. And then somebody else came, a man no longer very young, an old acquaintance who at the end of the vacation made a proposal to my youngest daughter, which she accepted, and thus she has resolved to resign at the end of this school year.

I am very happy about this. For eight years I have considered him my friend. The young

42. It was customary in Germany to address the wife of a man holding a military, professional, or academic title with the title of her husband; thus *Frau Dr.*

people did not want to understand this. But now Decker's sister writes, "I have never seen such a happy bride." Strange, our sober Tillie! I replied that I have a feeling that I could see it even more! And so they will be coming here for Christmas. He has ordered a Christmas tree especially for our young people. Louis and Emily are very happy.

As always, your sister, Jette.

Jefferson City
9 January 1880

Dear Heinrich:

We have a report from Mr. Adrian,[43] the older son-in-law of our deceased brother-in-law, G. H. Bruns, that they are satisfied if you want to transfer the part of the inheritance from Pastor Bruns to my son Louis. Do it as before—by draft on the bank in St. Louis.

We spent the holidays quietly at home in the family, mainly because of the weather. But it was not less pleasant. Ottilie had to hold school until Christmas Eve. And then when Effie's Christmas tree was standing there in all its bright magnificence, the chosen one appeared and to the amazement of the boys was introduced as "Uncle Hess." The next morning the couple was ready for their departure, and they arrived here at the designated time. Louis had a vehicle ready for them at the depot. This really opened people's eyes. Here, after dinner, they had a few hours to themselves. Emily took care of the tree. Hess arranged for the gift-giving upstairs in his room, where even his fiancée was not allowed to enter. He had brought along a big barrel from Toledo. When dusk came we were led upstairs, and there our eyes took in a glittering and shimmering of magnificent things.

Above all, for Louis and Emily, as a wedding present, a tea set of French porcelain, painted, a quite new fashion, then a tea pot, sugar bowl, a silver creamer, etc. Then it was Mother's turn with crystal pitchers, small *dépôt de menage,* three beautiful lamps, etc. Ottilie received a cookbook, a beer pitcher, a toilet set, ornaments for the parlor, a magnificent lamp, etc. etc. etc. (Wilhelm was favored with a smoking apparatus.) Hess and we were very pleased. Downstairs the Christmas tree was shining in its splendor; it had been decorated mainly for his sake since he had asked for it especially. Then we presented our little favors and remained together for a few hours, happily "at home," as he called it.

It is really good to see how happy he is, how completely relaxed. And our girl also acts as if this is quite natural, and one can see only little of the dignified behavior of the school ma'am. She is still tired and always has to rest and feels that she is pressured again. To be sure, everything will be all right eventually. Naturally she has resigned and will stay with her mother in order to acquaint herself with managing a house. Last summer I was concerned about her, since our niece, Effie Bruns,[44] died of tuberculosis. She was a teaching sister in Philadelphia.

In St. Louis all are well. The boys send greetings to the Grandmother in their letters. Their mother, Effie, and Mrs. Hildenbrandt, Decker's sister, will miss Tillie very much. Effie doesn't

---

43. Herman Adrian (1836–1888) married Elisabeth Bernadine Catherine Bruns on 6 April 1864. The second child of Dr. Bruns's brother Gerhard Hermann Bruns, she was born at Westphalia 24 April 1842 and died at Martinsburg 8 January 1903.

44. Euphemia Bruns, Sister Nazaria, was born in 1855 in Westphalia, joined the School Sisters of Notre Dame in 1872, and died in Philadelphia in 1879. She was possibly a daughter of David and Christina Bruns.

possess the energy of her sister; however, she has passed one of her pending exams successfully. I have offered her my help in her house for a while to relieve her, but only until spring comes.

We had some ugly weather, icy roads, rain, frost; so we were not at all tempted to go out, which Hess was enthusiastic about. He will soon have to go back until the middle of the summer.[45] If he were not tied down there, there would be no obstacle to their marriage now. But it seems that they want to wait a year. I do not quite like that. But he is so attached to this place. "This is supposed to be his home."

Louis and his wife find it quite far to the office, and they are rebelling a bit. However, he feels much better with these regular walks, and since we do live here where it is better in the summer than anywhere else, he will have to please the owner and stay here.

Mr. Lay, an acquaintance of ours here, a lawyer and member of Congress, died in Washington,[46] and today there is a new election. On the Republican side ex-governor McClurg,[47] of whom we have perhaps written earlier, stands again. The Democrats, among whom are the Rebels, went too far in their arrogance, and it had to be tolerated. McClurg will also receive the votes of the colored people, and they are not insignificant in the state. In general the black people are still very shabby, although certainly many of them are also quite respectable. Judge Krekel still endeavors to further the university[48] for them; however, he also goes too far in his judgment of them. It is after all a different race from that of the white, and equality often leads to unacceptable situations. You probably cannot comprehend that. In the east and in the northern states things are different. But in Missouri it is perhaps more noticeable than even in the South, where the black population still has a lower standing and still lets itself be ruled more.

I have not written to our sister Therese because it finally became too much for me. I shall make it up. For now, best greetings for the family von Hatzfeld. Enclosed are the pictures for you and for Johanna that I have gotten. Be cordially greeted from your sister, Jette

Jefferson City
7 March 1880

Dear Heinrich:

Your letter with the enclosed draft arrived safely.[49] Louis will send a receipt. He has immediately written to Westphalia. As for myself, I convey my best thanks. You noted that I

45. Carl Hess was associated with a wholesale crockery business in Ohio and involved in an ore refractory undertaking in Colorado before permanently resettling in Jefferson City, where he was superintendent of the Jefferson City Light, Heat and Power Company. Active in civic affairs, he served on the school board and promoted the bridge over the Missouri River. He died in Jefferson City 22 December 1904.

46. Alfred Morrison Lay (1836–1879)was born 20 May 1836 in Lewis County and graduated from Bethany College, Virginia (now West Virginia), in 1856. He practiced law in Jefferson City and took his seat as a member of Congress on 4 March 1879.

47. Joseph Washington McClurg from Camden County, Missouri, was elected governor in November 1868. Running on the Republican ticket in the 1880 election, he was defeated by the Democratic candidate, Thomas Theodore Crittenden.

48. In January 1866, at the suggestion of 1st Lt. Richard Baxter Foster, plans to found a university for blacks in Missouri were laid by members of the 62nd and 65th U.S. Colored Infantry, who contributed over $5,300 to the cause. On 20 February 1866 a Board of Trustees for Lincoln Institute was created, and Articles of Incorporation were presented to the Cole County Circuit Court on 25 June. On 17 September 1866 Lincoln Institute opened with two students. Foster, a native of New Hampshire, educated at Dartmouth, who before his enlistment had taught school in Illinois and Indiana, served as the institute's first principal, from 1868 to 1870. Judge Arnold Krekel was active in promoting Lincoln Institute and served on the board during its early years. See W. Sherman Savage, *The History of Lincoln University* (Jefferson City: Lincoln University, 1939).

49. According to a letter from Louis Bruns of May 1880, the draft was in the amount of $279.

should inform you when my situation is improved. This gives me food for thought. If you, or, more correctly, if the caretakers of the Stevermann Foundation are of the opinion that I should not file a claim because I live so far away from the home country in another part of the world, then I cannot object to that. If this, however, is not the case and I as a born Geisberg am equally entitled to it, then, to be sure, I have to ask to be considered. When they are married, the children often do not help their mother, or rather cannot do it, as is also shown in the case of Trude.[50] The same is true in my case. There is no lack of good will, God be thanked!

Louis has a hard row to hoe in the beginning. He is industrious, and in a few years they will probably get along. He is the one who supports me, since they are living with me. Tillie is now without an income, but she has, as long as she lives with me, contributed by paying the taxes. As I already reported, Wilhelm returned from his excursion to the west. He should not have done this, for since that time he has been rather inactive, and I have to do everything for him. His brother and sisters notice this unkindly, and he will probably have to start anew again. It was a great mistake that he resigned from Heinrich's office, particularly since the latter tried to keep him there. It worries me very much what will become of him.

It seems that in our country a new upswing is noticeable. There is a general hope that everything will improve. In the fall they were working on a new railroad line to the south-west. However, after a few months work stopped again. Since that time a rich New Yorker by the name of Gould has bought many railroads here in the west. Some of his employees are new. If I could sell my house soon and have approximately two thousand dollars left to me, would not the interest sustain me? Since I can rent out only a small part, the interest, the insurance, and the repairs consume the rent, and very little is left. (Perhaps I wrote in greater detail than you have to report.)

Now I shall try to write of more cheerful things. When the bridegroom-to-be spent several weeks here in the winter, it seemed to him finally that he would prefer to take our girl home in a few months. This was explained to me, and I could only say that I did not object in the least to the proposal. Thus the couple has thought over everything, and consequently the wedding will take place in May. —But now I am still being tortured a lot. I am not to come into the kitchen at all anymore, and constantly there are questions such as "Mother, how do you do this? How would one have to do that?" She wants to be informed in all things. She will make a capable wife. She has a strong will and endurance.

Spring is gradually making itself felt outside and makes me restive. The gardener was already here for a week. He has planted trees and pruned the old ones. To my great sorrow the garden was taken out and plowed, and a terrace was planted with sod. I planted shrubs and set out narcissus, hyacinths, and snowbells, which remind me of our mother, for in our little garden the first crescent-shaped flowerbed on the inside was surrounded by them. Do you still remember?

We shall try to spruce up everything so that it will look fit for a bride when he comes.

Effie's oldest, Harry, and little Ernst, the youngest, have been here for some months. They are going to school here so that Effie will have more rest. We are a big household. I saw in a local newspaper that Clemens Wesemann went to Leipzig. It will be hard on Johanna.

50. This is thought to refer to Gertrud Steinbicker Geisberg, wife of Franz Heidenreich Geisberg's son Franz, who lived in Oels.

Best regards to Auguste and all the others from your sister,

Jette

On 21 July 1880 Jette wrote to Catherine Dubbert[51] to inquire if Wilhelm was in Westphalia. He had left home a week before to find work with the railroad but had not taken along any clothes for a change. She asked Catherine to advance him money to have clothes made and send her the bill.

Toledo, Ohio
3 December 1880

Dear Heinrich:

I have been here with Ottilie for several weeks already. And since the young couple insists that I should not go home this year, I relented after serious consideration.

Since I received your last letter I have become somewhat melancholic, but I could not help it and was not capable of controlling my thoughts. I had been consulting with Jette for a long time about a trip to St. Louis. But then I went alone, and suddenly I found myself in a full, lively household at Effie's, where I was welcomed by the big and the little ones in the most endearing manner. Jette followed me a bit later, and since the teachers and the students were not home during the day, we whiled away the time quite well. It was soon a bit too much for me, and I left as I had planned, promising to stop over on the return trip. I wanted to return in three weeks, and now this is not possible. These two can get along without me most easily, but they do not want to hear that I am in their way. I would very much like to be active and helpful.

I want to be with Effie, but since she lives with her sister-in-law and I cannot pay board, this won't work. Later, perhaps! Effie has been transferred to a more distant school, where she teaches English as well as German. She does not see the boys now from breakfast time until late in the evening, and naturally she worries a great deal because of that. It is hard and worrisome. However, she was told it was the lowest step of the ladder and she would have to have patience.

Formerly I thought that I could probably not get along without the annual sum I am receiving from you from the Stevermann Foundation, but I would rather that you send it to Effie than to me *if that can be arranged!* You know she has three sons, who are already in need of instruction and clothing. She can provide part of her living expenses, but she does not have nearly enough from her income. I urge you very strongly to consider if you can help her by sending her my allocation.

Everybody now tells me that I should enjoy the good life and rest. If it were only possible for me! But I am not accustomed to that. And don't I still have worries about my youngest? It seems to me as if I am deserting him. To be sure, at age twenty-seven he ought to be independent and should have his career. Since this is not the case, it still causes me concern.

Louis and wife are striving ahead, and I am welcome with them. Hess and wife are well and very satisfied and happy. He is a capable man, always busy in his business, which is, as he says, blossoming. Strange, however, that he as well as Ottilie would rather be in Missouri.

51. Catherine Mary Dubbert, the daughter of G. Hermann Bruns, was born in Westphalia, Missouri, on 20 June 1846. She married Joseph Dubbert (born 14 February 1847 in Westphalia) on 8 June 1875. The Dubberts moved to a farm near Martinsburg in Montgomery County after their marriage.

I do not like it here as well as there either. The land and the people are different, more narrow-minded. However, this is judging the situation from a superficial point of view. I hope and wish very much that Hess can stand it for a number of years. His wife diligently endeavors to catch up with what she has missed because of her earlier professional duties. And so she is busy in the household and supervises a capable girl as well.

And what are you doing? We read of severe cold weather. To be sure we have that here too, and I cannot stand it so well. Otherwise I am quite strong. I wish you could be as strong as I am! Perhaps you are now? I imagine that you and your wife and the little ones are looking forward to a comfortable and happy holiday. And on this occasion I wish you good fortune from the bottom of my heart, and I shall be thinking of you. We here are considering what should be done to give the master of the house some pleasure. He is attached to the Christmas celebration with a childlike piety and is already forever talking about it. I only wish we could also have the boys from St. Louis here. Children are a part of Christmas Eve.

Once more I wish you happiness for the Christmas festival and for the New Year! Auguste must be satisfied this time with our best regards. The young couple sends regards to you.

After the New Year I would like to go home, and I hope that I will then hear from you again soon. With affectionate love,

your sister, Jette

Jefferson City
28 May 1881

Dear Auguste:

For several months I had been impatiently waiting and worrying about a letter from home, and I was just on the verge of writing you when I was interrupted by a visit from my daughter. And then finally a letter arrived from our sister Johanna, and soon after one from you and Heinrich. With that the worries were over. You must not believe that I hear about events there in threefold versions. Johanna writes only of her house, and Therese writes so rarely that I do not know whether it was her turn or mine last. However, she is a good narrator when she writes. From this you see that we receive news almost exclusively from your pen. Everything is interesting to me, and sorrow and joy probably touch me more than if I were back in the hometown. Thus it was rather strange to me when you said "Grandfather Bachofen." Naturally that is Carl von Bachofen, and why should he not be a grandfather? I have not seen him since he was at home as a young student. We were together a lot as children. Clemens visited me twenty-five years ago in Münster. Heinrich probably does not associate much with Carl.

You seem to think that we see each other frequently here. I don't know. Traveling by railway is not very difficult, and I can easily get away from here, and the daughters want to see me, and as to the main thing, there's always somebody who pays for the travel expense. So I can travel with an easy mind and take it easy. My wardrobe can quickly be assembled and does not worry me much.

Last fall I was somewhat unsettled and began to brood. I don't know what might have become of me if I had had to stay here. In St. Louis I became ill, and with that I developed patience. If Tillie had not really expected me, I would have turned around. And then when I was five hundred miles away, I gave in and realized that I could just as well spend the winter with the young people since they really wanted that. They, as well as I, felt strange in a strange city outside of the house. And perhaps we were not quite fair, but we prefer Missouri.

I have been here again since the middle of February. We also had a lot of snow and cold weather and a slow, beautiful spring. At present it is very beautiful here. We have improved many things and have attended to things, and we can see the rewards. Since both sons are interested in it, as I am, it affords us a great deal of entertainment and discussion. I have even begun again to pay attention to a kitchen garden, which I had not done for the past twenty years. Louis is taking care of raising flowers, and we have a tremendous number of roses and other bushes. It is almost too much of a good thing. There is always something that occurs to me that should be improved, and so I am never quiet in the house.

For a few weeks we have had new help, a girl fresh from Silesia, who now has some very serious difficulties. She is, however, good-natured, clean, and a good learner. And so it is only a matter of patience. We are now all obliged to speak high German. Otherwise it is unfortunately mixed a lot, especially with the young people, who speak English among themselves.

In a few weeks the school in St. Louis will close, and I can look forward to having Effie and her three sons here for the vacation. Our little girl is growing nicely and also likes her grandmother, for which she probably has good reason. On 25 May the Nitchys had another son: Franz Friedrich. Both his grandfathers and our grandfather bore these names.

All in the family are well, and so receive best regards from everybody.

Hold dear as always, your Jette.

Jefferson City
30 May 1881

Dear Heinrich:

By forgetting your letter to me, you caused me a lot of worry. I was quite nervous, which I never was earlier, and I thought of you every day and tried to figure out what might be wrong. Ottilie came here for several weeks, and then I was seriously thinking of inquiring, but finally a letter from Johanna arrived, and shortly thereafter the one from you.

First my thanks for the $27.90 I have received. This time I shall claim it for myself since Effie and the children will be spending the vacation with me here, which naturally sets me back. Later Effie should put in a claim for this, however, and I hope you will let her know in due time what information she will have to supply to you. In the future I shall then spend my time with any one of my children as they can decide among themselves. In my last letter from Toledo I already spoke about that, for with a special project I have planned, it seemed unfitting for me to continue to accept support from the foundation. Namely, my new son-in-law Carl Hess wants to provide a sufficient sum for a trip to the old country for his wife and for me! This is a strange idea. At my age, and they are a young married couple! I said in confidence that I would be very happy if they would have an heir. Although the first year has already passed, it is premature to imagine that this will not happen. —Well, although it remains doubtful, I still worry about it. Particularly since both of them consider it something so definite that they have ordered me there for the winter to prepare for the trip in the spring.

Would it give you great pleasure to have me there once more? Or vice versa? After twenty-five years? And alone this time? I believe it would be best if we would not continue to think of it and let it rest. —I thought it necessary to tell you about this, but I urge you to forget it. Since Bernhard died[52] I have often thought it would be time for me to say good-bye, since we are all, after all, already much older than usually happens in our family (except for the Hüffers). I am strangely strong, but I do have to take care of my health a little bit.

Enclosed is a list from us of our and brother Franz's children.[53] My young people would also like to know a bit more about the relatives over there. So if you have some time, sit down with your secretary and put together a list of names.

Do you often have attacks?[54] Perhaps you do not have enough time for recreation and you have to work too hard? This probably happens because your work is not limited to any one place. Do you have any hope that this will soon happen?

Now, farewell! Give our best regards to your family. We are all well, and we are anxiously looking forward to the arrival of the Deckers.

With love, your sister Jette.

P.S. A few weeks ago I received a card and a letter from Nettie, now Mrs. Henry.[55] Mr. Henry is a man well advanced in years, but he has a good business in St. Louis. He is a widower and has several children who are mostly grown already.

On 8 October 1881 Effie Bruns Decker wrote to Heinrich applying for support from the Stevermann Family Fund.

Toledo

1 March 1882

Dear Heinrich:

Yesterday I finally received some news about you by way of Effie. I had been worrying for the last few weeks about you and about her. She did not write at all, and her boys did not answer my postcards either. The oldest ones had been sick, and with teaching and caring for and worrying about the children, she had put me off. I had still thought that I would get a sign of life from you first, no matter what the results were concerning Effie. She sent me your letter and inquires what she should do. We are both grateful and are satisfied. It came to me quite unexpectedly, but it is very welcome. Hess offered to take Effie the amount when he is passing through. Thus we can, as you suggested, leave everything with you to be settled later.

We have reserved berths on the *Main*, a departing North-Lloyd steamer, and therefore will travel via Bremen on 11 March. We will probably be able to inquire aboard the ship which railroad we may take to you, possibly directly from Bremerhaven. You will probably

52. Jette's brother Bernhard died 18 August 1880 at age sixty-one in Marsberg, in the institution where he had been confined for over thirty-two years.

53. Enclosed with the letter of 30 May 1881 was the list of children and grandchildren of the Geisberg family in America that Jette had prepared. It contained a number of inaccuracies. A chart listing the Geisberg–Bruns families is provided on pp. 28–29.

54. Heinrich Geisberg suffered from rheumatic attacks, which led to almost complete paralysis.

55. Catharina "Nettie" Bruns, the widow of Jette's oldest son Hermann, married widower Peter Henry of St. Louis in 1881. Henry and Company was a well-established firm manufacturing excelsior for carriages, mattressmakers, upholsterers, etc., located at 1100 West Main Street in St. Louis.

be informed by telegram and will then be able to meet us in Münster. At least this is how we expect to do it.

And now all of you take good care of yourselves! We hope to be with you in three weeks. It is, after all, strange to me but nevertheless good that I shall see you again soon.

As always, your sister
Jette

Do give regards to everybody hither and yon.

Jette to her son, Wilhelm Bruns

Münster
21 April 1882

Dear Wilhelm:

It really is of no use if I accuse you of completely forgetting me, for I really do not know whether and when you have written to me. And so I now just have to let you know how things are. In Toledo I received the postcard of 26 January in which you informed me that you would write a letter to me in a few days. I waited for it, but then I did write you a last letter from Toledo before our departure, in which I asked you to write to me immediately to Münster, and I gave you your uncle's address. The above-mentioned postcard was the last that I received from you. I was already somewhat concerned in Toledo. And I have also mentioned this in a letter to Louis from New York, as well as one from here to Effie. And now there is still nothing!

Tillie received a letter from her husband in Texas, and yesterday she received newspapers and journals from Heinrich. So my children do have time enough to reciprocate a courtesy to their mother for which she longs every day.

There was high water even before we left America, and even though the Hubers are fortunately living high up, they may still have had to save some of their crops and animals. Tillie commented that perhaps the postal connections were delayed, which is also probable, but are you also sure you used the correct address in your letter? And where should I send this one now? I had been so sure that you would completely relieve me of my worries and that you had taken everything along except ink. Well, now I am waiting and waiting. But believe me that I am very cross, and I think a hundred times, "I wish I had stayed there." Well, enough of that!

We have been here for two days short of a whole month. We landed on 23 March, and then we went on a small steamer to Bremerhaven, and after a few hours went on by special train to Bremen. From there we went to the Osnabrück train station, and soon after left for Münster, where we arrived about six hours later. Tillie exclaimed immediately, "I see Aunt Therese," and she was right—there they all were: your uncle and his wife and both of the sisters, Caspar H. dressed as a soldier,[56] Felix O., two H. daughters, and two Geisberg children.[57] We see each other every day since the three families live close together, and I can tell you that we are very happy and enjoying each other's company. Your uncle looks quite

---

56. Caspar, Franz and Therese von Hatzfeld's second son, was born in Lüdinghausen in 1858.
57. The two Geisberg children were Maria and Max, ages nine and six respectively.

old and has been suffering again in recent times. Your aunts are hardly as agile as I am. We take daily walks together, and we often eat together at noon or in the evening. O. Hatzfeld is in Berlin; of the Offenbergs, only Max and Felix are here; Richard was here for two days. We live close to Aunt Johanna. In the beginning we were freezing a lot, although there were no more cold spells. The people here have been much more toughened to the cold than we. Spring is magnificent, but I believe you must be more advanced in the season. Now all the trees are in full bloom. People do a lot here for parks and flowers. We have seen many very splendid estates and frequently see beautiful gardens and parks. But it will become even more beautiful as the season advances. I am taking note of several bushes and flowers that I hope to bring along for H[ess]'s place and for Louis and Jette if I can manage it. Aunt Johanna has many things in pots in her little garden. Many houses in Münster have little gardens in spite of the narrow streets and the very tall houses. People are living together in such crowded conditions, but they are comfortably situated. They do not have as much and as fine fresh air as we have. I also see many people who are much poorer or who are doing rough work, and they are, of course, clothed much more poorly and wear wooden shoes and work much harder. Better society is just as it is with us, only they don't have anything to do with craftsmen and workmen, and those who have government positions are then really the masters, and they live with their ladies very comfortably. We in America have to work much harder and don't have as much free time by any means. All in all, everything has become quite foreign to me here. But later we will visit our hometowns of Oelde and Stromberg. We are expected by Aunt Hüffer, who has already written us. It now seems to me that we have spent an endlessly long time here, and I really do not have an inclination to get acquainted with new areas and new people. Perhaps this will change a bit later when I have heard all the good news from you. And because of Tillie I have pulled myself together. She seems to like it here very much and is quite lively. She is with the von Hatzfelds a lot, and also with the cousins, the two Petri girls and the Uedink girl, whose mother was a Geisberg. You will not understand all these relationships, but Tillie is gradually catching on. I am generally called "Aunt Jette" here, and Tillie is also addressed by the relatives with the familiar *Du.*

Now I have written you a long letter, and I only wish that I could dispatch it correctly and quickly and see that you receive it. But where should I send it? What are you doing? But surely you have told me all of this a long time ago.

Your loving mother,
H. B.

A note on the margin of the first page: I must surely assume that you are well again and have regained your strength since the winter has passed. And I do hope that you take good care of yourself.

Münster
5 September 1882

Dear Auguste:

We are already completely enraptured with music. A large number of strangers blocks our way, and particularly noticeable among them are the gentlemen of the clergy. Many remind me of old times with their stockings and buckled shoes. Again, many are quite young. But all look lively and seem to enjoy the exhilarating occasion. I seriously endeavor to find understanding and pleasure in the presentations, but I still cannot change the opinion I formed at first, namely that boys can never substitute for the full sound of the female voice, and also that a greater perfection could be achieved by a mixed choir in these compositions, particularly under such direction as this. This morning there was a Mass, a *Te Deum*. This afternoon there is a rich program, and it will probably be interesting, as Dr. Bäumker also thinks.[58]

Yesterday afternoon everybody went to Handorf except Johanna and I. We met Agathe at the railroad station as planned. She looks peaked and haggard, so that each cousin exclaimed with great amazement at the other's appearance. Elisabeth will stay for a few days after her husband has departed. We miss you every day, and we do not yet quite know how we are to manage our afternoons.

I write you this long letter so that you too can think of us. I shall be happy to continue if Caspar will consider giving me some ink. The chest for the children's dresses has not yet arrived, and we do not know how to find it. If we catch Lisette[59] she may perhaps be able to tell us. The mother bird has left her young ones in the lurch.

Now farewell! With this good weather we are hoping for the greatest success for Heinrich and wish you all a great deal of fun. Best greetings from us to you from your,

Jette

Münster
15 September 1882

Dear Heinrich:

The days are slipping away. The last week has started for us. You had only a few days of relaxation. I had to decline Auguste's invitation, which worked out well since Marie has left in the meantime to be with you.

We here try to remain happy and unworried, in which we easily succeed as long as our nieces are here.[60] But yesterday Elisabeth took her leave. It was rather hard on her, and I was annoyed with Therese, who laughingly pointed out her tears. It might have been for the best. Agathe will leave on Sunday. I am already becoming quite sober, and I no longer know what to say. If it would be possible for me, I would like to take going away from you light-heartedly. But I have my doubts.

Will you spare me the farewell completely? It seems to me it would be better. And then I wish from the bottom of my heart that you could be spared these drudgeries for a bit longer. A few weeks more of rest and enjoyment would strengthen you very much, even if it would be too late to go swimming. Do write me immediately concerning this. I am very serious about it.

I am no longer worth much. At the beginning, after your departure, I missed you very

---

58. Professor Clemens Bäumker married the third daughter of Therese von Hatzfeld, twenty-three-year-old Wilhelmine, in 1883.

59. Lisette Schumann was the nursemaid in Heinrich and Auguste Geisberg's household. She had been with the Geisberg family since 1852.

60. The nieces were Agathe Offenberg, born in 1852 and married to Clemens Wesemann in 1873, and Elisabeth von Hatzfeld, born in 1854, who was married to Judge Adolph Freusberg of Limburg/Lahn.

much, and even now the spice of the conversation is missing. I still would have liked to ask many a thing and would have liked some more explanations. But we must part! Sincere greetings to Franz and Phina and little Malchen.[61] I enclose a picture for Phina, which is probably very sharp. But I cannot really be satisfied with the eyes. In case Malchen should like to have one, too, I would send one in exchange for one of hers.

As always, your sister, Jette

Jefferson City
December 1882

Dear Auguste!

The holidays are approaching. I would very much like to send you greetings on this occasion. Often it seems to me that we are very much occupied.

The luxurious life, the boundless pleasures, which we were able to enjoy this past summer in the cozy circle with all of you, has changed very quickly for us. Both of us have returned to everyday life now, and we have found, just as other people, our share of worries and hardships.

It is not really a shock for Ottilie, but nevertheless quite hard that she found her husband suffering so much. Now, to be sure, he has improved in some respects. A chronic abdominal complaint has been remedied, but there is still a great weakness and frequent pains in his legs. And then the strong man is discouraged, obstinate, and out of sorts. The worst thing, however, is that he does not want to consult a doctor, and when Ottilie sent for a doctor he immediately explained that the visit would be very agreeable to him, but only as a friend, and he would not want to have anything prescribed. We have to bear this patiently.

I—well, there is not anything big that bothers me. I would like to see Wilhelm placed better. But he is working not far away, and he often writes to me. The others are well except for Louis's smallest one, Clarice.[62] To be sure, there are many little things that one does not mention except at the appropriate place. However, I cannot hide the fact that my thoughts are often occupied with these during the day and at night. Particularly for Tillie's sake, I try to appear quite happy and in a light mood, but it doesn't come from the heart. Best of all, I would like to stay quietly at home and live on memories.

We do have some very dear friends here, and we must not withdraw. The family alone is sufficient for entertainment and for an exchange of news about what is happening. —I am very much amazed at the great luxury here. The people live in splendor. I did not notice it as much earlier. Now I make comparisons. The cut of the dresses is more graceful and not at all stiff. We are, I believe, ahead of you. Naturally, these are the ladies of fashion.

What are you doing now? I hope you and the children are well. I hope you are braving the storms of winter, which you are probably having now. May I assume that Heinrich is free of any discomfort? I doubt it! I am often still sorry that our departure was not favorable for a consistent treatment at the baths. Now he has to suffer through the winter and is often confined to the house and cannot improve. If only I could hear from you immediately!

You will have to write to me a lot, dear Auguste. I am with you a lot in my thoughts. It

61. These are Jette's Boner relatives in Trier.
62. Clarice Bruns was born 12 October 1881 in Jefferson City.

seems to me that I could understand you quite well if I could be with you. I would not always agree with you, but it would cheer me greatly. I am not at all as even-tempered and as happy as I was before our trip. Everything goes somewhat more slowly with old age. It often seems to me that I have gotten old only now. But I submit to this.

You will not need an assurance of how happy we were because of your loving attentions. If only we could show you how we could reciprocate. It remains an everlasting happy remembrance. If we could only be assured that we always showed how highly we valued your love.

Now farewell and remain good to me.

From the bottom of my heart, your Jette

Jefferson City
12 December 1882

Dear Heinrich:

How are you? Well, we had a letter from Henriette[63] that you are ill again. I had been afraid of that. If it had only been possible for you to have remained at the baths longer! It bothered me that we and the weather were obstacles to you.

I miss you so often. In Münster I often did not know how to find the proper tone. Now it seems to me that I should have been able to discuss so many more things and should have been able to listen to more things and to inquire about things for my own satisfaction and quiet consideration. A thousand thanks for everything that you have done for us. To be sure, we happily accepted everything. But we cannot reciprocate. Only then would it be all right.

This last trip affects me much more seriously than the first visit with my husband. Here I alone am the older one, while with you that was different. It is a harsh homesickness, which I have to fight against. I wonder whether I can regain a joy for living on? I wonder whether this letter will reach you for the holidays? I hope so. I wish you both much happiness and blessings for the New Year!

In political affairs there are all kinds of confused things. Our state is going highly Democratic. And then this temperance[64] business! After New Year's the legislators will sit again. During the summer the city grew in the number of houses and inhabitants. I myself got very much into arrears with our house and had to take care of many repairs. I had thought that would happen. It will take some time before it will balance out.

I shall try to write more frequently and will try to interest you more in our acquaintances and our happenings.

I am looking with impatience toward Christmas and news from you.

I hope that you will be feeling better.

As always, your sister, Jette

(Henriette forgot to add "Missouri" to the address. This is absolutely necessary!)

---

63. Henriette, the third child of Jette's sister Therese and Franz von Hatzfeld, was born in 1857.
64. Germans were generally opposed to temperance efforts, which jeopardized businesses and traditional social practices.

Jefferson City
3 March 1883

Dear Auguste:

When I see your dear handwriting unexpectedly, I always get a scare. But this time it was a joyful surprise. For I was already thinking, "You will have to get along without pocket money." I had nothing but worries for the New Year. Necessary repair work had to be done on the house, and I had to take out a loan to pay the insurance. I will not be straightened out financially until the end of this year. I should really have a business.

Recently I keep thinking, Heinrich must be feeling better, for spring is coming. If he could travel to visit us and take baths, then he would be healed. After all, last year mineral springs that are highly praised were discovered approximately thirty miles from here.[65] They will quickly provide for the reception of guests, just as in Werne.[66] It is a magnificent location, "Aurora Springs," and the railroad from here goes close by. It is scarcely worth the trouble for me. Only my shoulder causes me some pain, but otherwise I am well. The only thing that cannot be remedied is my age, almost seventy years, which can not even be described as an evil. So what should I do about that? And yet in me there is such a striving spirit that I cannot be inactive from one day to the other.

Our son-in-law, God be thanked, is better. He still lacks strength, but he shows a blessed appetite, and his wife does everything possible to make him comfortable so his strength will gradually return. After a month he will leave us for a while and devote himself to a more secure occupation. Let us hope then that things will be better than in the last year!

Ottilie is busy; she occupies herself very busily with her household, and is very precise and clean. There's only one thing she does not understand: giving orders. This will have to be learned, too, and I often have a secret malicious pleasure when I see the girl is not doing well enough in spite of all of Ottilie's admonitions. Thus she does a great deal herself so that it will be done the way she wants it. She also keeps chickens, and so every day they count how many eggs have been laid and say what an advantage there is in keeping chickens, but now Jose also knows what the neighbors' chickens are doing.

It is now almost a year since we left Toledo and went to sea. The weather this year is much more beautiful here. We still have cold nights, and the earth is not yet free of frost. This is unfortunate for me, for I would like to have a few trees planted. If we could have such a spring as we had last year with you! There were no setbacks after the little buds and blossoms showed up. Here, however, the climate is frequently treacherous.

Our legislators are still here, and that makes it more lively in the city. Also, many elegant ladies have accompanied their husbands.

The day before yesterday we went to a concert of German musicians. What they presented was very good, but brass instruments in an enclosed room and nothing else! We have few things that cheer us, and the Nitchy children did not at all know what Mardi Gras is. And so I made up a big tale for them and told them how the brothers Franz, Heinrich, Bernhard, and many others ran behind the Kurk.[67] They called, "Fool, Fool, Fool," they

65. Aurora Springs, near Eldon in Miller County, Missouri, was laid out in 1880 by Abram Fulkerson. Its success was almost immediate, and it developed into the largest town in the county during the 1880s and 1890s because of the mineral springs and enterprising developers.

66. Werne, a town approximately thirty miles south of Münster, was known for its thermal baths.

67. Read "Turk," a colorfully dressed character, named for a master mason of Oelde, appearing in the pre-Lenten procession. This custom is no longer known in the Westphalia area of Germany.

threw snow balls, and the poor fool danced, all made up, in his colorful garments and held the broom upright in his hand, and marched along with the people walking in pairs, accompanied by music, etc., etc.

So our best thanks, dear Auguste, for the check. Since it will be entirely for my personal use, I shall always think of the sender. My daughter will speak for herself to her uncle.

All here send best regards to you and to Heinrich. In the near future I would like to hear a lot more about the children. You do not say anything about them. Greetings to both of them.

With love, your Jette

P.S. You will have to tell me all the news when you write. The others often forget to do that. There is still no letter from Johanna.

Jefferson City
5 March 1883

My dear Heinrich:

First, many thanks for the things you sent. I was already beginning to wonder whether they would come, and I thought that my brother might not find it suitable to send anything to such a far-off country when there are people in need so close by, etc., etc.

I am still in need, to be sure, and I often feel depressed that I only live from the kindness of my children. And then I would like to work and earn something. But my daughter says, "No, I am working now, you did it before."

But soon spring will be here, and then I can be outside. I am already looking at trees and bushes and contemplating and trying. But it is still cold in the womb of the earth; it is too early. You had a bad winter. I thought of you so often. I did not guess, however, that such continuous confinement to your room was torturing you. In the last letter from Auguste she said that you had improved somewhat. If the spring is not so cold and wet, you will be able to visit some baths early. A friend of ours from here has already gone to take baths. His legs and shoulder had been swollen.

Hess is usually well now but not quite strong. He took some iron after the fever. In about a month he will go to Colorado to the mountains. He is not so quiet and depressed anymore and goes out and seeks company. We think that he is making progress in regaining his old energy and will create a new sphere of activity for himself. But it is questionable whether he will stay here.

I myself would like to be able to devote myself more to Wilhelm. It is often bitter for me that he is not good enough for the brother and sisters. If only I could have my own household! I often tell him that he should just look for something for himself and I would go with him.

You write, dear Heinrich, that we had not visited enough and had not talked to each other enough. This has often occurred to me too. In spite of the fact that we were with you for such a long time, there was really no quiet time together. I had in some ways become estranged from you, and if the close ties that had bound us together made it possible for us to speak openly and freely without reservation, on the other hand there were so many events on both sides to interfere. These we were not able to share, at least not in the same way as if I had remained near you. Very often now, something occurs to me about which I would like to have your opinion. I miss you!

A long time before we took our leave, never to return, the departure was on my mind. I had to control myself, and when I said a word now and then, Johanna replied, "We mustn't think of that." It would be hard on me indeed if I could not think that you would be feeling as I do now. But nevertheless not quite as I do—you are not so lonely! —And it is only fitting that I suffer more by the separation. It was I who went away from you. And now I lack the support, the help! —When I am a little calmer, then I only remember everything dear and beautiful that we had through you. Ottilie often mentions something, and tells Carl about you and how it is there. They both send their best. Also Louis and the Geisberg brother and sister. From the bottom of my heart, your sister, Jette

P.S. Again I forgot the pictures. Heinrich chose "The Card Players," Louis liked "Cinderella," Jette immediately decided on "The Death of Wallenstein," and thus only the "House of Mourning" remains for Wilhelm.[68] They all thank you sincerely.

Jefferson City
12 May 1883

Dear Auguste:

Indeed you know what is needed. For quite some time I had not heard from you, and I became worried and received quite a fright when Bäumker's announcement[69] arrived, but was reassured immediately.

So Heinrich is still being tortured and is housebound. And now you are collecting all your money and getting ready to take the trip to the baths. May it be successful! If only I could prescribe good weather for this purpose. I can still not get over the cloudy, cool weather of last year. But it was really good that we were with you. Now we all again go our own paths, which are sometimes sad. I have still not regained my courage, but I cower down and look for a little pleasure and joy in life and in people and nature. The reunion was quite a setback. The winter gave me a cramplike, dry cough, which sounded uncomfortable. It will not yield, and I have to take it easy, which really does not appeal to me. I think of Johanna, how she fussed when she went into her little garden. I am learning this.

Our spring is also cool, and nothing will grow. Perhaps I am only impatient because I was so quiet and inactive for so long. The German kernels and seeds refuse to come up, except for a few flower plants. The garden is my realm. Ottilie has a flock of chickens. She will raise far more than sixty, and the little creatures are so lively and tame. We would like to have a cow,[70] but Hess advises against this, and so we will have to see how we can dispose of the rich feed. The clover is over a foot high, so the thought very easily occurs that if one goes through it, one might step on some kind of snake, which would be hurt and could bite. After all, all around us is still a wilderness where such animals could flee and not be disturbed by anything. Later we will have to keep the chickens up higher.

68. Heinrich Geisberg owned a collection of 311 copper engravings, mostly inherited from his uncle Caspar Geisberg. He sent selections to Jette's and Franz's children.

69. This probably refers to Professor Clemens Bäumker's engagement to Wilhelmine von Hatzfeld. They were married on 20 August 1883 in Münster.

70. In a letter of 8 July 1883 to Auguste, Ottilie reports that she had bought a cow to try the "milk cure" for Effie, who was in Jefferson City for the summer. The boys were "growing fat," but the diet seems not to have had any effect on the adults.

My Wilhelm is here at present for our protection. After Carl's departure, we were descended upon by thieves. Jette offered her Walter, and Effie wanted to send Gustav. But neither of them is particularly heroic as yet, and thus we preferred to have their uncle. It is a special pleasure for me to have the boy here for several weeks. If only he would not be so good!

Hess has been gone for two months now and is quite healthy again. He traveled constantly at first, but recently he has settled and is building a quartz mill in the mountains of Colorado. It is good that he has taken up some activity, but he still cannot have his wife there. He will probably return next winter.

We are quite lonely here, and Tillie goes out very little. She joined a little singing society in order to practice. I'm very pleased that you are getting the children to play the piano, for it fills the free time so beautifully. I am also back to it again, that is, I give piano lessons to Effie and Ida Nitchy, and they and I work very seriously.

In four weeks the schools will be out in St. Louis, and Effie Decker will come here with her three boys. Then it will be lively enough. It is getting time for Harry to decide whether he should continue studying or whether he should make himself useful in some other way. He is now in high school. I hope that in a few years the boys will begin to maintain themselves and will make it easier for their mother. She is not very strong.

It seems that the stork has announced his arrival at Louis's soon. At first Emily protested against this. Miss Elsie was taking too many walks alone, which terrified her mother. Last week I took a big bouquet of snowballs, iris, honeysuckle, etc., to her, and the child kept the flowers in her arms all morning. Her little sister sits and crawls around patiently. The Geisberg boy[71] is growing strong after a long struggle. His mother thought that he had a despotic nature. Franz Nitchy came to visit by himself already. He is very good-natured.

21 May

I have not had the courage to complete the letter, for I was, and still am, ill. I am not in bed all the time. I took quinine, but I am so nervous, tired, and exhausted that I cannot take a single step. For hours I lie on the sofa, but I do not read and only dream with closed eyes. Then I jump up and look around and see what's going on outside, but then I lie down again. All night long I lie as if I am dead, and I neither hear nor see anything. I always intend to have the doctor come, but then I don't get around to it, and every day I think it must get better. And it surely will. I can eat something, and this is probably the best sign. And since I attracted this illness through overexhaustion, I will have to keep quite calm, which I hope I will succeed in doing. I should not have said anything of this, for poor Heinrich has been miserable for the past five months. Perhaps you are now going to the baths if the sun is warm enough. Our spring is still not perfect. There are still cold showers. Today we lit a fire because I was so cold. And then we constantly read of tornadoes, which demolish houses and kill people. I wonder whether we might be hit some time too? Kansas City had losses last week, and then St. Louis, and then Texas, etc., etc.

I will soon write more and hope I will be able to report something good. And please, dear Auguste, let me be at the top of your list of correspondents. I would be so grateful for that,

71. Charles Henry Geisberg was born 16 September 1881 to Heinrich and Amelie Geisberg in Jefferson City. The family believes he was the last to bear the Geisberg name born in America.

and I would reply immediately. I hope for everything good for all of you, and particularly for my dear brother. If only he could be healed and could walk again strongly! Do tell me what God wills.

Give him my best regards, also to the children and to all from all of us. Your Jette

P.S. You have given me great joy by sending me the picture of Aunt Phina, for now one can shove her sad figure into the background and imagine that she still looks as fresh and youthful as she did in the picture. Do write her how I like to look at her. I wish I could encourage her and sit patiently with her.

Jefferson City
19 September 1883

Dear Heinrich:

I have been looking forward to a letter from you with great anxiety. To be sure, I hoped and expected that you would arrive back in Münster strengthened and vigorous again. And then they said that you are so relaxed and even happy. I can imagine—and yet! I could weep for you. You still have to suffer so much pain. And now having to lie in bed; what is going to happen? What does the doctor say? It seems to me that I should be there. After all, I like to chat with you so much. I neglected to discuss so many things and didn't tell you enough about things that happened during the twenty-six years since we had seen each other. And I am accepting of things from you that I do not like to hear from others. Only you must not tell me that I hurt you. Do keep the memories that comfort you. I do indeed mean so well, and love you all so very much. Do let me keep a little bit of my will, which has been steeled by sad blows of fate—I hope to stay that way.

If I had not been interrupted so much, I would have thought of reporting several things from here; for instance, the reunion of the Confederate soldiers that took place here.[72] The city was flooded suddenly with approximately three thousand Rebels. And there were speeches and serenades. —Well, Missouri is a southern state, and the southern element is very strong. It seems comparable to the Luther celebration, of which we get to read a lot. Only that doesn't bother you because you live so far removed and are so strong in yourself. We, on the other hand, have to duck down. —In the near future I shall write down what seems suitable for you.

I am much with you in my thoughts and I wish and hope for improvement for you.

From the bottom of my heart, your sister, Jette

Jefferson City
22 September 1883

Dear Auguste:

I am pleased that your good humor still holds. Heinrich can be considered fortunate in that. This and his steadfast, even temper permit you to take so many things more easily than is the case with others. May God grant that he will improve somewhat.

72. The reunion of Confederate soldiers took place in Jefferson City on 28 and 29 August 1883 and attracted well over four thousand veterans.

So the resignation has been handed in.[73] If he becomes capable of using his limbs again, he will not be inactive. Perhaps he will be able to occupy himself in more intellectually rewarding ways and more pleasantly than at the academy. Thus we are already attempting to think of something to shove away the misery. If he would spend a summer here, that would cure him. —I myself have perspired honestly, and it has done me good. My limbs are nimble again. Now I fear the winter. To be sure, we are well sheltered. For the past two weeks we have been living in our old house again.

This has come about quite unexpectedly for me, and I was not even pleased by it. For four and a half years, I was outside the city limits with all my belongings and properties and kept house and arranged things pretty much according to my own mind. But now we are city folks again and are hemmed in by people. Ottilie claimed the whole house and has so many things that it is completely filled. She should really sell a lot, but Carl won't hear of that. I was surprised that he agreed that we should leave the country. We felt too lonesome and unsafe without him. He has not come back yet and will probably not come for a few months. The letters going back and forth are doubling in number.

It is a new undertaking, it demands a lot of capital and much work, and it is highly questionable whether there will be a significant profit from it. But he will have to persist until everything is on the right track. Whether he will then continue to participate, we will have to see. But without doubt he will then take his wife along if he goes back. It is horrible to us that they have to live separated from each other so long. In the last letter he talked about taking a Sunday tour. He climbed Bald Mountain (fourteen thousand feet) and saw snow-covered mountain peaks, beautiful valleys with rivers, and even a few villages. There was a view of approximately seventy English miles. The weather in Bonanza is rather cold. They had snow in August.

Except for your announcement of Wilhelmine's wedding and the humorous poem on the occasion of the festivities, which we read with great amusement, we have not heard from them since. Every day we waited for an announcement.[74] So we have been forgotten. Now there is a letter ready for Henriette von Hatzfeld. Have you heard recently from Trier how Uncle Franz Boner and Aunt Phina are getting along? —My Effie was here with the boys during the summer, and then it was lively enough. But most of the time we stayed at home because Effie was in ill health. At last she seemed a little stronger, and now she is back in harness. I often worry whether she can stand it. Gustav, the second son, has stayed with us. The family often gets together. There is Heinrich Geisberg with his family, the Nitchys, and Louis and his family. The latter has been increased by a son, which makes both of them very happy.

Dear Auguste, do let me have frequent news from you. If it won't work any other way, I shall be satisfied with a postcard.

From the bottom of my heart, your Jette

Regards to Marie and Max from Ottilie and myself.

---

73. Because of continued ill health, Heinrich Geisberg resigned his position as treasurer of the Academy in 1883.

74. Bertha, the daughter of Dr. Louis Petri and Antonie Geisberg, married the attorney and notary public Clemens Cruse on 1 September 1883.

St. Louis
15 November 1883

Dear Auguste:

Still no letter! It makes me so restive that I don't want to wait any longer to write even if the letters cross in the mail. I do worry so much. Surely Heinrich cannot possibly still be bedridden, although Therese had still reported he was. Now the cruel winter is at our door, and what will happen? Are you occupied so much by Heinrich and otherwise, or does your happy mood leave you occasionally? I would not like to think this. With everything that has happened to me in my life, with hard trials, heavy losses, I always found strength and courage at the right time and was never completely discouraged. It will be the same with you. You will make the difficult hours of the long illness so much easier for both of you by your untiring humor and your constant cheerfulness, since you both need this so much. Do write in more detail what the doctor is doing and what he thinks of Heinrich's condition. I often think I would like to come over for a moment. If only we were still in Oelde!

Look, dear Auguste, how well you are advised. And you can rest periodically for a few days, compared to my Effie, who in similar circumstances could not afford rest and therefore suffered for years and finally resolved to take a cure and has called for me to come to her here. She had an operation on 6 November, which she happily survived. Now she is extremely exhausted. There is no longer any danger, and she begins to have an appetite again and is free of fever and at times very vexed, which also is supposed to be a good sign, only I would like to be vexed now and then but do not dare show it. We therefore hope for success, but the doctor would like to have her lie still for at least four weeks, and perhaps have an even longer rest. This won't work very well in her situation. For the time being her sister-in-law has arranged a leave of absence from the school board, and thus she receives half of her salary. Ottilie writes that she is working out something with her brothers and with Heinrich Geisberg to cover her expenses for now. Later, other arrangements will have to be made. She just inquired to whom I am writing, and she sends her best regards to her aunt and uncle.

Up in Jefferson City Tillie is alone with Gustav and they miss Grandmother. Carl is getting quite impatient in Colorado, but he will have to persist since his partner is not back yet. All work is already discontinued in the mines since it is very cold there. Great success can probably not be expected until next year. We are very anxious about what he will decide to do next. I would not like to go west without Wilhelm and perhaps without Effie and her children.

We have our first big cold spell here, but it is dry. In secure expectation that there will be an answer for me within five weeks, I send my love, your Jette.

P.S. Regards to Marie and Max.

Jefferson City
24 September 1884

Dear Heinrich:

The day before yesterday I received your letter and was doubly pleased, and so that our letters will not cross again I will try to get ahead of you. And I certainly do not want to hurt you, but I would rather always send you some balsam, since I, after all, know from experience how it is when a letter is lying at hand that one can take now and then in one's hand and pursue in thought and embellish. And in this respect your dear better half is a special treasure, who is always ready to send a little letter full of light humor and interesting news. That you are able to write yourself now and no longer are so shaky is a particularly good sign for me, and I assume that you are strengthened after the twofold treatment at the spa in the winter. And now in your letter there is a sign of life from you yourself for the older sister.

You say, "Ludwig Offenberg introduced his bride to his mother and to us." It has been two years since I received anything from Johanna except for a little enclosure, and it almost seems to be a rule that my dear brother and sisters each report for themselves. Well, that may be all right, but it should not be so sporadic and the intervals so long.

You were at the cathedral for the Catholic convention, for the art exhibit. How I would have enjoyed that! Since Effie has returned to St. Louis again, we live as isolated as possible. However, since the fall is approaching I have lived up to my promise, and I am presently writing from Louis's house, where I am staying for several days, and then I shall go to the Nitchys' in the same manner. This does me good, and I am very welcome and feel at home with the big and the little people.

Fall is here and is really quite decent. During the day there is a warm sun. In the morning and the evening there is a dusky coolness with floating gossamer and a lurking quietness. It is a real Indian summer, or as you call it, "Old Women's Summer" [*Altweibersommer*]. However, it is not as pretty where you are. The German spring, however, is by far to be preferred.

In a week I shall take possession of a few acres of land with a little house on it. For the time being I have ordered manure. I very much insist on that. Then there will be plowing. Asparagus beds will be prepared and mulberry trees, etc. Wilhelm is busy for the time being, but he will come later and will work the property. It is very much on my mind, and calculating takes many an hour of sleep. But even though it involves difficulties, it will be tried!

Farewell, many regards to yours and to all. With love,

your sister, Jette

Enclosure in a letter of 8 March from Effie

Jefferson City
22 March 1885

Dear Heinrich:

Since my daughter delayed so long, my last letter will have arrived at your place a long time ago. She is now well again. The cold was very hard on her.

We still have winter; last night there was a severe frost. It curbs our impatience since we want to move in nine days and really could not do anything until now.

I had planned to raise silkworms with Wilhelm and therefore looked around for land and for trees that I could plant for this purpose. Last year I planted one hundred fifty young mulberry trees. Carl dissociates himself from this, Wilhelm does not know about it, and they always tell me, "You are too old for this." I torture myself very much because of that. I don't mean that I have to care for the youngest since he doesn't do it himself. Once he is located somewhere in a good position, he will get ahead. I will immediately go with him if we see that we can live together.

Thus, one year after the other goes by. I wonder how many more there will be? If it doesn't work out again, I will naturally go back to the Hesses and can make myself useful there. But I will not be satisfied.

For the time being, after a great deal of consultation, the Capitol will remain here, but the legislators made no concessions for the enlargement of the government buildings. There are many intrigues going on to transfer it to Sedalia, and this causes pressure on everything here.

Two weeks ago there was a railroad strike here, and no trains were running except for mail trains. The governors of Missouri and Kansas were petitioned to give the citizens of St. Louis, Sedalia, and Kansas City protection. Thus troops passed through here. When the train stopped here, one saw that many very young fellows were among them; among others there was a friend of Harry's, the son of Judge Rombauer,[75] who shouted to him to bring him something to eat. Another one forgot where he was and stepped onto the platform and greeted Louis, for which he was put under guard. They looked very serious when they heard that there were approximately a thousand men on strike in Sedalia. Since that time, things have worked out and the workers have been reemployed.

I shall write to Therese as soon as we are settled for the summer. Now, best regards to all of you, and let me hear something good from you soon.

With love, your sister, Jette

Spring 1885

My Dear Brother Heinrich:

Although the longer letter to your dear better half is also meant for you, I still want to enclose a few extra lines for you. I feel as if you were feeling a little better. May I conclude this from the address that was written to me? Your hand apparently no longer hurts so much while writing. Or do I imagine it because I so longingly hope for your recuperation? At any rate, this may well be assumed in view of the spring with its gentle breezes and warm rays of sun.

We are very much at a disadvantage this year. There was such a consistent and grim winter in Missouri. We are very impatient and no longer know what we should do. And then the husband of my daughter is often not here, and so we feel quite lonely and not very happy.

In the course of the summer there will be some building going on, and we are anxious to see what progress they are making with the U.S. courthouse and post office buildings, which lie across from us. Heinrich and his office will also be moved there. During the two district and circuit court sessions, which take place twice a year in longer session, many people will come here, so that we will probably get to see more than we have.

Jette is envied for the beautiful historical engraving, "Wallenstein's Death." It is really very grim—we very much like the lady, with her goodness of heart and her fine sensitivity. But she has a very great weakness for her young people, whom she torments very much.

75. Roderick E. Rombauer, born in 1833 in Hungary, came to the United States in 1851. After graduating from the Harvard University Law School in 1858, Rombauer was admitted to the bar in Missouri on 19 May 1858. He served with the Missouri Volunteers in the Civil War, was elected judge of the law commissioner's court in St. Louis, and in 1867 was appointed judge of the circuit court in that city, an office to which he was subsequently elected.

Effie is almost grown up now and is a good girl. Walter, who is more reasonable than the Decker boys, and whom I often call Caspar without wanting to, will soon make himself useful.

In Ohio there is so much misery again because of the high flood stage. It will take a long time until the poor people who were driven away get back to normal. The water of the Mississippi had spread to twenty-five miles at one point, and on the Missouri there are still ice floes coming down.

I wish we too could experience such a celebration as you had, with a bishop here sometime.[76] The only things that occur here in the course of the summer are the conventions for the impending elections of both parties. I would very much like to have some prospects for Wilhelm; he does not achieve anything, and yet he would very much like to.

Your faithful sister, Jette.

Jefferson City, Missouri
15 September 1885

Dear Auguste:

Still, nothing has arrived from Bad Werne. Therefore, you have apparently had some necessary rustic rest. However, as a precaution and in order not to fall behind, I have sent a postcard to you. We are now getting back quite to normal and try to catch up with everything that had to be postponed.

Effie and her two sons have gone back after spending almost three months of vacation here. And now the short summer heat is past and has given way to rainy weather, which is quite out of the ordinary. During the Indian summer we usually have an extensive drought. Therefore it has been necessary for us to stay in the house, although quite frequently— through petulance and with some disgust—we go to get a new ribbon for our dress. Such a place is after all a great burden, and the weeds are growing everywhere. Well, one should really let them stay there since they won't do any harm any more and will soon be suppressed by winter. But often I bend my stiff back and tear out the offending plants, and Carl does likewise. He has an aversion to plantain and the sticky plants that deface the lawn and make the hay unpalatable. Ottilie limits her activities outside to the strawberries and raspberries. To my great joy I always have some very fine monthly roses and flowers, which smell good. And on Sunday without fail there is a vase with the best flowers, tastefully arranged, in the parlor. In that, they all let me rule the way I want to.

Unfortunately Ben, the horse, is still lame, for which the boys, who did not tie him up well during the summer, have to be blamed. Therefore, if we want to see our people, we are forced to make the trip on foot. I imagine that I cannot walk so well any more as I used to, and I always threaten that I shall not come back. Well, this cannot be helped, and so, with Effie and also otherwise, I have gone to town several times. If my nephew learns about this in some way, then he always takes me home in his buggy.

Harry Decker, who has a job here in the city, owns a boat. And thus we frequently had little trips on the water—at first on the creek and later on the river. Effie was always greatly

76. Dr. Wilhelm Cramer, the cathedral deacon and regent of the seminary in Münster, was installed as suffragan bishop of Münster in December 1884.

worried then, especially when the little one, who can swim only very little and is also of a restless and daring nature, was included. Carl then always preaches that the boys have to try everything. And so Mama and the aunt were invited, and at other times Jennie Bruns and Effie Nitchy. Even Grandmother had to go along once. But I did not want to go to the bridge, and so I went down the hill with them. But at the end it was almost perpendicular over big rocks down to the bank, and that was more than enough for me. But the rowing went magnificently until the sun had set, and then they set me ashore with Wilhelm. We thought they were behind us, and so we slowly climbed the hill. And then we saw a steamboat coming. We shouted but received no answer. Wilhelm went back. And then they landed, but they had had a few races first since we had two boats. Well, this is youth for you! Effie has to get used to the fact that her sons will "gamble and dare to test their good luck."[77] Well, you will experience this too, and I can see it come—how desperate you will be, and how you will yield to things as they occur.

We have received the announcement of the engagement of Ludwig Offenberg to Lieschen Brixius[78] and were very pleased, and we almost thought Aunt Auguste could have given some assistance if she had thought it necessary.

But we have not heard from you nor about you. It's beginning to worry me. Probably the letters will cross in the mail. If not, then I urgently request that you take pen in hand immediately. Has your practice of painting already been shelved? You still have a lot of free time to indulge in such pleasures. However, here too it has become fashionable. A lady from Boston gave lessons and everybody participated, young and old. It is amazing! Only Ottilie remains aloof from such amusements. And yet it would be good for her. Perhaps she will participate in a reading club. Best regards to all, and I hope for a nice letter.

Your Jette

Jefferson City, Missouri
6 December 1886

My dear Brother Heinrich:

It has taken a long time for me to answer you. In the beginning I wanted to write immediately, but I was saddened by the contents of the letter. So I told you a great deal in my thoughts and tried to calm you and did not get to the writing. I live in a constant turmoil of activity, and I was often very tired, so that the subsequent rest was absolutely necessary for me. Wilhelm had to be out of town, and so I was alone with some strange help. For several weeks now we have been harvesting everything at Stromberg[79] and have stored it, and I am back with Hess. I would rather have stayed on the place there if the house had been in shape and if Wilhelm could have been there. Now I'm supposed to stay here for three months, and then we will begin to work our place anew. Here grim winter has appeared, and so I often think that it might be much worse with you, and I wonder how you are managing.

77. Jette is quoting from Friedrich Schiller's "Das Lied von der Glocke," a very popular long ballad written in 1799.
78. Ludwig Offenberg, born 31 October 1855 in Münster, married Elisabeth Brixius of Lutzerath on 18 August 1886. She was the daughter of the senior judge of the county court, Eduard Brixius, and his wife Maria (née Boner) of Kleve.
79. Jette named her property in Cole County after her hometown of Stromberg.

You seem to have gotten little relief from the baths, and you are apparently still suffering quite a bit, and naturally because of that you are probably feeling quite melancholic. I often think that I wish this life were over, but I don't mean that you have reached the stage to have the same wish. It is not worry for the family alone that holds you. Your participation and cooperation in the development of your children must also make you hope that you are kept for them.

I on the other hand am not needed. Even Wilhelm, whom I assist now, can get along without me. But how? A week ago he became thirty-three years old! And as much as I worry about him now, it will probably remain this way as long as I live. And yet it is really not so bad. He keeps himself decently, only he has no steady income. Perhaps I shall live to experience that yet. And then I would like to close my eyes and follow the many dear ones. And you must not be saddened about me.

My life was very difficult, even though there were many happy days. I have always endeavored honestly to do my duty, and more if the opportunity was offered. It always seemed to me as if our parents were urging me on in sad days, for I know a great deal more of them than all of you. I remember how Father read to me from the odes of Klopstock[80] and how his eyes glistened. And our young mother! If I hurt somewhere, it seemed as if she had placed her hand on the shoulder of the lonely one and whispered, "Be calm, my child." My dear, dear parents. It is not necessary to remind myself of them. And when my hour strikes, I hope that I can enter the uncertain beyond calmly.

I often talk about you, and there is so much that I would like to tell you. You would not tell me again that we find so little to talk about. I am withdrawing more and more into my own self, and I participate less in daily activities. And then my thoughts go back into the past.

I really would like to know a little bit more about your activities and your daily life. Do you always have pain? And more at night? Are your hands lame and your feet too? Can you go out? Writing is difficult for you, but it makes me so happy when I see something from you.

I wish you happy holidays! And a blessed New Year to all of you.

With sincere love, your sister, Jette

Jefferson City
8 December 1886

Dear Auguste,

Joyous holidays! All of a sudden December has come, and now I have to hurry, although a little earlier I thought that I could launch my letters in peace. Since the beginning of November I have again been with Ottilie, and that brought all kinds of commotion. She had been away for about six weeks and found all kinds of things to get straightened out in the house, as I did. Now she is happy that I am here. We do everything so calmly and neatly. It is very comfortable here. Carl also seems to find it so. He's always in good humor, part of which is due to his love for teasing his wife. And then she often cannot defend herself. She is stronger and looks better than during the past summer, when she frequently had too much to do. It is strange how everything outside has to be put in order so exactly. They have

80. Friedrich Gottlieb Klopstock (1724–1803), sometimes called the German Milton, reawakened interest in religious poetry. His *Odes*, glorifying religion, friendship, and nature, restored emotionalism to a major place in German creative writing during the eighteenth century.

raised over one hundred fifty chickens. Recently there were still over twenty roosters run-ning around. We had food in abundance. And now Ottilie has filled a number of tin cans with chicken fricassee. The garden was worked down to a depth of two feet with manure, and new asparagus was planted as well as strawberries. Carl is always figuring out how he can lay out things and how he can spend. That is no great art if one can employ people.

At our Stromberg it also looks better than it did a year ago. All kinds of things have been planted, and the soil has been improved. I have a special partiality for manure. In the beginning Carl made fun of me, but now he imitates me. We grew all kinds of things on an experimental basis. Fine white silver onions, sage, horseradish, potatoes, cab-bage, popcorn, corn, and, out of curiosity, sweet potatoes, which grew so well that one was as big as a child's head. We were amazed. And then I unselfishly set a few hundred plants of tobacco for Wilhelm. So there you see what can be done, but it does take a lot of effort.

How entirely differently you are occupied. At the very most you look at the flowers in the garden or at some things for the kitchen. You probably had a very lively summer. First you had little Marie's first Communion, on which I congratulate you and which reminds me of my youth when Father and Mother stepped toward me in the house and embraced me, full of emotion. Three weeks later our dear mother was dead.

And then there was Aunt Phina. I would have loved to have been there to see her become stronger than she was when we saw her in Trier. It seemed to me that she would have liked to be happier if she had felt tolerably well. Do give my regards to her and also to Schilking,[81] who seems to enjoy visiting you.

Then another sad case has been reported. I could not at all comprehend at first that Max[82] had to go, and I find it so natural that his mother has become so restless.

Every week now, as a recreation, I go to a whist party; there are two German ladies and one American lady. At the request of Ottilie, they came to our place this week in the after-noon and were entertained elegantly and magnificently. Otherwise I go there in the evening and spend the night at Louis's place. We have so much fun.

Everything is going well in St. Louis. Effie is with her sons, and Harry has gotten a suitable position. It was better for him there. And Ottilie says that they all play music in the evening; Harry and Gustav play the violin, and the little one plays the piano. Ernst has a particularly good ear for music, only he likes to play without notes.

I wonder if anyone will send me a note for the holidays? Hardly! But I shall not cease to write until everything is taken care of, and that is really an art!

With love, your Jette

Jefferson City
6 March 1887

Dear Heinrich! Dear Auguste!

Many thanks to you and your secretary for the draft. It came at a very opportune time again, although I doubt whether I will ever see anything of it. I wonder whether we'll ever get out of these tight situations?

81. Heinrich Schilking, born in 1815 in Warendorf, became a well-known painter in Münster. A friend of Heinrich Geisberg's, he died 3 October 1895 in Oldenburg.

82. Max Offenberg, the oldest son of Jette's sister Johanna, was born in Ahlen on 1 December 1841 and died in Münster on 23 August 1886.

I was again waiting for Effie, who is moving and is always somewhat upset. The old year brought many good things over there and here. But the new has not begun quite as well, for a bill in Congress was passed in the House proposing that the U.S. court would establish two new offices in Missouri. Heinrich Geisberg and my Louis are very much affected. The Senate has since agreed, and only the signature of the president is needed to put the new law into effect in a few months. Naturally both of them have reported to the judges concerned. But here in Jefferson the office will bring in only half, and at best Heinrich would have to move to Kansas City.

Presently the legislature is in session here, and last Tuesday they voted that the Capitol should stay here. There had been quite a bit of excitement and debate for a long time. Sedalia, a city farther west, claims the seat of the government. The governor submitted a proposal that the Senate should approve $250,000 for improvement and enlargement of the buildings here. This the opponents seemed willing to defeat. The city is showing itself in its best light. Society, entertainment, two new railroads, a waterworks, electrical light, besides the gas works; in short, there is an upswing in everything. We hope that the summer will draw much life and a work force to the city. Also, a bridge across the Missouri is being planned. We ourselves are watching the activities and are pursuing our own business.

For two weeks already I have been back at Stromberg. Trees and bushes are being planted. Wilhelm is working outside the city. We are satisfied here. This spring I can already harvest some asparagus. If it does not sell well here, we will ship it or can it.

21 March

We have a very late spring. This morning we had snow. It is all right that it is still cold, for then we will not have any setbacks later, and finally after five years we can expect a good peach crop.

Two hundred and fifty thousand dollars has indeed been approved for the enlargement of the Capitol by both houses. In the evening there was a great celebration, illumination, etc. So this will produce work and life. In St. Louis the Sunday Law will be enacted. This will result in some rebellion! Here we have become accustomed to this for years. For the time being the sale of drinks is still permitted, although the restaurants will have to pay very high taxes. However, there is a great deal of temperance education, and it could happen that no beer or wine may be had. Curious!

The Japanese pines have been planted, dear Auguste. They are already blooming at the Hesses. I have a young little tree growing. Last year there was very little time left to plant anything pretty. I recently got myself some roses and plants from Hess, and I sowed grass and planted an oval bed with flowers. Until now we only sorted and laid out things. Now it is the garden's turn, but it is supposed to stay small. I shall make it easy for myself. Hess has planted a great many fruit trees and bushes. He also had some sent for me, and he even sent a man around to plant them for me, and everything is free of charge. While doing this he looked so grouchy, and yet he is always here at the right time.

I am glad that I have no silkworm eggs. They all advised against it. Emily's brother promised me some, however. I had the beautiful idea of enclosing a few for Auguste, as a punishment because she does not know that the eggs will sit calmly on the paper all year long and hatch only when spring comes and grow and eat for the next five weeks until they are big, then will spin a cocoon, burst out of their cocoon, and lay eggs for the following year.

If only we would not have such a changeable climate! I shall keep the mulberry hedge for the time being. They will probably produce fruit this year. Soon more!

With sincere greetings and kisses, you sister, Jette.

Jefferson City
4 December 1887

Dear Heinrich:

As I wrote to Auguste, I have been in the process of reading, putting in order, and destroying old letters in expectation of an impending, blessed end. But as I got more and more deeply involved, I became more serious, sadder, and more nervous. Old wounds are breaking open again. Events that were forgotten or had been pushed aside torture me anew in my futile desire to make up to you, to our dear uncle, and the others, what we have involuntarily caused. I wonder whether I will have to carry this burden into my grave? Without a doubt! And I see again in every letter how you are: so unselfish, so noble, sacrificing for me again and again. And now there you sit, miserable, needy, poor.

A few years ago I was given some prospect for a pension, but it was false hope. Considering back pay since the death of Bruns, it would have amounted to four thousand dollars. Just imagine, if I could have been able to send this to you! This would really have been something. I am beginning to speculate on something. Many take out stock in mines in Colorado. If only I would have the means to do that, I would still do it. I also read of our brother Wilhelm again. You and our uncle wrote concerning him. All the things that you have had to endure!

From reading the letters I became somewhat sick. Now I am better again, but dull. Strange, I get nervous so easily without noticing it, and then I am not worth a thing for a while. I no longer know myself.

But now it is getting time for me to send this off. From the bottom of my heart I wish you happy holidays and a happy New Year! You will certainly write me again: "I am so much better now, without pain, and I walk daily for several hours in God's free air."

I would be so glad to relieve you, but I cannot even visit you. Otherwise you would see how I, with Auguste, would tease you every day and how we would compete in bringing you back to good humor.

Your children are growing up. Marie has probably grown up completely. And what about Max? May God bless him so that he does not get into new difficulties. I hope he has not suffered any damage from his fall?[83] A greeting from Niedieck is missing this Christmas. Their daughter still sounds very depressed.

As always, your sister Jette.

Jefferson
25 February 1888

Dear Heinrich:

Two weeks ago your letter arrived with the draft. Thus I send you my own and Effie's best thanks. We have very serious concerns about Effie, so that I immediately sent her the whole

---

83. Max Geisberg fell from a tree and injured his knee, necessitating a long stay in bed.

amount. The plan in St. Louis to ban the German language from the schools has gone into effect as a result of a new election for school officials, and the German teachers were suddenly unemployed. An English exam has been approved, and they may be able to get vacant positions eventually. However, Effie has become so timid, and although she had spent a great deal of effort and expense earlier in preparing herself, she now explains that she has become too old, etc., etc. For the time being she is giving private lessons to German children in school. We will have to see how long this will last. They don't like to make facilities available for that purpose. Hess is offering his house for her stay, but what good would that do? The sons, of whom only Harry has an income, want to work, and this will probably be their only prospect during the summer. We attempt to encourage her, since in the beginning she was quite beside herself. In her last letter she said that she wanted to come here and stay with me until the fall if these private lessons do not continue. Well, for Heaven's sake! Strange, she is already saying that the sons want her to do this. Later she wants to be with them and keep house for them. She has always liked to do that, but it also proves to me how very much affected she has been by this affair.

We are approaching spring, although we had frost again. Wilhelm is making all kinds of preparations, and I am lying down on the job because the feverish condition I have had several times is making itself noticeable again for the third time since we have lived here. I try to cure myself, but that is not sufficient. Ottilie promised to go and get a prescription from the doctor today.

I hope that this year will be more favorable than the last ones. The summer drought often continues too long. The trees have grown very little. However, if the frost does not kill the peach blossoms, we can expect these, and berries as well. Wilhelm and I spend a great deal of our time making plans. He puts it down on paper after he has determined the exact feet and inches, and I criticize. To be sure, we have to make an addition to the house. We have joined a building cooperative so that we can borrow money at a lower interest rate. But at first we would like to see some profit from our land so we can help ourselves. We also have added many conveniences in the house. We could stand it quite well here if we had an extra room. The bad thing is that Wilhelm always has to stoop over in the kitchen and the dining room, and he often forgets to do that!

Our city is becoming splendid. The water works will be started in the immediate future. The legislature has approved the construction of a bridge over the river. Naturally this will give jobs to many people. Perhaps it will also draw some capital and factories here. The gas works have been united with the power and light works. Hess, as the superintendent, has a lot to do, and for this reason has been in Chicago and St. Louis several times already. The Capitol is now ordering electric light, and a wider chimney will have to be built, etc. It is just the very thing that Hess has to have, an urgent job! He is so thorough.

If only I could be as relaxed as you are. There you sit, and it seems you cannot even get around by yourself without some help. So it is worse than it was earlier. Will the summer not bring some relief? I do hope so. And you will be constantly treated with salve and massage.

I too feel the nerves, but little of my rheumatism. My knobby fingers are considerably smaller than those of my sister. But I do not at all possess patience, and much less now than earlier. The reason for this probably is that we have to do so much more and have to arrange so much more now. Day and night we are thinking of our work. If only I stay well and strong for a few more years! But I am seventy-four years of age! I often think of Niedieck's sudden end. This New Year I still wrote to the children. But now that is over.

Louis, his wife, and four children were here on Sunday. They send their best regards. Also Hess. I have not seen the Geisbergs since they were here at Christmas. Their son, a dear boy, was ill recently. The Nitchys are moving ahead. The girls are diligently helping their mother. If only their father would not be so full of jokes.

I hope to hear some good news in the near future. The treatment with the ointment, the help to get to bed, and even help to maneuver up and down the stairs are sad to think of.

As always, sincerely, your sister, Jette

Enclose always, if you can, something when Auguste writes.

Only a part of the following letter to Auguste survives, beginning in the middle of a sentence and describing a return to Westphalia, perhaps on the fiftieth anniversary of the founding of the church.

no date[84]

. . . with whom I had not associated for many years. We had a lot to tell each other and could not finish everything because we thought that we had experienced so many important things. She had news that her brother Wilhelm, the bishop of Münster, celebrated his fiftieth anniversary as a priest last August.[85] You will know that. Heinrich has been acquainted with him since childhood.

Dinner was in the open air under tents. In the evening there were illumination, speeches, fireworks. Most of the farmers stayed on so their wives and children could see something new. We drove in bright moonlight to the Bruns's farm. Harry was completely ecstatic about the landscape. We went to the cemetery, saw the graves of my five children, of my dear cousin, etc. On the return trip next day a young priest boasted about his home, where a spring flowed from under the church, the Pader. So I could not restrain myself from participating in the conversation, and we talked very pleasantly during the remainder of the trip on the boat. It was Brackmeier from Paderborn.[86] Well, I probably will not be able to go to Westphalia again.

There are a lot of new things here in our city. Approximately two hundred paces from our apartment a big tower for the water line has been completed. The tower was finished today, and we are glad that the incessant hammering will stop. Later, when everything is in operation and everything has been leveled again, it will be very pretty here. Our area is now called Tower Park, and we even have a streetcar that goes down the main street every hour from

84. Although this fragment of a letter is undated, we place it in 1888, which marked the fiftieth anniversary of the establishment of St. Joseph's Catholic Church in Westphalia and the arrival of its founder, the Jesuit missionary Father Ferdinand Helias, in central Missouri in 1838. Further evidence as to the date is provided by the fact that electricity had come to Jefferson City in 1887. Other improvements in the capital city around this time included street cars for public transportation, a modern waterworks, and a significant enlargement of the Capitol, all seen as the dawn of a new era for the city.

85. Dr. Wilhelm Cramer, bishop of Münster, celebrated the fiftieth anniversary of his ordination in 1888. We have not been able to determine the identity of his sister.

86. The river Pader has its springs in the center of the ancient city of Paderborn, whose name literally means "Spring of the Pader." The young priest, a native of Paderborn, was Carl Brockmeier, who on 18 November 1882 had become the first resident priest of Saint Clement in Pike County, Missouri.

here to the prison. I wonder whether this will continue? Now the streetcar is well used, and I also like to spend my five cents twice.

The Capitol will now receive two new wings and a new cupola in the middle. It seems to me that it will no longer have such good symmetry; as to style, it is similar to the post office in Münster, but larger. The State House is supposed to be finished for the session this coming winter.

You are tired from reading, dear Auguste. So this shall suffice for this time! We shall become happy again! I wish that you too would have a good reason for happiness. Hold dear your Jette.

P.S. The present pastor is called Diepenbrock.[87] He comes from Everswinkel.

Jefferson City
1 October 1888

Dear Heinrich:

Well, it is good after all that I waited. For several weeks I had resolved to write you, but I was prevented from doing so. All summer long I did not hear how things were with you. I assumed, to be sure, that you were making another pilgrimage to Werne. But now your letter has arrived. The baths did not have the beneficial effects that you had expected, and you continue to suffer and are even more paralyzed. It is so sad, but Auguste does not complain and does not say what you are doing to try to relieve your pain, but only that she dreamed you were able to get up by yourself once. I probably know little of how bad it really is with you. So you are entirely helpless! I have been thinking every day about this. Auguste still has the courage to console herself that there are greater crosses in the world. I often tell myself the same when I am depressed, which unfortunately has often been the case recently.

I do not at all see that we are achieving anything or that Wilhelm is succeeding in anything. I am beginning to see that my effort with this property was a vain attempt on my part. He thinks that he could get ahead in a new and bigger city. He is not sufficiently interested in our project here, he is not practical and diligent enough, and so here I sit. We shall probably spend the winter here together; we have supplies, and in the spring there will be new ideas and new prospects. Louis's departure[88] has probably upset Wilhelm too.

Hess is always at the right spot, and in his sharp manner he thinks a lot and acts a lot for us. He always says that I could have a home with him. Not only that, but he also does a lot for the Deckers. Effie was here for half a year, and as soon as the vacation began, Gustav and Ernst also came. Effie has begun to keep house in her home in St. Louis now. Hess has advanced her some money for a start; and Gustav, who as a future lawyer still has no income, is working in an office. The boys are quite hopeful and happy with their mother and are not strangers any more.

I shall not be writing more now. You probably have some entertainment and visitors from France. Both sisters are home, after all. They do see you every day. I would I could do that!

Farewell, remember and think often of your sincerely loving sister, Jette.

87. Rev. Anton Diepenbrock was born 19 November 1856 at Everswinkel, a small town about ten miles east of Münster. Shortly after his ordination in St. Louis on 7 March 1883, he came to Westphalia. As its first diocesan priest, he served St. Joseph Parish for almost forty years.

88. Louis Bruns moved to Seattle, Washington, where he became superintendent for the Ferdinand Sander Company.

Jefferson City
25 November 1888

Dear Heinrich:

Auguste does not write at all, and that worries me. We are having a magnificent fall. There is still bright, beautiful weather, a little frost but not too much to prevent us from doing some fall work. There is always something that occurs to me that I would like to have done. We have to set out a few dozen raspberries, set out asparagus plants where they are missing, and plant sixteen cherry trees. Then vegetables will have to be harvested, put into the ground, and covered for the winter. The newly planted grape vines must be wrapped, and the flowers must be taken into the house, just as if we were quite a few people and pursuing big plans. And then, needlessly, I receive good lectures that I should not do this and should not do that myself, should make it simpler, should manage more simply, etc., etc.

Well, finally I do use a little intelligence and do only what I cannot resist doing. It is strange—such a little place demands constant attention and offers so much to think about.

In the fall when Wilhelm wanted to follow Louis, we both became neglectful and depressed. Things were to stop here, and the place should be rented or sold. It got around, and then Wilhelm suddenly said we should after all see what success our plantings might have and he would rather stay, and so there was nothing left for me but to agree. Since that time we are back to our planning and striving again and are satisfied again. This year brought several deaths of dear acquaintances so that I did not like to go to St. Louis in spite of urgent invitations from my daughter and nephews.

Effie went from here with the firm determination to live alone with her sons in her own home, which had stood empty for a long time. Her sister and her mother contributed in the beginning, and more important help was given by her brother-in-law. They still had furniture, etc., in St. Louis. She moved in after it became livable again. She also was immediately able to rent the better half of the house. Then a sudden offer was made for her property. The buyer let her live there till spring as a renter but he paid immediately. Thus she was able to pay off her debts and could invest the profits, which Carl did for her. Effie and her boys are happy that they are rid of the house, for there was much that would have had to be repaired. Harry and Gustav are contributing to the household, and they think that they will be able to manage. They are earnestly trying. They are happy that they can live together, which they have not been able to do since the death of their father. It seems to me we can let the additional money from the Stevermann Foundation go now, although I still have to claim it for myself, which perhaps will not attract as much attention since I am an old person with fewer opportunities. Should it turn out that I can give it up, I would rather do this than apply for it.

In advance I wish you the very best for Christmas and New Year's. If only it could be granted to you to spend a few more years with your family in better health! I keep thinking so much about how helplessly and in how much pain you have to spend your days. Auguste must inform me in greater detail about your condition, but you must always add a little, even if it is only as little as in the last letter.

In everlasting love and faithful sympathy, your sister, Jette

P.S. Also best wishes for your wife and children. Everybody here joins me in that wish.

St. Louis
28 December 1889

Dear Heinrich:

Once more a Happy New Year! Several weeks ago I wrote to you. At Christmastime, or rather a little before, a letter from Therese arrived. I immediately thought that I should be satisfied with that. But several days ago a great-nephew, J. H. Bruns, wrote that the estate of Uncle Pastor had finally been concluded because of the death of the executor Wieschhölter.[89] He reported that in Lippstadt they had already gotten their share. I assume that you have not received any notice of this because Wieschhölter's son spoke of a new authorization and had simply put you into the land of the blessed. This gave me a few restless days, and I was looking forward anxiously for the mail carrier three times a day. This has now been going on for five days, but the letter from Lohne was dated 29 November. Thus I have concluded with Ottilie that my nephew had not been told the truth, probably in order to exclude the Americans. My nephew offers that if we cannot employ anybody in Westphalia to take care of this, he would make an attempt to get the money with a court order. The entire matter is a question of 1,324 marks and 27 pfennig, two-ninths for my children and two-ninths for G. H. Bruns's heirs. This to be sure is no big sum. The junior Wieschhölter lamented mightily that there were some insecure notes, so that the people in Lohne gave him a certain amount as a present, and he wondered whether the people here would drop their claims. This will have to be left up to you. I am not in favor, but I have written to my niece Catharina that she could leave it either to you or to a nephew who has been authorized by you to determine the final outcome. This they will probably do. The brothers and sisters are scattered so widely that it will make it more difficult and more expensive to obtain a new power of attorney. Since you are now prevented by your paralysis from looking after this, I therefore ask what should be done, but I will yield if it is fitting. Old man Wieschhölter had probably been drinking, and thus the sons will have to struggle.

So we are now standing at the end of the year, and this is always a serious time. We spent the holidays at home, the evening with Effie's children and sister-in-law and Nettie with her daughter and two stepchildren. Our boys are growing magnificently. They are solid and active. I hope for the best, and especially for better times for Effie since she is becoming stronger and more active. I myself cannot complain, but I have to rest more frequently, as if this too is a job. In a few weeks I shall go again to the Hesses. The letters can be forwarded there.

And how are you? Is the pain still there? Particularly at night? Does the weather have any influence, as it usually has with rheumatic cases? I am often so impatient, and I would like to know exactly.

Now, may God keep you! Imagine frequently how I would stand there and look at you with love and care in the hope of making it easier for you.

Best regards and wishes to Auguste, Marie, and Max. As always,

Your sister Jette

89. Franz Wieschhölter of Liesborn, near Wadersloh, had been named executor of Pastor Hermann Bruns's last will, executed 6 November 1874 at Wadersloh.

Jefferson City
30 January 1890

Dear Heinrich:

And now you have given me great joy by writing yourself, and such a long letter as I have not had in a long time. It probably did not come easy for you; I can see that. I still have a letter from Uncle Caspar that was also written with a trembling hand. I myself am often not so sure about my hand either. How much I treasure these two letters!

So you enjoyed Bentheim.[90] If only the baths would have straightened you out! I wonder how you are getting along now? The winter does not make your condition any worse? But to have oneself shoved day after day from a bed of pain to a sofa, and not to be able to find any peaceful sleep because of the cramps! I cannot imagine such a condition. May God preserve your quiet resignation and make it tolerable for you. Perhaps it will get better. That is to be hoped.

For a few weeks now I have been back in Jefferson with the Hesses after I spent almost five months with Effie and her sons in St. Louis. I enjoyed being there, although I had a great deal to do. Effie has become quite well again, thank God, but is still weak. The boys are all very dear and did not want to let me go. Harry has received a raise in his salary to sixty dollars. Gustav is taking his last exam as a lawyer this summer, and Ernst is earning his four dollars a week. He works hard and gives half of it as his board, and so does Gustav, who works in a rather large legal office nearby.

Everybody is awakened in the morning at six o'clock. A good breakfast is prepared, and a sandwich with cold cuts and fruit is packed for lunch. Then in the evening there is dinner. Afterward there is music or conversation until one's eyes fall shut, which in the case of Ernst occurs right after dinner. They all three sing so well. They are very contented at home—more than we wish at times. The sister-in-law, Lena Hildenbrandt, does not live far away and is a great support for Effie and the boys since she is a teacher in high school and has more opportunity to stimulate them intellectually.

I know they will miss me. Gustav promises to write a letter each week. His mother is usually somewhat negligent, but she has already written a double sheet. Here I have my big room and all possible conveniences. My son-in-law is attentive, and my daughter even more so. Only I have nothing to do. Perhaps I am still somewhat lazy. Today I was outside with the gardener and had him prepare a few hotbeds, and I have already written for some seeds. Flowers are my department, for the garden is taken care of by Tillie and me. The winter was as mild as it has hardly ever been before. There will be no ice. It is strange, for they write from Washington State that they had deep snow and frost, which they have not been accustomed to. I am glad that Wilhelm is also there. He is delighted with the area, with the sailing ships and the icebergs. He found a job immediately, and young and old say, "Grandmother must come." As if twenty-five hundred miles miles were just a jump for a seventy-six-year-old woman.

Yesterday I went to Stromberg. It makes me sad that I cannot be there since Wilhelm is gone. We were so content together. And it has been arranged so beautifully and would be so rewarding now.

90. Bad Bentheim was a health spa near the Dutch border, approximately thirty miles northwest of Münster.

The children of Dr. Bruns do not want to have their two-ninths from the estate of Uncle Pastor, and they wish that their uncle, authorized to represent them, would take their share for his trouble. But I cannot say anything concerning Hermann Bruns's heirs in Westphalia. The daughter Catharina has written me that they wish the share to which they are entitled would be sent to me. It would not be worth our while to provide a new authorization. I only fear that there is not much to be gotten from the junior Wieschhölter. Otherwise you probably would have been informed by the court, as those in Lohne have been.

Ottilie, Hess, Jette, and Heinrich join me in sending their regards. From the bottom of my heart, your sister Jette

P.S. I would like to ask Auguste to write also. I would like to hear more of her brother.[91]

Jefferson City
12 October 1890

Dear Heinrich:

I received your letters this morning, and I thank you so much. I am quite ashamed about it. You will probably remember quite well that almost fifty years ago you loaned eight hundred dollars to Bruns. I do not know whether interest was paid, but I do know that I asked my husband to repay the money. He agreed. Perhaps it was already too late, and he never got around to it. This has always rankled me very much, and then you also made a present of the amount that was saved from the bankruptcy. I do ask you to tell your wife about this.

After the death of my husband I struggled, I worked, I raised the children. The years went by without my suffering any need, at least I did not feel any. The children pursued their occupations, became independent, and are all good to me. I probably never have had anything extra, but I have never lacked for anything. After the departure of Wilhelm I sold the little property. The house provided me some interest, and now, as I reported to you, the Union pays me a pension. If I wanted to scrape everything together, I could live quite splendidly. But this I am not accustomed to doing anymore.

You will probably understand that I consider it my absolute duty to return to you some of my abundance. If I had received the back pay, as was the former custom, for twenty-seven years, then it would be different! But I am quite satisfied this way. Hess is the first to agree with me that I should think of you! He is and says he is a rough fellow, even though well educated and secretly quite sensitive; he doesn't care for family but in spite of that maintained his sister for years, then helped his nephew, who unfortunately had to die during his last year at the university, etc., etc.

Effie, who can use it most of all, is always afraid that Mother will shortchange herself if she does this or that. Her boys come from a noble race. If only they can get through with all their goodness and straightness; they are trying their very best. I shall soon go there again. In preparation for the weddings, which are both going to take place within a month, I put on a stiff silk dress to satisfy the wishes of my daughters. Both brides are well-situated, which pleases them and me. I was still able to carry out a few honorable courtesies. I remembered Wilhelm with a sum, which Louis will invest for him since Wilhelm was very much involved

91. Max Boner, born 17 May 1833 at Herten, died in 1920. He worked as an engineer in Rostov on the Don and cofounded the Association of German Engineers in 1856.

in Stromberg. I have informed my sons of everything, for after all I am I! I believe I gradually feel that it is going to be comfortable not to be entirely without means.

While reading your dear, dear letter and your wife's even stronger one, I felt very embarrassed (as Uncle Caspar had felt when he presented a golden watch to Aunt Therese and a gold piece to me). Well, this was not intended that way. You have nothing to thank me for; I can only praise a fate that gives me the opportunity to show you that I have treasured the many proofs of your unselfish love and that I always loved you as much. And this you also know. What will now happen after half a year, you can leave to me without any worry. My children will not let me come up short, and I still do not know myself how things will work out. It is not worth mentioning.

Your new treatment could turn out well. If only it would return movement to your limbs!

Once more I thank Auguste for the manuscript,[92] and I shall study it in peace. Tillie is already into it. What I have written is just as long,[93] but I want to add to it and shall try to copy it down or have my daughter do it.

I now conclude and will soon write more to Auguste. I only had to report immediately that you are very much in error, for I shall always remain in your debt.

With faithful love, your sister, Jette

A letter of 7 June 1891 from Ottilie to Auguste reports that Jette had gone to visit Louis and Wilhelm in Washington State. Ottilie had opposed the trip of "3,000 English miles," but the doctor felt that the change in scenery would be better for Jette than any medicine.

Seattle
c. 1891

Dear Auguste:

Here is the view of the city where Louis lives with his family. He would not take it very kindly if he knew that part of his letter goes along, especially since he is very weak in German; but in spite of that, he keeps it up just for me. He always threatens that he will study it more and then will instruct his wife in the language. But he has made derisive remarks concerning her style several times, so that Emily will write only in English. Since your Marie is learning English, we hope that she will soon introduce herself to us. Ottilie would be delighted and would surely answer her immediately.

What a joy for you that you hear more frequently now from your brother. It seems to occur frequently in our family that the man marries late. Your cousin Mr. Savels seems to have good taste.[94] Our father was twenty-eight years old, our mother sixteen, when they were joined in matrimony.

I shall remember to send you a photograph from here. Richmond Hill [in Jefferson City], with the water tower, looks beautiful, but they have placed a huge mound of earth with the

92. Heinrich Geisberg wrote "The History of the Geisberg Family," which was edited in a lengthened version by Carla Schulz-Geisberg in 1958.

93. In fall 1868 Jette wrote an autobiography in German, which has been translated by Adolf E. Schroeder. Sections of the autobiography introduce periods of her life covered by the letters in this collection. A copy of her complete autobiography has been deposited in the Westphalia Museum.

94. Max Boner was forty-six years old when he married Emma Vidulitsch in 1879. August Savels, born in 1847, married the twenty-two-year-old Seraphine Kochs at age forty-two.

water basin exactly in front of Hess's nose, which completely takes away the view, and will also stop the fresh air next summer.

Regards to the children. Hold dear your Jette.

Seattle
8 August 1891

Dear Auguste:

Time flies, and my stay here is coming to an end. I have decided that I will depart on 24 August, which will make exactly three full months here.

Recently a letter arrived from Effie's sister-in-law, who is taking a vacation trip this year to somewhere near San Francisco, California. She is very enthusiastic about the area and everything there and immediately makes comparisons, but nevertheless longs to return to Missouri. It will be different for me. To be sure, I also prefer to go back, because Missouri is closer to me. However, I will have to think about this place a great deal, about the busy people, the magnificent forests, where civilization is gradually making its way, the endless water which borders the area and carries the wealth of the land to all parts of the world. When my sons tell me, and prove in round figures, the extent of the exports, I become dizzy. I wonder what will come of all this?

The city is well situated for its development. Presently the harbor is laid out on a broad scale. Many vessels will find places here, and for miles they prepare docks and sites for the construction of ships and warehouses. Wilhelm has accompanied me along the wall. I tried to look around on all sides.

The city has over one hundred miles of streetcar lines, and so we sometimes go here and there for very little money. The view is usually splendid. The streets have been laid out in a regular pattern. From the bay, Seattle is laid out like a fan. The straight lines move up the hill. To be sure, one has to overlook the dips and should not think that there is an uninterrupted row of houses. That will take a long time to achieve. At first I objected to the fact that next to pretty houses tree stumps and the wilderness remain, and also that except on the main streets the buildings have been built of boards, although frequently in a grand style. It is almost funny how dainty, and at the same time how solid, such a building is. At least it looks that way. At times there are houses that were built a bit askew. I don't like to see that very much.

Mr. Sander is taking a tour with his wife to the National Park at Yellowstone, where art has helped nature so that tourists stream there in large crowds during the summer. Since the Sanders had a daughter a year and a half ago, they don't like to be gone very long. A professional nurse will be engaged and will receive twenty dollars a week. The aunt will supervise, and every day Louis will have to send a wire. Since Louis has returned, he is free to accompany us to the famous waterfall of Snoqualmie. Tomorrow we will go there by railroad.

Recently I wrote to Toni Petri and recommended the Price family in Berlin to her.[95] I

95. Toni Petri, Jette's cousin, was born Antonie Geisberg 3 March 1819 in Cappenberg, the daughter of Franz Heidenreich Geisberg and his wife Maria Westendorf. Col. James Barry Price was born in Virginia 19 January 1832. He fought for the Confederacy, was widowed in 1870, and in 1873 married the widow of his cousin, Gen. Thomas L. Price, of Jefferson City. After a fruitless odyssey through Germany and France in search of a cure for his cancer, he died in 1892 in Denver and was buried at the Price Cemetery in Jefferson City.

hope if her son is not there she will have some connection there. I did not know Toni's address in Münster, and so I thought that I might address it to Heinrich. If she does not receive the letter, she should inquire at the post office.

Colonel Price of Jefferson has cancer damage and is looking for help in Berlin. I was asked for recommendations. Ottilie is very worried about it. And so I wrote to Louis Bischopink,[96] whom I personally met at the von Hatzfelds. But at this time I neither knew the exact address nor what has happened to him since 1882.

Ottilie is afraid that the colonel will not survive, and then Lucile would be alone. To be sure, she is very independent and is somewhat capable of handling the German language. They probably also had recommendations to Minister Phelps of Missouri,[97] and I thought that in the long run this might be sufficient. But since Tillie is urging me, at the request of Miss Lucile, I could not refuse.

How is Heinrich doing this summer? So you are back again at the *Domplatz*.[98] I wish you could make yourself comfortable in those quarters for always. Have the wounds healed? I ask you to send the next news to Missouri again. If only Heinrich could walk a bit! Is your health now tolerably good? I hope that Marie is back home again? I enjoy hearing a lot about your children.

Emily, my sons, and the children are well. For myself, the trip was indeed worth the trouble. Now I can at least picture how and where they live. Wilhelm still has not succeeded in getting a good position, but his older brother and his wife have influence on him. He is now lodging with them, which is a great relief for me. It is also good for the children.

Many sincere regards from all of us to you and Heinrich. Louis will soon write to his uncle. I will have to take the return trip by myself. It will take four full days, but there will be a change of coaches only once, in St. Paul. That, after all, is not so terrible. God bless you! With love, your sister,

Jette

Jefferson City
20 September 1891

Dear Heinrich:

A week ago a letter from you arrived from Seattle, and now one came directly more quickly. I have been here since the beginning of the month. I had decided to stay there three months, but Louis could not get a lower berth in the sleeping car for me for the 24th, so I waited for two days. If I were twenty years younger, I would not have objected to staying in Seattle. The youthful, strong striving, the healthy breeze of the sea air, all appealed to me

96. Louis Bischopink was a brother of Maria Boner, who had been married to Jette's cousin Max Boner in Hovestadt since 1841.

97. Jette is apparently in error here regarding Phelps's Missouri connection. William Walter Phelps (1839–1894), a native of Pennsylvania, graduated from Yale University in 1860 and from Columbia University Law School in 1863. After a successful legal and business career, he was elected to the House of Representatives as a Republican in 1872. In May 1881 he was appointed minister to Austria-Hungary, but he resigned within a year to reclaim his seat in the Congress. Having served effectively as commissioner to the Berlin Conference on Foreign Affairs in the Pacific in 1889, he was appointed minister to Germany.

98. During the summers, the Geisberg family lived at the von Nagel residence on Cathedral Square because the apartment was accessible by wheelchair.

very much. I came back very satisfied, but I was very, very sorry to have to take leave of them. They are my only sons. I wonder whether I will ever see them again? And Emily and the children?

I do not know what to tell you of the return trip. I was quite indifferent and dull and was not at all looking forward to Missouri, but I had good company. After much chatting and reading, I arrived Saturday evening in Minneapolis, where I had to change. Since it was a Saturday and there was no through train, I preferred to spend the night there. I had a good hotel, but the electrical light in the room bothered me. The next morning I went to church, and in the afternoon I walked and rode around. It is a magnificent city! The private residences look so friendly. All are individually surrounded by lawns. The streets with their posts are so clean and quiet. The public library, a very impressive building of red granite, caught my attention. The streetcar took me outside town for four miles, but I calmly stayed on the car and rode back because I did not dare to use another line. After supper Miss L. Black, the bookkeeper, took me to the depot. That was very kind, but since it was now a day later I was not able to obtain a lower berth. I did not want to climb up, and therefore went into the day coach. I thought I could surely stand it for a night. Afterward I almost regretted it, although I saved three dollars. The wire to the Deckers brought two Deckers to meet me on Monday evening. And then we were at Effie's immediately.

Her sister-in-law, Mrs. Hildenbrandt, arrived on Sunday from San Francisco. Originally we had planned to make the return trip together, but she took the Southern Pacific Railroad. Neither of us had to complain about the heat on the trip. She described the abundance of fruit in the vicinity of the big city. It was actually dumped into the water. In Seattle they had many vegetables and fruits from California, but they were very expensive. Apples were doled out to the children in a frugal fashion. In a few years this will probably change. Around Seattle there is a great deal of clearing and planting. This destruction of timber is on a large scale. Louis had four large fir trees on his street cut down, which will provide him a supply of wood for a year. Perhaps in another year this will stop. Labor is expensive, even though the wood does not cost anything. Next door he grew his supply of potatoes. The property is not fenced, is not plowed, and has only been cleared of the underbrush, which is then piled in a heap. The new, sunny land produces so well.

One other thing struck me very much—everything that was planted succeeded, flowers as well as bushes, in the middle of the summer. Louis has a faucet in the garden from his well so that they can sprinkle the garden with a hose every evening during the drouth. The lawn, as well as the entire area around the house, is fresh. The natural playground for the children is the forest. There is a swing. They build houses in the branches and collect flowers. I wonder how long this will last? To be sure, thousands of building lots are for sale. The Japanese are very well suited for clearing the land, and they ask forty dollars per acre. In the city the Swedes keep the prices down. The speculators keep the prices of the building lots high, and therefore the present slowdown. The operation of the mines is in full swing again, and the big harvest of hops has begun. For this purpose hundreds of Indians with canoes came to work. But they are bothersome people. They buy clothing and blankets from their wages and spend the remainder and then move off again. A few work in the big sawmill at Port Blakely. There are still more Chinese, some Swedes, as well as Americans. The latter, however, have a higher status. This sawmill is said to be one of the biggest in the world. Mrs. Sander, who took us there because her parents live there, said that they ship timber all over the world. Six big three-masted ships were waiting to be loaded. Her father, Captain Hall, a man from the East, has been living there for fifteen years. He is a shipbuilder. He builds four-masters, and one had just been finished. They buy what they do not cut themselves from the mill next door. Thus the masts were over one hundred feet high. These magnificent trees are moved by machines. He does everything on a large scale and employs over one hundred men. The family lives elegantly up there. They have a Chinese cook who does all the cooking, washing, and ironing, and even works in the garden for some thirty-five dollars a month. Three times a day a steamer goes to Seattle. It was a splendid trip, and one really becomes aware how well the city has been laid out. The harbor stretches for miles and is very busy. The traffic is already over forty million more than Tacoma, Portland in Oregon, or San Francisco. Recently there is a considerable yield of iron, silver, and gold from the mines. Seattle also now has a German daily newspaper, which Louis sends me so that I can keep up with the local news.

Louis's brother-in-law will travel to New York in September. He always travels with his wife since he fears that he may suffer a sudden end because of an earlier internal injury. Since they now have a little daughter, there is a trained nurse there during their absence who receives twenty dollars a week, and Louis sends a telegram every day. The brother-in-law seems to be getting stronger, and Emily thinks that he will reach a decent age. It was pleasant for me to be able to discuss things with him. He also said that he valued Louis very much, that his services were very satisfactory, and that he could have complete confidence in him. To be sure, Louis felt this very much since the brother-in-law leaves everything to him and always says everybody should go to Bruns because he will know what to do. It's true others know this also, and Louis has had all kinds of offers that would perhaps make him more independent. But naturally he does not think of changing and leaves it to the brother-in-law to do what he considers fair. He pays Louis three hundred dollars a month. This helped him obtain his property, and even with the high prices there he can still save after paying life insurance and investing. To be sure, he is very much tied down and has to be in the office all the time and frequently has to work at home in the evening. Mr. Sander seems to realize this and wants to get someone else for the bookkeeping. And Louis is supposed to look more to the work out of the office. He is supposed to supervise the building of a new railroad that has been started along the Sound. As Louis said, he has also found an occupation for Wilhelm that can last. Both sons are so much taken with Seattle that they would not want to return for any price.

I once wondered whether there was not a lot of poor trash hanging around, but no, they cannot last there because they would have to work. Well, this is another question. But Louis maintains that there are very many intelligent, fine people from the highest circles of all countries, also many rich, who like it there and take an interest in helping the new, wild country get ahead in comparison to the everyday activity back home. The police are strangely strict.

To be sure, since both sons were very much tied down, many excursions were omitted. I would have liked to go to Victoria in British Columbia, which is on Vancouver Island. An excursion to there was made, but the people returned seasick. Louis took a tour with us to the Snoqualmie Falls, which was really magnificent. The white foaming water rushes down, forced down by steep rocks two hundred feet high, and forms a double rainbow at the bottom and flows into a flat valley where there is a great deal of cultivation. Our path was high above, surrounded by sky-high firs. The railroad will be built to continue toward Canada, where there will be a connection. We did take a tour to Ravenna Park by railroad during the last week. There only a few paths had been cut. From both sides little brooklets were streaming down together, a little dammed in and forming waterfalls. One very strong spring containing sulphur increased the water. There were a few benches and tables where we served ourselves. It was quite wild there, and sky-high trees grew between thick underbrush—gloomy, cold, but picturesque. I wonder what will still come?

On the 20th, the day we wanted to go to the park, we were passing the office and Louis found a telegram for me, in which Gustav Fischer, Jr.,[99] announced his entrance into the world: "Mama and I are well." So I am a great-grandmother!

I have already seen the young fellow twice, a strong little fellow with dimples in his cheeks and very good. The parents are happy, but it is also noticeable how happy the grandmother is. It seems that she shook off all worries and cares and is really coming alive now. Ottilie drives me there; she said it would be too far otherwise. I also visited Mrs. Burger, of whom I wrote once before. She is older and was suffering more miserably from rheumatism than you. This summer she is so improved that she can carry on her domestic work.

The end of the letter is missing.

Jefferson City
22 September 1891

Dear Auguste:

In order to make it come true that you will receive the next letter, I shall begin immediately. First it occurs to me that I expressed myself somewhat flippantly concerning the supernatural medication that you would like to use. Even though I always preferred to use natural means, I should, after all, consider how you have tried everything for years with great trouble and great expense and painful trials. Don't take it amiss. How little one can imagine from this distance how miserable Heinrich's condition really is, how much he suffers, and how you have nursed him for many years with unselfish love, with hope, and with worry. I wonder if these wounds can ever be healed? Will the pain become more unbearable? It seems to me there could not be any more pain than he has already had to suffer.

Today was the great parade and picnic of the blacks. They celebrated their emancipation.[100] From far and near they came streaming in—over five thousand. Who can begrudge them this? Even so, one would rather like to see the whole matter transferred somewhere else.

The 28th
Your letter to Ottilie arrived. Since she is a little slow, is busy with all kinds of things in the household, and is planning a trip to the St. Louis Fair at the beginning of October, for which

99. Clifford Hess Fischer was born in Jefferson City on 8 September 1891. His parents were Johanna Henriette (Jennie) Bruns and Gustav A. Fischer. The grandmother was Jette's daughter-in-law, Nettie Henry, the widow of Hermann Bruns.

100. The celebration was held on the anniversary of Lincoln's Emancipation Proclamation, which was issued on 22 September 1862.

purpose she naturally has to have a new dress, it will be better if I continue this letter and let it sail off.

At first, in reference to the answer regarding your highly valued efforts for Miss Price: you are indeed a splendid woman! Where others have formalities and delays, you go directly to the point. It could be that later your magnificent recommendations could be used. So far, as I reported to Heinrich, Mr. Price has been referred from Berlin to a hospital in Vienna, and from there to Paris, where he wants to wait for the return of a famous surgeon. At this time he is in London, from where he wrote to Carl, who answered him and mailed it to London. With all his misery and probably his poor prospects for recovery, the man still has energy and whiles away his time with travels and new impressions. The poor daughter is sickly and has not yet recovered. She was completely exhausted at the death of her stepmother, whose long care she undertook in spite of all admonitions and the help that was offered. The doctor had told her that she would have to spare her strength for more difficult things she may still have to face. Demands were always made on Lucy, and she was always there. The father said when taking leave that if he could not find a cure he would return immediately. Thus we assume that a decision will soon be made. I shall write more about this. His house here, next to the one that we had formerly, stands dark in its magnificent surroundings, as if it were dead. It is locked up.

I cannot help it that I still think back to Seattle with the greatest interest. Missouri is not nearly as dear to me as it used to be. I am a pioneer by nature, but we after all have withstood a beginning here. That magnificent wilderness surrounded by the great water! The mild healthy climate where everything that man attempts to raise succeeds!

My Wilhelm, in his quiet contemplation, has already written to me, but the others are still waiting. It now takes only four days for a letter to arrive here. Yesterday I saw a young friend who was also traveling through the area. We shared our views of Seattle. He became rich through an investment in Montana. He told me that so many intelligent and even rich people were leaving for the West, particularly from St. Louis, in order to get out of the everyday routine back home. And then after that they gradually move their families.

Yesterday we finally had the rain we had wished for all month, and now the temperature has dropped from 100 degrees down to almost freezing. We have a tremendous climate here!

You probably have moved by now.[101] That is a lot of trouble. Perhaps you are already accustomed to it, and when you have poor Heinrich safely tucked away, then the rest follows easily. I like to hear that Max shares the inclinations of his father. His sketches give us a great deal of pleasure.[102]

Hess and wife send their best regards to you. Recently we have seen no one else but each other. The heat, the dust, and our disposition kept us at home.

With love, Jette

St. Louis
12 October 1891

Dear Heinrich:

Since the 7th I have been here at the Deckers with Ottilie. Carl urged his wife to take a fall trip. She always postponed it as long as possible for all kinds of reasons, and because of this

---

101. At the end of the summer the Geisberg family moved back to their house at Hörsterstrasse 25.
102. According to family members, Max Geisberg was gifted with extraordinary artistic talent.

has met with rather poor weather several times. This time she went earlier, and since I spent only one night here on my return trip from the West and had promised a later visit, I joined her, although I really would have enjoyed a bit more rest.

There is a big difference between the two big cities. Here everything is so regulated, so solidly rich, heavy and cold. There everything is easy and difficulties are quickly shoved aside. If it doesn't work going over the mountain, then one goes through it and the valleys are bridged over. A lively, happy life, as if the people were concerned with each other and wanted to fight the battle with primeval nature together, wanted to subjugate it, and wanted to make it yield to civilization. It does not surprise me at all that my sons are so enthusiastic about the new land. They are progressing with its progress and are participating in the progress. Louis sent me a check for you, which I am forwarding to you from him. By the time you receive this letter you will have received the check. Gustav took care of this for me through an acquaintance in a bank in Münster. Four hundred twenty-five dollars equal seventeen hundred seventy marks. This is what he said, I believe. It pleased Louis that he was able to achieve this for you. He sends his regards and will write to his uncle soon.

You will probably have moved into your new house again by now. I think this might be rather difficult. Now you are sitting up there, glued to the spot, and can only breathe God's fresh air through an open window. Does the cold affect you very much? I wish I could be with you and entertain you during these long, hard winter days. My visit should not be tiring for you. We would not even chat all the time but would look at each other and bring back the times of our youth.

I often feel quite lonely at the Hesses, since I cannot even go to visit Jette or Jennie. The horse has been put out in the pasture for the winter. Ottilie likes to go walking.

A project for electrical lamps and streetcars has been accepted by the board [in Jefferson City]. I wonder whether it will pass in such a little city? Well, we shall see. If it passes, we will profit by it.

Effie and her sons are well. Gustav has been installed as a lawyer. Ernst was to go to New York for a semester this winter to take a course in plumbing. He can use the tools only after he has passed this. We very much advised him to do it. He is industrious, and although he is having a somewhat difficult time, he is not discouraged, but remains the happiest of the brothers. Harry acts quite the senior. He is even-tempered. We would so much like for him to learn to dance so that he would not stand around so stiffly. I enjoy hearing that Marie and Max are doing things nicely for you. They will, after all, always be able to do that. And this will always cheer you up.

In a few weeks we will be back in our winter quarters. Tillie is recuperating gradually, but she is still rather weak and thin. Carl would like for her to visit his relatives in Toledo. He seems to be planning a surprise for her at home.

Farewell, and think lovingly of your sister, Jette

Jefferson City, Mo.
13 November 1891

Dear Auguste:

It gives me just as much joy as it gives you that the draft has arrived and has fulfilled its purpose. But I missed something in your letter. You are not at all sarcastic! You will have to make up for it right away, for this has its good side and in many respects is to be recommended. With the pictures I sent a piece of moss from a tree in Seattle, which I found so beautiful. Elsie brought it to me. I took some of it with me to St. Louis, where they planned to use it after it had been moistened to decorate a picture or something of that sort. It can be drawn and pulled into all kinds of forms when it is wet, and then dried afterward. Perhaps, however, it was ruined by the trip.

We have been here again since All Saints' Day. Carl would not give us any rest until his wife went on a trip, and since he absolutely refused to be of any company to me, I found it advisable to go along. We honestly tried to amuse ourselves, and after a week Ottilie went to visit Hess's cousin in St. Charles. I, in the meantime, caught a cold and fever. After Effie and I went to get Ottilie back, I found a doctor at my bed one evening. And so then I had to take medicine. A bad cough did not let me rest. After two weeks I was well enough again to make the return trip. Carl met us, and there were surprises in the house and outside. He likes to do this by himself. His wife acknowledged everything joyfully, but he has not quite finished it. The dining room has become very comfortable and fine now. They have a group of several pretty plants and flowers around a big rubber tree. Only our mood is somewhat forced. I tell myself that I shall be improving with every day, and I come to the table, but I cannot eat well. I no longer sleep so much but I am very inactive. Ottilie got a tumor on her neck. The doctor explained that it was a boil, and so we made compresses and opened it and then put compresses on again. It seems to be getting better now, and she is of the opinion that the poisonous materials that stayed in her body since her attack of the flu have now found a way out and that her condition is already better than during the summer. We let ourselves be visited now, and they all came except for young Fischer and his mother. As his grandmother says, they are very cautious.

2 December

The day before yesterday your and Heinrich's letter arrived. I was very pleased to get it although Heinrich's condition is really pitiful. A few days ago I went to see Miss Burger, who a year ago was miserable and always crying. Now she is up and around and takes care of her household, but since her circumstances are not good she will probably soon spoil it for herself again. She is older than Heinrich.

In the meantime I have gotten stronger, and if I had not become so delicate and short of breath I could accomplish something again. But I am constantly turned away, which surprises me. So I began to prepare a rug for Effie. That was easy. And now I have to sew some. I wanted to make some underwear for myself, but then Nettie said, "Why don't you leave that alone?"

To come back to my return trip, that was as safe and comfortable a tour as is possible. Nature is so grand that you can't imagine it. But in the midst of it, all along the way, people work and make useful things. There are probably no longer any wild animals around their cabins and fences. I looked at my travel companions somewhat distrustfully in the beginning, but gradually, as they talked with me so simply and sympathetically about the purpose of my trip and the return, I became less worried. There were only ladies around me. I traveled first-class, Pullman-sleeper. And then there is a car for dining, elegant and abundant, as in the biggest hotel. So it went for four days. But then in Minneapolis I had to change trains; on Saturday the train went only to Burlington, so I was much better taken care of in the first city. To be sure, the next day I missed my bed because the sleeping car was over-crowded, and I preferred to take the second-class tourist, which was somewhat difficult for me. It seems that one travels here more comfortably than where you are.

And now it occurs to me, since you mentioned it, that Wilhelm must resemble his uncle and godfather. Only his size is extraordinary: six feet two inches. Louis is smaller, but he is above average. Do send me a little picture soon. I have prepared an album especially for little pictures. It gives me particular joy that you will chaperon your daughter and that she enjoys her youth and has joined a singing society. Are you still sickly and weak? Last Thursday we had a big dinner, but because the young families are somewhat cross or jealous and do not harmonize, Carl invited a few American families and left all the relatives at home. Ottilie had done everything possible, and her husband voiced his approval. She is indeed magnifi-cently supplied with porcelain and silver and everything glittering. Soon more from your

Jette

Jefferson City
2 December 1891

Dear Heinrich:

Now we have some really ugly weather, constant monotonous rain. It is not at all normal since we usually have very little cold, but clear and bright weather until after Christmas.

I have completely recovered from my fever, and I eat celery several times daily and won-der whether this will help me too. However, that is not figuring correctly, because with you it is supposed to drive away rheumatism and with me it is supposed to repair my stomach. I think of you at each meal and wonder whether you also have such beautiful yellow crisp roots as Ottilie grew herself and bleached.[103]

So you still have sores? They apparently don't want to heal? And with that you also have pain. However, as you said, we hope that everything will improve. It is such a relief to me that you find pleasure in your wife and children. Now again: my hearing has suffered. If I were the only one! But you and Therese are also experiencing the same. Your remark con-cerning music and the singing of birds fits my situation exactly, only it is intensified by the ringing and noise of the railroad as if a wild chase were thundering by.

I also sit here a great deal without participating, and so I let things wash over me until I catch a few individual words and turn to Tillie for an explanation. Carl then shouts so loudly that it embarrasses me again. It is not always so bad, and often with others I hear everything. Recently Wilhelm wrote that I should send him your address because he would like to finish a letter since Louis had too much to do and would probably postpone it even longer. That is just how the boy is, always considerate and good. If only I could be with him! And now I shall never see him again during my life. He writes to me frequently.

I am glad that you have taken the money. There is no more risk now, and just as Auguste says, it comes at an opportune time. Louis was pleased with his success. He thought you would do something especially for yourself because this came as an unexpected gift. Their installments will not stay as high, as they said themselves. When more funds become avail-

103. The commonly used European cultured celery has big turniplike roots and short stemmed leaves and is most frequently used in salads or soups.

able, it will decrease. Fred Sander's company has real estate and banking businesses. By 1 December they will have finished a ten-mile-long electrical streetcar line. Louis is supposed to become the superintendent. He is going up the bay. But whether he will be able to get out of the office is questionable.

Louis and his wife are both members of a musical society that wants to give Haydn's *Creation* at the end of November. Louis has a very pleasant baritone, and his wife sings soprano and learns very quickly. Unfortunately, rheumatism prevents her from playing the piano for any length of time. Now their two oldest girls are practicing piano, and little Louis sings in the boy's choir.

I hope that Miss Price will have answered Auguste, for she intended to. We often get news of father and daughter. They are in Paris and will stay there for the time being since a doctor has started a treatment. The latter did not consider it malignant cancer but rather a bad ulcer that could be healed. They rarely say anything concerning his condition. Recently the second son was here to take care of matters pertaining to the estate. The mother had designated fifteen hundred dollars for a public fountain, and a piece of property of ten acres just a few blocks above that of Hess, outside the city, has been prepared for a park, with a burial plot for the family with three obelisks.

The Deckers are struggling along bravely. Harry is the housefather. Gustav leaves more of his salary for his mother than he really should. A friend and colleague recently named him guardian of four minors. That was his first case.

After New Year's, Ernst will go to New York to a technical school where he wants to study mechanics. This is necessary for his career.

Finally, our best wishes for the holidays to all of you. I thank you very much for your long letter, and I seize new hope from it. If only our Good Lord would make it easier for you.

With love, your sister Jette

Jefferson City
16 April 1893

Dear Heinrich:

First I want to tell you that you really know how to appreciate a picture. While sitting for it I thought only of you, and I sat once more for you. What do the young people know of that? They think I would look this way at age ninety. The eye speaks to you although wrinkles and seriousness are probably frequently also there. In general I maintain a cheerful attitude, much of which can be explained by my generally good health. I really should be much more serious, and I tell myself every day that in the late fall I shall be eighty years old. In the morning I begin by singing the school song: "Mein erst Gefühl sei Preis und Dank" ("Let my first feeling be praise and thanks"). But soon thereafter all kinds of gay and worldly thoughts occur. I live for the present, but I still enjoy reminiscing. I often tell myself that it could suddenly be that I will have finished my earthly career, and what good would I then have to show for the dark beyond?

It is true that what I have accomplished in earlier years, when I struggled and strove to fulfill my tasks, must be credited to me. Today I live quietly and in seclusion, for myself, and I have and seek no opportunity to do much good for mankind except for those nearest me. Every morning after breakfast I take the Thomas à Kempis (following the example of our dear father, who after church always first took *Philotea* and other devotional books in hand),

and I try to remember something for the day. I would like to know whether St. Hieronymus and other hermits did not also find pleasure in contemplation of nature? For me, my thoughts immediately fly outside and far into the world. My reading does not only treat science and progress; I also relate to the fate of human beings and how they dealt with their joys and passions. I then make comparisons, and I find a lot is true, and I drop silly things. I really do not like to read a lot. It strains my eyes and in general does not give me much pleasure. I am becoming so indifferent. I would like to be able to look toward the future calmly. I cannot understand how many people, even quite pious people, have such a great fear of death.

I went to St. Louis in February under some kind of a pretext and remained there five weeks. I was quite pleased with the simple way of living and the almost constant sitting at home with Effie and her three young fellows. Then Jette wrote that she was with the Hesses and that Ottilie was sick but was improving. And so in spite of protests I traveled back in snow and frost. It took only a little more than four hours. Tillie was up but very weak. I thought that I would nurse her, but instead I myself contracted fever immediately and got a cramplike cough, which tortured me for over a month. Now, though, we are both ready for spring. But there is no lack of mutual admonitions every day. Winter will not yield here. Severe storms are raging all around us without having done any special damage to us here.

In Seattle they had deep snow recently even on Easter Day. The exhibition in Chicago will soon begin. Nettie, Mrs. Henry, wants to go there. She knows and is very much interested in machines. Otherwise there is no one whom we know well going from here. Hess does not want to go, and his wife says that she is not yet strong enough to enjoy it. The travel costs are minor, a room from six to seven dollars per week. But board and extras will amount to something. Are there any who are eager to travel among you? And who would consider it worth the trouble to travel in a group across the sea and steer this way? One reads so much about this. There is probably a great deal of humbug, but also much that can be seen only once in one's life.

Effie's sister-in-law and her daughter want to rent a room there for six weeks. It is really worth the trouble to be able to see everything in peace.

And what are you planning for the summer? Are you again moving to the Domhof? I hope so. Johanna told me that she found you fresh and eager. Some relief can really come. And if you really could walk again! Or even if the cramps in your legs would only cease, so that you could rest at night!

I think a lot of Therese,[104] and I would like to be at her side. She is not endowed with a strong constitution as Johanna and I are. The sketch of our house in Oelde satisfied me. I could see immediately that the children's room had a deeper corner. Strangely, when my memories are unsure, I brood about it and cannot get it off my mind. Often there is only one word missing in the chain.

Best regards, soon more. I remain always with sincere love, your sister, Jette

Jefferson City
22 July 1893

Dear Auguste:

First of all, many thanks for the new picture. [This photograph was taken in 1893.] You appear there in a new stage. Heinrich is now a portly old gentleman, extremely well

104. Jette's sister Therese had been widowed in 1886.

taken care of, and apparently well satisfied and well kept. His wife seems to have had worries, and looks as if she had been more seriously affected, but is still cheerful. The fine young fellow above them is still so slender. Perhaps he may now be somewhat broader and more mature. That will come! The picture seems so natural to me and always gives me a great deal of pleasure. Should it be destined that Heinrich will yet be able to make use of his limbs, I would like to see all four of you standing side by side. I like to see tall people! And there is my little son-in-law, quite a different type. They are the same size. Ottilie and Hess would like to be remembered to you.

Now we are in the middle of the summer, and since spring was late and brought with it a long period of wet weather, there was an extraordinary amount of work to be done, of which Tillie particularly got her share. I became stronger with moderate exercise outside. We are now both tired of it and threaten to do nothing. But the reward for our effort already shows in the great abundance in the garden. Several gallons of cauliflower were put into vinegar, as well as beans and cucumbers, and masses of raspberries were converted to jelly, even six quart jars for her sister. And then Tillie says I really did myself honor with raspberry vinegar, which is refreshing for the sick and cooling for the healthy. There is little fruit this year. Tillie bought a new horse, and so she can call for her husband daily at noon in the city. And in the evening we can go for a ride.

I don't believe that I have told you anything more of Colonel Price. A year ago when he returned from Paris he took a doctor from New York along to Denver. His second son, John, lives there. Lucy was always with him and kept house for him until finally his suffering was ended. His body was brought here. Lucy went with her oldest brother to Louisiana, where he owns a plantation. Recently John and his wife came from Denver, and Lucy also came to see them and to take care of the significant inheritance. They all say that she sacrificed her youth to her parents, who made so many claims on her. She is rather delicate and not so strong. She plans to go to Berlin again later, to the same institution she liked so much before. However, who knows whether the rich heiress cannot be held here after all? The family is very attached to Hess. Their father saw him daily, and the children seem to have had a great deal of trust in him.

Our Effie recently got a widow's pension approved for herself. Decker contracted a heart problem in the service that troubled him to the end. I had scarcely thought that her claims would be considered. She was very excited about it. There is so much swindling going on with these approvals. It is not so much what she gets, ninety-six dollars a year, but it is something secure. The monetary situation here is very depressing. Many banks have failed, and silver is very low. This will limit visitors to the World Exhibition. Nettie told us many interesting things about it, but even for her it was tiring. One would think that in the fall more people would stream there. We are tired of the continuous reports in the newspaper.

We hear only good things from Seattle. They celebrated the Fourth of July with fireworks at the house. Here the celebration was completely rained out. There was to be a big parade, and over thirty businesses had decorated floats on wagons. I had somebody take me to Jette's, but when they had gotten into position a severe thunderstorm broke loose. The city was full of people from the country.

In a short time we expect Effie and her niece, J. Hildenbrandt. Harry will probably also be coming, but only for one day. The others seem to be tied down. Gustav has recently gotten a better position and must be quite diligent. I thank you for the good wishes on my name day and reciprocate belatedly. I am surprised at your uncle; I am not that strong. To be sure, I have the good will to make myself useful, but then I tire very quickly. And my daughter also does not allow me to do too much, which worries me, for I feel so lonely and I have to rest my eyes and am not permitted to read much.

With love and regards to all of you, your Jette.

P.S. Dear Heinrich, when you write yourself it always pleases me so much. Who knows, perhaps you can still become tolerably well. I hope that you keep on hoping. As always, with love,

your sister Jette

Jefferson City
17 September 1893

Dear Heinrich:

Yesterday your letter and the little picture arrived. The little picture, which really pleases me, is quite good. And it is so similar to those of Louis, who sends snapshots that he has taken himself or that Wilhelm has taken, which always allow us to recognize a few large and small figures, as well as see the landscape with houses and surroundings. If my eyesight were better I would very much like to try to take some pictures too. Photography has become much easier since most things needed can be purchased ready-to-use. But my eyesight is getting weak; it worries me much. Last year I took a stronger pair of glasses, but now I have to strain. I need stronger light and should not read at all in the evening. What should I do then? Usually we are quite silent here. Ottilie finds time for reading only in the evening, and we live too far removed for me to make evening visits. Even during the day she does not let me go, since afterward I do not feel so well.

We had to live through another grim summer. In the spring there was a great deal of rain, which brought such lush vegetation that we had a great deal of trouble keeping our property in check. The workman, Tillie, and I each did on our own part the best we could until we were completely disgusted. And then a drought set in, and the normal heat started. During the last four days we had 28 to 29 degrees Reaumur [98 degrees Fahrenheit] and a disgusting wind, like the sirocco from the desert. This burned everything. The grass is crisp, and there are cracks in the soil. A passing thunderstorm brought some relief elsewhere, but with a change of the wind it only brought a significant drop in temperature here. In the morning it was 10 degrees R. Well, this is how it is in Missouri.

Hess's sister from Toledo, Ohio, came with her little daughter to visit us, stayed for about three weeks, and then went on to the World Exhibition in Chicago, accompanied by my daughters. Ottilie had invited her sister. They were completely satisfied with it but were tired, particularly Effie, who has never had the opportunity to get out. But she also proved to have more endurance than Tillie. The visit here was not so pleasant. Brother and sister were too great a contrast. While Carl says too little, Mrs. Hassenzahl says too much. This constant chatting made Tillie quite nervous. I was pleased, however, that she at least remained somewhat polite toward the visitor. Many people are going to Chicago, and the variety and size of the products of nature, of art, and of science, which have been brought from all parts of the world, are supposed to surpass all similar exhibitions ever held. The Missourians are not satisfied with their part. The state approved the third largest sum for the construction of a building, but something did not go right. The state of Washington distinguished itself by enormously high, slender trees and by the way in which the arrangement attracted attention. I almost felt the desire to go there too. The prices have been very moderate. I fear, however, that it surpasses my strength, and to ride around in a wheelchair is not appealing. Several old acquaintances fainted and had to go to the hospital.

Recently I had to live through some very difficult times. My Wilhelm wrote that he was suffering want with the hard times and unemployment. I immediately wrote back to both sons. Because of my fortune, accumulated from the sale of the house, which I distributed among my five heirs (who, however, left it with me, wanting to let it grow here, except for Wilhelm, whose share is encumbered with Louis's), and through a sum from the sale of the Stromberg property, we hoped that Wilhelm would have a nest egg if he could not ever achieve anything else. I transferred it to Louis and advised him to use his discretion and let the capital grow if possible if he could not invest it in Wilhelm's favor. Well, now I live so far away, and the boy who played many a prank on me but is really basically so good is in need. For three weeks I had no news, and now Louis writes that he wants to intercede again. I should be calm about it, but it is indeed a hopeless situation. I was already making plans to travel there, but at age eighty, alone and incapable of accomplishing anything. — Is it a consolation that one can see other similar cases? Certainly not. One has to experience this oneself. I write all of this to you because it relieves me since I know that you sympathize with me, but I really would not like the others to know about it—just as they do not know here.

I am on the verge of going to Effie's to spend a few months with her. Her sons were here recently one after the other, and they urgently requested it. Since, however, they intend to change their residence, it is better to postpone my trip. And we are nearly finished with canning for the winter. The garden furnished everything possible. There is very little fruit. That is, there were enough apples and peaches. In the cellar we have sixty-one quart jars filled with them. Tillie also canned cauliflower, beans, pickled cucumbers, and little onions in glass. We shall not starve. In the stable there is enough hay, oats, corn, and wheat for horse, cows, and chickens. It is a comfortable household. The housewife takes great care of everything and is loved for that. She is truly getting to resemble me more and more. I have been demoted to the flowers; it affords me great pleasure to compete with some friends.

During the summer we had discomforts at times, such as malaria, fever, rheumatism. I am always afraid that Tillie will overexert herself. She really would not have to; she accomplishes more than her girl. Hess is enthusiastic about his work. For such a small city, so much is done for water and light. There is also a great deal of building going on.

Nitchy has been suffering for several years with rheumatism, usually in his legs. He took a recommended medicine, which however was so strong that he became quite ill, although he was free of pain. The inner organs have been affected. He can eat almost nothing and has to keep on a very careful diet. We shall hope that he will gradually improve. The family must try to get by. Jette is also often sickly. She is entirely too lenient with her girls, who make more claims on her than would be necessary. Since it makes me angry I go there less frequently in order not to know about it.

When I read Thomas à Kempis I wonder at the many passions and temptations of which he speaks. After all, those should be lost in old age. To be sure, a secluded life is wholesome, and when I go out I am always uncomfortable afterward. The chapter on love pleases me exceedingly, as well as St. Paul's epistle on the subject. The Geisbergs of the Cappenberg line are all gone since Toni's death.[105] We people from Oelde must be stronger. A young girl came back from Europe from the province of Posen or Pomerania and reported that there was a Lieutenant Geisberg on the steamer. I wonder whether that is the son of our cousin Franz? Probably. And on the record player a piece of music by a Professor Geisberg has been playing.[106] Heinrich went to hear it. I hope to be able to hear from you soon. I hope that it will be something good.

With love as always, your sister Jette

Jefferson City, Mo.
25 November 1893

Dear Heinrich:

It has been almost four weeks now since I celebrated my birthday, showered with attention. For three days I have been back here again where, as the youngest one explained, my home is. And so I am sitting again in my own room, with everything so clean and orderly. My own bed, my own desk, many memories that have been guarded, my books, and a few dear pictures. I am not insensitive to all this, but for the time being I am still suffering from homesickness. I was so very much at home with Effie. I fear that in the beginning they will miss me there. It was always a bit turbulent. Effie got the flu (it was mild, however), but in the house below it was worse—the children got scarlet fever in addition. When I left, there was a warning notice on the door to keep strangers away.

A few weeks ago I was at the eye doctor's. He explained that my eyes were suffering, caused by something, and that he could not heal them, but that by treating them they probably would become somewhat strengthened. Thus I was discharged, to report back three months later. I must say that I still cannot get used to this. I am only permitted to read and write a little, but especially not in the evening. Also I am not allowed to do needlework. I am primarily to avoid things that would strain the eyes.

Many thanks for your congratulations on my birthday. You took the eightieth so seriously that I myself did too, and even though I did not get to go to church, I still allowed for some serious meditation, a conclusion of times past, which lie behind me with their joy and sorrow and lead perhaps, of late, a short distance downhill to the end of my earthly career. Well, that is all right, if only I could tear myself gradually, peaceably, and quietly away. However, there is still much that pleases me greatly and much that worries me. After all, I need not be indifferent to the fate of my fellow men, my beloved ones. Tell Auguste and your children how much I was pleased to get a greeting from all of them. Later I shall write more. Has your condition improved? The recent indications did not promise anything good. You must have been home for a long time now and more comfortable? Farewell, my dear faithful brother. If

---

105. Antonie Petri died 8 August 1893.

106. Leo Geisberg, professor of music in Munich, was the son of Carl Geisberg, who had emigrated to Missouri and then lived in Milwaukee before returning to Germany.

only I could do something good for you to raise your spirits, to make it easier for you. From the bottom of my heart,

your sister Jette

Jefferson City, Mo.
10 June 1894

Dear Heinrich:

I am thinking about your letter of February. I have written you an answer. The new letter from Auguste does not bear one syllable or a greeting from you. However, I see that you are back at the *Domhof* again. You still go out for rides, and at night you always have a nurse, and you have very crooked legs. I am after all much better off, and I should console myself with that, and yet I cannot be resigned that my eyesight is so weak that I am permitted to read so little. I have to let everything be done for me. However, every morning I look gratefully to the trees outside, I look at the tapestry and the pictures to see whether they are clear, and then I have my meditation for the day, as our father did, and then if possible I go outside.

At the request of the eye doctor I was recently in St. Louis again, the third time. He now gives no hope for special improvement. (And, after all, how should that be, at my age?) However, I again got some drops, and I am to report back to him later. The worse thing is that I lack something to do. Here in the house it is very quiet. Ottilie only rarely allows me to assist her in the household. In the evening there is some reading for recreation or the two of us talk. When Carl is there, he listens quietly or he speaks in English with his wife. The hard times have brought him losses, and so he cannot control his moods. But we do have a new house companion. Carl asked Ernst Decker whether he wanted to enter the electrical profession. The latter has prepared himself for this for over a year; now he is taking it up anew, and for the time being getting practical experience. Ottilie and I told him how difficult it is. He accepted it with a firm determination and is getting a good salary. He lives here but he has to be at work all night long. In the morning at four o'clock he comes home and steps into my room: "Good morning" (a kiss). "How did it go?" "Good." "Are you tired?" "Yes, now I'll go to sleep."

At noon or later, he is refreshed again. In the beginning the whole matter bothered me as much as if I too were working. And I could not lie still, and as a result of this I was worn out. But now it is already better. Strange, his mother is satisfied that he has prospects. Because of the knowledge he brought along and the present arrangement, he has better prospects for the future. And then having the supervision of his uncle is not to be slighted. But his young happy life is past; he has become very serious. We are expecting his mother very soon to spend the summer here. Heinrich Geisberg maintains it is the best appointed factory that exists in this field, the Light, Heat, and Power Company. If only the city would be bigger. But the Capitol, the courts, and the penitentiary need much.

You are worried about Max. But just imagine what kind of support your children have! First in you, and then in a circle of friends, in good schools and recreation, while Effie has had to struggle since the death of her husband with worries, above all about feeding the family, and has had to experience deprivations of all kinds. She could not prevent her boys from feeling that deprivation, and later they avoided the invitations of relatives and friends whenever possible because they could not appear as their friends did. Harry particularly is very withdrawn, and with him no invitation and no meeting him halfway helps. Only music fascinates him, and under the direction of an excellent violin player he has gotten himself pretty far and likes to give us recitals, which make Mama nervous although she does not like to admit it. But he has a voice! The finest, the loveliest tenor, only not strong. He suffers chest pains. For years he was the greatest support of his mother, but because of the fire at the store he lost his investment and is now very depressed. At present he is traveling for the firm, which helps his health.

I wonder if what I am telling you here is not perhaps for my own recreation? (As you have said also—it may be.) The boys are very close to me, and it is fortunate that they can turn to their uncle and can always ask for advice from him. Now Carl says he wants to make a real man out of Ernst if grandmother and his wife would not spoil him so much. It is funny! And yet he himself is so worried that he is not shortchanged.

The bad times continue. Great numbers of unemployed (mostly tramps) move about and force the railroads to carry them. The military should really interfere. No groups have yet passed here. Daily, however, hungry people pass, and they always receive something here. You do not know such things. In all bigger cities here, organizations have been created to give the fathers of families work and bread.

Jette Nitchy, a widow since March, moved with her two daughters and little son to her son-in-law, Dr. Porth.[107] We consider this to be very good since her health has already suffered for some time. Her husband's constant sickness is to be blamed for her situation, as far as inheritance is concerned. However, Nitchy had gone to the office until a few days before his death. Two life insurances now assure her an income if she moves back home in the fall or winter. Heinrich, her brother, is also a big support. We like the Geisberg house much better in recent times. The wife, although always an excitable person, has already proven to be a magnificent mother. The three children are quite nice.[108] The oldest, almost grown now, is very sweet and natural. The son Charles (Carl) has been my travel companion twice already and also a companion on trips to the eye doctor. His eyes are getting to be better. The little one, a pretty child whose picture we have sent you already, is a chatterbox with a clever head. All three of them know how to chat. It is strange, the father is so quiet! Yesterday he came by car and took Jette and me for a ride for a few hours. It was so refreshing.

I hope that the summer will also bring you good days. Do let me know soon. And hold dear as always your sister, Jette

An appendix to the letter of 10 June 1894

Dear Auguste:

It's true I have waited for a letter. I too did not know anything special to report. Ottilie is still not strong and complains that she is always deadly tired. However, she does not let this

107. Henriette Nitchy's children were Ida, Hilda, and Franz Friedrich. Her husband, Henry C. Nitchy, had died 5 May 1894. Dr. Joseph P. Porth (1865–1923) was born in Osage County, Missouri. He graduated from St. Louis Medical School in 1887 and took postgraduate courses in Berlin and Greifswald, Germany, as well as in Vienna and Paris. Upon his return in 1888 he began to practice medicine in Jefferson City. In 1890 he married Effie Henriette Nitchy.

108. The three Geisberg children were Gertrude (born 1876), Charles (1881), and Claudia (1889). Another child, Ada, born in 1878, died in 1879.

interfere. It is with her, however, as with you—her courage is lacking. I have to say that it worries me very much when you are depressed. This is so unnatural. Perhaps it is also not so bad as it seems if one reads about it, since after all you have to go out frequently.

Ottilie is too lonesome here. She admits it herself. Gradually she is getting to be just like her husband. They lead the lives of real hermits. To be sure, besides us two people she has two cows and a calf, approximately one hundred fifty chickens, eight cats, and a flock of singing birds in addition to three canaries. And then the place is so beautiful. A big catalpa tree is in full blossom. There are bushes, flowers, and vegetables, which are arranged between fresh stretches of grass. Only there is no fruit this year except some berries. Should this not be sufficient, and should not one be able to live without worries?

My dear sisters distinguish themselves again through their silence, so that I have to urgently request that news not be kept from me, particularly about the family. I don't know at all where Johanna is. A little Bäumker writes that Grandmother will come.[109]

You seem to think that the first signs of old age are past checking in with me. Didn't you know that my hearing makes it impossible for me to participate in a normal conversation? So there I sit, and I catch a few individual words and sentences and then I probably ask a question, but usually I am silent until Ottilie gives me some information afterward. They often speak louder for me, and Carl then shouts so much that it frightens me. To be blind, however, is worse. Now it is still tolerable. I distinguish the colors, but frequently I pull flowers instead of the weeds, and I cannot distinguish anything among the many beautiful pictures. But it could be much worse.

In a few weeks Effie will come, and in general there will be more change. I shall then try to write an interesting letter if I can hit upon the right thing. I also ask for the same!

Greetings to your young people, as always your Jette

Jefferson City, Mo.
1894

Dear Auguste:

Although I was of the definite opinion that I had expressed my sincere thanks for your courtesy in sending me your and all the others' congratulations in a letter to you and Heinrich at the end of November, I am now becoming doubtful whether I was not thinking of writing a special letter and then did not follow through. I note every day that I have not yet received any kind of a sign of life from Europe in the New Year. I therefore begin to be concerned—what might have happened? Besides, I am worried about my sons since Wilhelm writes that Louis had a chest fever and got up too early and now has suffered a setback. Wilhelm took a fall and has been incapacitated for three weeks. I have not received an answer from a letter I wrote to Emily a full week ago. And now I endeavor mightily to remain calm, and I tell myself that I can resign myself to the will of God in anything that might befall me, but that is hardly true.

Since I returned from St. Louis I have been using the eye doctor's prescription diligently, on the outside as well as the inside. To be sure I do not see any improvement. My vision

109. The reference here is most likely to Jette's sister Therese von Hatzfeld.

seems to be weakening. Every day I see with happiness the smallest branches of the trees, the needles of the cedars, and more without glasses. If, however, I want to read or I want to make a few stitches, then this won't do, even with strong glasses and bright light. I am not supposed to. And so there I sit, and I arrange and fold rough things, I read some things with large print, and then I listen and shake my head, and I live from the past. What a rich life lies behind me. That way I dwell almost more in the home country than here. How good we all were! I wonder whether I really deserved that?

Strangely enough, winter will not come here at all. Over in your country and in the west here it is probably very cold. We still have not seen any snow, but a few times there has been a light frost. And now we think every day that bad weather will come and we prepare ourselves, and again and again the wind blows away the cover from my flowers, and I arrange it anew. I mainly worry about the fine roses I left in the bed. Ottilie's garden has been spaded up. She specializes in trees, planted fruit trees, grafted, pruned. Her husband is still building his tornado cellar; he always calls that room "his room." He wants to move his writing desk, his books, and a sofa there later. For the time being he is lucky to have dry weather so that the new German workman who scraped off the old parts can now put up a new ceiling to his heart's content. The whole thing could have furnished a new modern house. But his wife agrees with his ideas in order to keep him in a good mood. I, however, say quietly, "If he had only kept his good money in his wallet!" That is how people act who do not have to worry for their children.

We often wondered if any one we knew would make a trip to Chicago. So many went from here and from all the other states. We have heard our fill of tales, and all brought beautiful memories back. Even Emma Geisberg[110] told me with great humor how all the people were so lively and were so ready to enjoy everything. Effie and her two sons were also sent off.

In a few weeks I will have to go to the doctor again although I consider it superfluous at my age. However, I shall continue to go although there is after all no operation for it.

Many regards to Heinrich, the children, and you. I hope you don't take my forgetfulness amiss since I know that you particularly endeavor to please me. I ask you now to send me a happy letter as soon as possible. Otherwise I shall write again.

From the bottom of my heart, as always, your Jette.

P.S. Thanks also for the little pictures.

Jette to Max Geisberg

Jefferson City, Mo.
24 July 1894

Dear Max:

You belong among the number of my dear nephews who joined in remembering me on the occasion of my eightieth birthday, and so you must not be surprised if I present you with a picture of myself and of your two cousins, my daughters. I hope that it will please you.

I often hear through your parents that you are growing in every respect. In a few years you

110. Jette is probably referring here to Amelie Guyot Geisberg, the wife of her nephew Heinrich Christoph Geisberg.

will have established a stable course. I follow everything that occurs with great interest when your mother reports it.

Do keep me in your memory and be assured of my affection. With love, your aunt Jette.

Jefferson City
1 September 1894

Dear Heinrich:

I received your letter of August, and at this time I shall reply to your remark concerning the "American Protection Association."[111] To be sure, a secret alliance against foreigners, and particularly the Catholics, exists here. I read about that in the *Forum*,[112] an excellent journal by an absolutely neutral author who responded to the appeal of Catholic priests. He says that the above-mentioned association developed first in Clinton, Iowa, and is supposed to have a membership of two million members, and it could become serious, although right-thinking Protestants are unanimously against it. Then he mentions various deplorable situations in the Catholic Church that the priests should remedy or remove, because otherwise he fears that a serious conflict could take place. The big city of Chicago is full of anarchists and rubbish of all sorts. As an example he cited that three-fourths or more of municipal employees are Catholics, whose power, which is constantly increasing at the polls, is being abused. It is entirely different in St. Louis. There also are many churches and monasteries and just as many bigoted bums. But there is another element there, the descendants of Frenchmen, of Germans, and naturally also of Irish and others, old families who are favorably inclined toward the Catholics and demand, by reason of their position and their fortunes, a respectable position for the entire church.

As to the big railroad strike, this is an unforeseeable misfortune for the entire country. It will last a long time, if ever it is worked out. And then we do not have any such prompt law enforcement as you have. They beat around the bush for a long time until they are tired, and then the whole thing dissolves into nothingness.

In general to this day the majority of immigrants have not left their home without some stain, and it is not amazing that we, the older immigrants, feel the same as the Americans and consider new immigrants with some distrust. It is also a great misfortune that so many families who do not at all belong there remain hung up in the cities instead of pursuing their former professions as farmers. And here they could easily obtain property in a rich, wholesome area. In this section of the country many settlements developed that are doing very well. Most of them are Catholic, but there are also others; it depends. And then soon a church is built. Two daughters of my brother-in-law married well. They moved away from Westphalia. The older, Mrs. Adrian,[113] now a widow, has become very wealthy; she lives near

111. The American Protection Association was founded at Clinton, Iowa, in 1887 by Henry F. Bowers for the purpose of reviving the Know-Nothing party's campaign against what was perceived as the increasing power of Roman Catholicism in schools and other public institutions. A secret organization, it grew slowly in the Middle West until the Panic of 1893 caused native Americans to fear economic rivalry from immigrants and their American-born children. By 1896 the organization claimed to have over two-and-a-half million members.

112. *The Forum*, a monthly journal established in Philadelphia in March 1886, printed an article by Frederick R. Coudert, "The American Protective Association," 17 (July 1894): 513–23.

113. Elisabeth Bernadine Catherine, the oldest daughter of Gerhard Hermann Bruns and his wife Anna Maria Lückenhoff, was born at Westphalia 24 April 1842. On 6 April 1864 she married Herman Adrian. The couple moved to a farm near Martinsburg, where she died 8 January 1903.

Martinsburg and sends her daughters to the convent for their education. A son is now in the seminary. The other, Mrs. Hageböck, lives upriver on this side, near Sedalia.[114] Getting out of Westphalia is a bit more difficult because of the hilly area.

This summer we had a great drought, so corn and hay crops failed. And now for the past two weeks we have been enveloped in smoke. Now news reaches us that in the north there were large forest fires that destroyed entire areas and killed many people. Yesterday we finally got some rain; however, it is too late since we usually have to fear some frost in October.

And how is the summer weather treating you? You are probably ready to move back into the old residence, and then you will be condemned to stay in your room. I would so much like to visit you, and Auguste would read to me. It seems that I have to give up using my eyes for reading. It makes me cross about many things. Yet again I am so grateful that I can still see so much. And in addition it is fitting that at my age I should have rest, which I unfortunately do not have. In the end it would be better if some misfortune befell me so that I would have to practice patience. As God wills it!

More to Auguste. As always in faithful love, your sister Jette

Jefferson City
8 September 1894

Dear Auguste:

The evil deed will now be balanced. I sent a little picture to all the nephews and nieces. Since recently both a letter from Seattle and one from St. Louis got lost, I would like to hear from you at your convenience if the letters arrived. We have a new postmaster and new personnel.

Jette Nitchy's third daughter was married to a Mr. Culkin.[115] Except for us and the Geisbergs, a niece of Nitchy's, and two strangers, no one else was there. Jette herself was still in deep mourning. A few hours after the wedding the couple left for St. Louis, and then embarked on a long trip to the north and east. They had been engaged for three years. He distinguished himself by frequent gifts of flowers from the south, but is otherwise a very respectable, likable businessman. So we hope that Ida drew a good lot. Through a double insurance Jette is now better off than we had thought earlier. Her deceased son Walter[116] left his mother twenty-five hundred dollars. Jette has settled all back bills and lives for the time being with her son-in-law, Dr. Porth, in order to strengthen her health. The youngest son, thirteen years old, promises to become a capable man. He learns well, will probably be as tall as your Max, and is handsome and friendly. Since he is here with his brother-in-law, he comes out frequently. He is called Franz Friedrich.

Ottilie's brood of one hundred sixty young chickens has already been decreased a lot. First many of them were fried, although neither Hess nor I like to eat them. And now even Tillie and Ernst are hesitating. There were so many roosters among them that Hess gave her permission to sell some of them, only he did not want to know about it. Several also disap-

114. Maria Catherine Wilhelmina, born 2 May 1856 at Westphalia, married Bernard Hageboeck 2 September 1879 and died at Montrose in Henry County, Missouri, 14 March 1941.
115. Ida Jennie Nitchy (1873–1959) married Anthony F. Culkin (1862–1935).
116. Walter Henry Nitchy, born 25 April 1870, died 19 June 1892.

peared, which annoys us. But the first brood is already beginning to lay the dearest little eggs, and the young hens are sitting so importantly on their nests, just like the old ones. Now the older ones will have to be gotten rid of. Recently we finally had some rain. Everything was dry, the grass, the garden, the flowers. For many things it is too late, and I now begin to plant the flowers for the winter, which we keep under glass to protect. I have planted endive and horseradish in the flower beds because I was so annoyed. Ottilie also set out fifty celery plants rather late, which will have to be bleached later. She is very careful in the garden, and I say quietly, "This she has learned from me."

Effie also has a hobby of working in the garden and with flowers. Last week they moved to a small apartment where she has a little garden. Harry has accepted a better position, which will let him overcome his setback. Gustav is waiting for clients. The bad times brought a subdued mood. It is rather difficult to become known when there are a few hundred colleagues. A friend just married in spite of that, and now they are bad off. Young Hildenbrandt[117] became sick in Heidelberg and Stuttgart, and then he went to Rome and Venice and took care of an aunt's estate, and then returned. Now finally fifteen thousand dollars has arrived. Over there it is quite difficult and ceremonious. He was there recently.

The young people are becoming important politicians who want to represent the Republican party in a decent way, which indeed was needed. Gustav did not want to leave his ward when they moved.

The exhibition in Chicago will not be surpassed easily. You should not have passed up the opportunity to come, at least somebody should have come. Nature and location cannot easily be surpassed. If only I could distinguish the pictures and sketches well! That would be a quiet pleasure!

Please write soon to your loving Jette.

St. Louis
4 January 1895

Dear Heinrich:

So now we have entered the new year, and in spite of my resolution to send you greetings before that time, it was not done. You will have got together for Christmas and New Year's, and in spirit I was with you!

In person I have been here with Effie for over a month and am quite satisfied with the change. Mother and sons are very considerate and are constantly thinking of entertaining me since the loss of my sight takes away all my pastimes. Usually I knit with closed eyes, I occupy myself in the house, and that is all. People read to me, they play for me. In the evening they play cards. Recently I contracted a cold, had rheumatism, and was quite impatient with that. I think less of your long-lasting suffering than of my Wilhelm. You have a wife, children, little nuns, who surround you, who console you and seek to give you relief. He, however, was struggling for months by himself, was starving, and was only barely supported by Louis until he was confined to a hospital for two months and recuperated. It is not astonishing that I would have liked to venture on a trip. Now he writes that he is employed on a range and

117. Ernest Hildenbrandt (1863–1916) was the surviving son of Theodor Hildenbrandt and his wife, the former Lena Decker of St. Louis.

hopes for better times and hopes that he can visit me in another year. I thank God for the consoling news. Louis also complains very much concerning too much work and the bad times. He blames everything on the Democrats. But in spite of the changeover, there is no immediate change. Here there is also a great deal of need. Effie moved into a smaller, homey apartment. The oldest one is contemplating marriage and brought the chosen one to Jefferson City at the suggestion of his uncle. She is a gentle, dear girl, but without means. She has a house, which is rented out well, but this does not count with us. Harry must be able to support himself. I preach patience, just as we have practiced it too. But we old people are planning ahead. What pleases him most is the fact that she is an ardent Catholic.[118]

People think that the tariff bill will have good consequences. In Jefferson the legislature has convened. The state has become very Republican. The old regime is still ruling in the city, but they are very subdued.

God protect you and bless you with relief and many good things that are unforeseen for the New Year. For myself, I wish that I may have patience and humility for that which may befall me. All here send their greetings with those of your sister Jette.

Jefferson City, Mo.
12 February 1895

Dear Auguste:

It was with regret that I heard that you were ill. I know several cases like yours. Here, we are tolerably well. Sometimes I am often very short of breath, which amazes me and does not seem to me to be fitting since I always used to move quickly. I returned from St. Louis somewhat depressed because there seemed to be no hope for any improvement in my vision. I am eagerly endeavoring to make the best of it. But I also have letters and other things read to me. I knit with closed eyes, one pair of socks after the other, and I see the figures in the tapestry, on furniture, and on the carpets. I am so happy that it is not getting worse.

For two weeks now we have had a deep cover of snow and severe cold. To be sure we can stand it well, but the newspaper reports give you a bad feeling. The river is said to have two feet of thick ice. From Seattle they complain about much rain. Wilhelm is better and is employed. He wants to visit me in about a year. This is a great consolation to me although it may be doubtful.

I wonder how you can stand the eternal sitting at home? Heinrich, with his infinite patience, is happy if his condition is tolerable. You probably have gotten very much accustomed to that. And then you have a special attraction yourself so that dear visitors come who can shorten the time and make you happy. We are missing this more. Ottilie did not dare go to town. Even her husband went in the morning with a fur cap and earmuffs and did not return home until evening, which was very much against his custom and his inclination. Ernst is standing it well, and he has received the good news that soon he will work during the daytime. Electricity will be used more and more in various businesses and concerns.

On Wednesday, the 13th, Jette Nitchy came to visit us in the evening, against her usual custom and without her husband to call for her. And I shouted after her, "Be careful!" But approximately two hundred feet down she did fall and could not get up, and in spite of her

118. Harry Decker married Veronica (Vera) Byrne on 22 June 1895.

calls for help she lay for half an hour in the snow until a man came down the street. They brought her home on a little hand sled with difficulty. The doctor wanted to straighten out her joint, but she would not have it. In the morning after an examination it was found that her hipbone was broken near the joint. It upset me terribly. She has the best of care but will probably have to lie in bed for several months. Are you now completely healed of the boil? I wonder how something like that can develop!

Ottilie reads to me in the evening. In her club they are discussing Russia, and we have already started several things at home relating to that. We would like to be clear where your brother lives, the province, the city, the climate.[119] You did once write that the daughter looked so southern; well, perhaps she resembles her father, certainly however the grandfather, who was dark and such an imposing man. Please tell us more about the family.[120] Was he back for a visit? Hardly!

Now when after so many long years I must dream so much, it comes back to me how your father was so good, at first to my mother and then to me. How he looked after the young country violet in Münster, which pleased Aunt Therese very much. In the club, in society, at the castle, always.

The end of the preceding letter is missing. On the day the following letter was begun, Heinrich Geisberg died in Münster.

Jefferson City, Mo.
914 West Main Street
14 May 1895

Dear Heinrich:

I was pleased by your letter. Since that time we have become accustomed to spring, which this time has advanced slowly, as with you, without any mischievous attacks. A great abundance of blossoms surrounds us and seem to forebode much good. In the garden we dared do all kinds of additional things, and they are doing well. Harry was here again on his big tour. He threatens that he will marry during the summer. This gives us some disquieting thoughts. Mother will then be alone with Gustav, who is not yet capable of making his own way. Ernst regularly sends his contribution. He will be promoted to day work beginning 1 May. He is already breaking in his successor. However, because of that there is more to be done, since the governor has called the legislators back for a special session. The residents seem to support the construction of the bridge; in general the city is lively and active in spite of the threats that the Capitol might be moved. Some rich people bought approximately fifteen thousand acres around Sedalia and now want to let the entire state dance to their tune. Infamous! St. Louis also protests against that. Naturally the swindlers swarm over the land from all sides in order to influence people. The election will be held in the fall of 1896.

My eyes seem to remain at a certain point. Every day I think about that. I cannot read and cannot do any needlework, but I do see the objects and colors, to be sure somewhat indistinctly, but I can see. Outside I have to substitute with touch. It just cannot be helped. I am so happy that you with your great many sorrows can see so well and that you have a wife and

---

119. Max Boner lived with his family in Rostow on the Don River in southern Russia near the Sea of Azov.
120. Emma Boner was the daughter of Sabin Vidulitsch from Trieste and his Italian wife, Theresia Rocco.

children. I often think I cannot bear it. Ottilie reads to me at times. They are such quiet people. It often is difficult for me to keep my gay composure, but then even the young people say Grandmother is frivolous, and this after all means only that I always come home with an empty purse, which pleases them and me no end.

The 22nd

Our little city indeed managed to muster one hundred thousand dollars worth of shares to make the construction of the bridge possible. Today is the celebration of the first groundbreaking at the site selected for the construction.[121] The salutes are already thundering from the Capitol, and railroads are screeching from both sides of the river, and several steamers are whistling. Bright, warm spring weather invites participation. At two o'clock the procession will move from the Capitol and will go up six blocks to the bluff at the river. Mrs. Effie Porth invited us to come to her balcony. My dear niece seems to want to raise her head again after three months of painful confinement. It is probably no great pleasure. She has become very weak.

Since the shares for the construction of the bridge have been set at only ten dollars, rich and poor on both sides of the river have participated. The legislators are still here and are very much in conflict with each other and the governor. This time the Republicans in the state—and therefore also here—have won by a great majority. I wonder whether that will do any good? The young fellows participate eagerly and seek to prevent special tricks so as to strengthen the party. Well, I have gossiped about all kinds of things. I wonder whether this interests you?

With Auguste I am still at the masked ball; I shall look for news to be able to tell her something so that she will kindly answer me.

Sincerest greetings from Ottilie and from me and all the others. In old love, your sister Jette.

St. Louis
6 June 1895

Dear, dear Auguste:

So, suddenly the inescapable has happened, and you stand alone. In spite of the many troubles your dear husband brought you, he was also a support to you. I have to put myself in your position; you do not at all know what is to be done and are completely lost. In the beginning the news of his death shook me very much.

Now I am calm, and I do not begrudge him relief from his misery and eternal rest—or you the freedom and the end to the many troubles and worries you had for him for so many years, and during which you relieved his pain so very much. I have to tell you that I shall always be grateful to you for this. You have borne much and have suffered along with him, you have cheered him up by giving him a change, have invented things, have tried things that always bore the hope for improvement. Is it not a great comfort to you now that you have tried everything for him?

121. As late as 12 April 1895, according to the *Jefferson City Daily Tribune*, there was considerable doubt that the residents of Cole and Callaway counties could raise the one hundred thousand dollars required to begin work on the bridge. However, by 5 May over ninety thousand dollars of the stock had been subscribed, and on 23 May a six-column front page article in the *Tribune* announced the success of the "movement which gave us the bridge."

Other women of your age could have enjoyed life in many ways. It was your fate to endure your days with a sick person. It was doubly difficult with your happy nature. But the fact that you have made him so happy will always be a great satisfaction to you. This thought will remain with you for the rest of your life. Now, in the first pain of the new loss, and later it will strengthen you and steel you for everything or anything that could happen.

If only I could hope that you can live without great financial worries for your children! Do not let me remain entirely in ignorance. I have not heard anything from our sisters, and I am longing for news. You have done me an infinite favor by reporting immediately and in detail. I also believe with you that it was the wish of my dear deceased brother that you write to me immediately. We always loved each other so very, very much. I long very much to follow him, and I have to hold myself together to show an interest in the present.

Ottilie will write to you. I have been with Effie for some time. The letters were forwarded to me. Effie asked me to tell you that she feels the most sincere sympathy.

Regards to Marie and Max. You will hold together firmly.

God console you and protect you! In sincere faith and love,

Jette

A fragment of an undated letter, from late May or June 1896

On the 27th a tornado passed over the city of St. Louis,[122] causing terrible desolation, particularly in the southern part. In the house where Effie lives, the second and third floors collapsed. She lived below and did not suffer any damage. This is almost all we know, but they found shelter with Aunt Lena. All illumination, all streetcars stopped. What a terrible night for the people who were under the debris. Nearly two hundred bodies have been found, and all the hospitals are full of injured people, many of whom are unconscious and probably will die. Three days afterward there was good weather, and much could be organized and done. Other cities wanted to help; however, St. Louis will help itself. Help is offered and is arranged in the most liberal way. Thousands work for the poor. The police are guarding the streets. Commissaries have been set up where supplies of foods will be distributed. Big businesses, factories, and the rich will pay thousands of dollars to help. Electrical light is already restored from the demolished powerhouse, the streetcars are running again, and traffic is beginning to flow. But it will take a long time. The loss is estimated to exceed fifty million dollars.

On 8 December 1896 Ottilie Hess wrote the family Christmas letter to Auguste Geisberg: "Mother is still occupied with her flowers every day. I believe that we will have about a hundred plants in pots. But she gets quite dirty with transplanting, watering, and other jobs that go with her hobby. Last week the girl was beating the carpets and then Mother's gardening dress. Effie maintained that there was more dirt coming from the dress than from the carpets. But it is a true blessing that she can still keep busy. And even if you cannot read the letters she writes, it nevertheless gives her a great deal of pleasure to write them."

---

122. A tornado struck the south side of St. Louis on 27 May 1896, causing extensive damage and loss of life.

Jefferson City
10 June 1897

Dear Auguste:

Today is a work day. Therefore I have everyday activities, beginning with the morning prayer, a Lord's Prayer, and the Ave Maria. Then the electrical bell rings below. Ernst answers his uncle the same way. It is six o'clock. Getting up is getting somewhat difficult for him, which you probably know from Max. After breakfast I lay the beds out for airing and open the doors and windows. Effie prepares Ernst's room next door, and takes fresh water to him, etc.

We are through with washing and ironing. The garden beds have been cleaned. We are waiting for rain. In the meantime cherries are being picked, of which we have plenty. Ottilie is filling quart jars.

My vase is filled with the most beautiful roses, a smaller one with carnations and heliotrope. I frequently put my nose into them with pleasure. Then I put my hands in my lap and think. Involuntarily the melody of a hymn or a worldly song comes to mind and I drum the beat with my hands or feet.

This is enough of everyday life.

Nettie had to take over a stretch of land of one thousand acres in lieu of a debt. It is located below St. Louis. She sent Gustav there to look at it. It is said to contain lead. She is being advised not to sell it yet.

The end of the letter is missing.

Jefferson City
27 February 1898

Dear Auguste:

Finally your letter arrived. [The letter continues in Ottilie's handwriting.] You see that I must answer indirectly, but let us not grieve. For the past two weeks I have been back in Jefferson and they are all tolerably well. Spring is coming unexpectedly to us, if it does not mischievously bring us snow and ice later.

The bridge over the Missouri River is almost completed, and we think that we will have more lively traffic, although rich capitalists want to deprive us of the investment through money and intrigues. In November the people of Missouri will vote concerning this. It would be a severe setback for the city.

We hear with joy how Max is getting on, that besides his serious study he does not neglect the arts.[123] I surely would have thought that Schilking would have given him something as a present, but there probably wasn't very much there. I wonder how much the picture of Stromberg would cost without a frame? If it doesn't cost too much, Ottilie would like to buy it. Because of the construction of the bridge and other expenses, our means are somewhat limited.

123. Max Geisberg, while a fourth-semester student at the "Royal Academy," was commissioned to be in charge of archaeological diggings in Münster. On 5 January 1898 he began the excavations at the *Kreuztor*, a medieval city gate that had been part of the fortifications erected in the twelfth century but destroyed in 1770. By the end of the first day of digging his team had discovered a system of brick walls and raised two sculptures of angels. This promising undertaking later produced a number of art objects, some of which had been part of the portal of the *Überwasser* church and are housed in the *Westfälische Landesmuseum*. Max Geisberg describes his findings in his autobiography, *Meine Jugend im alten Münster,* ed. Paul Pieper (Münster: Aschendorff, 1984), pp. 155–63.

In the future you will always have to tell us more about your children. I follow their continuing development with pride. Since we are now already at the end of the month, you will hardly be able to write before the beginning of April, but I hope that later correspondence can be regulated better. I shall answer immediately. I trust that you will have left the flu behind without any further consequences. Here difficulties frequently arise because of an illness that follows it.

With best greetings and wishes for you, and with love,

Your Jette

Epilogue ·

From Ottilie Hess to Auguste Geisberg

> Jefferson City
> 8 November 1899
>
> Dear Aunt:
>   A quarter before seven
> o'clock in the evening our
> dear mother closed her eyes
> forever.
>   Your Ottilie

Index

About the Editors

Adolf E. Schroeder is Professor Emeritus of Germanic Studies at the University of Missouri in Columbia. He has written extensively on the immigrant experience in America and on nineteenth-century German literature.

Carla Schulz-Geisberg is a private scholar in Muenster-Nienberge, West Germany, who has spent many years studying and documenting the American letters of the Geisberg family.